11 윤미경

BRIDE of the WATER GOD

story and art by

Mi-Kyung Yun

MO-RAN (PEONY)
—BY SEOL-DO

WHEN YOU WILTED AND BEGAN
TO FALL LATE LAST YEAR,
I WET MY PAPER WITH THE
SADNESS OF PARTING TEARS.

WHAT CAN I DO TO SEE YOU AGAIN?
IT'S AS IF A FISHERMAN IN MOO-REUNG
HAD TO UNEXPECTEDLY SAIL TO FIND
DO-HWA-WON.

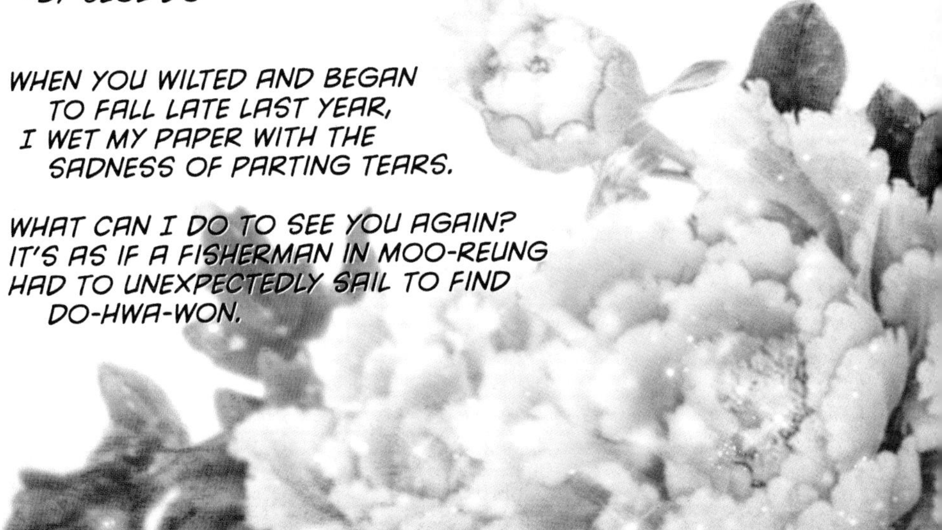

translation

Julia Kwon Gombos

English adaptation

Philip R. Simon

lettering

Studio Cutie & Betty Dong

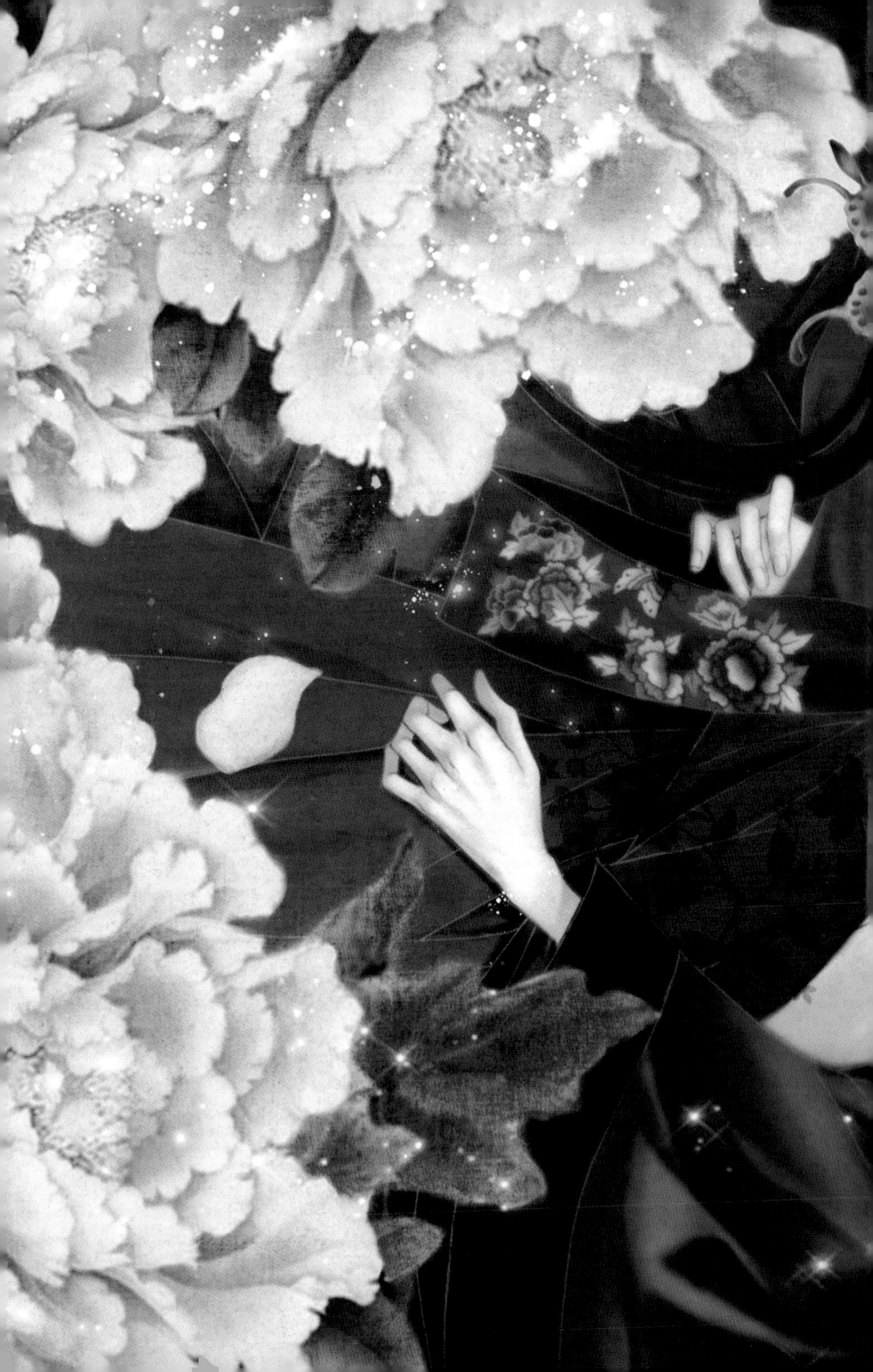

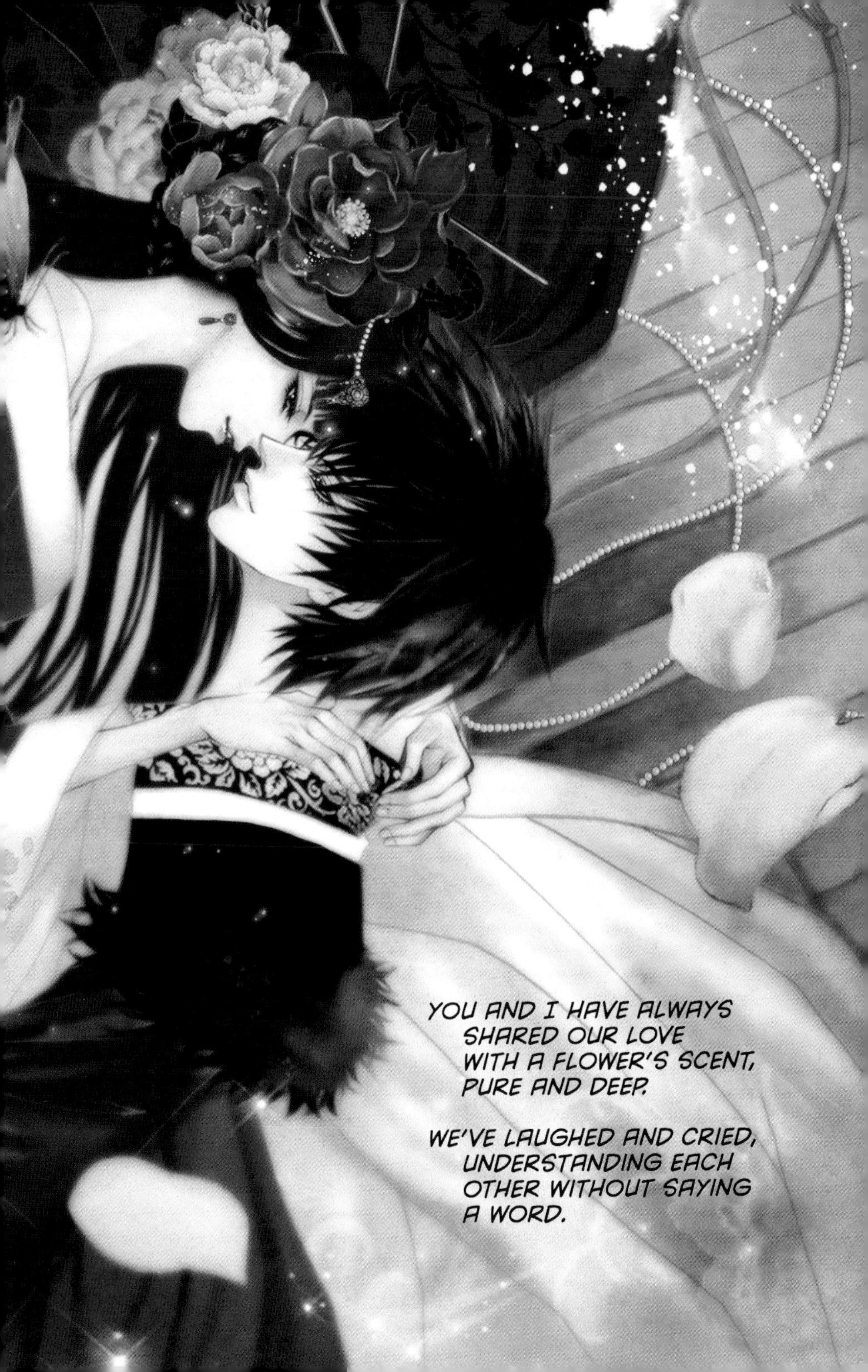
YOU AND I HAVE ALWAYS SHARED OUR LOVE WITH A FLOWER'S SCENT, PURE AND DEEP.
WE'VE LAUGHED AND CRIED, UNDERSTANDING EACH OTHER WITHOUT SAYING A WORD.

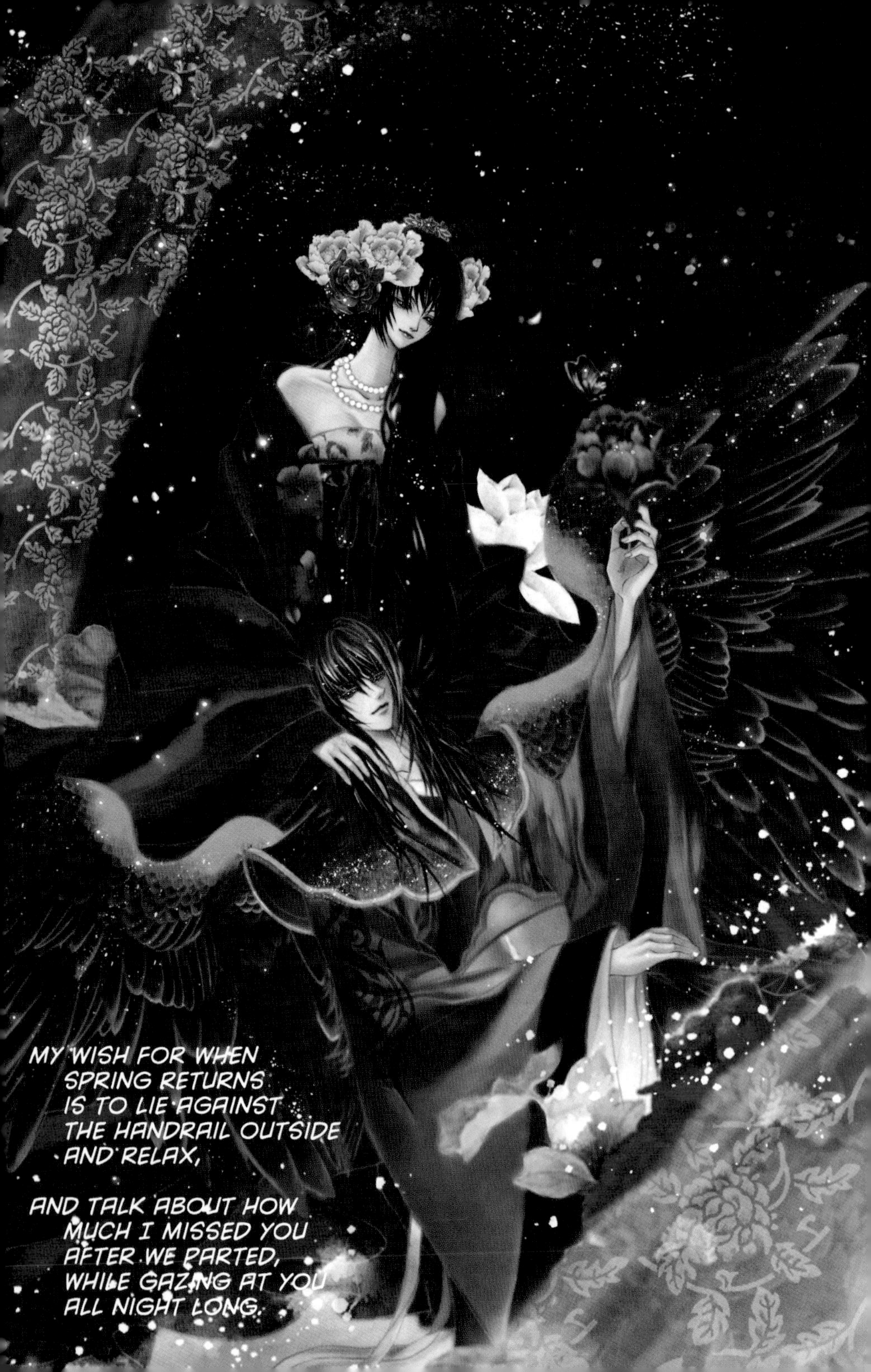
MY WISH FOR WHEN
SPRING RETURNS
IS TO LIE AGAINST
THE HANDRAIL OUTSIDE
AND RELAX,
AND TALK ABOUT HOW
MUCH I MISSED YOU
AFTER WE PARTED,
WHILE GAZING AT YOU
ALL NIGHT LONG.

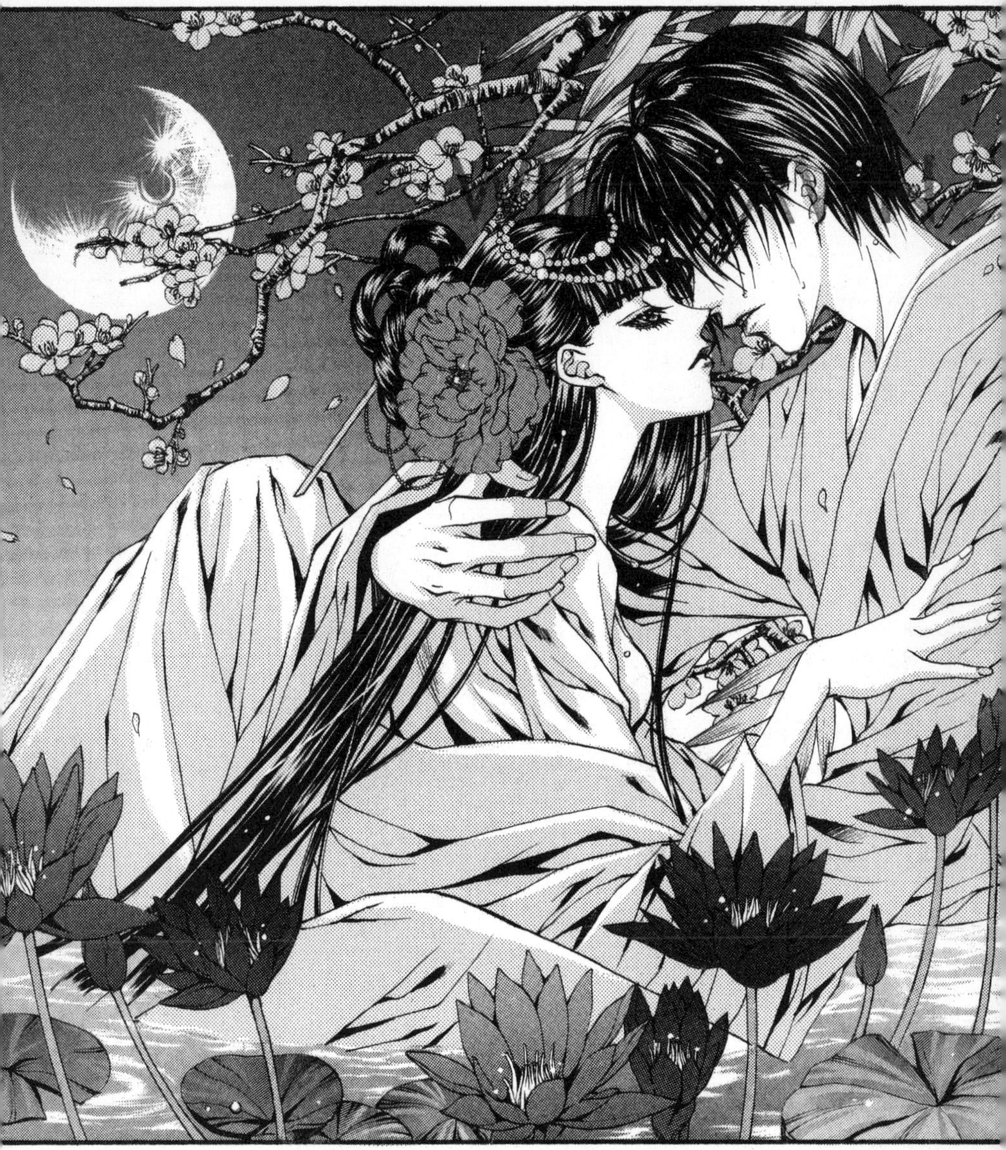

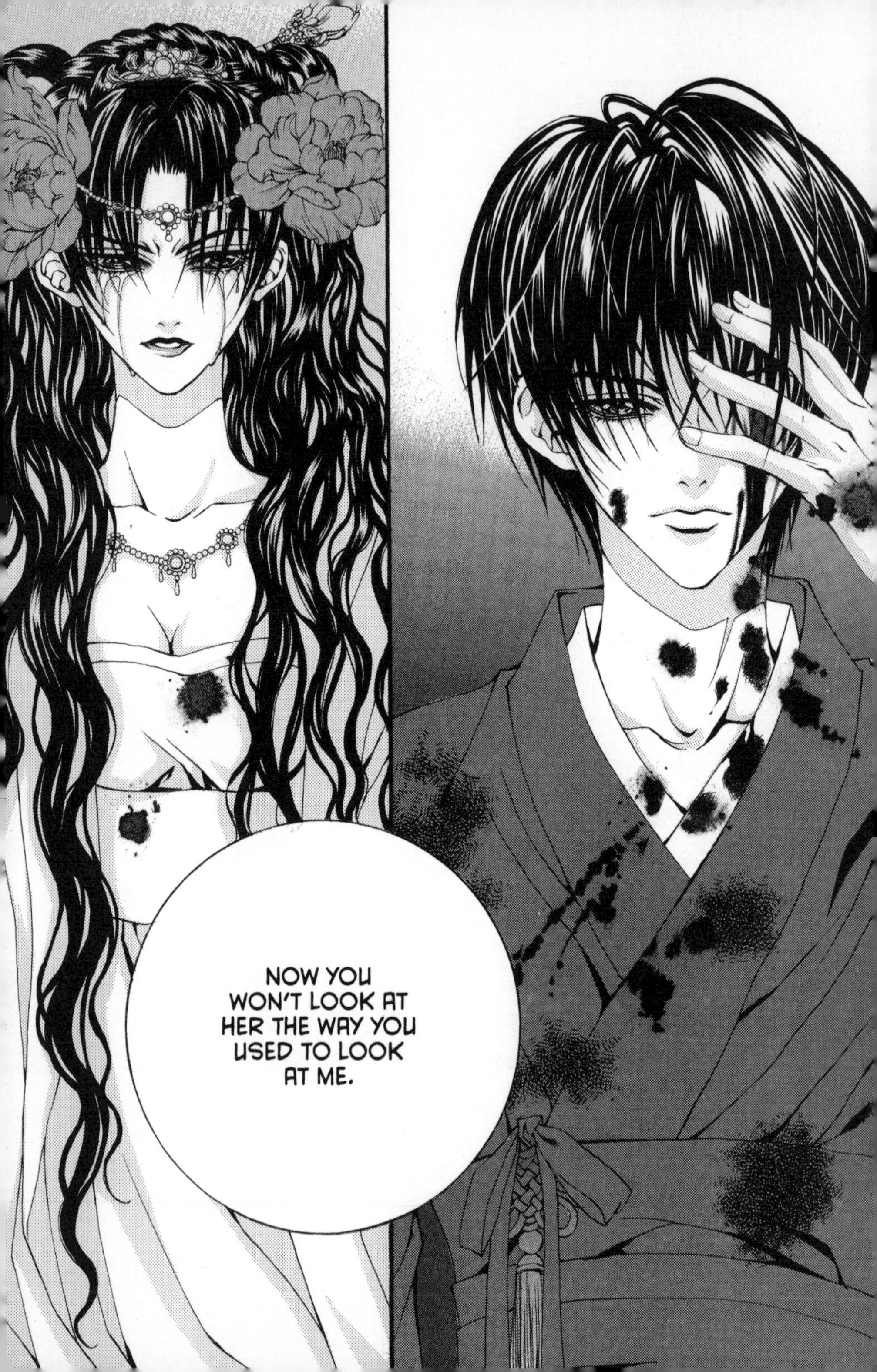
NOW YOU WON'T LOOK AT HER THE WAY YOU USED TO LOOK AT ME.

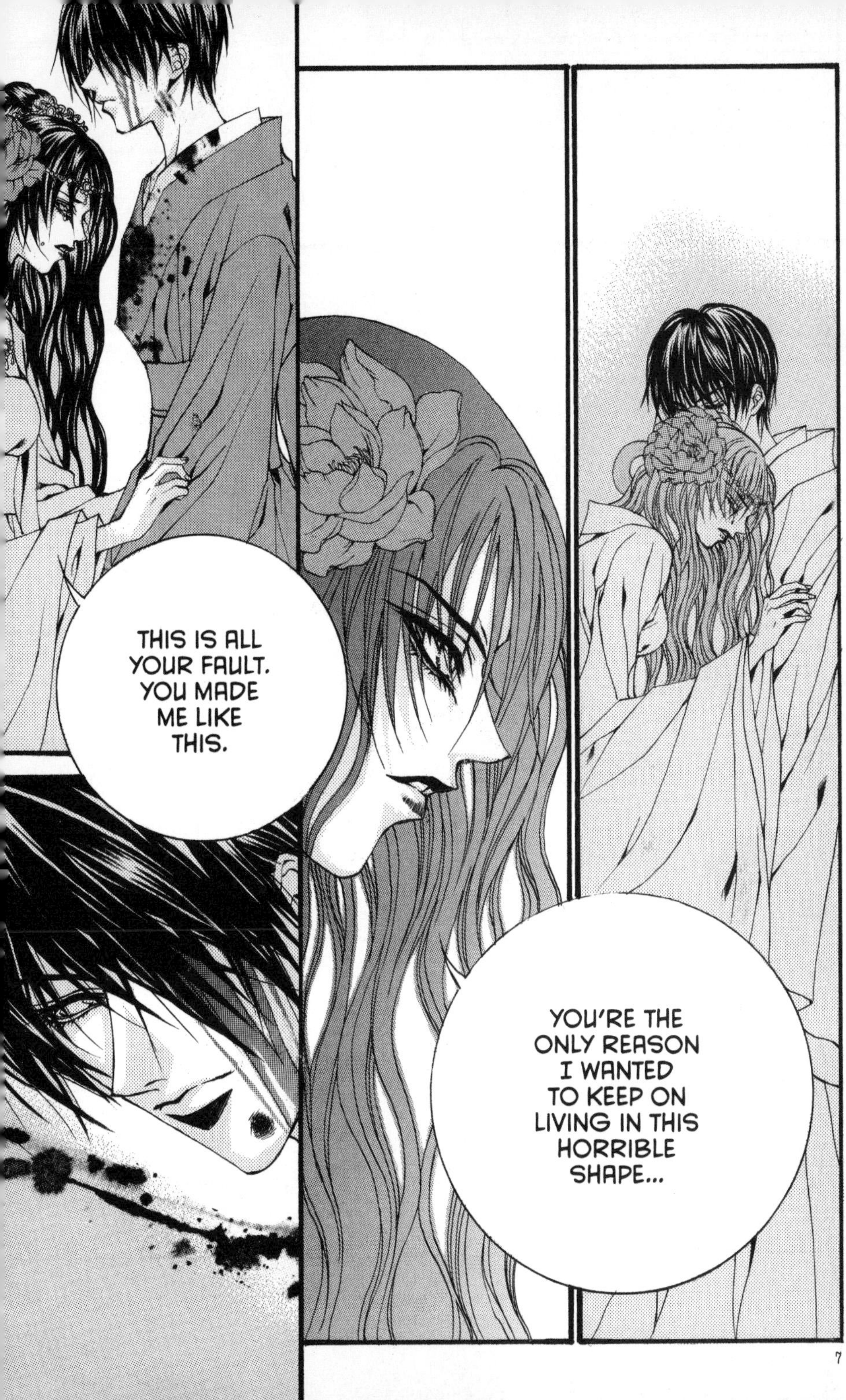
THIS IS ALL YOUR FAULT. YOU MADE ME LIKE THIS.
YOU'RE THE ONLY REASON I WANTED TO KEEP ON LIVING IN THIS HORRIBLE SHAPE...

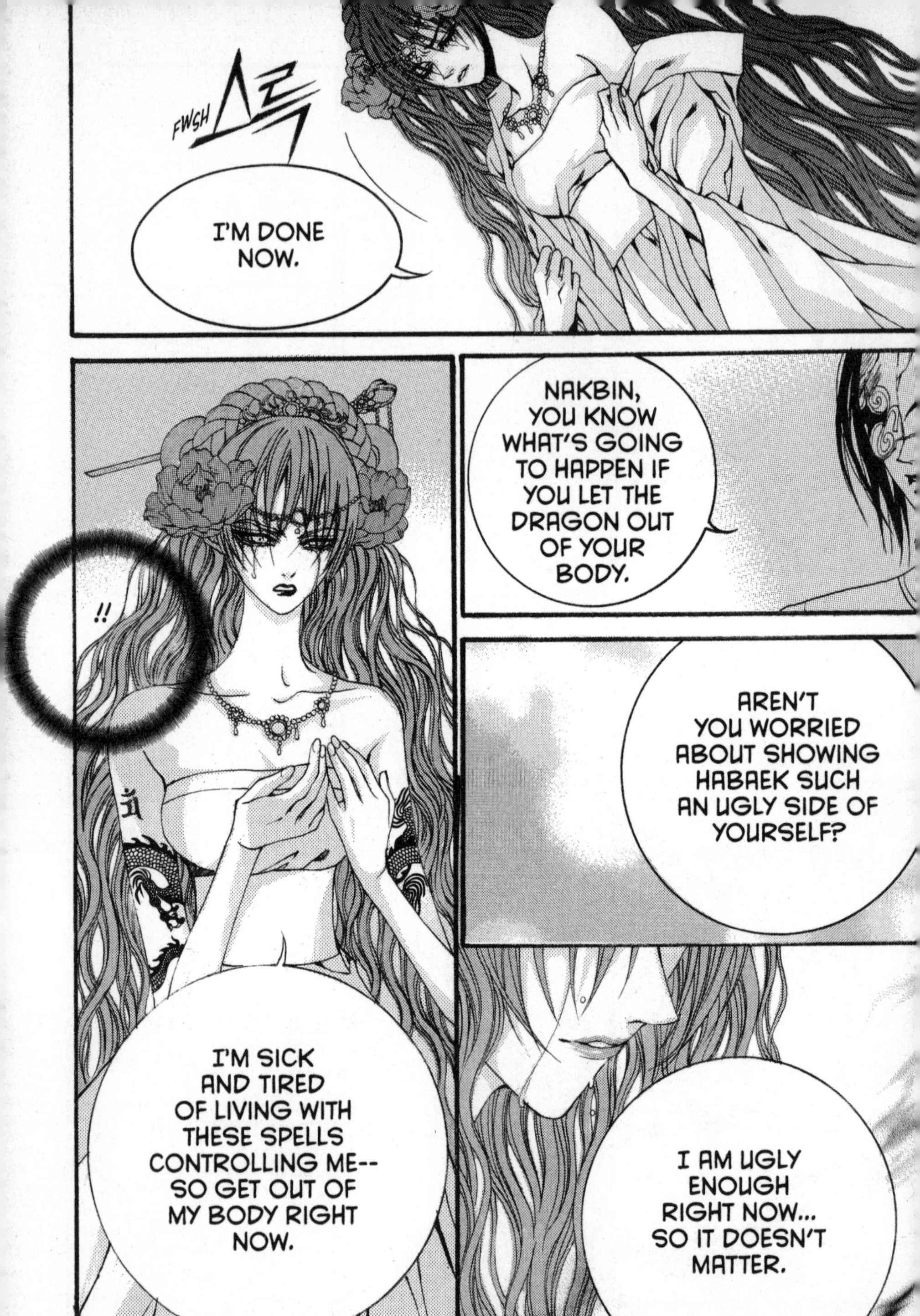
FWSH
I'M DONE NOW.
NAKBIN, YOU KNOW WHAT'S GOING TO HAPPEN IF YOU LET THE DRAGON OUT OF YOUR BODY.
AREN'T YOU WORRIED ABOUT SHOWING HABAEK SUCH AN UGLY SIDE OF YOURSELF?
!!
I'M SICK AND TIRED OF LIVING WITH THESE SPELLS CONTROLLING ME-- SO GET OUT OF MY BODY RIGHT NOW.
I AM UGLY ENOUGH RIGHT NOW... SO IT DOESN'T MATTER.

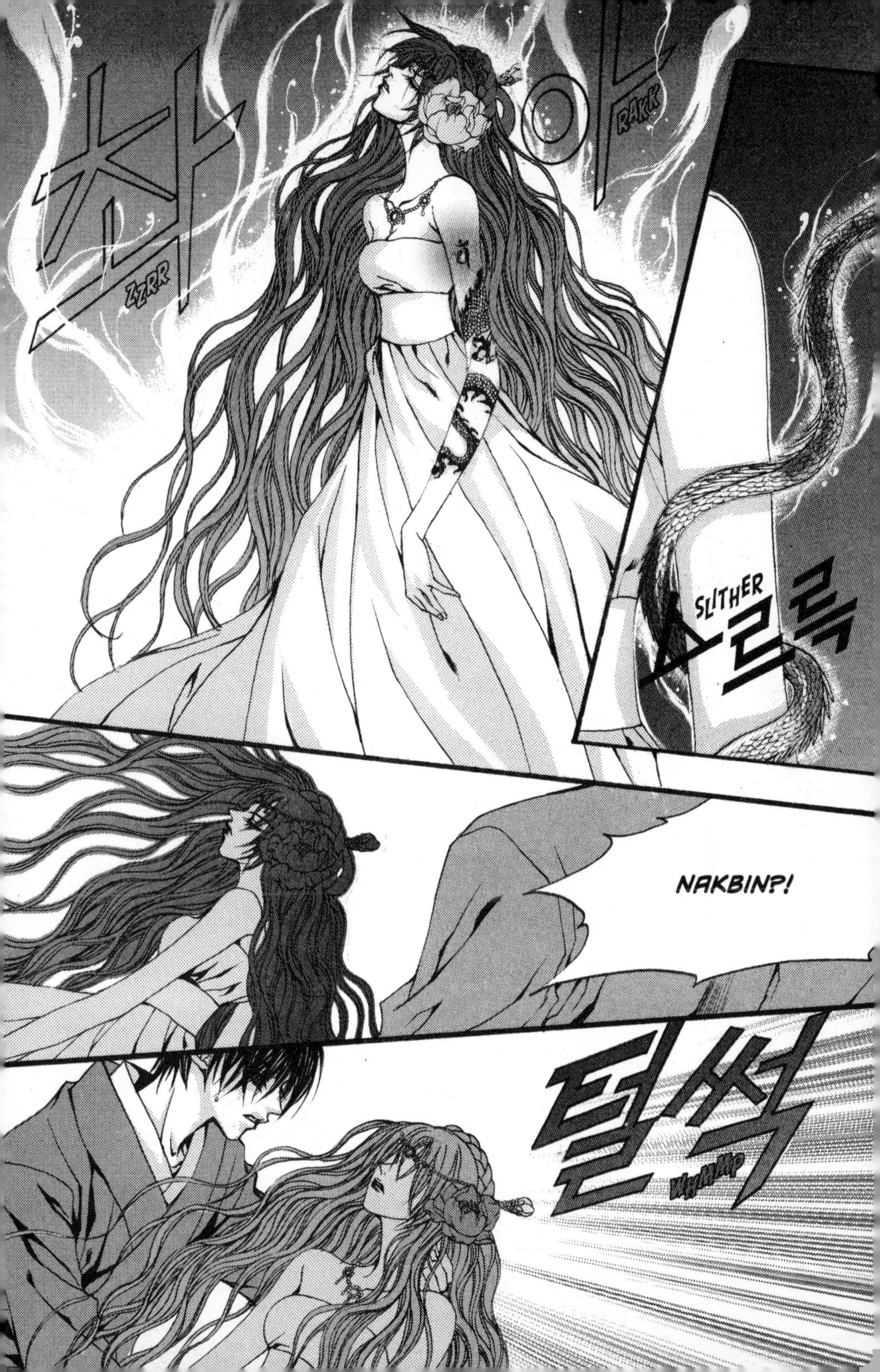

RAKK
ZZRR
SLITHER
NAKBIN?!

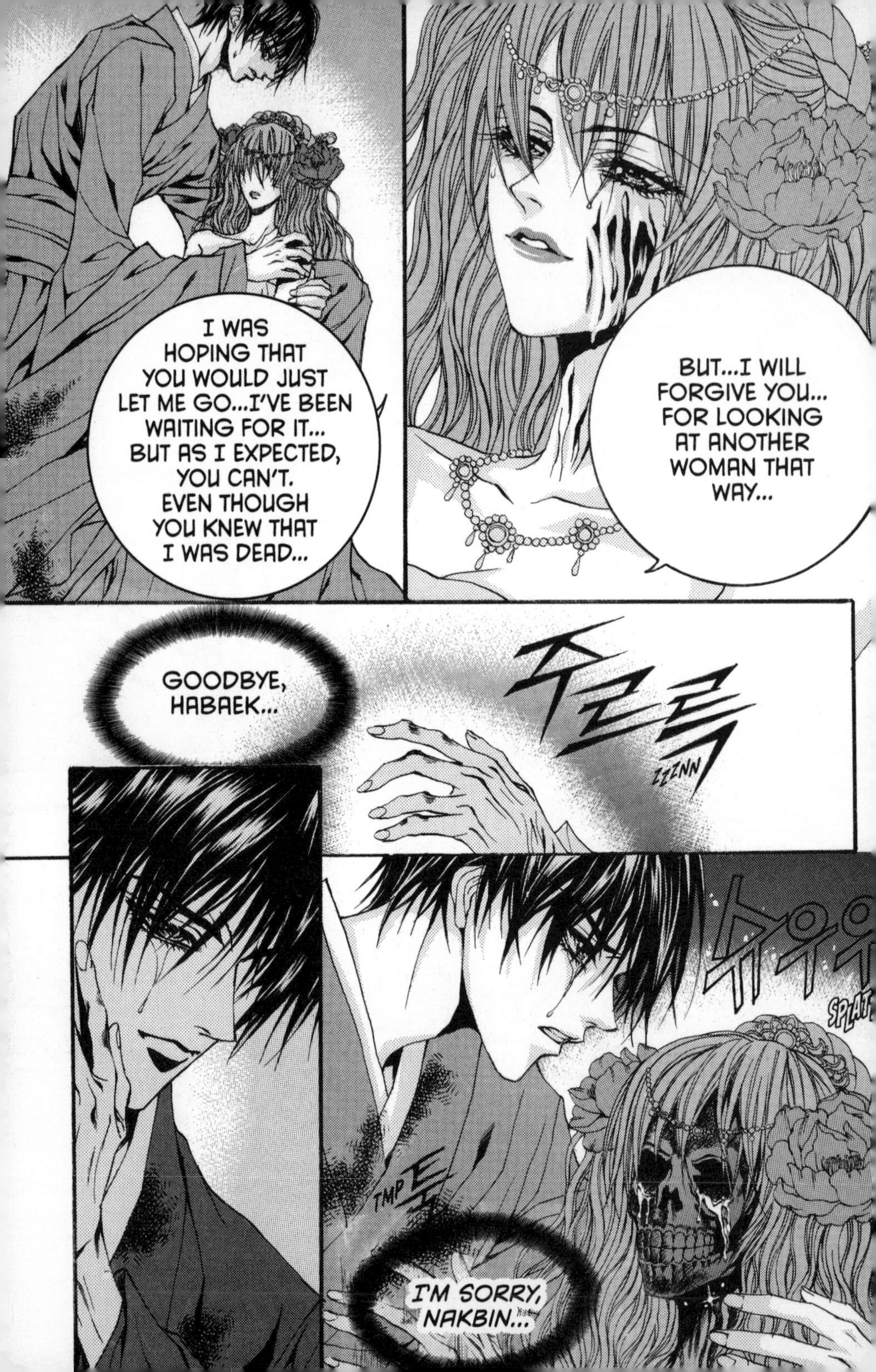
I WAS HOPING THAT YOU WOULD JUST LET ME GO...I'VE BEEN WAITING FOR IT... BUT AS I EXPECTED, YOU CAN'T. EVEN THOUGH YOU KNEW THAT I WAS DEAD...
BUT...I WILL FORGIVE YOU... FOR LOOKING AT ANOTHER WOMAN THAT WAY...
GOODBYE, HABAEK...
ZZZNN
SPLAT
TMP
I'M SORRY, NAKBIN...

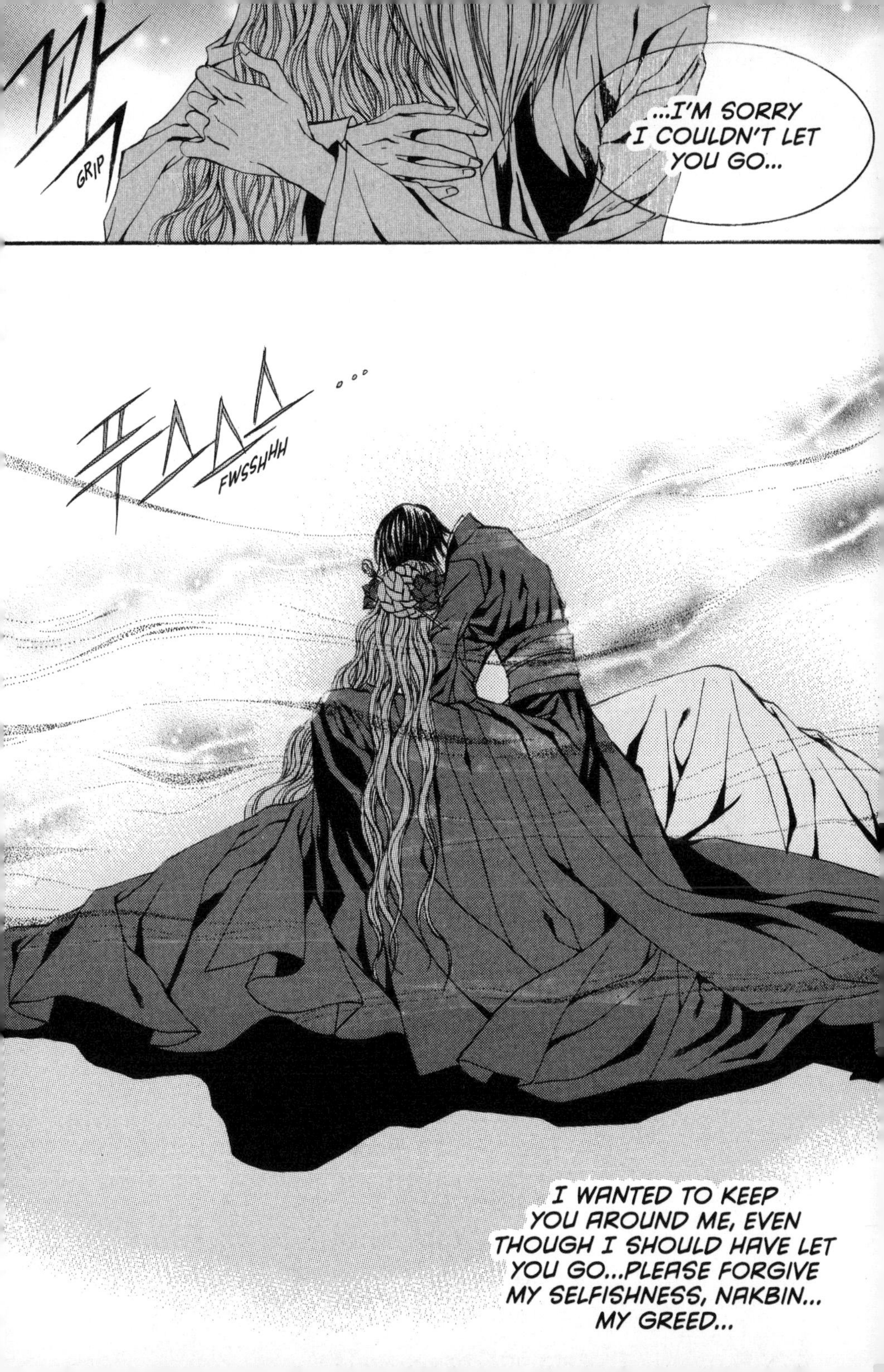
...I'M SORRY I COULDN'T LET YOU GO...
GRIP
FWSSHHH
I WANTED TO KEEP YOU AROUND ME, EVEN THOUGH I SHOULD HAVE LET YOU GO...PLEASE FORGIVE MY SELFISHNESS, NAKBIN... MY GREED...

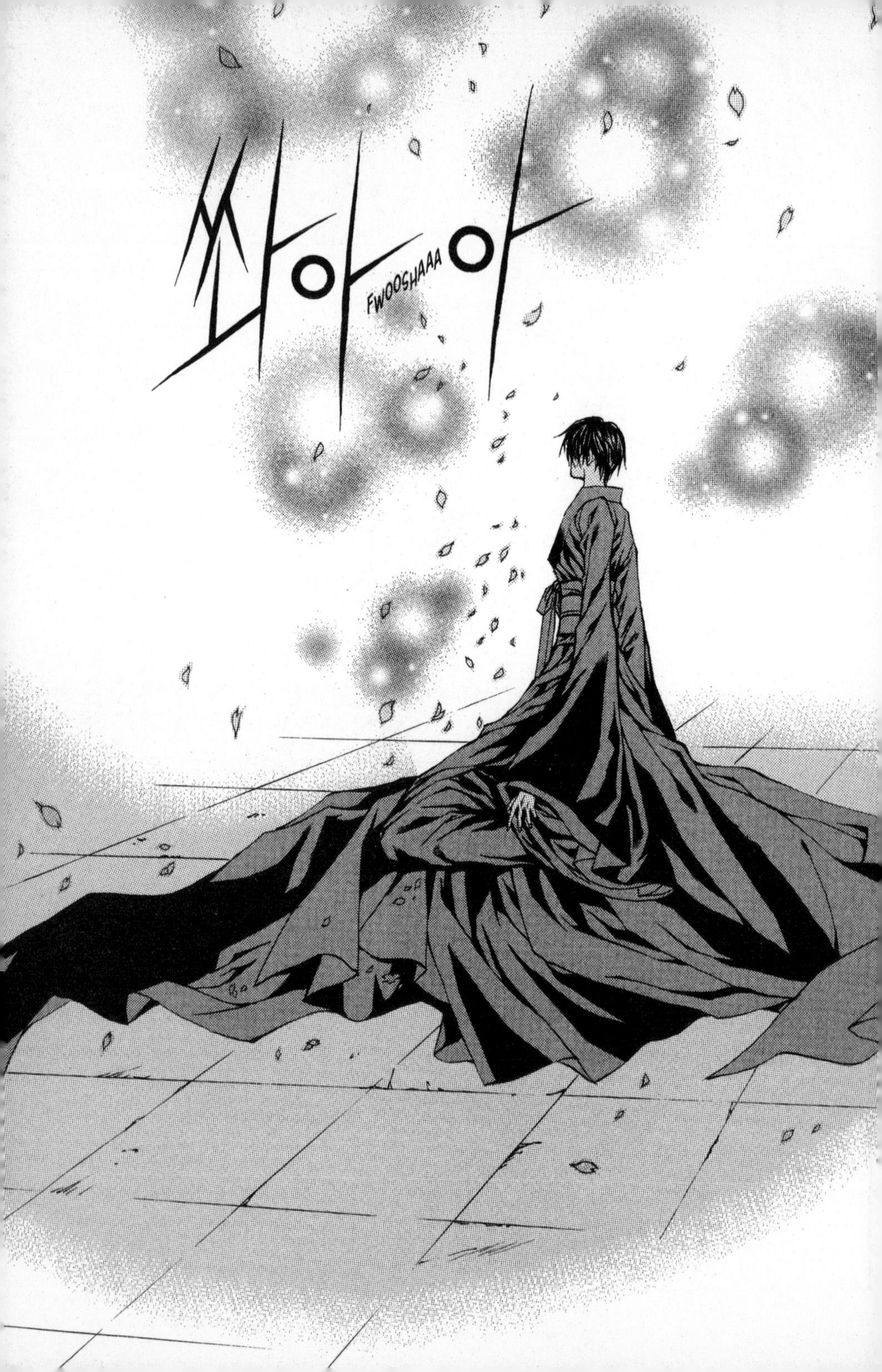
쏴아아
FWOOSHAAA

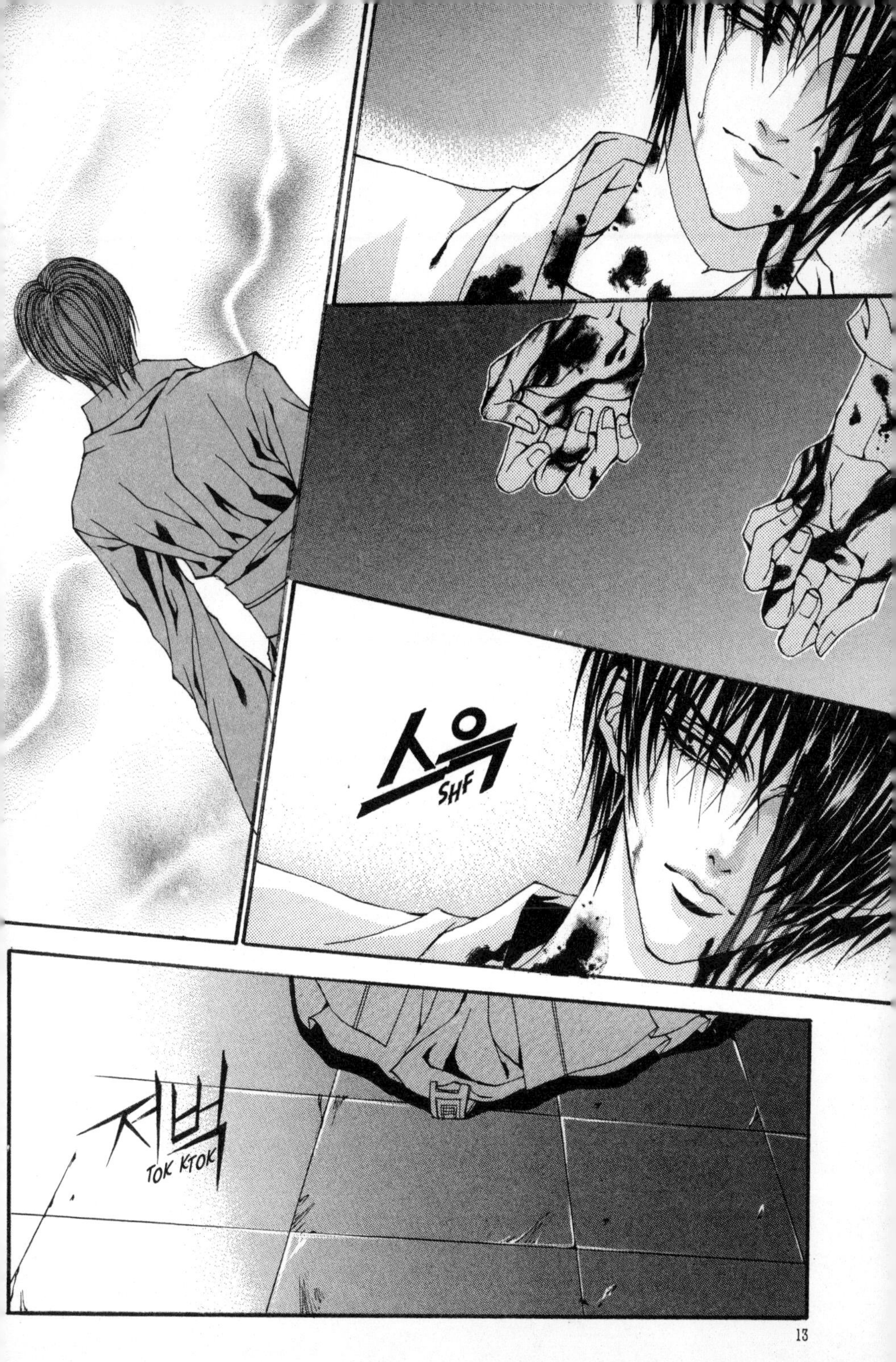
슥
SHF
저벅
TOK KTOK

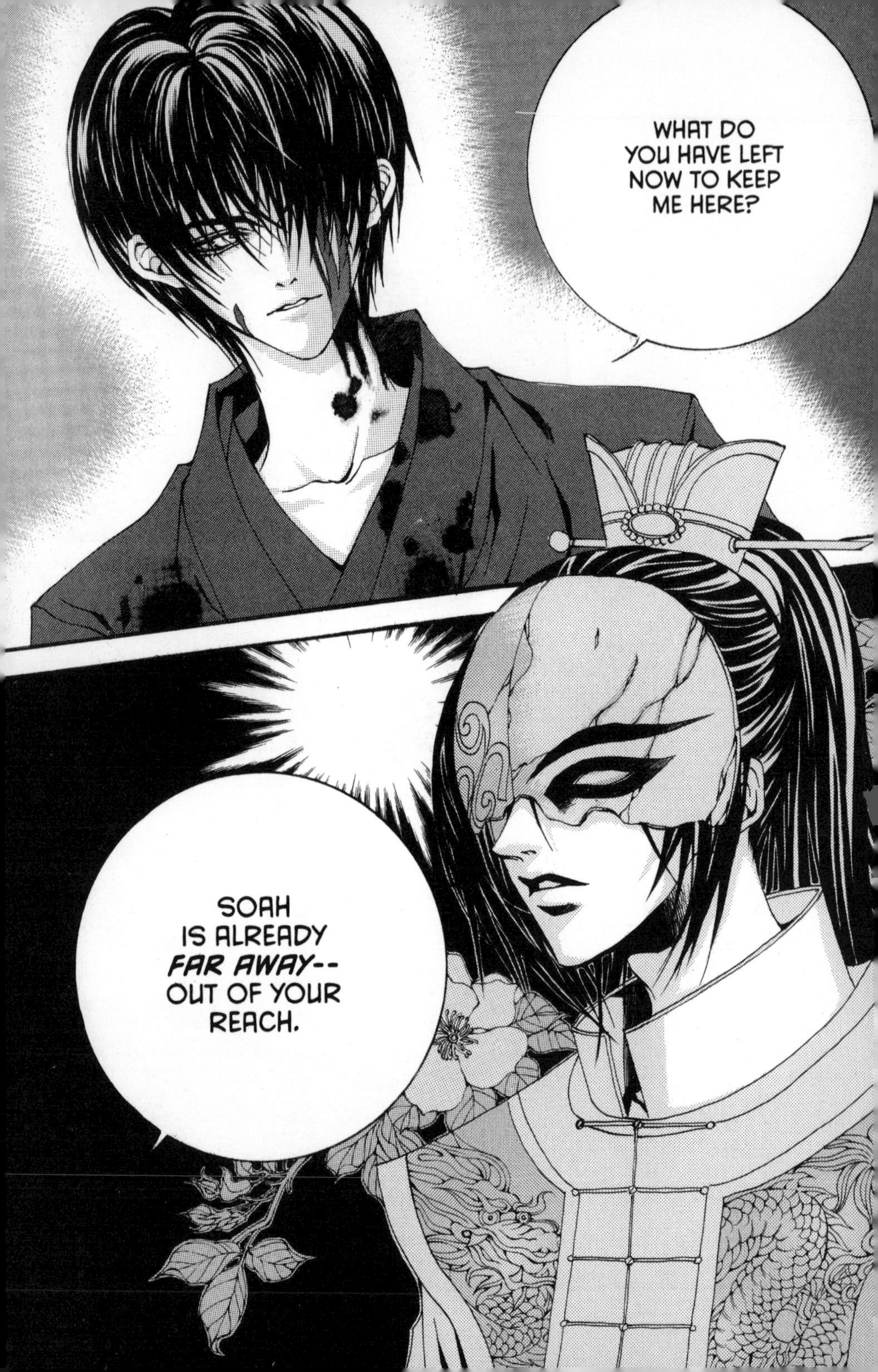
WHAT DO YOU HAVE LEFT NOW TO KEEP ME HERE?
SOAH IS ALREADY *FAR AWAY*-- OUT OF YOUR REACH.

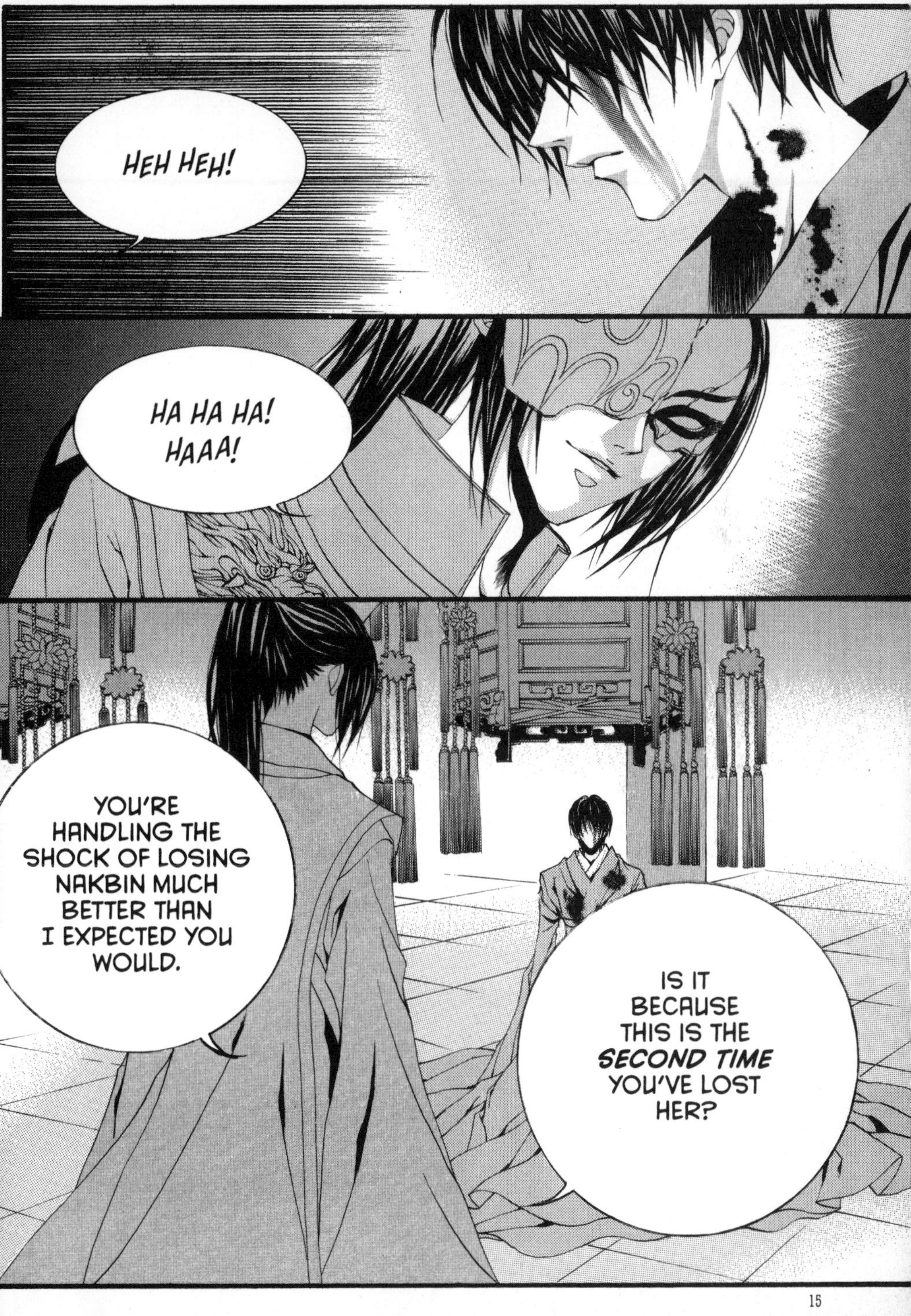
HEH HEH!
HA HA HA! HAAA!
YOU'RE HANDLING THE SHOCK OF LOSING NAKBIN MUCH BETTER THAN I EXPECTED YOU WOULD.
IS IT BECAUSE THIS IS THE *SECOND TIME* YOU'VE LOST HER?

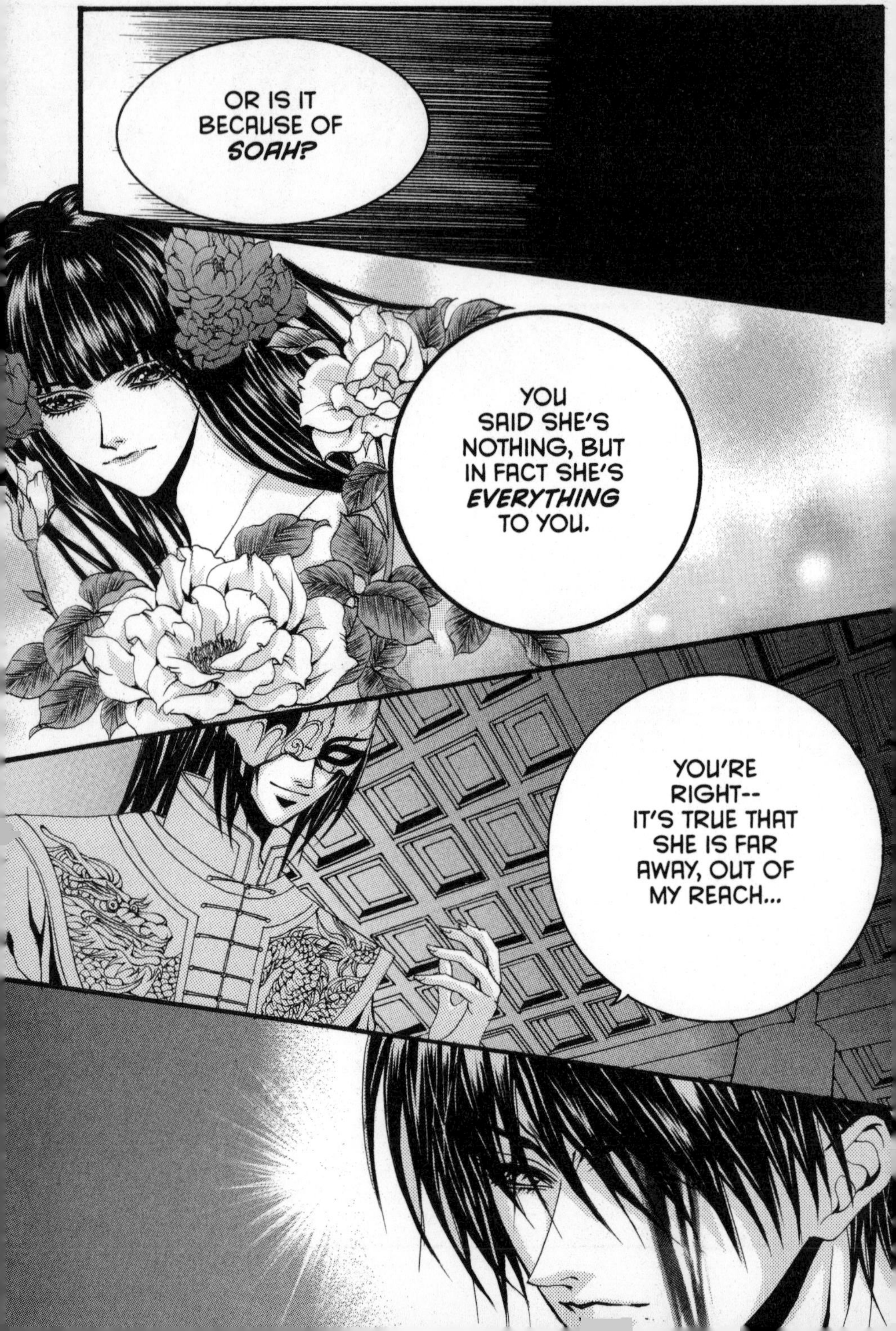
OR IS IT BECAUSE OF *SOAH?*
YOU SAID SHE'S NOTHING, BUT IN FACT SHE'S *EVERYTHING* TO YOU.
YOU'RE RIGHT-- IT'S TRUE THAT SHE IS FAR AWAY, OUT OF MY REACH...

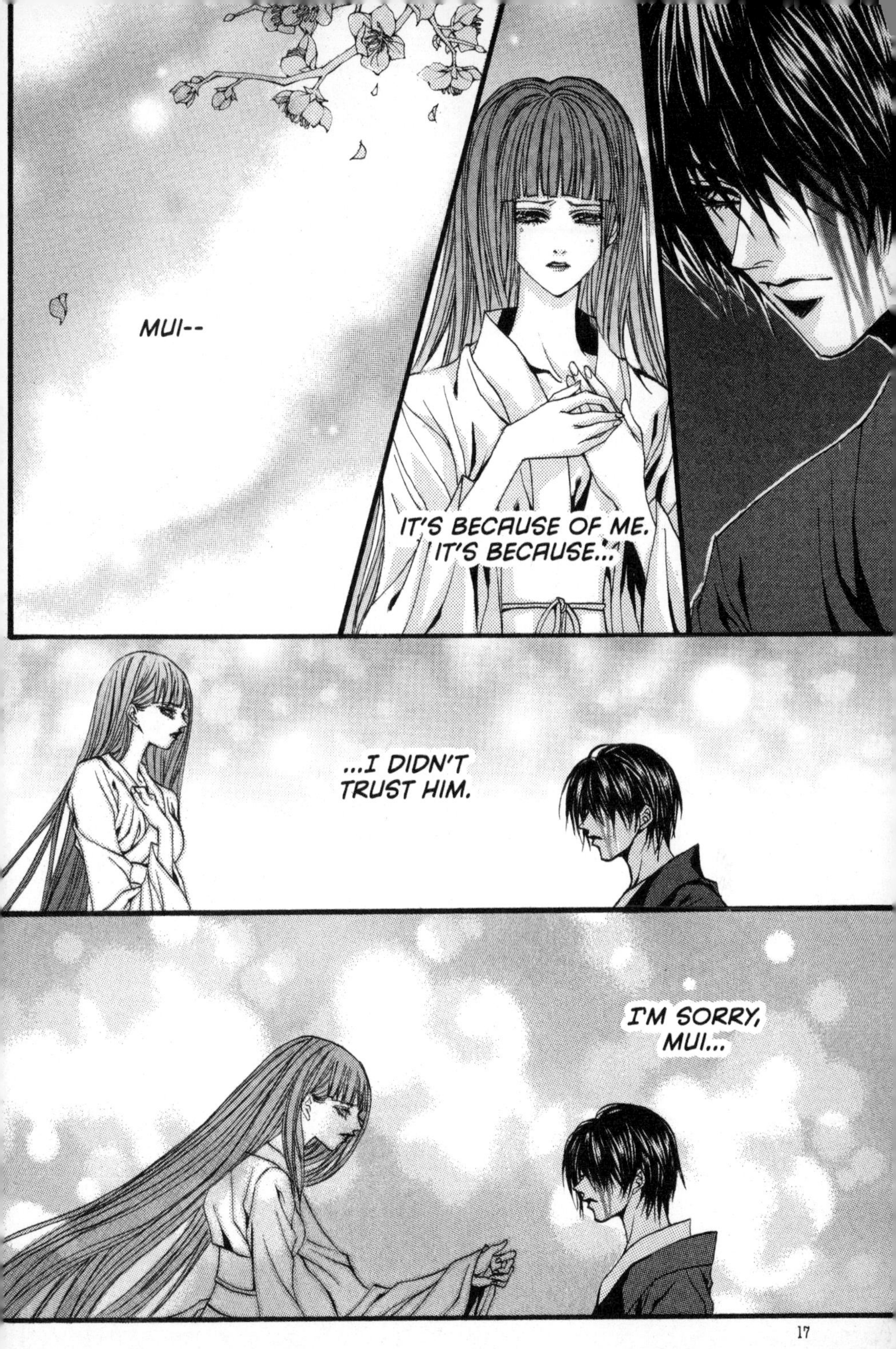
MUI--
IT'S BECAUSE OF ME. IT'S BECAUSE...
...I DIDN'T TRUST HIM.
I'M SORRY, MUI...

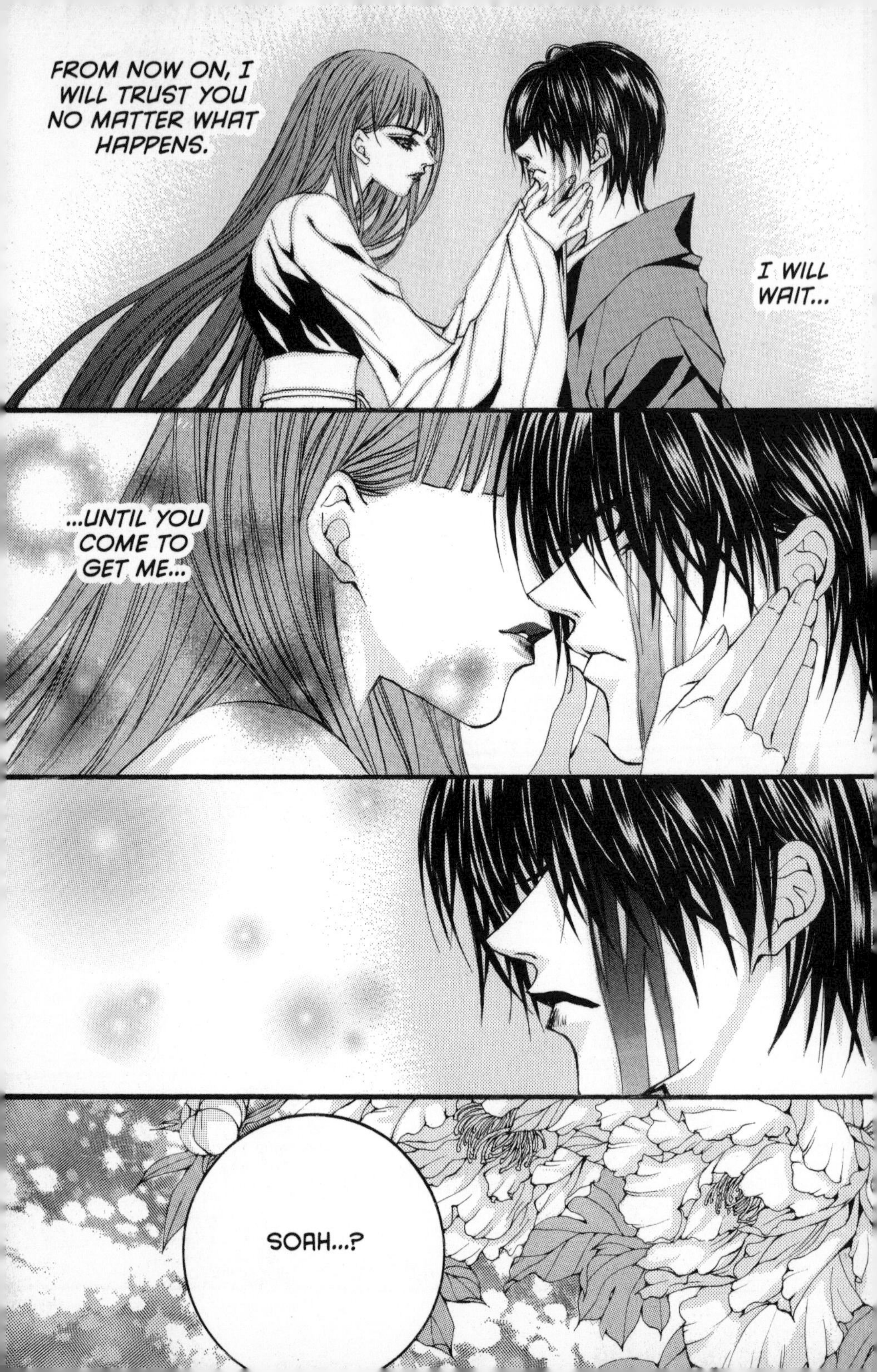
FROM NOW ON, I WILL TRUST YOU NO MATTER WHAT HAPPENS.
I WILL WAIT...
...UNTIL YOU COME TO GET ME...
SOAH...?

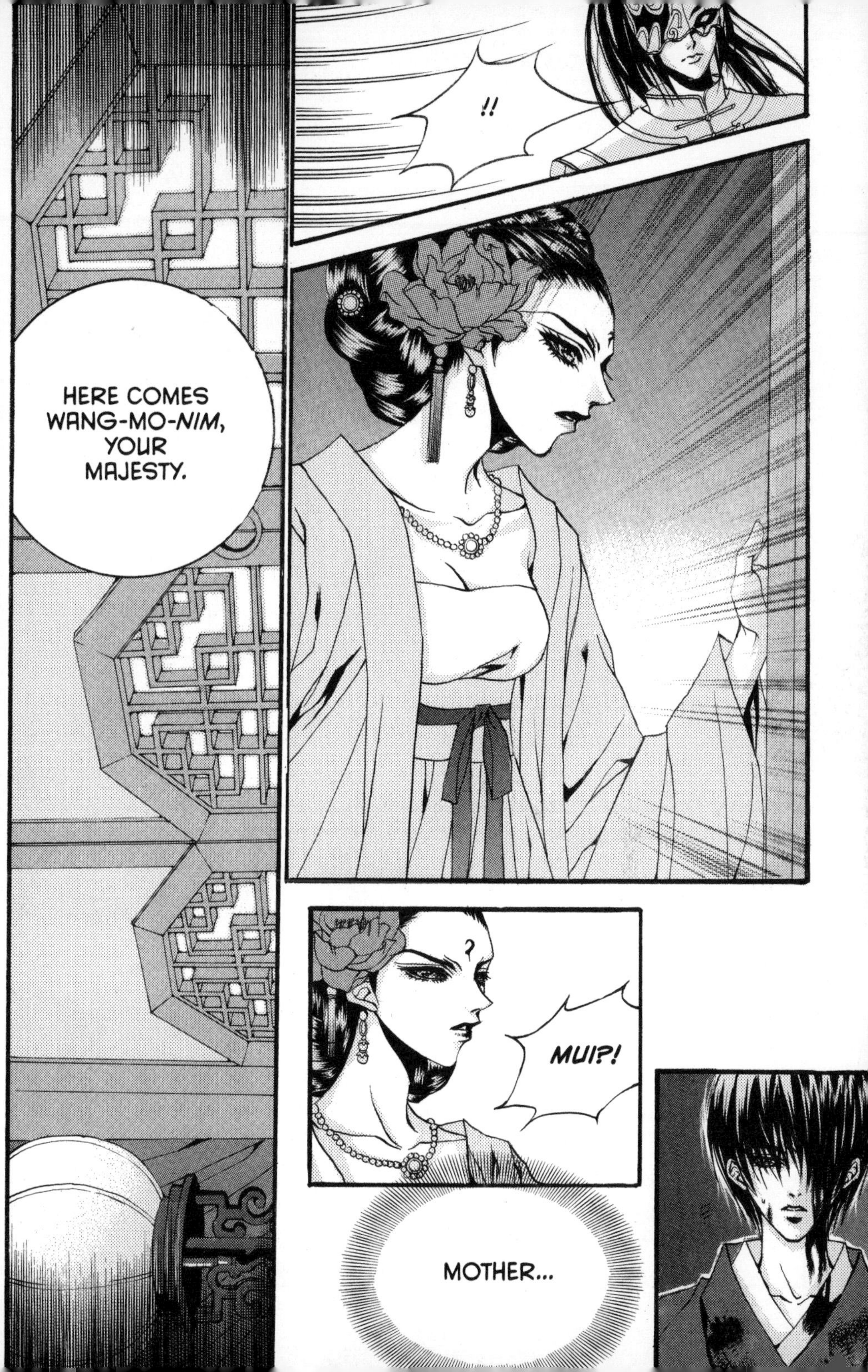
!!
HERE COMES WANG-MO-NIM, YOUR MAJESTY.
?
MUI?!
MOTHER...

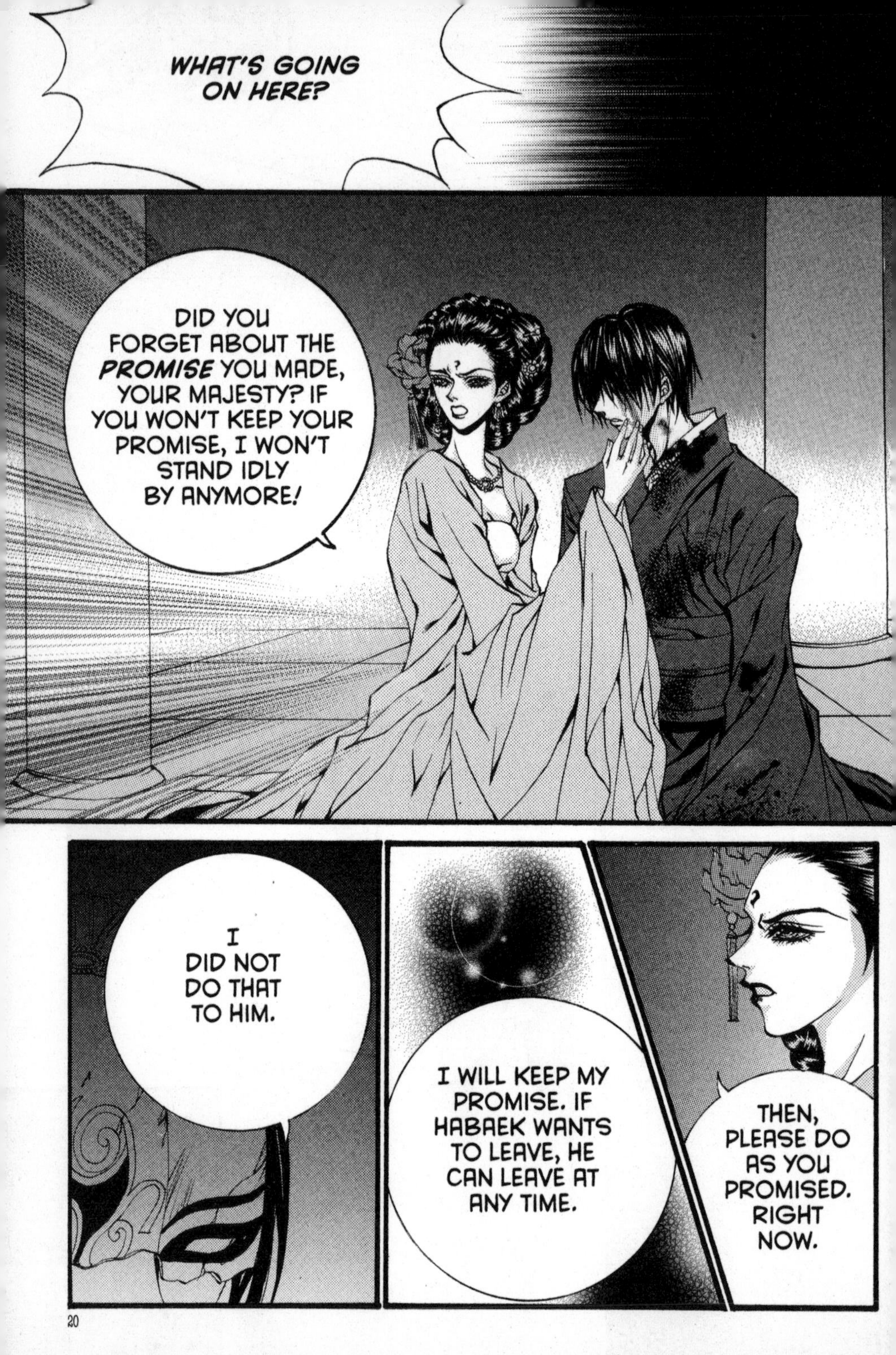
WHAT'S GOING ON HERE?
DID YOU FORGET ABOUT THE PROMISE YOU MADE, YOUR MAJESTY? IF YOU WON'T KEEP YOUR PROMISE, I WON'T STAND IDLY BY ANYMORE!
I DID NOT DO THAT TO HIM.
I WILL KEEP MY PROMISE. IF HABAEK WANTS TO LEAVE, HE CAN LEAVE AT ANY TIME.
THEN, PLEASE DO AS YOU PROMISED. RIGHT NOW.

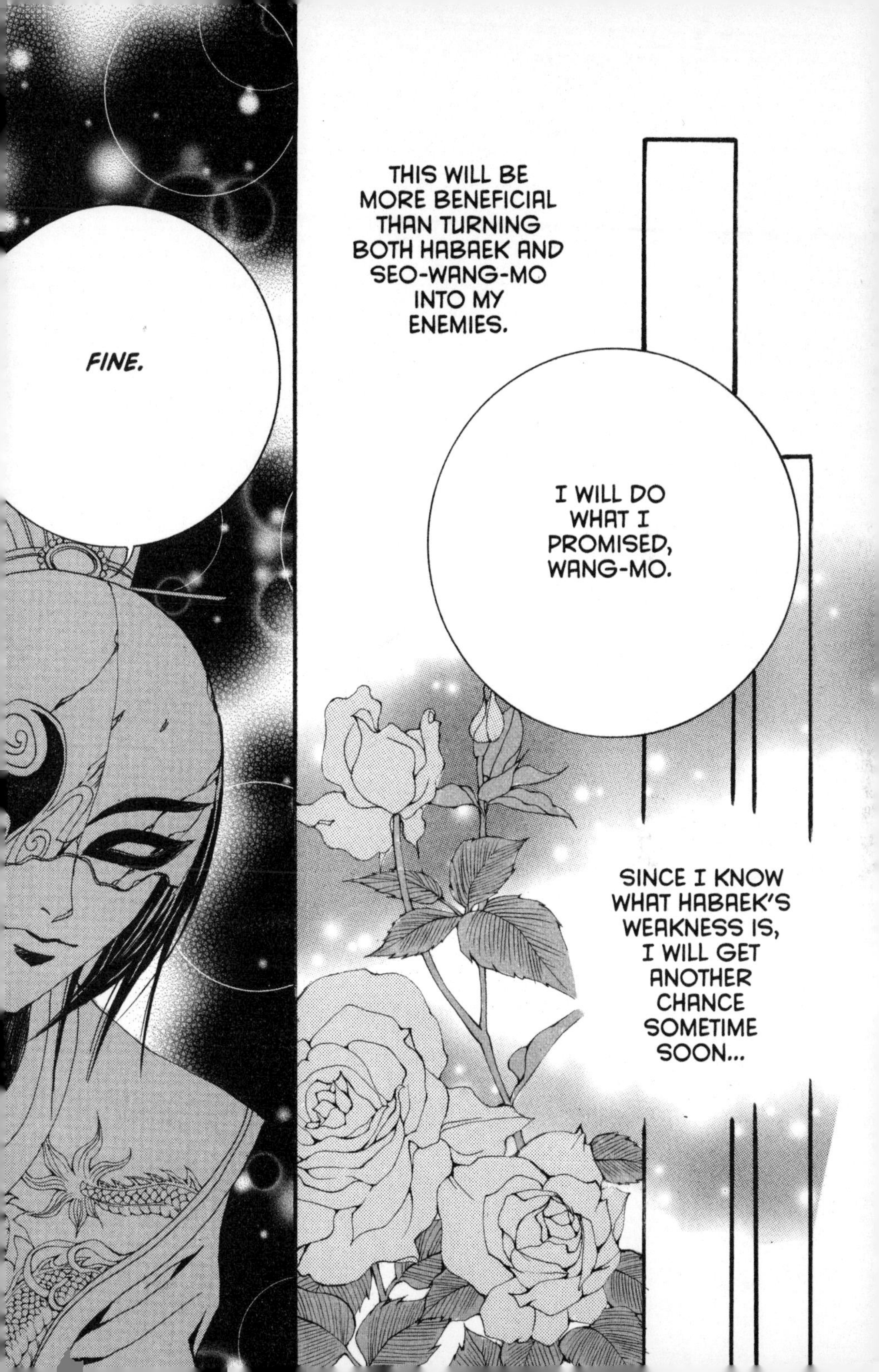
THIS WILL BE MORE BENEFICIAL THAN TURNING BOTH HABAEK AND SEO-WANG-MO INTO MY ENEMIES.
FINE.
I WILL DO WHAT I PROMISED, WANG-MO.
SINCE I KNOW WHAT HABAEK'S WEAKNESS IS, I WILL GET ANOTHER CHANCE SOMETIME SOON...

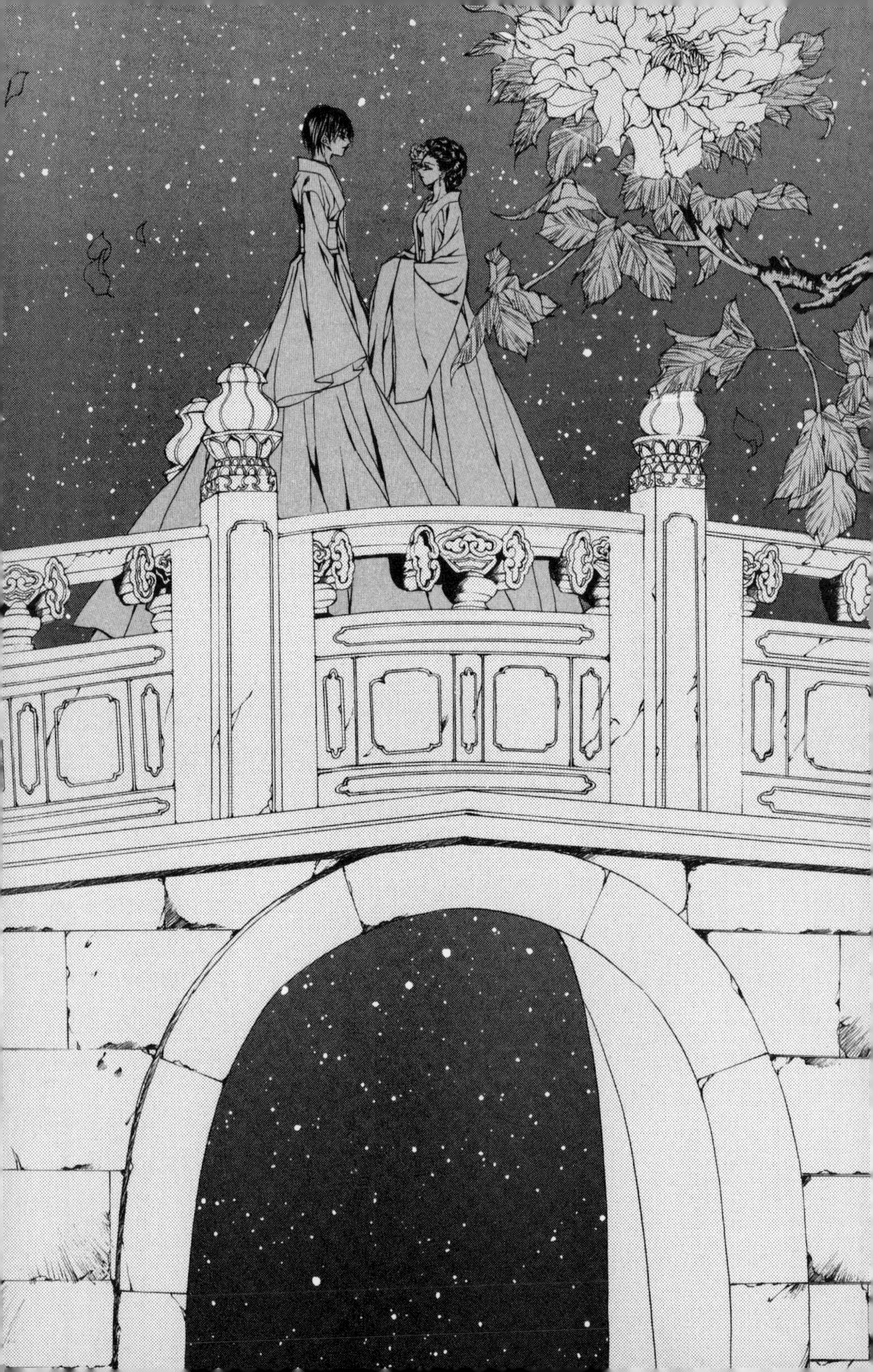

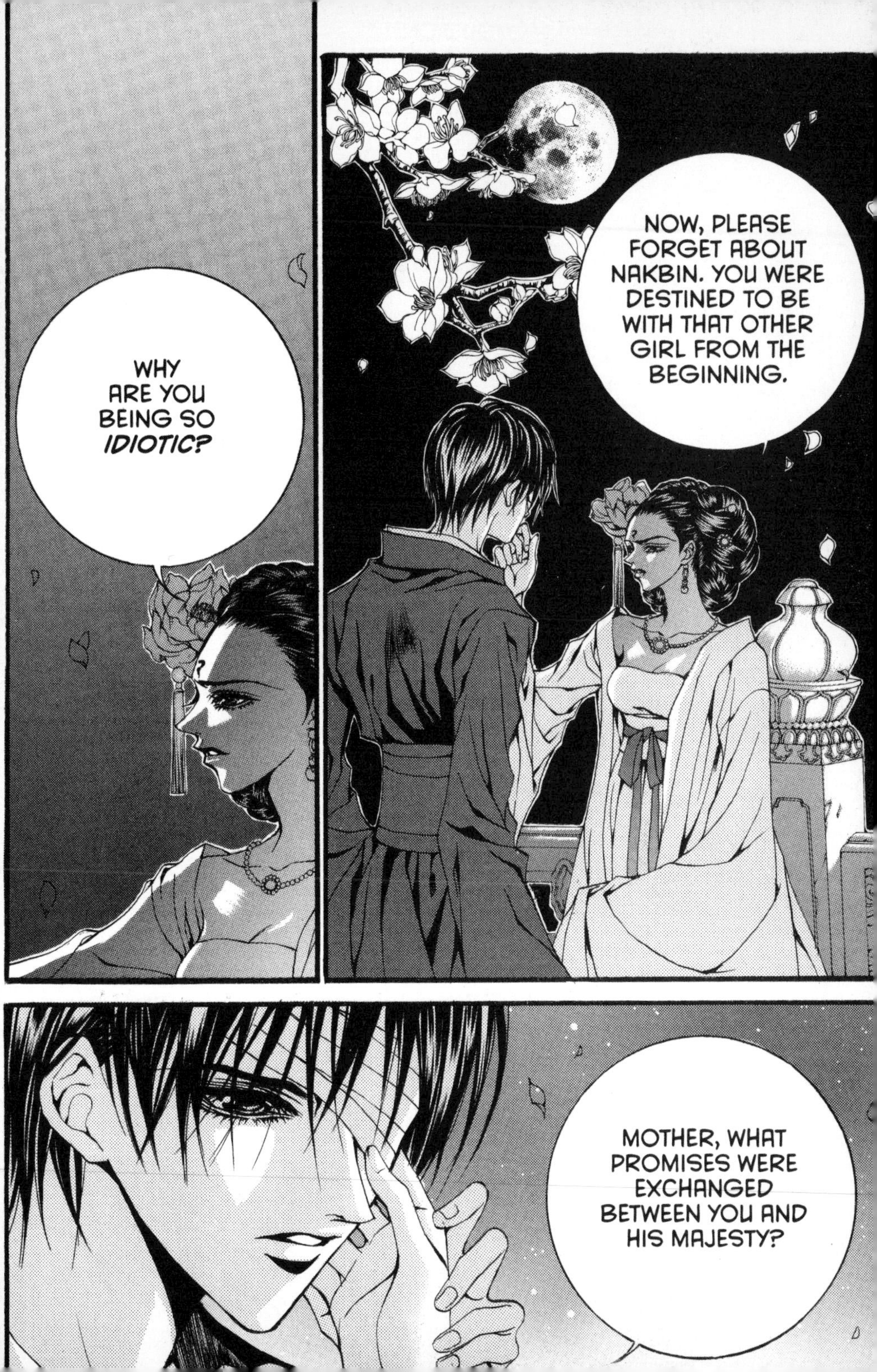
WHY ARE YOU BEING SO *IDIOTIC?*
NOW, PLEASE FORGET ABOUT NAKBIN. YOU WERE DESTINED TO BE WITH THAT OTHER GIRL FROM THE BEGINNING.
MOTHER, WHAT PROMISES WERE EXCHANGED BETWEEN YOU AND HIS MAJESTY?

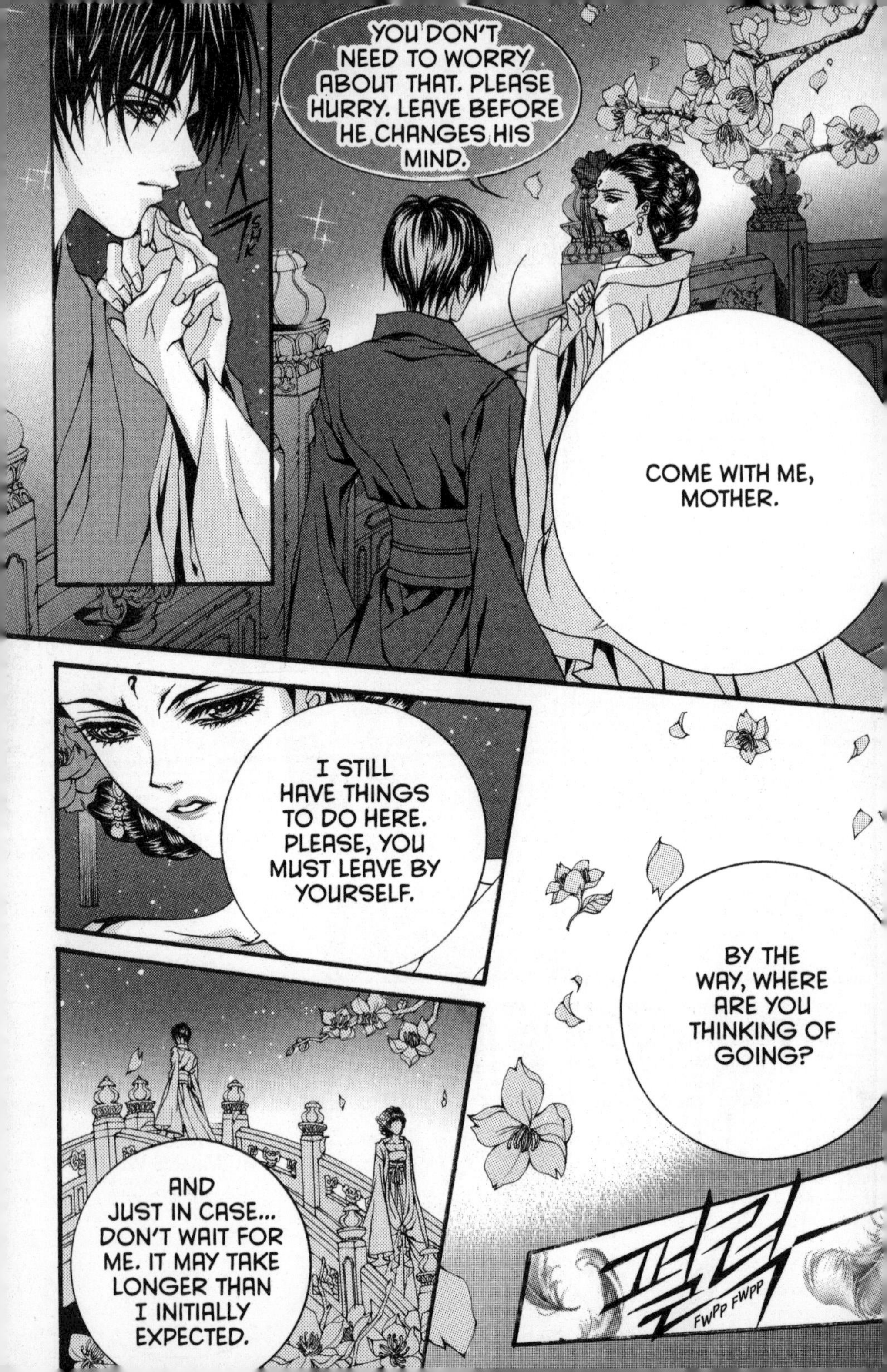

SHK
YOU DON'T NEED TO WORRY ABOUT THAT. PLEASE HURRY. LEAVE BEFORE HE CHANGES HIS MIND.
COME WITH ME, MOTHER.
BY THE WAY, WHERE ARE YOU THINKING OF GOING?
I STILL HAVE THINGS TO DO HERE. PLEASE, YOU MUST LEAVE BY YOURSELF.
FWPP FWPP
AND JUST IN CASE... DON'T WAIT FOR ME. IT MAY TAKE LONGER THAN I INITIALLY EXPECTED.

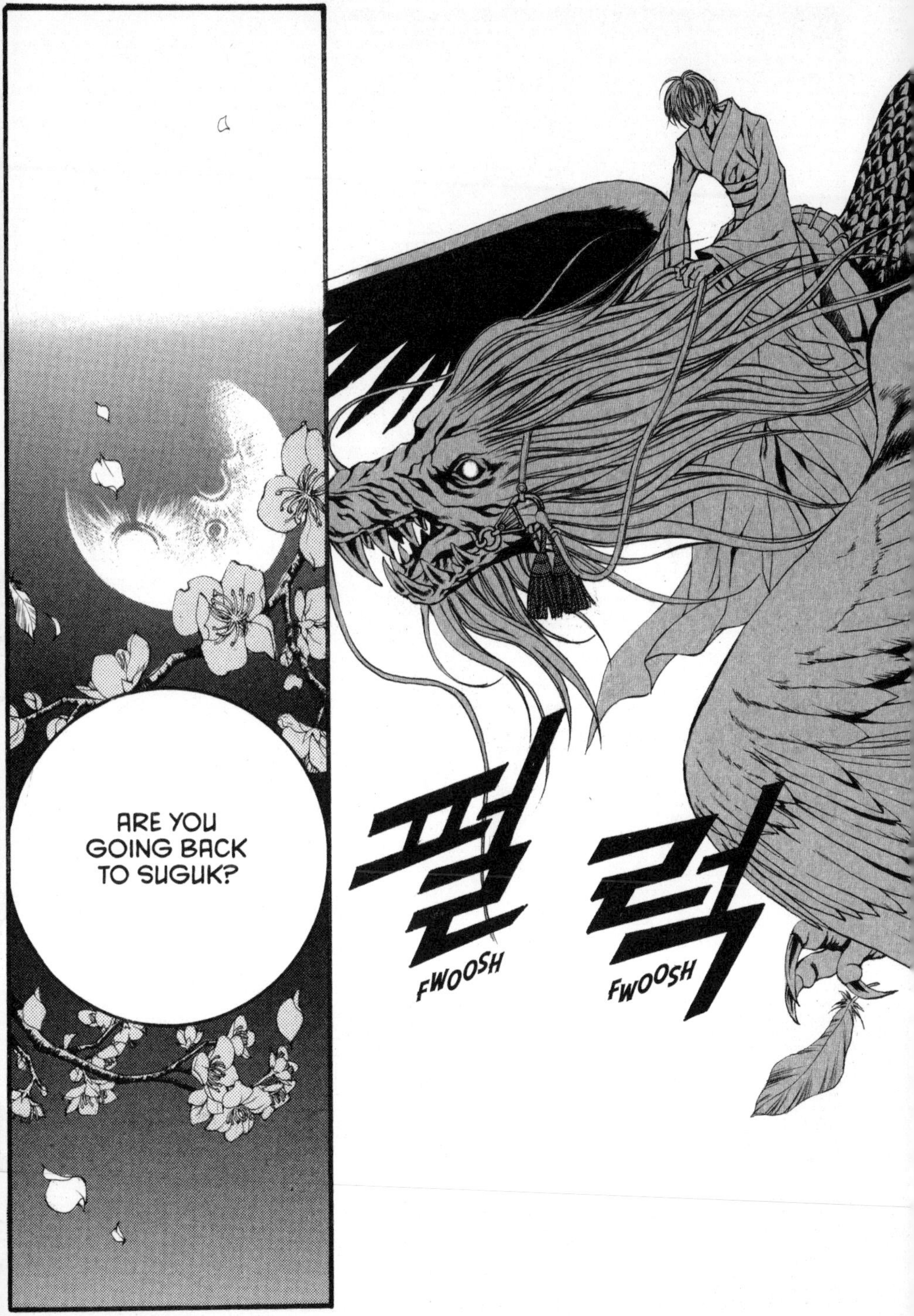
ARE YOU GOING BACK TO SUGUK?
펄
FWOOSH
럭
FWOOSH

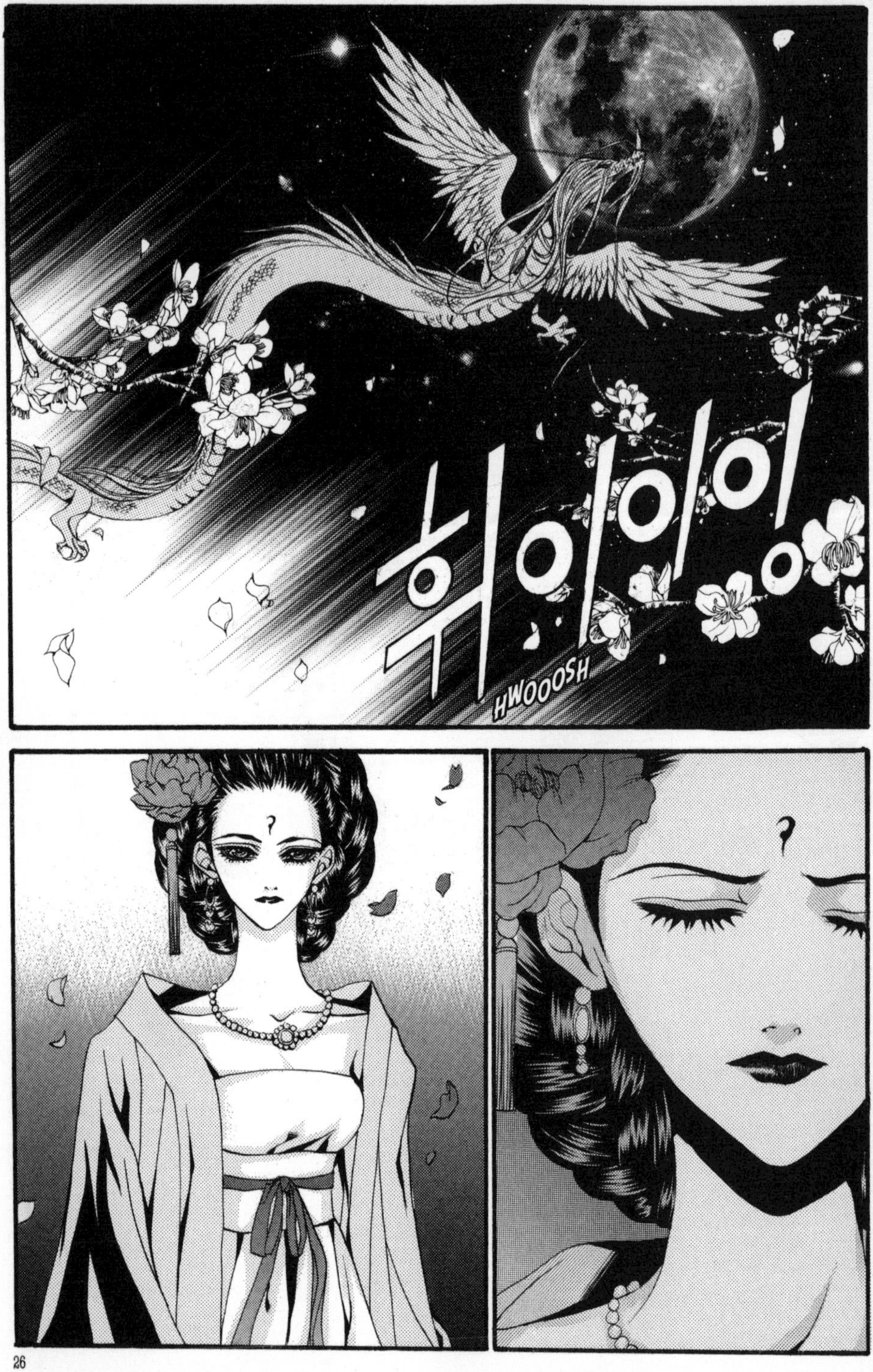
휘이이잉
HWOOOSH

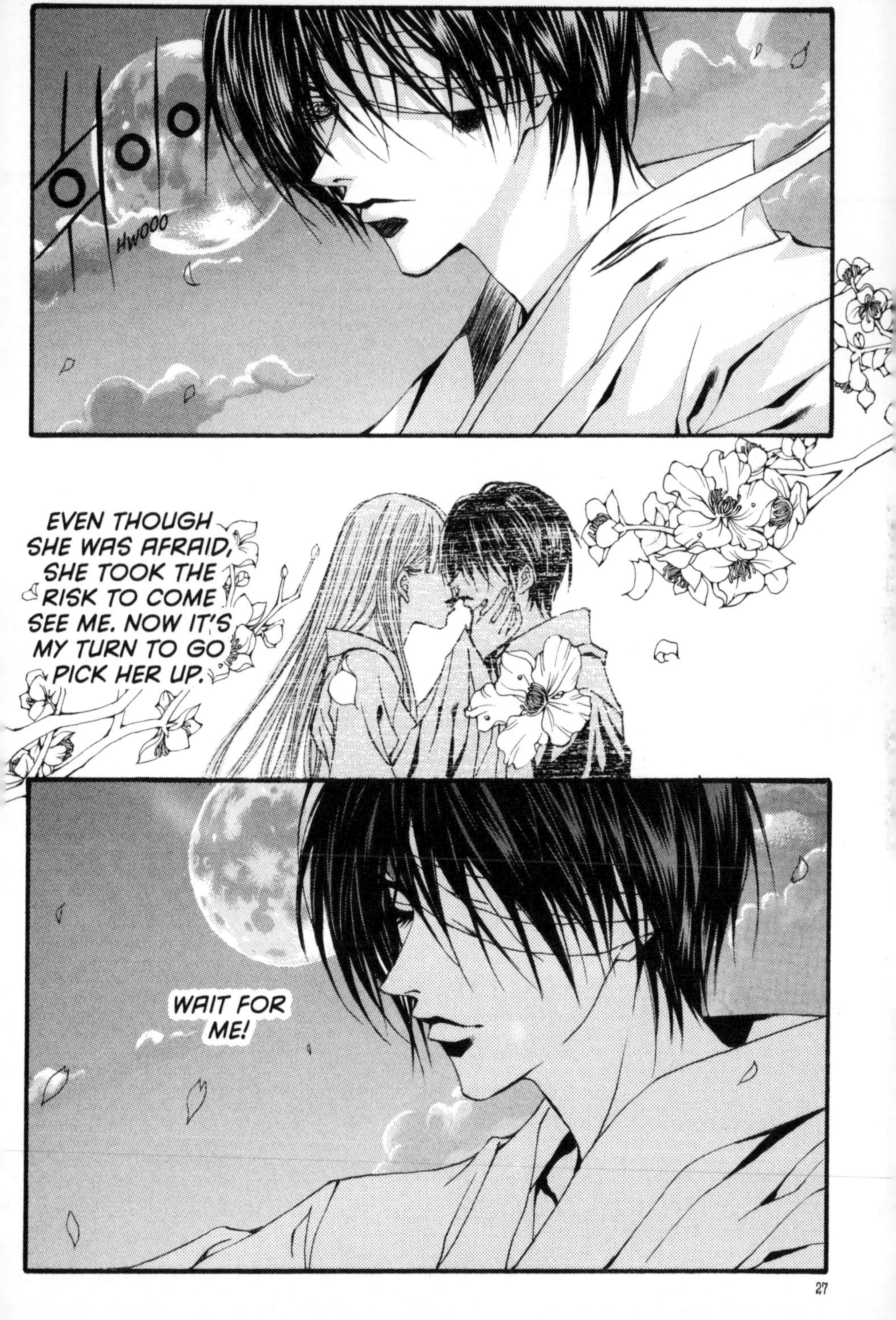
HOOOO
HWOOO
EVEN THOUGH SHE WAS AFRAID, SHE TOOK THE RISK TO COME SEE ME. NOW IT'S MY TURN TO GO PICK HER UP.
WAIT FOR ME!

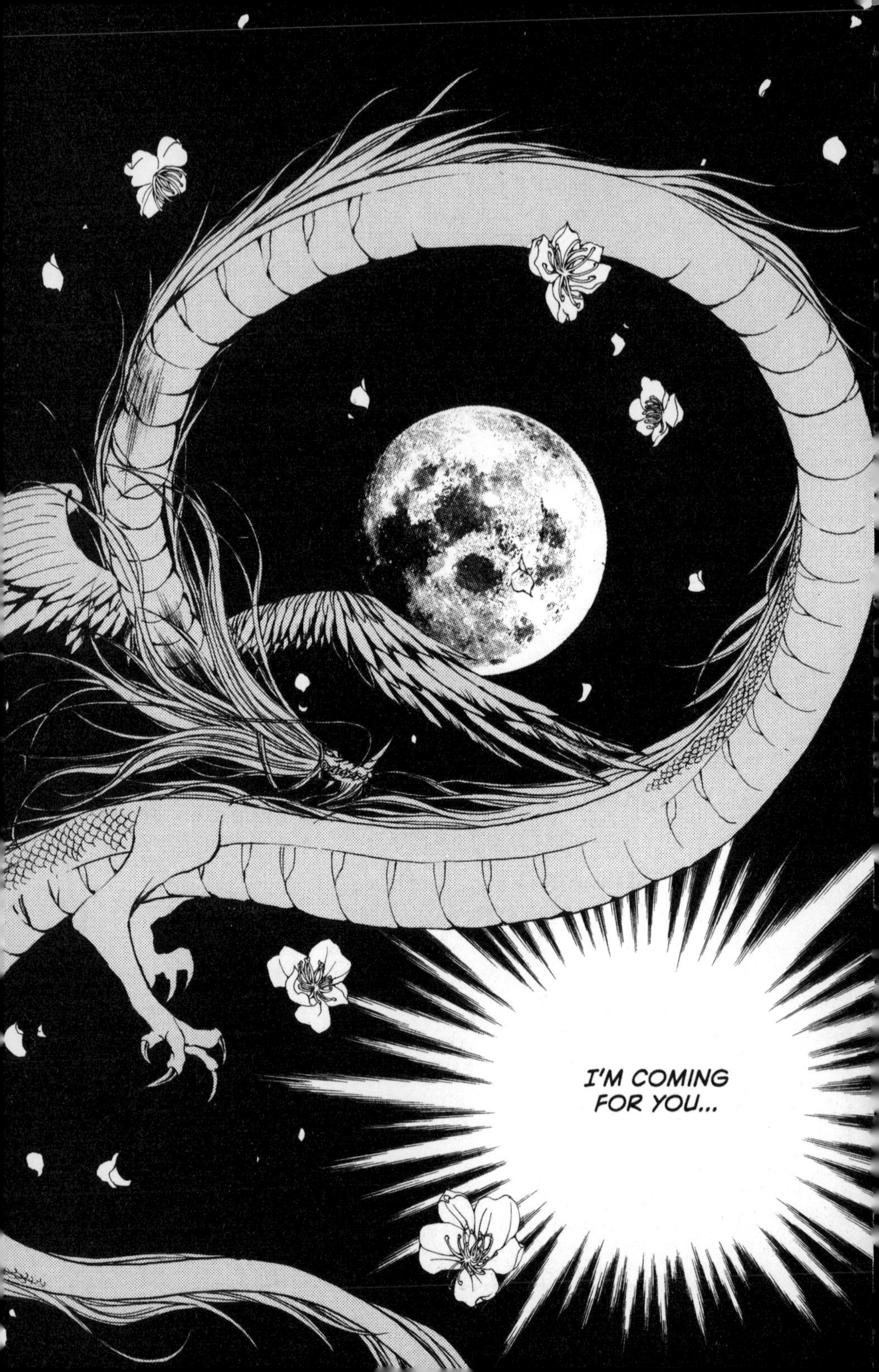
I'M COMING
FOR YOU...

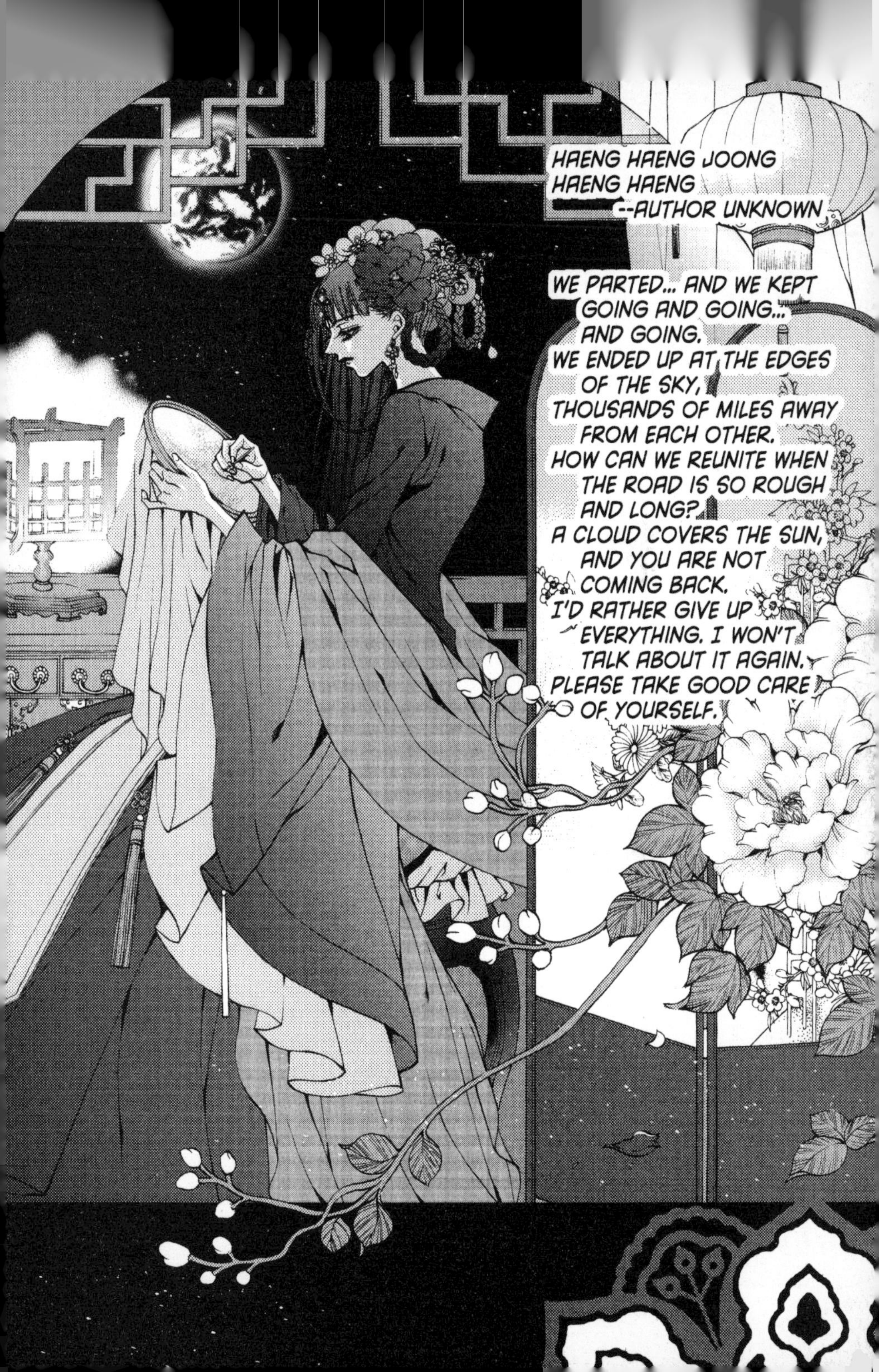
HAENG HAENG JOONG HAENG HAENG
--AUTHOR UNKNOWN
WE PARTED... AND WE KEPT GOING AND GOING... AND GOING.
WE ENDED UP AT THE EDGES OF THE SKY,
THOUSANDS OF MILES AWAY FROM EACH OTHER.
HOW CAN WE REUNITE WHEN THE ROAD IS SO ROUGH AND LONG?
A CLOUD COVERS THE SUN, AND YOU ARE NOT COMING BACK.
I'D RATHER GIVE UP EVERYTHING. I WON'T TALK ABOUT IT AGAIN.
PLEASE TAKE GOOD CARE OF YOURSELF.

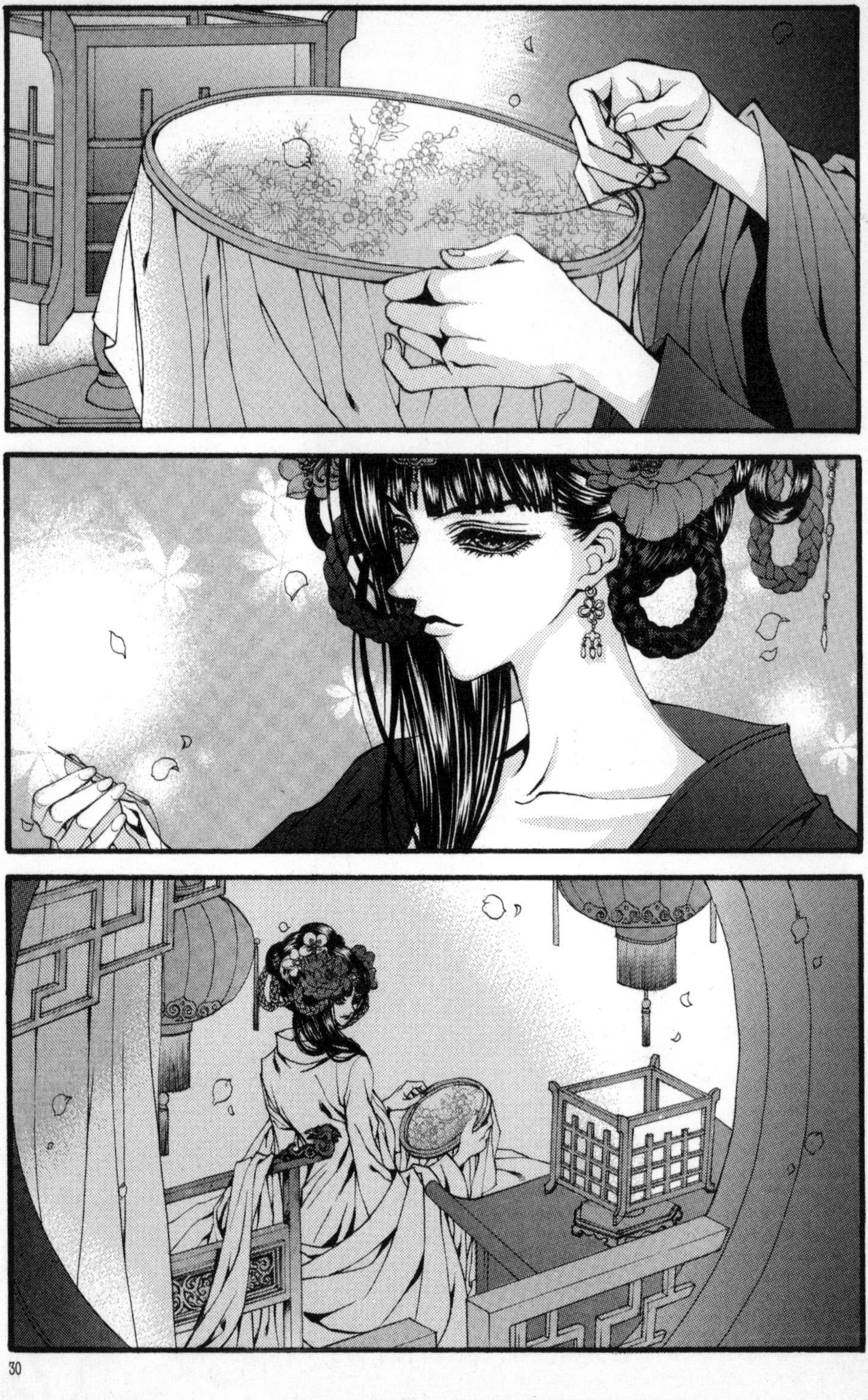

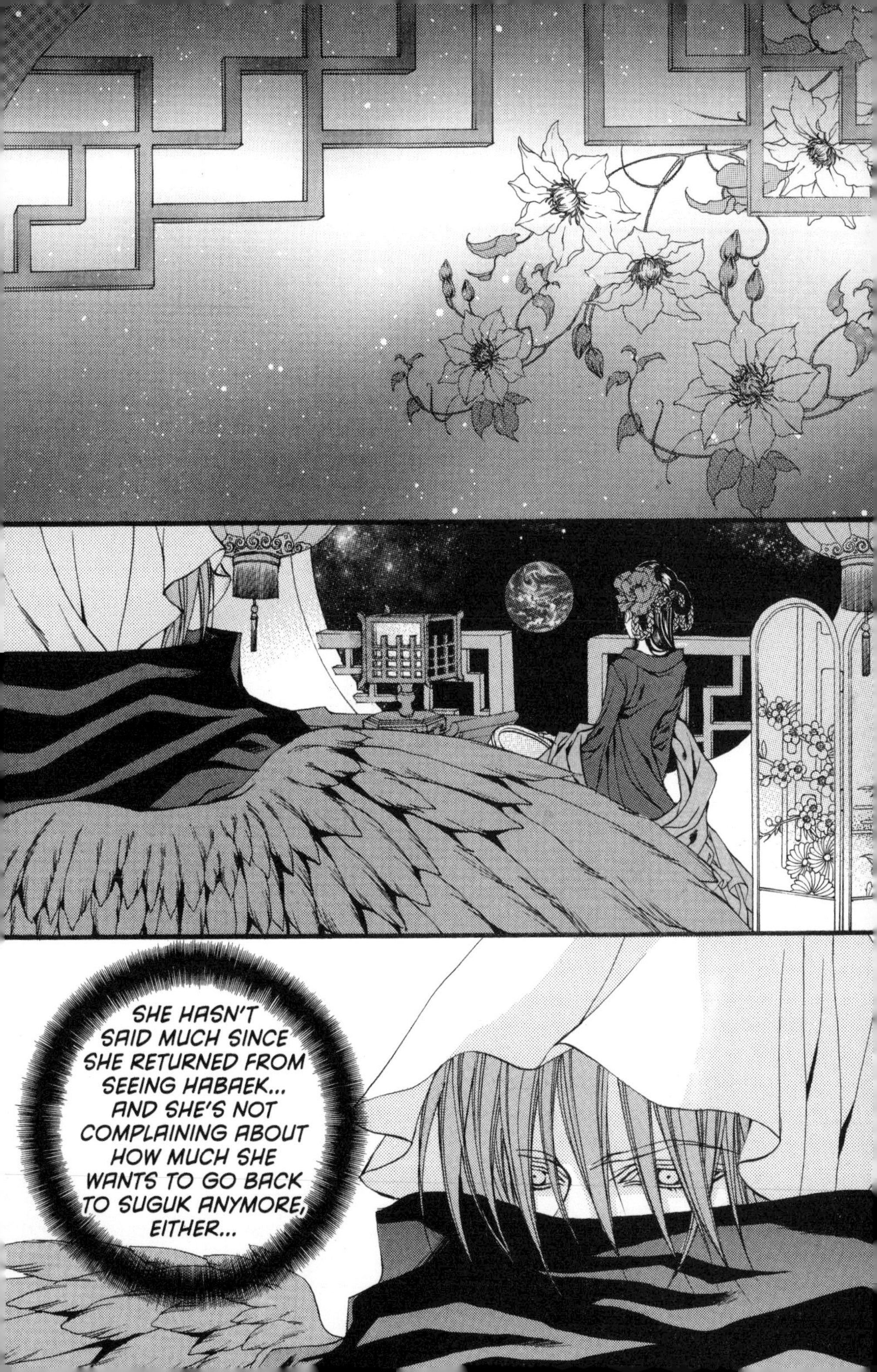
SHE HASN'T SAID MUCH SINCE SHE RETURNED FROM SEEING HABAEK... AND SHE'S NOT COMPLAINING ABOUT HOW MUCH SHE WANTS TO GO BACK TO SUGUK ANYMORE, EITHER...

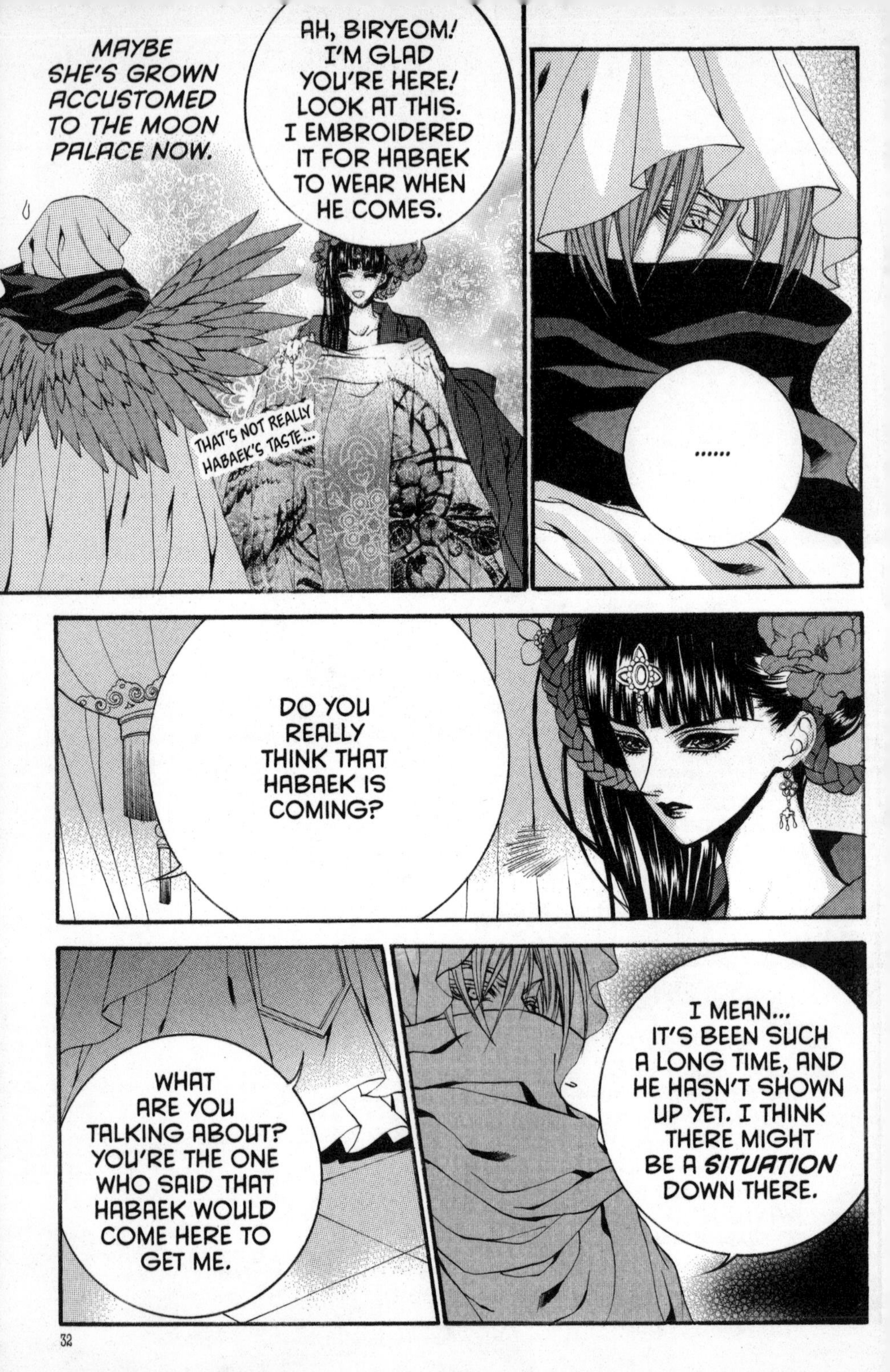
MAYBE SHE'S GROWN ACCUSTOMED TO THE MOON PALACE NOW.
AH, BIRYEOM! I'M GLAD YOU'RE HERE! LOOK AT THIS. I EMBROIDERED IT FOR HABAEK TO WEAR WHEN HE COMES.
THAT'S NOT REALLY HABAEK'S TASTE...
......
DO YOU REALLY THINK THAT HABAEK IS COMING?
WHAT ARE YOU TALKING ABOUT? YOU'RE THE ONE WHO SAID THAT HABAEK WOULD COME HERE TO GET ME.
I MEAN... IT'S BEEN SUCH A LONG TIME, AND HE HASN'T SHOWN UP YET. I THINK THERE MIGHT BE A *SITUATION* DOWN THERE.

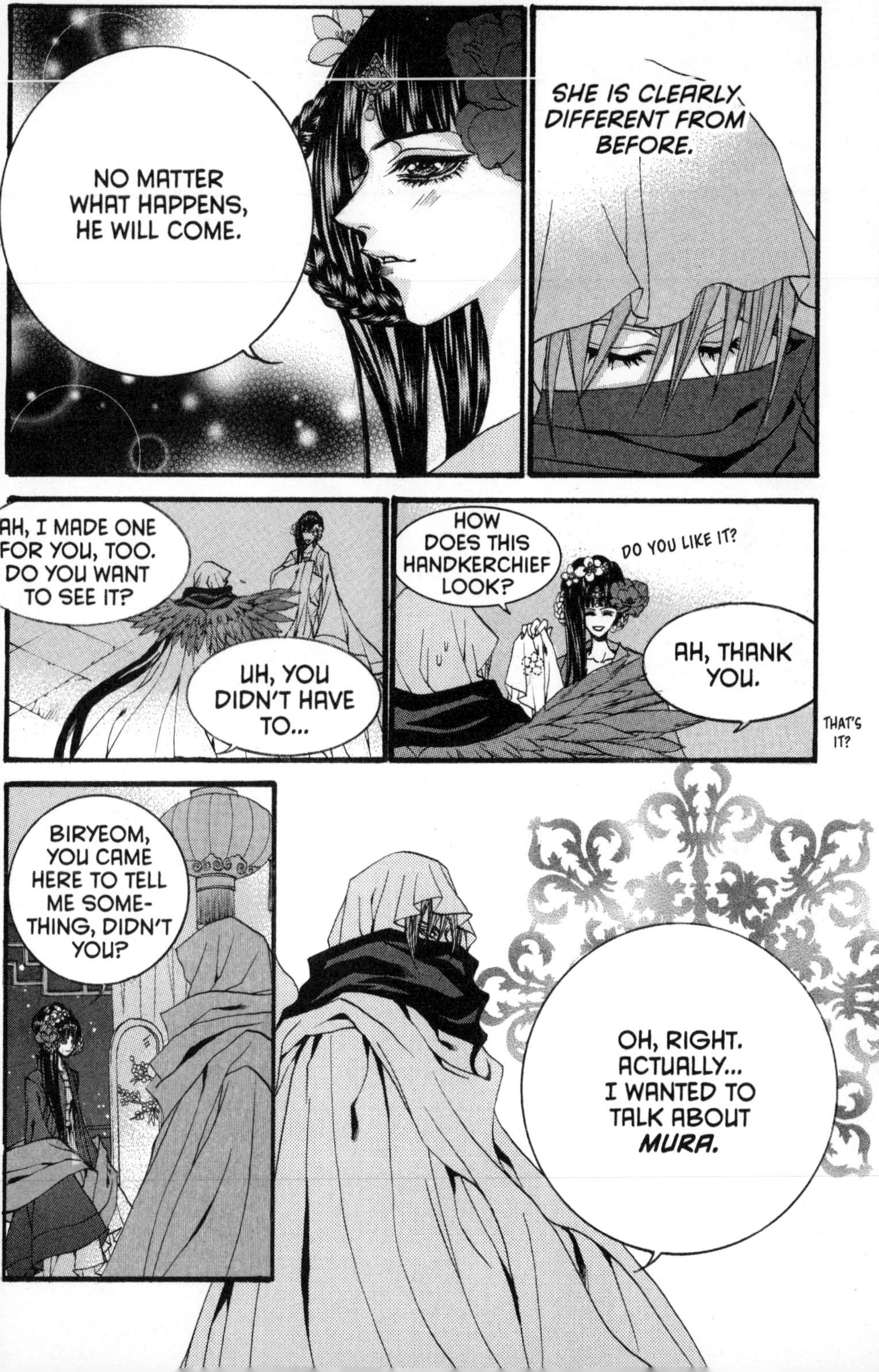
NO MATTER WHAT HAPPENS, HE WILL COME.
SHE IS CLEARLY DIFFERENT FROM BEFORE.
AH, I MADE ONE FOR YOU, TOO. DO YOU WANT TO SEE IT?
UH, YOU DIDN'T HAVE TO...
HOW DOES THIS HANDKERCHIEF LOOK?
DO YOU LIKE IT?
AH, THANK YOU.
THAT'S IT?
BIRYEOM, YOU CAME HERE TO TELL ME SOME-THING, DIDN'T YOU?
OH, RIGHT. ACTUALLY... I WANTED TO TALK ABOUT MURA.

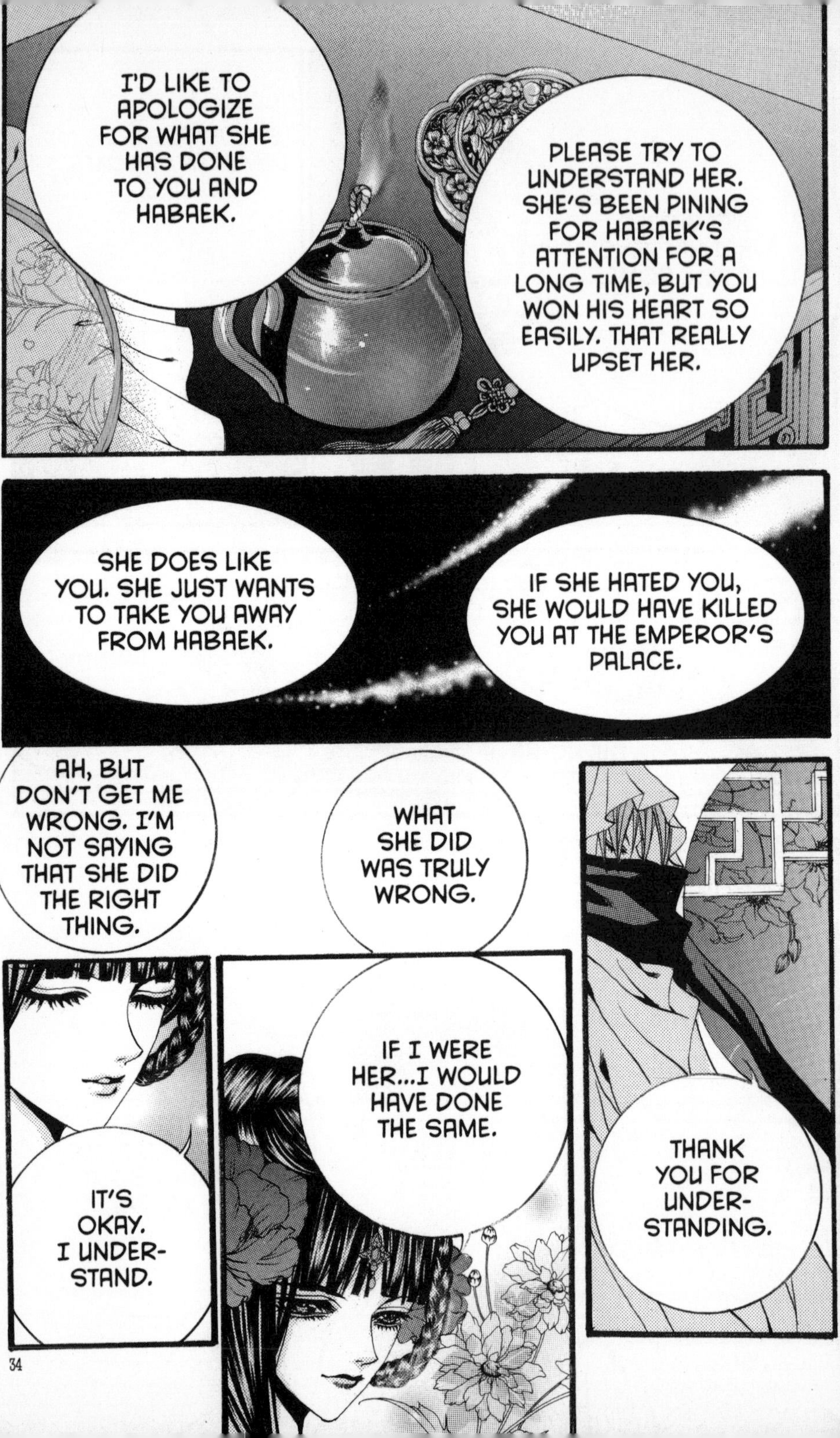
I'D LIKE TO APOLOGIZE FOR WHAT SHE HAS DONE TO YOU AND HABAEK.
PLEASE TRY TO UNDERSTAND HER. SHE'S BEEN PINING FOR HABAEK'S ATTENTION FOR A LONG TIME, BUT YOU WON HIS HEART SO EASILY. THAT REALLY UPSET HER.
SHE DOES LIKE YOU. SHE JUST WANTS TO TAKE YOU AWAY FROM HABAEK.
IF SHE HATED YOU, SHE WOULD HAVE KILLED YOU AT THE EMPEROR'S PALACE.
AH, BUT DON'T GET ME WRONG. I'M NOT SAYING THAT SHE DID THE RIGHT THING.
WHAT SHE DID WAS TRULY WRONG.
IT'S OKAY. I UNDER-STAND.
IF I WERE HER...I WOULD HAVE DONE THE SAME.
THANK YOU FOR UNDER-STANDING.

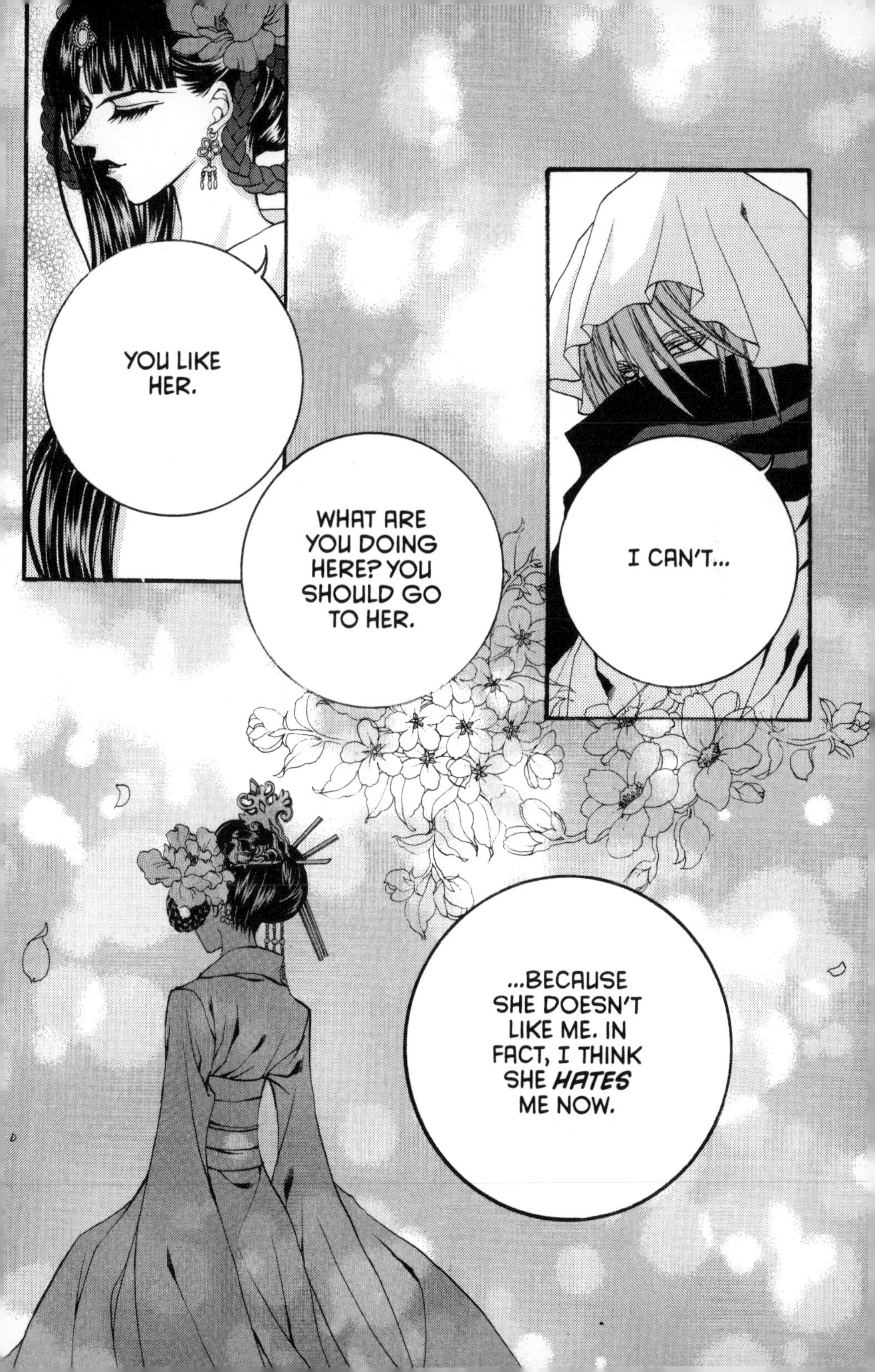
YOU LIKE HER.
WHAT ARE YOU DOING HERE? YOU SHOULD GO TO HER.
I CAN'T...
...BECAUSE SHE DOESN'T LIKE ME. IN FACT, I THINK SHE *HATES* ME NOW.

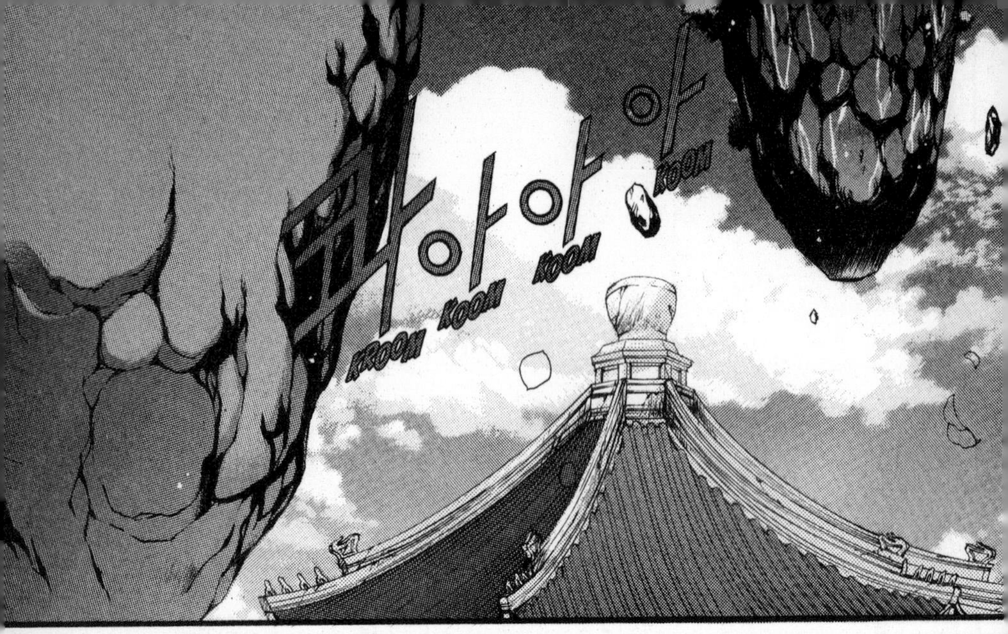
KROOM KOOM KOOM KOOM

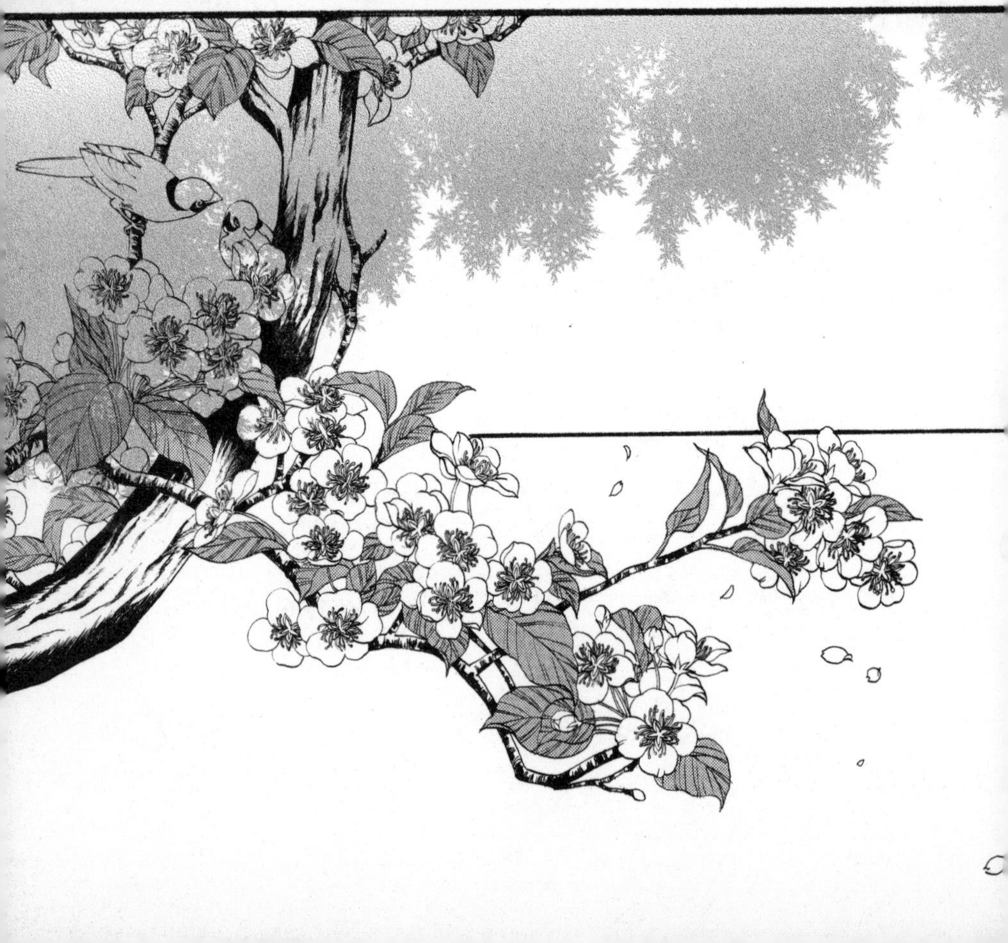

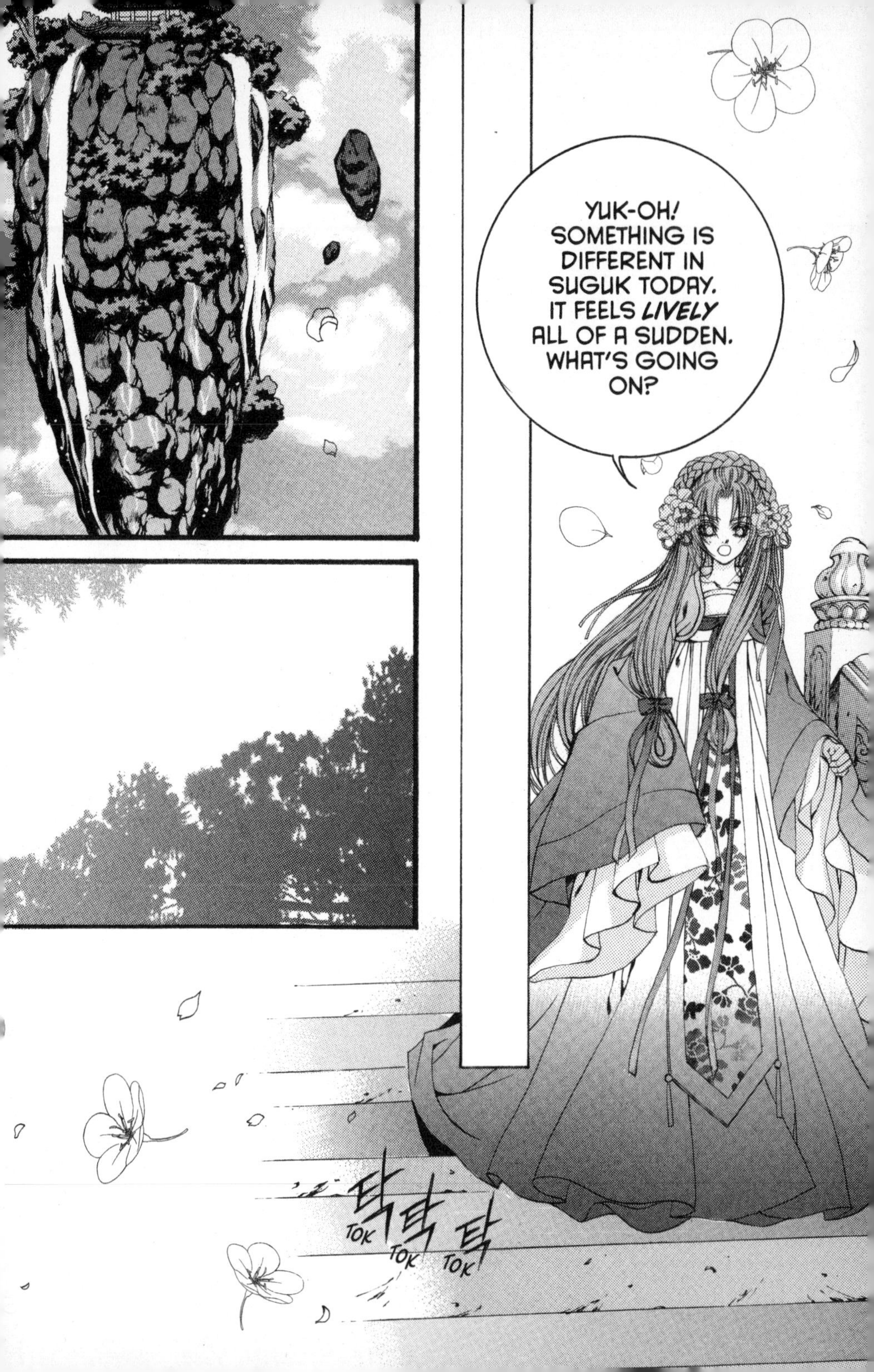
YUK-OH! SOMETHING IS DIFFERENT IN SUGUK TODAY. IT FEELS *LIVELY* ALL OF A SUDDEN. WHAT'S GOING ON?
탁 탁 탁
TOK TOK TOK

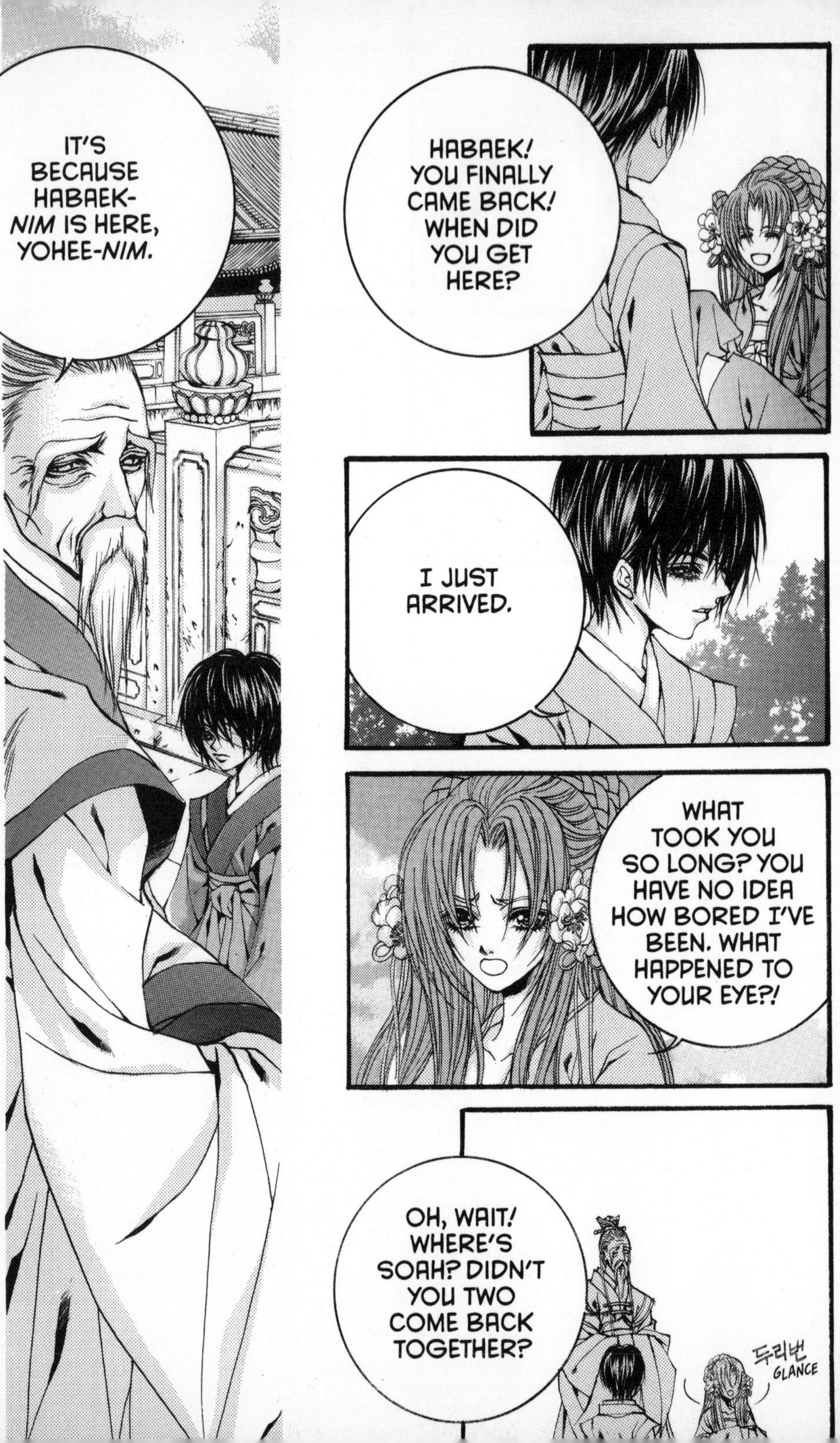
IT'S BECAUSE HABAEK-*NIM* IS HERE, YOHEE-*NIM*.
HABAEK! YOU FINALLY CAME BACK! WHEN DID YOU GET HERE?
I JUST ARRIVED.
WHAT TOOK YOU SO LONG? YOU HAVE NO IDEA HOW BORED I'VE BEEN. WHAT HAPPENED TO YOUR EYE?!
OH, WAIT! WHERE'S SOAH? DIDN'T YOU TWO COME BACK TOGETHER?
두리번
GLANCE

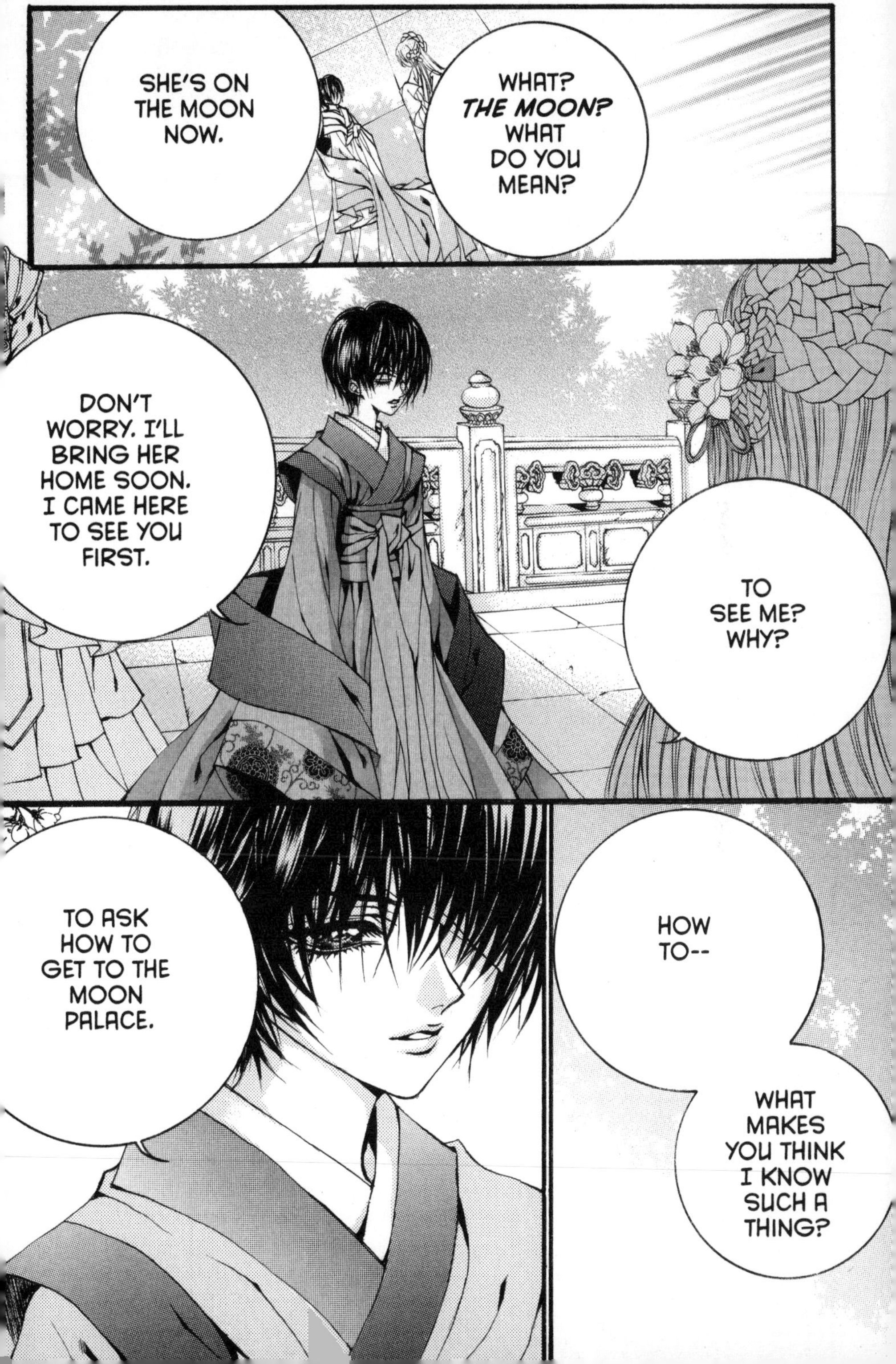
SHE'S ON THE MOON NOW.
WHAT? *THE MOON?* WHAT DO YOU MEAN?
DON'T WORRY. I'LL BRING HER HOME SOON. I CAME HERE TO SEE YOU FIRST.
TO SEE ME? WHY?
TO ASK HOW TO GET TO THE MOON PALACE.
HOW TO--
WHAT MAKES YOU THINK I KNOW SUCH A THING?

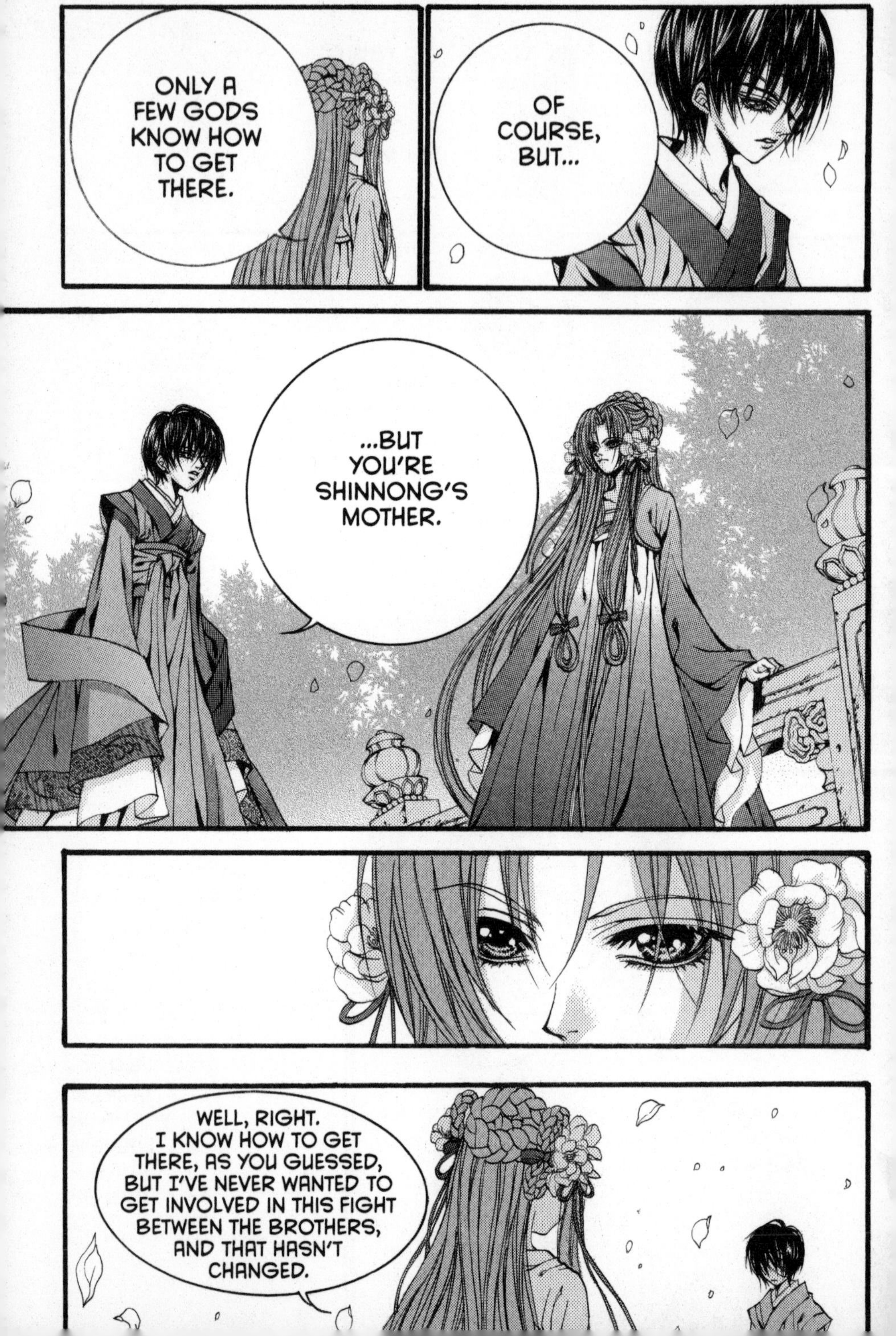
ONLY A FEW GODS KNOW HOW TO GET THERE.
OF COURSE, BUT...
...BUT YOU'RE SHINNONG'S MOTHER.
WELL, RIGHT. I KNOW HOW TO GET THERE, AS YOU GUESSED, BUT I'VE NEVER WANTED TO GET INVOLVED IN THIS FIGHT BETWEEN THE BROTHERS, AND THAT HASN'T CHANGED.

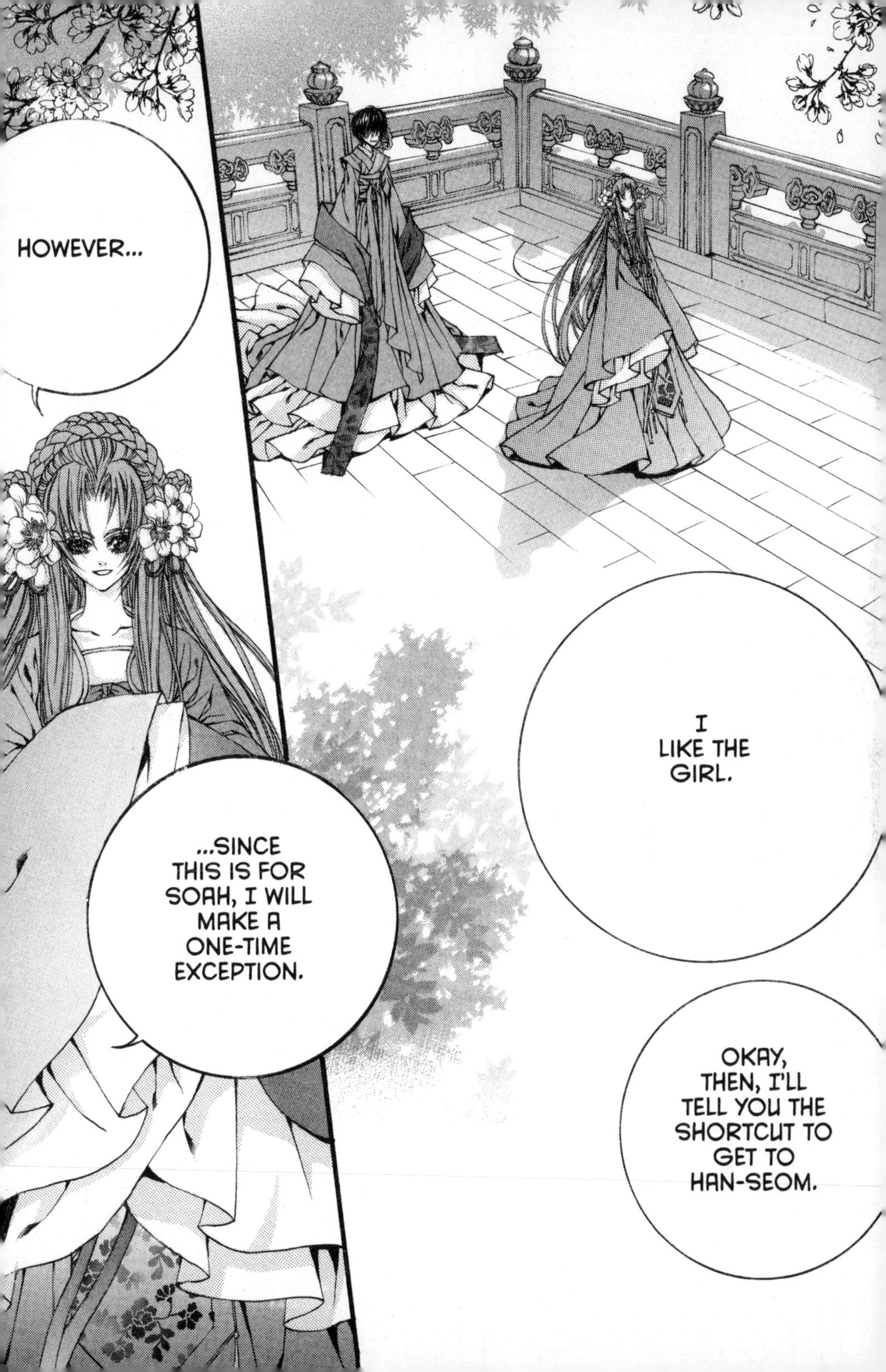
HOWEVER...
...SINCE THIS IS FOR SOAH, I WILL MAKE A ONE-TIME EXCEPTION.
I LIKE THE GIRL.
OKAY, THEN, I'LL TELL YOU THE SHORTCUT TO GET TO HAN-SEOM.

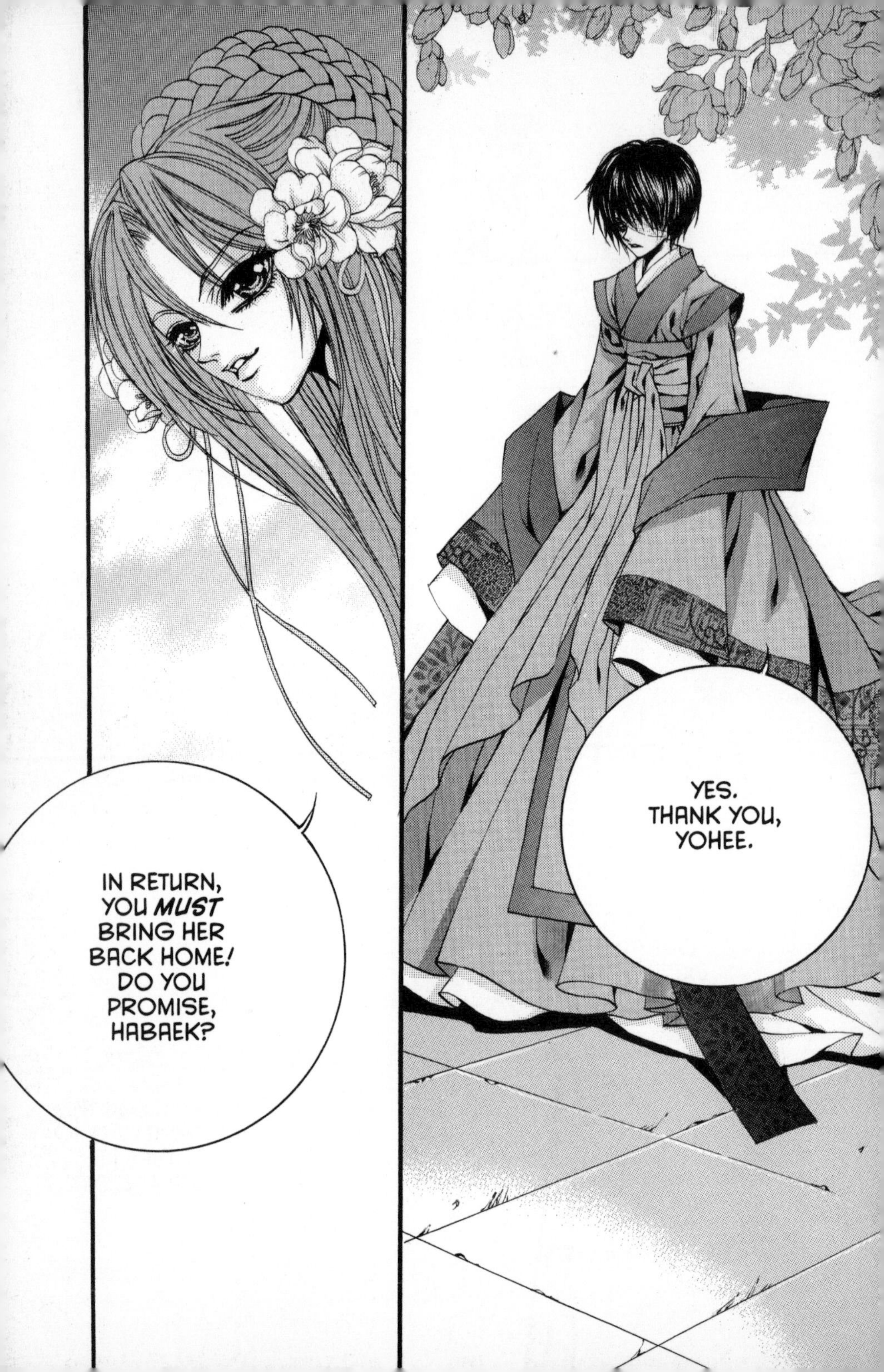
IN RETURN, YOU *MUST* BRING HER BACK HOME! DO YOU PROMISE, HABAEK?
YES. THANK YOU, YOHEE.

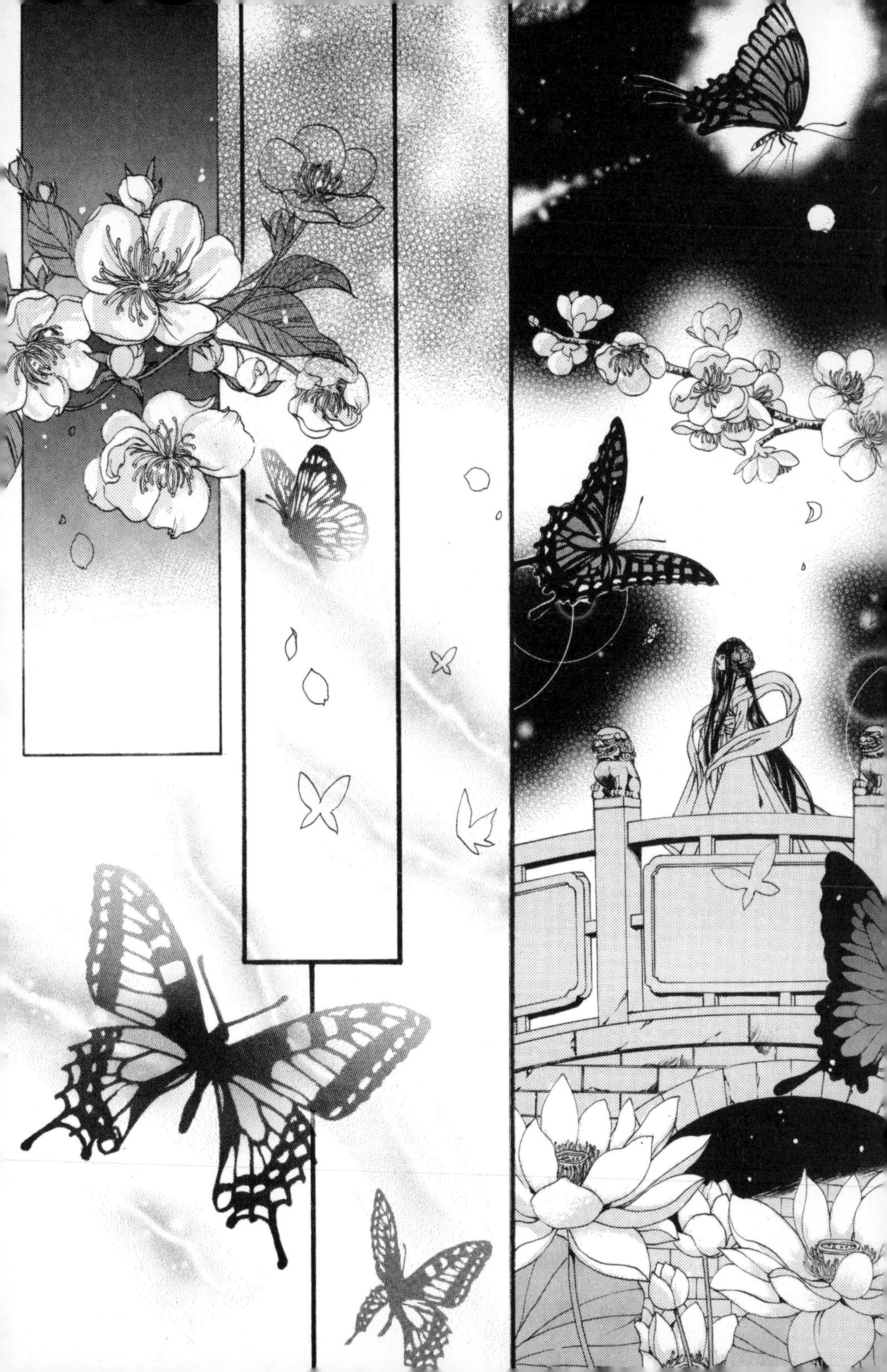

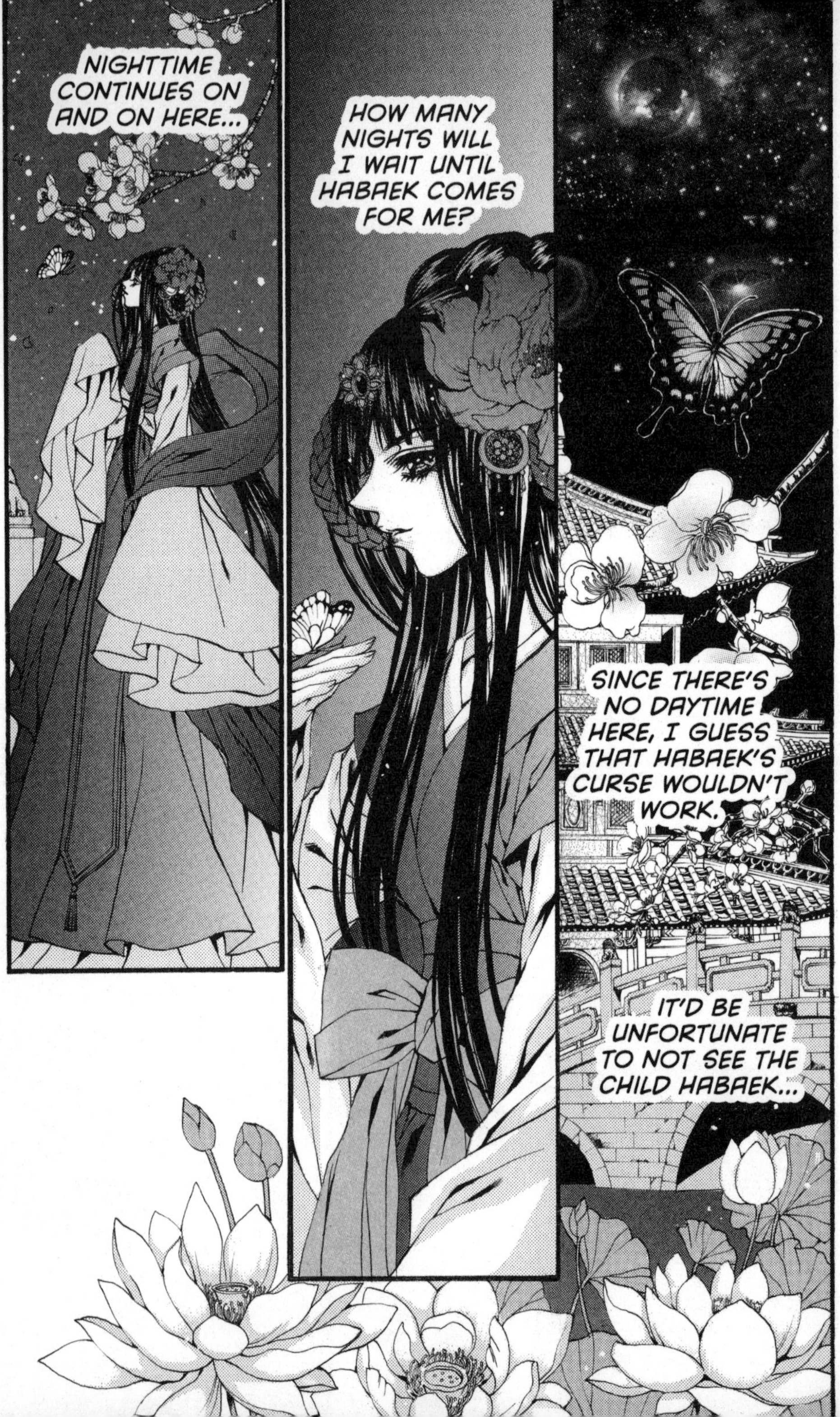
NIGHTTIME CONTINUES ON AND ON HERE...
HOW MANY NIGHTS WILL I WAIT UNTIL HABAEK COMES FOR ME?
SINCE THERE'S NO DAYTIME HERE, I GUESS THAT HABAEK'S CURSE WOULDN'T WORK.
IT'D BE UNFORTUNATE TO NOT SEE THE CHILD HABAEK...

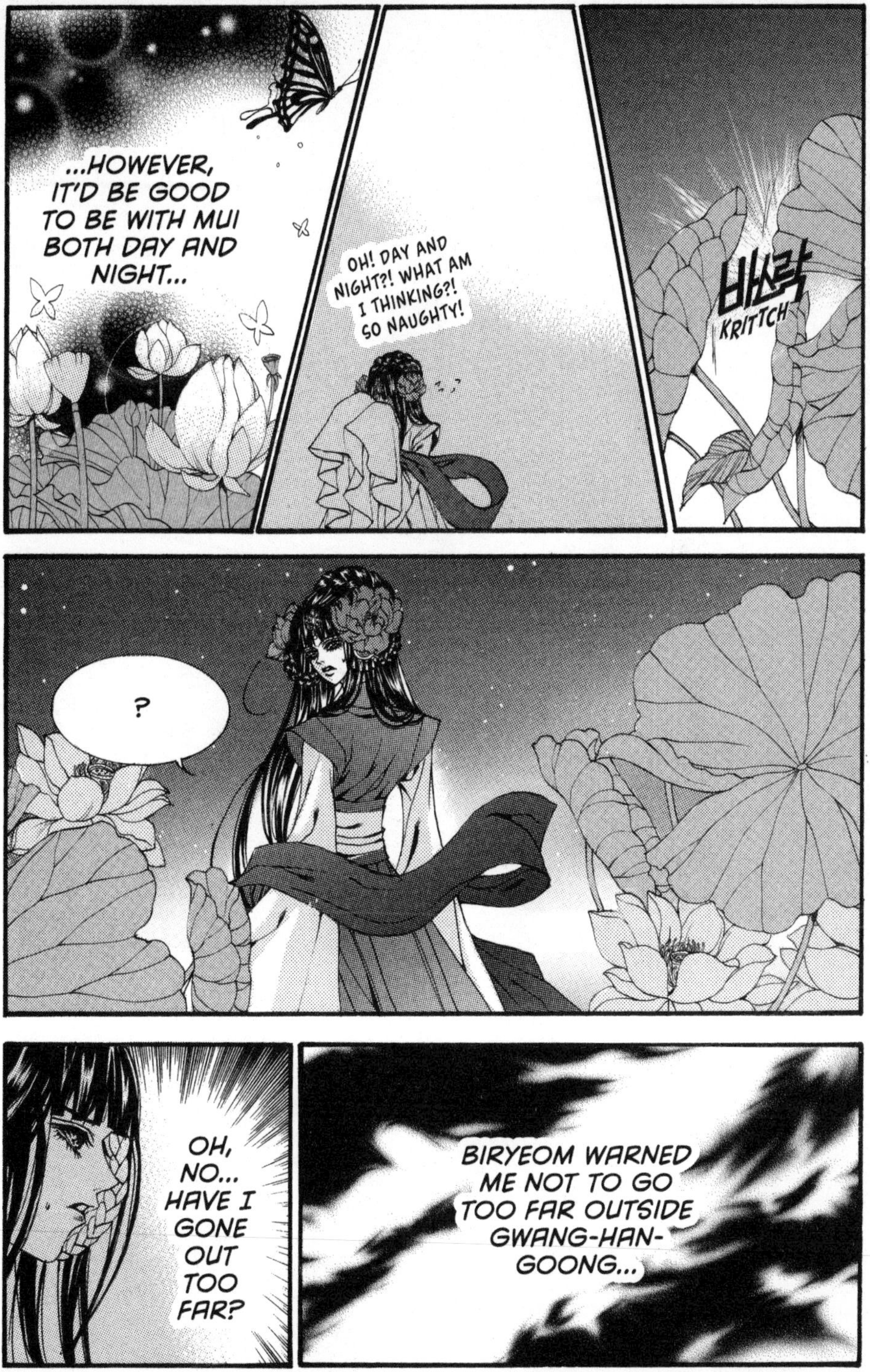
...HOWEVER, IT'D BE GOOD TO BE WITH MUI BOTH DAY AND NIGHT...
OH! DAY AND NIGHT?! WHAT AM I THINKING?! SO NAUGHTY!
바스락
KRITTCH
?
OH, NO... HAVE I GONE OUT TOO FAR?
BIRYEOM WARNED ME NOT TO GO TOO FAR OUTSIDE GWANG-HAN-GOONG...

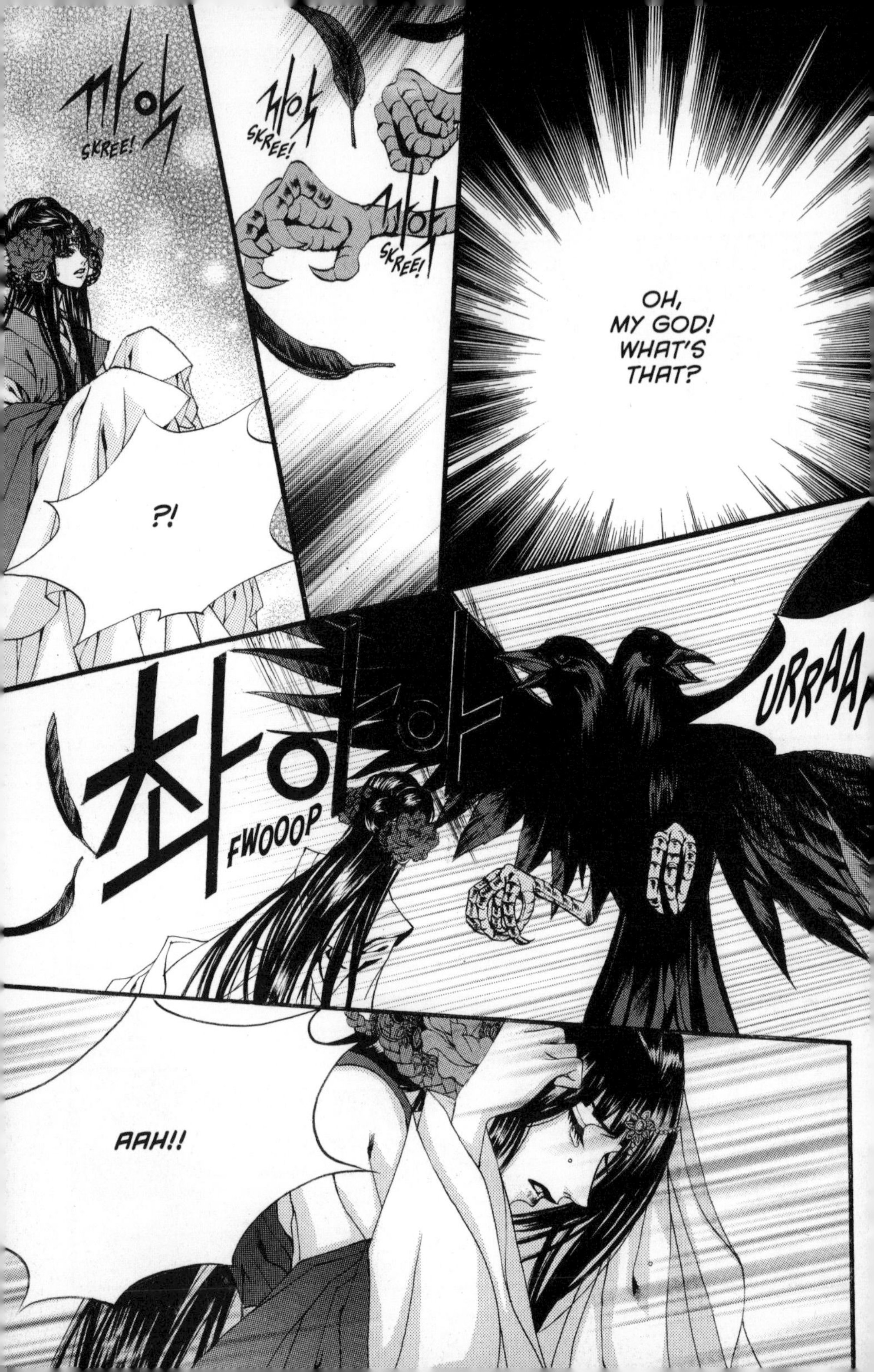
SKREE!
SKREE!
SKREE!
?!
OH, MY GOD! WHAT'S THAT?
FWOOOP
URRAA
AAH!!

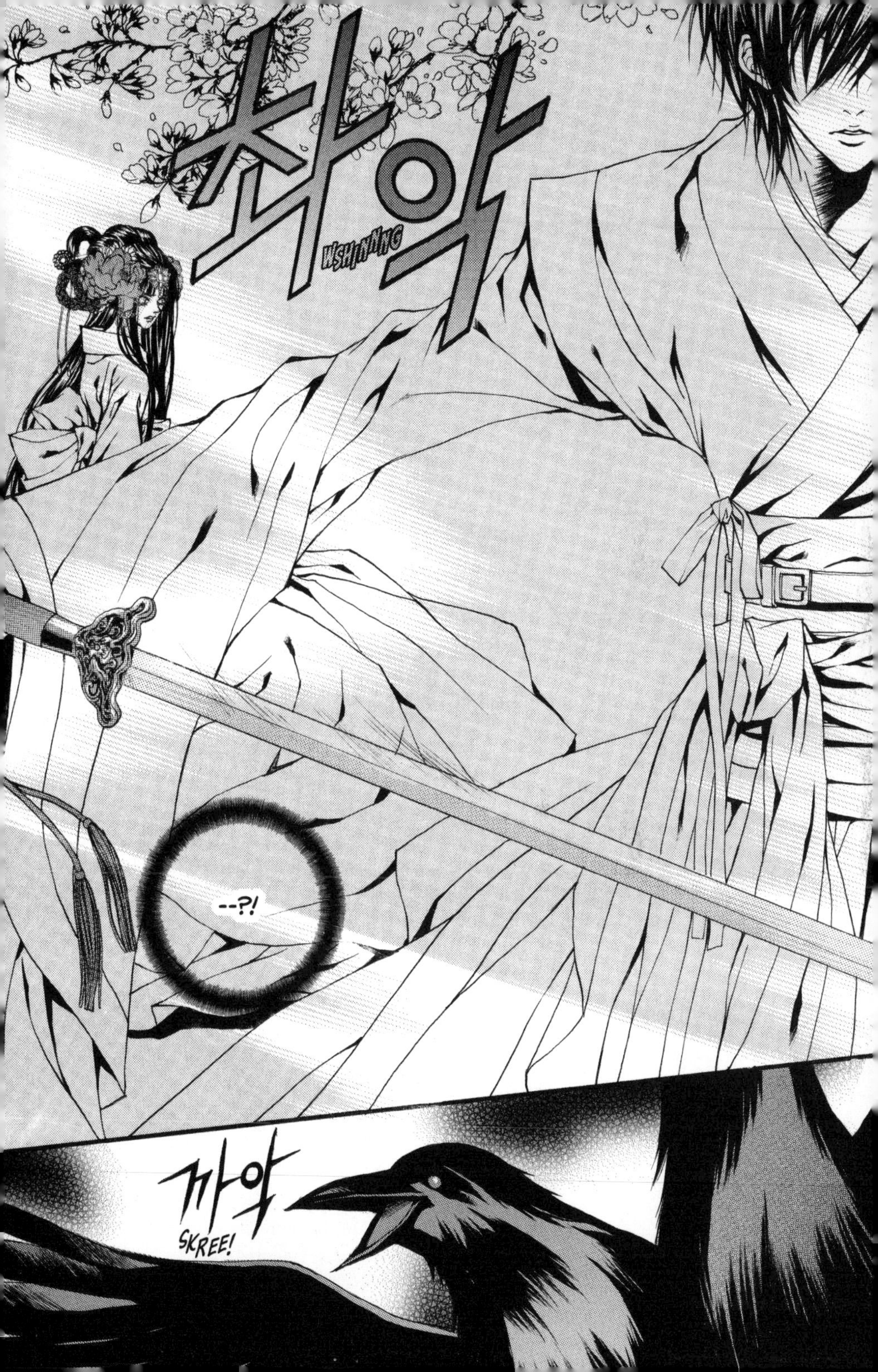
쇄아
WSHINNNG
--?!
까악
SKREE!

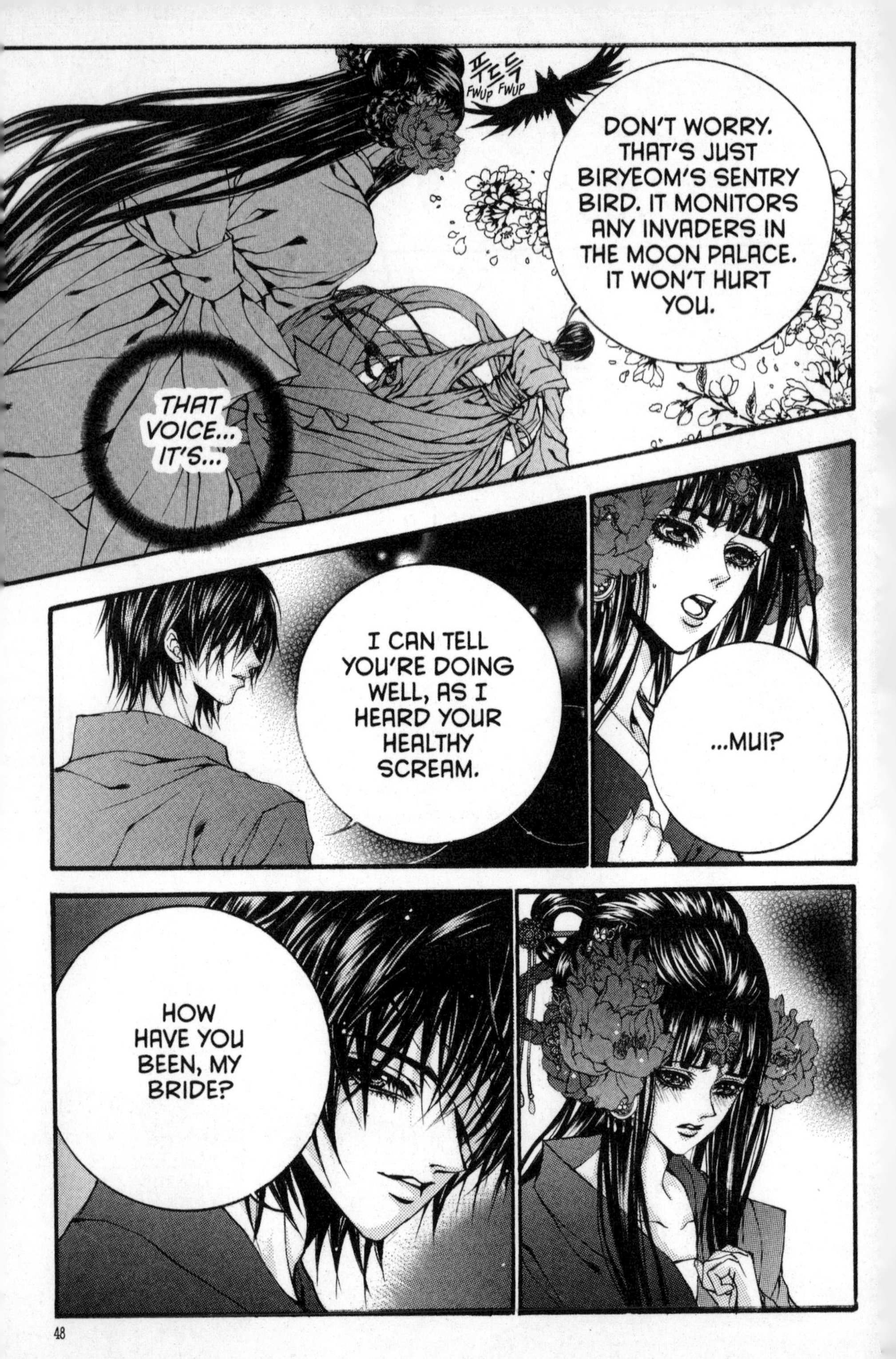
푸드득
FWUP FWUP
DON'T WORRY. THAT'S JUST BIRYEOM'S SENTRY BIRD. IT MONITORS ANY INVADERS IN THE MOON PALACE. IT WON'T HURT YOU.
THAT VOICE... IT'S...
I CAN TELL YOU'RE DOING WELL, AS I HEARD YOUR HEALTHY SCREAM.
...MUI?
HOW HAVE YOU BEEN, MY BRIDE?

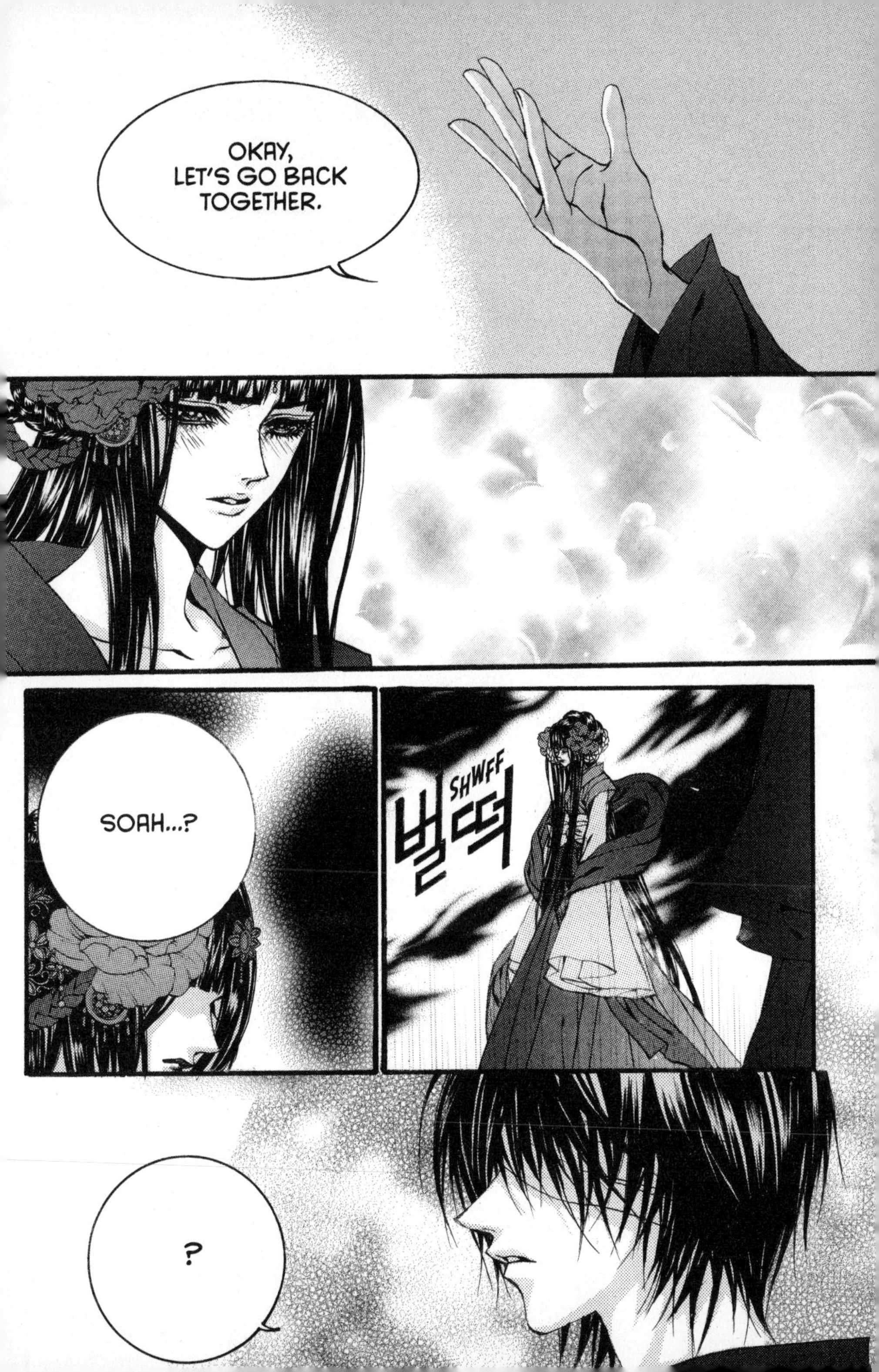
OKAY, LET'S GO BACK TOGETHER.
SOAH...?
SHWFF
벌떡
?

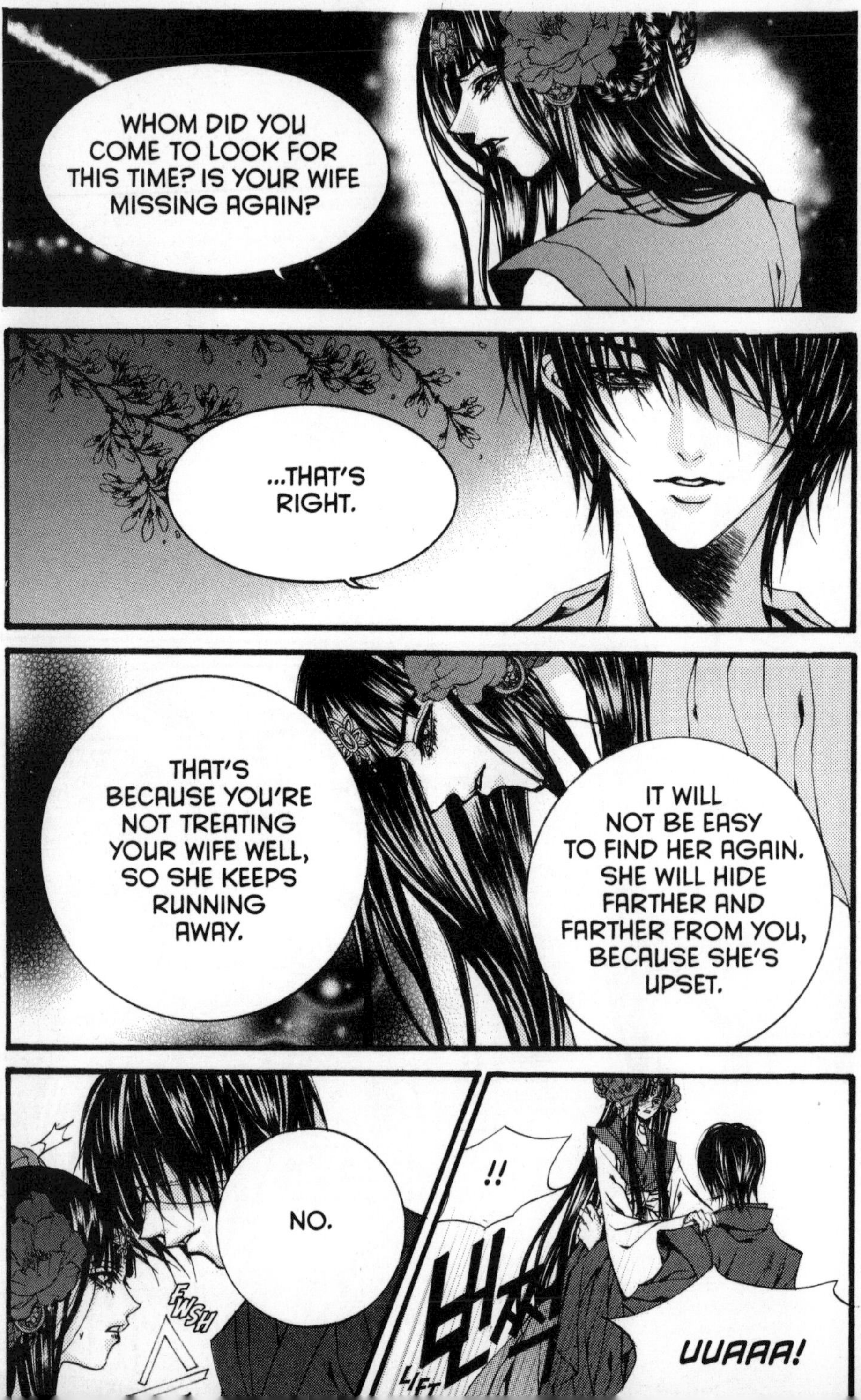
WHOM DID YOU COME TO LOOK FOR THIS TIME? IS YOUR WIFE MISSING AGAIN?
...THAT'S RIGHT.
THAT'S BECAUSE YOU'RE NOT TREATING YOUR WIFE WELL, SO SHE KEEPS RUNNING AWAY.
IT WILL NOT BE EASY TO FIND HER AGAIN. SHE WILL HIDE FARTHER AND FARTHER FROM YOU, BECAUSE SHE'S UPSET.
NO.
FWSH
!!
LIFT
UUAAA!

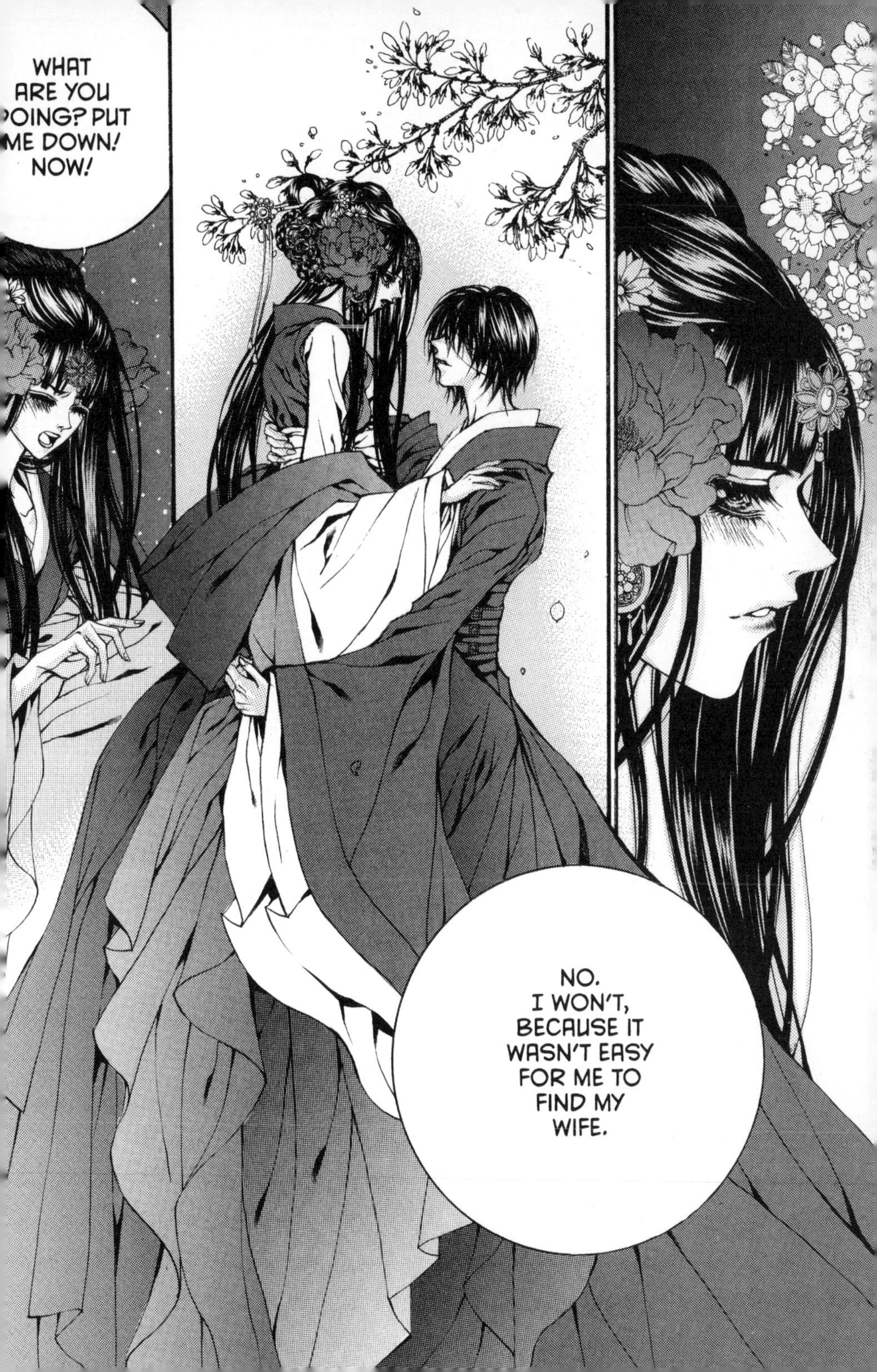

WHAT ARE YOU DOING? PUT ME DOWN! NOW!
NO. I WON'T, BECAUSE IT WASN'T EASY FOR ME TO FIND MY WIFE.

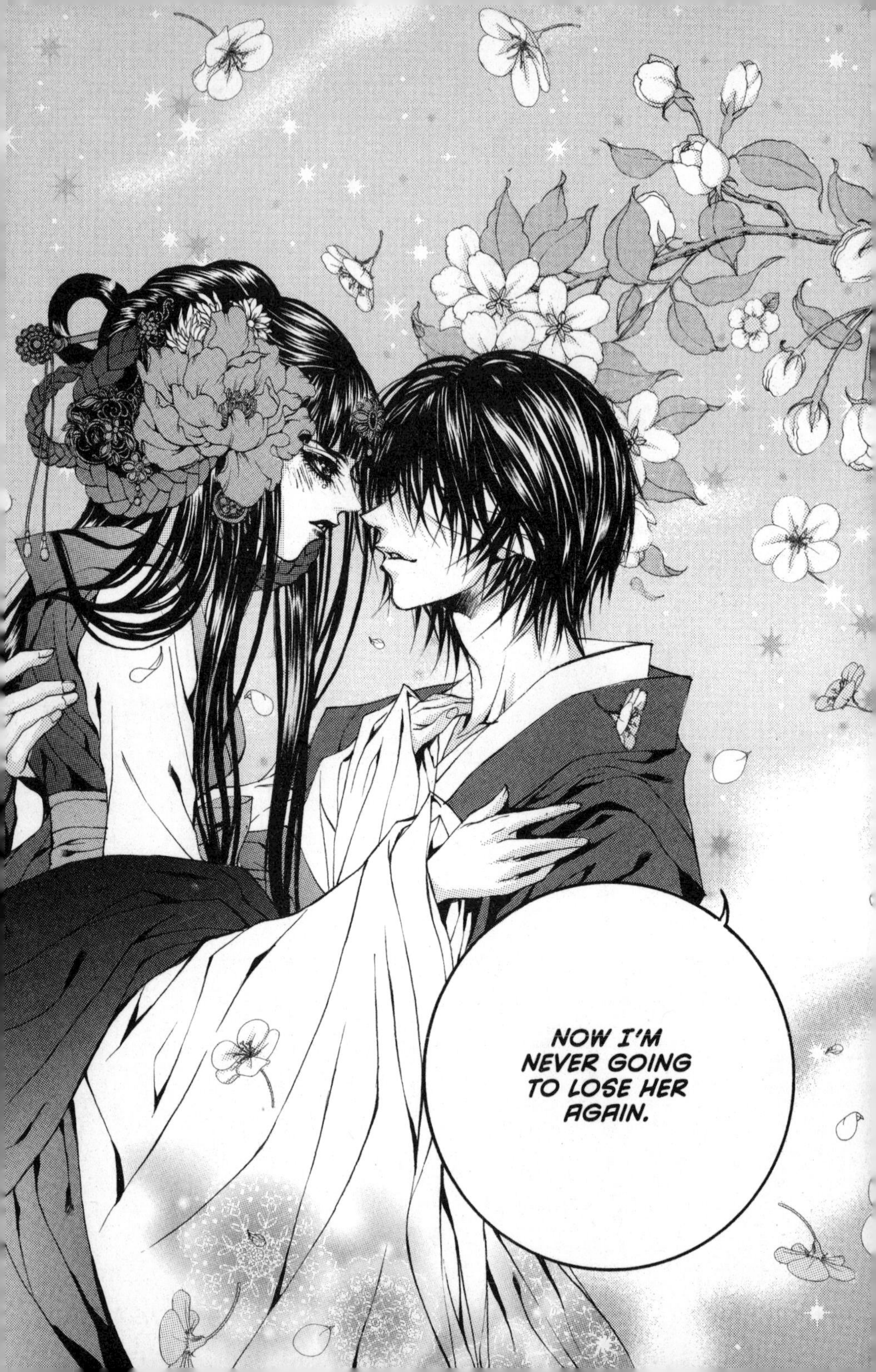
NOW I'M NEVER GOING TO LOSE HER AGAIN.

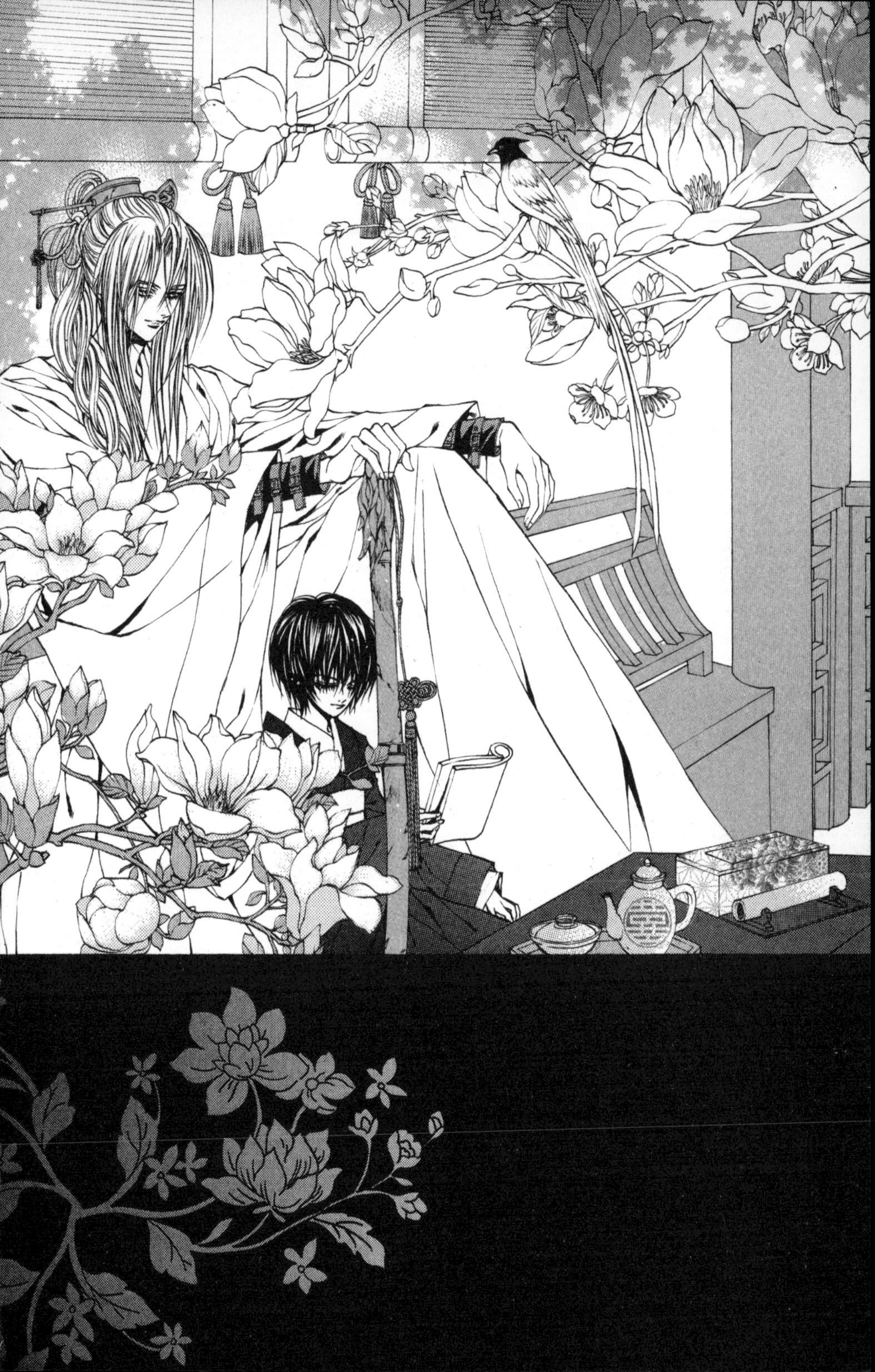

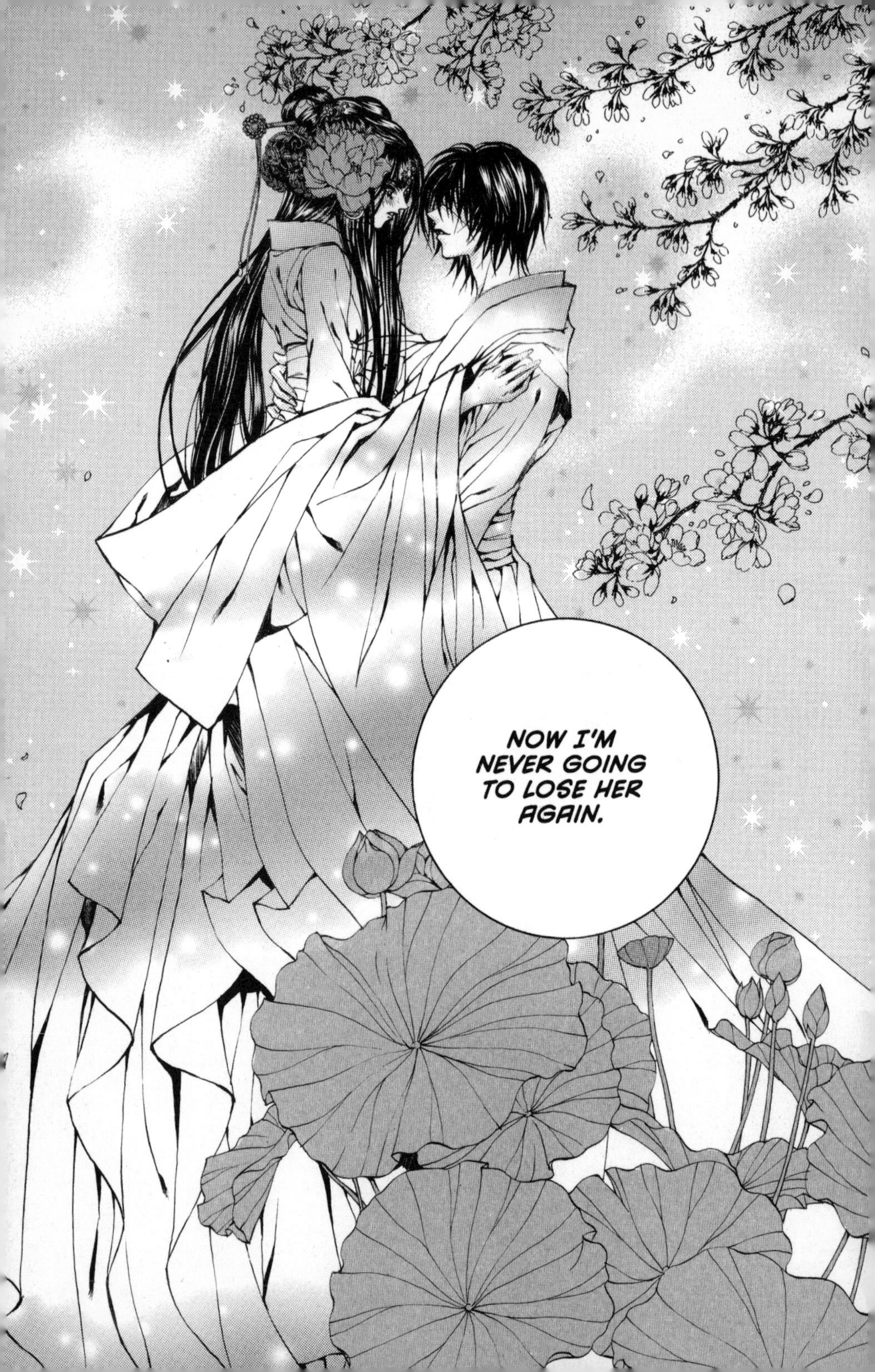
NOW I'M NEVER GOING TO LOSE HER AGAIN.

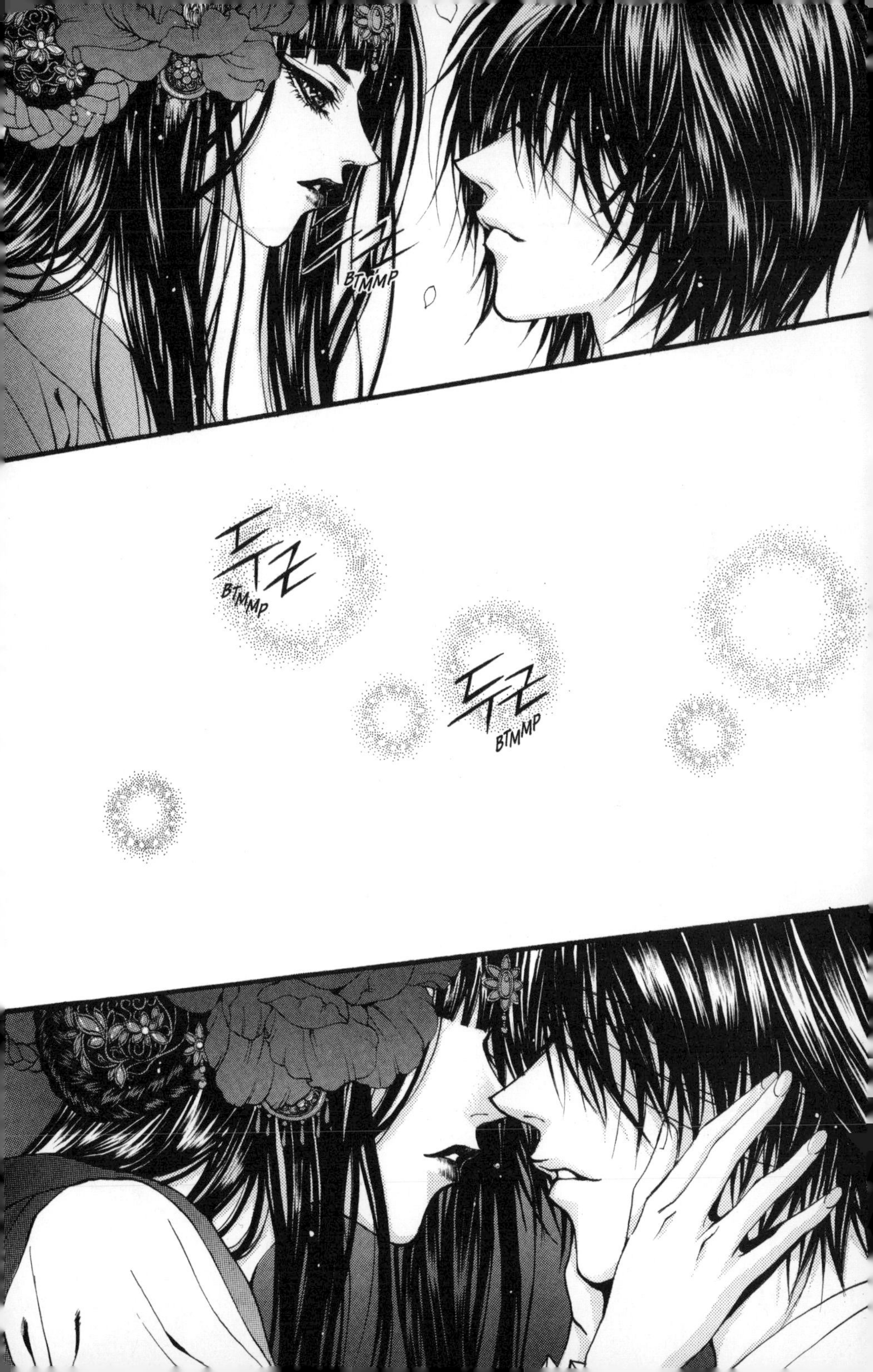
두근
BTMMP
두근
BTMMP
두근
BTMMP

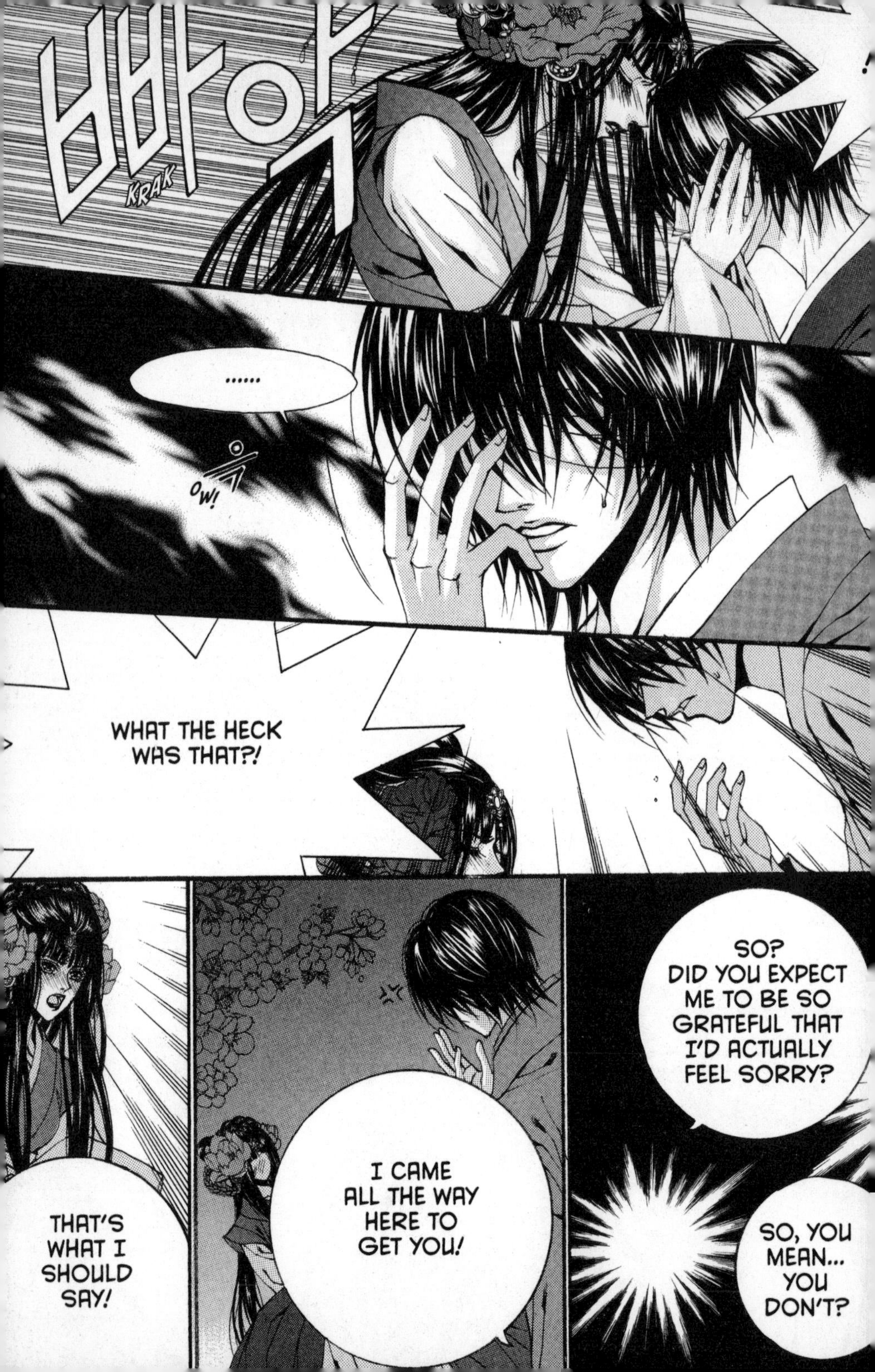
KRAK
......
OW!
WHAT THE HECK WAS THAT?!
THAT'S WHAT I SHOULD SAY!
I CAME ALL THE WAY HERE TO GET YOU!
SO? DID YOU EXPECT ME TO BE SO GRATEFUL THAT I'D ACTUALLY FEEL SORRY?
SO, YOU MEAN... YOU DON'T?

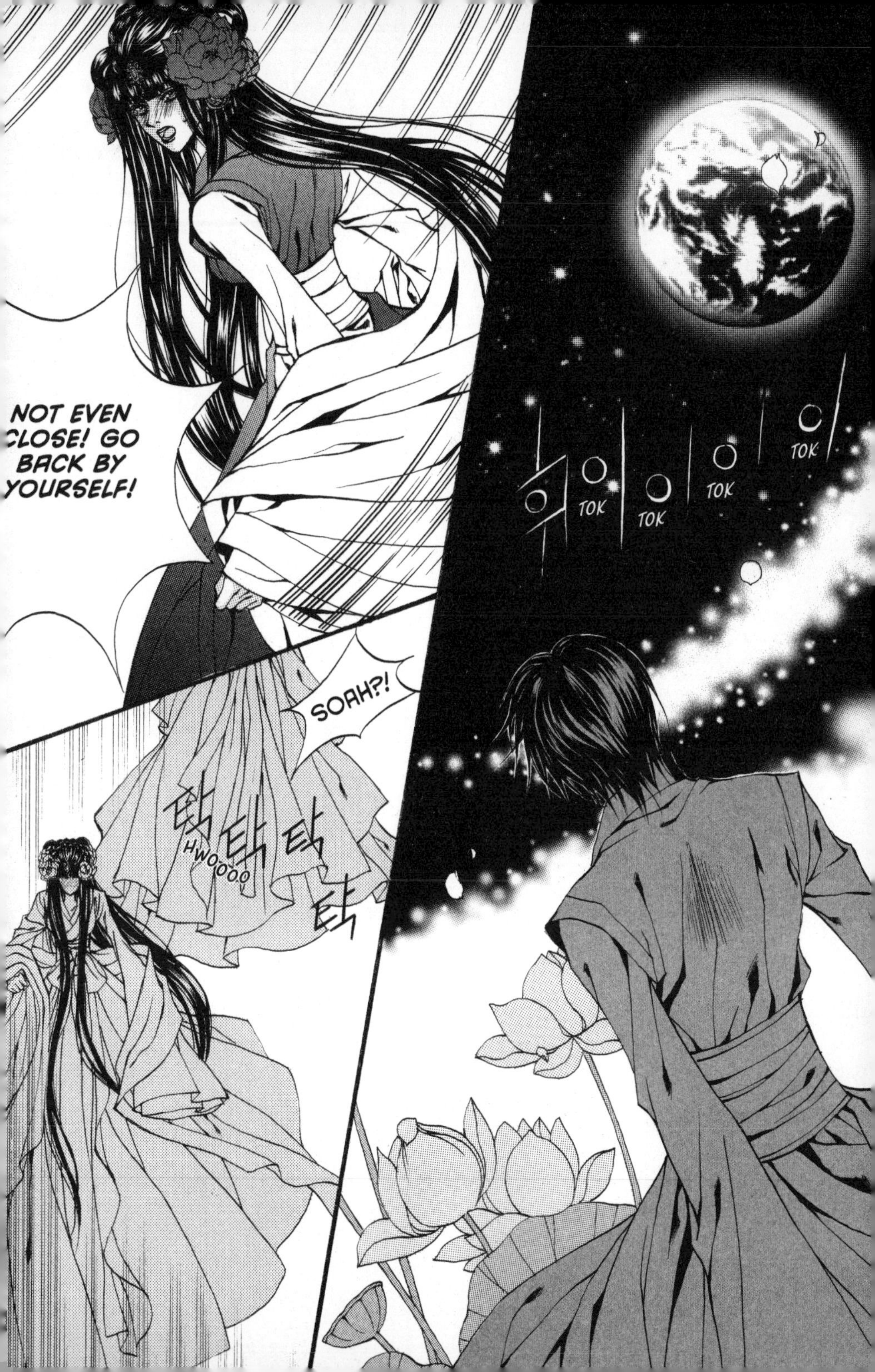

NOT EVEN CLOSE! GO BACK BY YOURSELF!
SOAH?!
HWOOOO
TOK
TOK
TOK
TOK

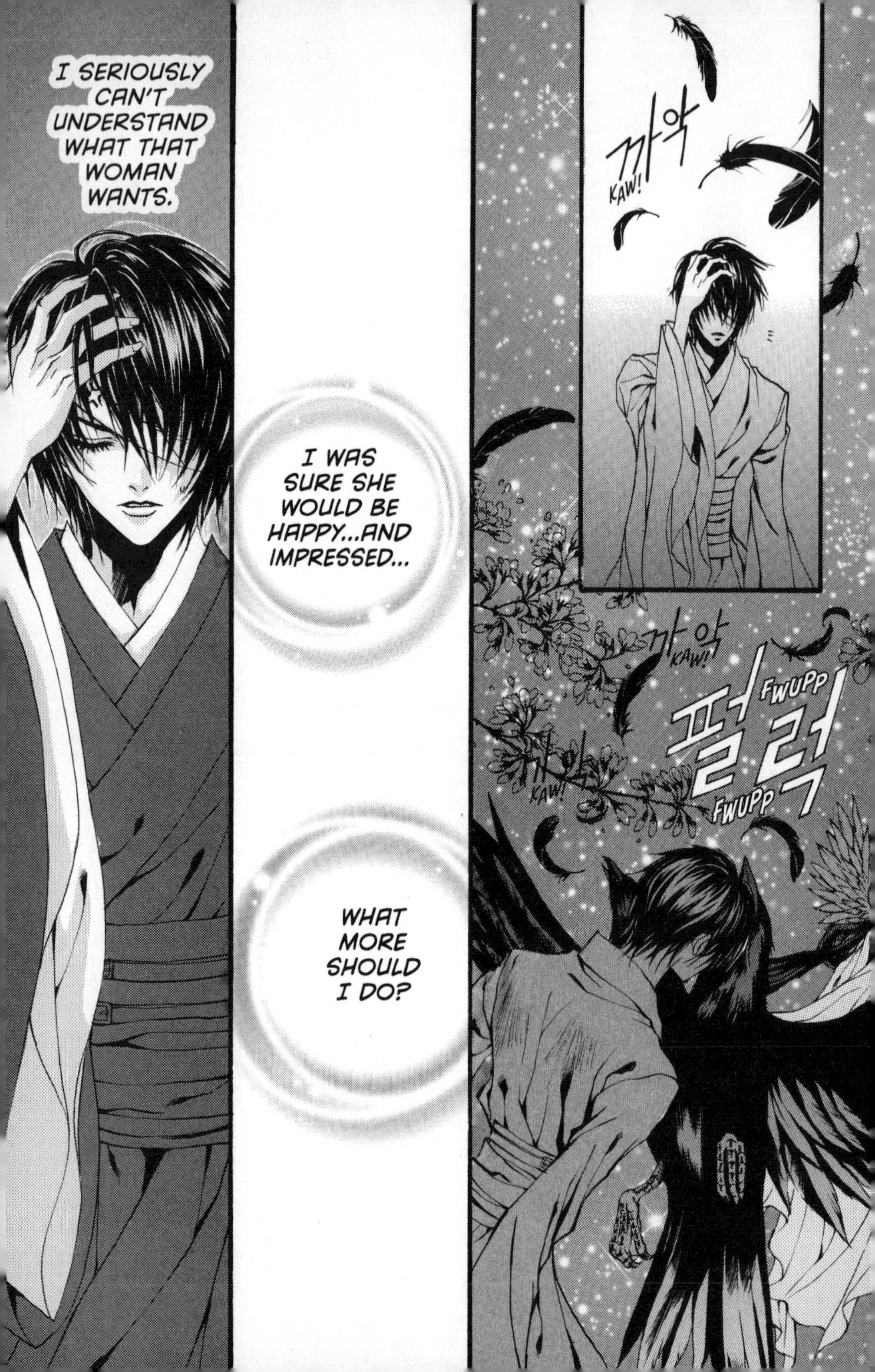
I SERIOUSLY CAN'T UNDERSTAND WHAT THAT WOMAN WANTS.
I WAS SURE SHE WOULD BE HAPPY...AND IMPRESSED...
WHAT MORE SHOULD I DO?
까악
KAW!
KAW!
KAW!
펄럭
FWUPP
FWUPP

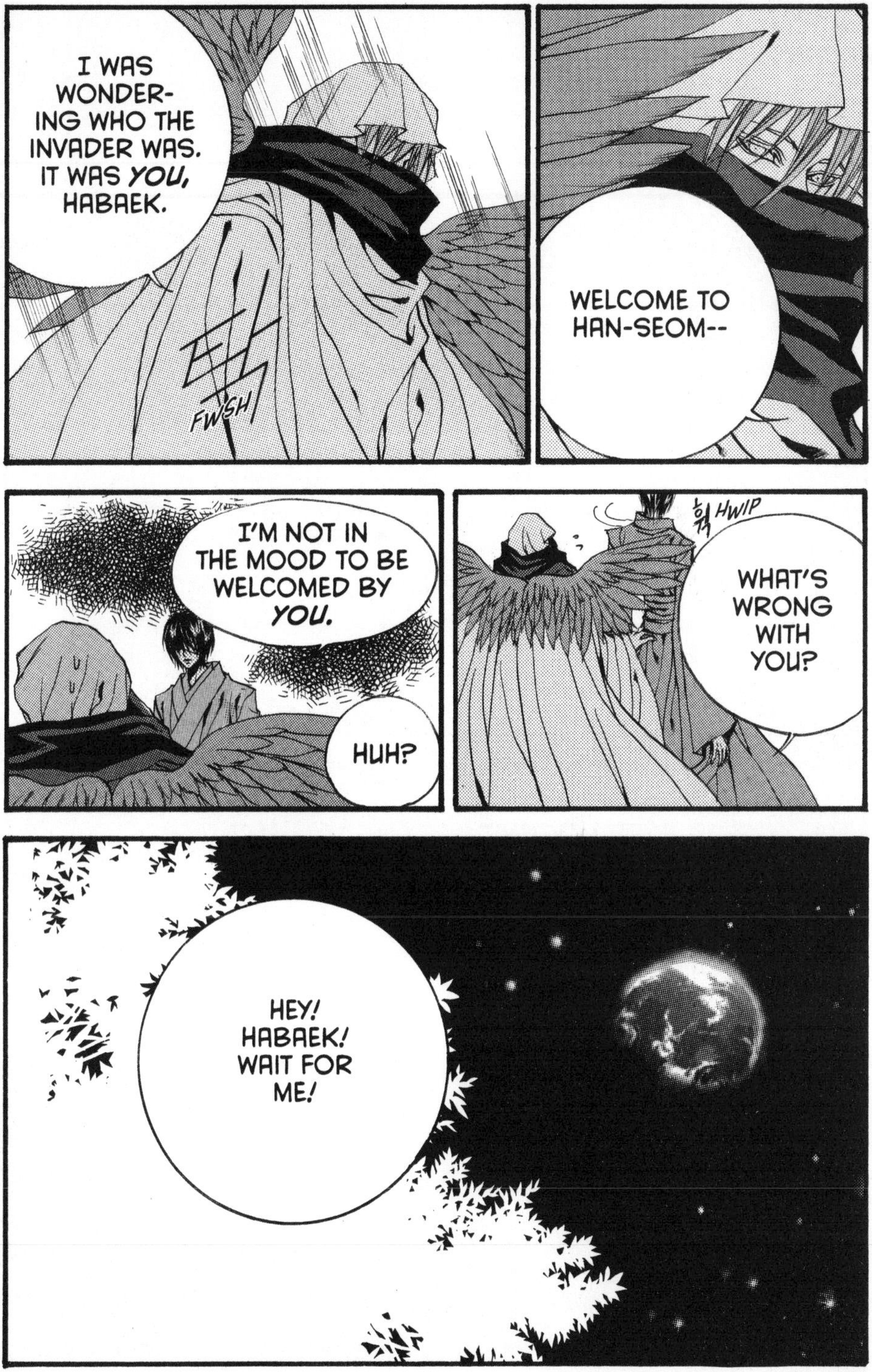
I WAS WONDERING WHO THE INVADER WAS. IT WAS *YOU,* HABAEK.
FWSH
WELCOME TO HAN-SEOM--
I'M NOT IN THE MOOD TO BE WELCOMED BY *YOU.*
HUH?
휙 HWIP
WHAT'S WRONG WITH YOU?
HEY! HABAEK! WAIT FOR ME!

I'M SORRY, MUI...

YOU CAME ALL THE WAY HERE FOR ME...I WAS HAPPY.

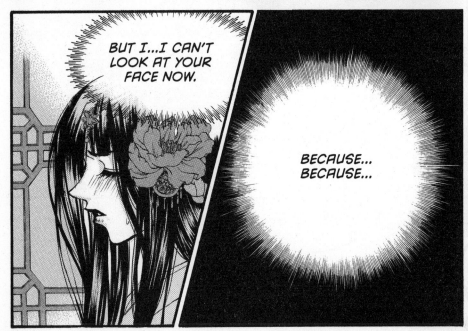

BUT I...I CAN'T LOOK AT YOUR FACE NOW.

BECAUSE... BECAUSE...

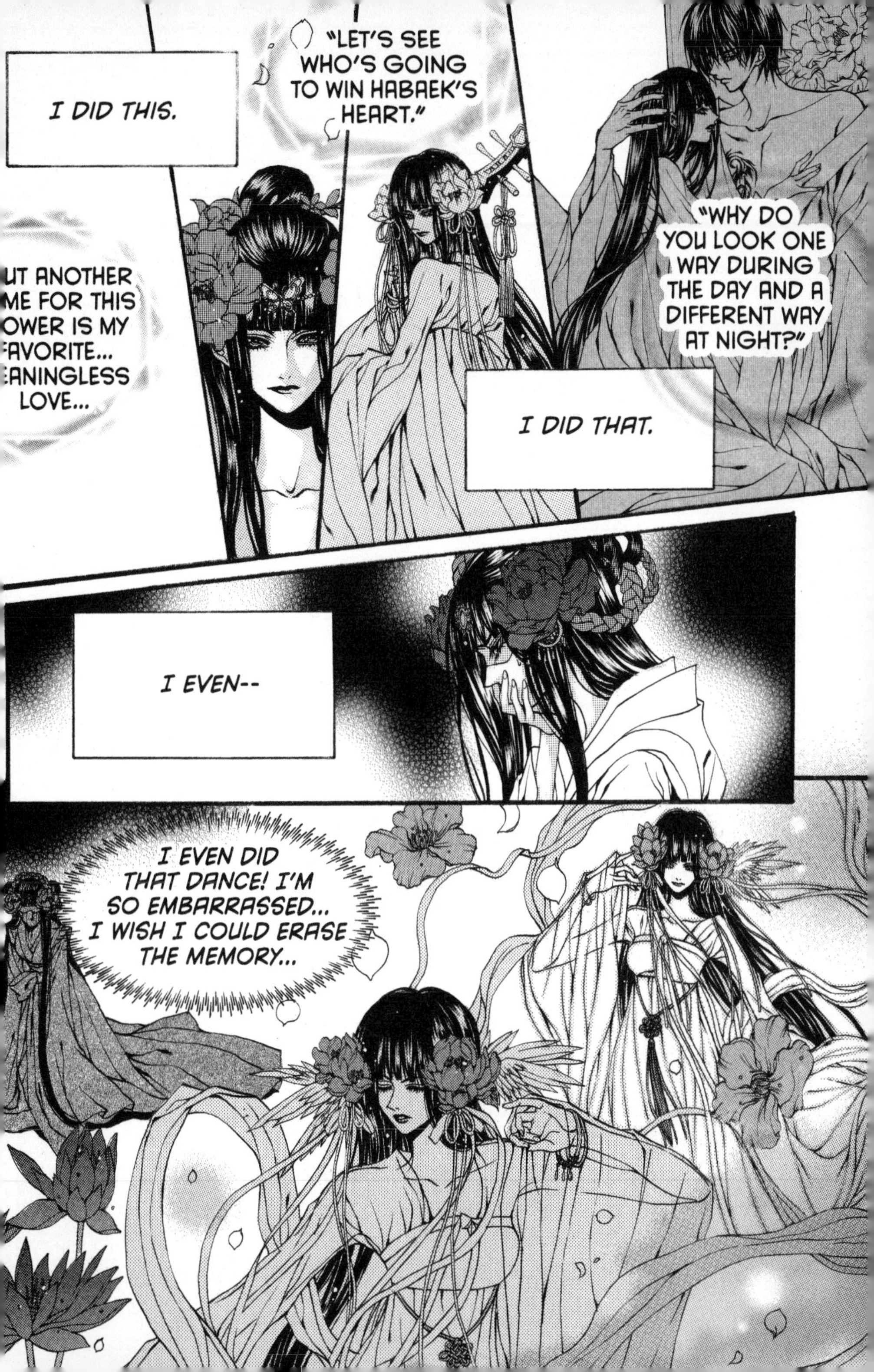
"WHY DO YOU LOOK ONE WAY DURING THE DAY AND A DIFFERENT WAY AT NIGHT?"
I DID THAT.
"LET'S SEE WHO'S GOING TO WIN HABAEK'S HEART."
I DID THIS.
UT ANOTHER
ME FOR THIS
OWER IS MY
FAVORITE...
EANINGLESS
LOVE...
I EVEN--
I EVEN DID THAT DANCE! I'M SO EMBARRASSED... I WISH I COULD ERASE THE MEMORY...

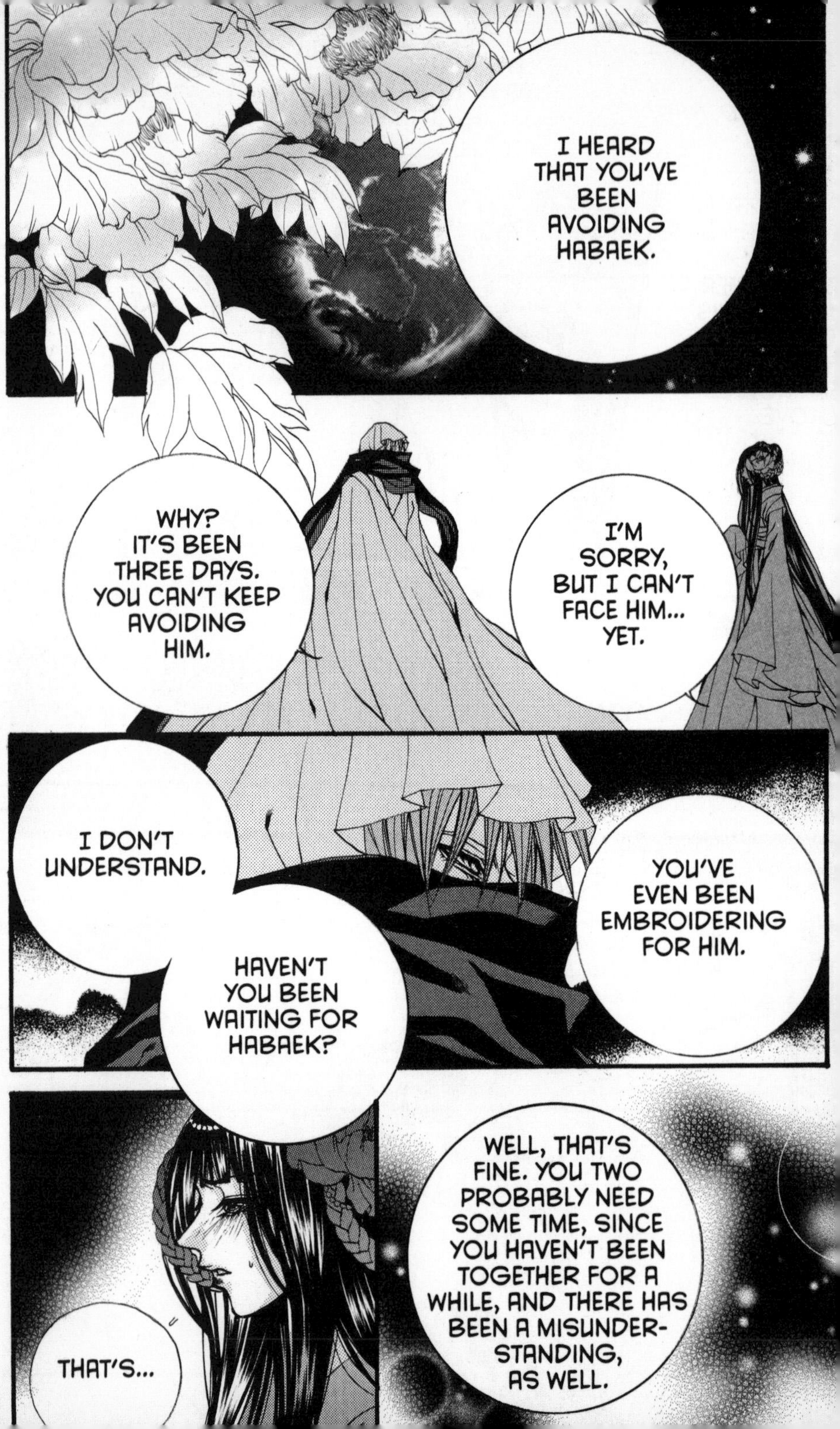
I HEARD THAT YOU'VE BEEN AVOIDING HABAEK.
I'M SORRY, BUT I CAN'T FACE HIM... YET.
WHY? IT'S BEEN THREE DAYS. YOU CAN'T KEEP AVOIDING HIM.
YOU'VE EVEN BEEN EMBROIDERING FOR HIM.
I DON'T UNDERSTAND.
HAVEN'T YOU BEEN WAITING FOR HABAEK?
WELL, THAT'S FINE. YOU TWO PROBABLY NEED SOME TIME, SINCE YOU HAVEN'T BEEN TOGETHER FOR A WHILE, AND THERE HAS BEEN A MISUNDER-STANDING, AS WELL.
THAT'S...

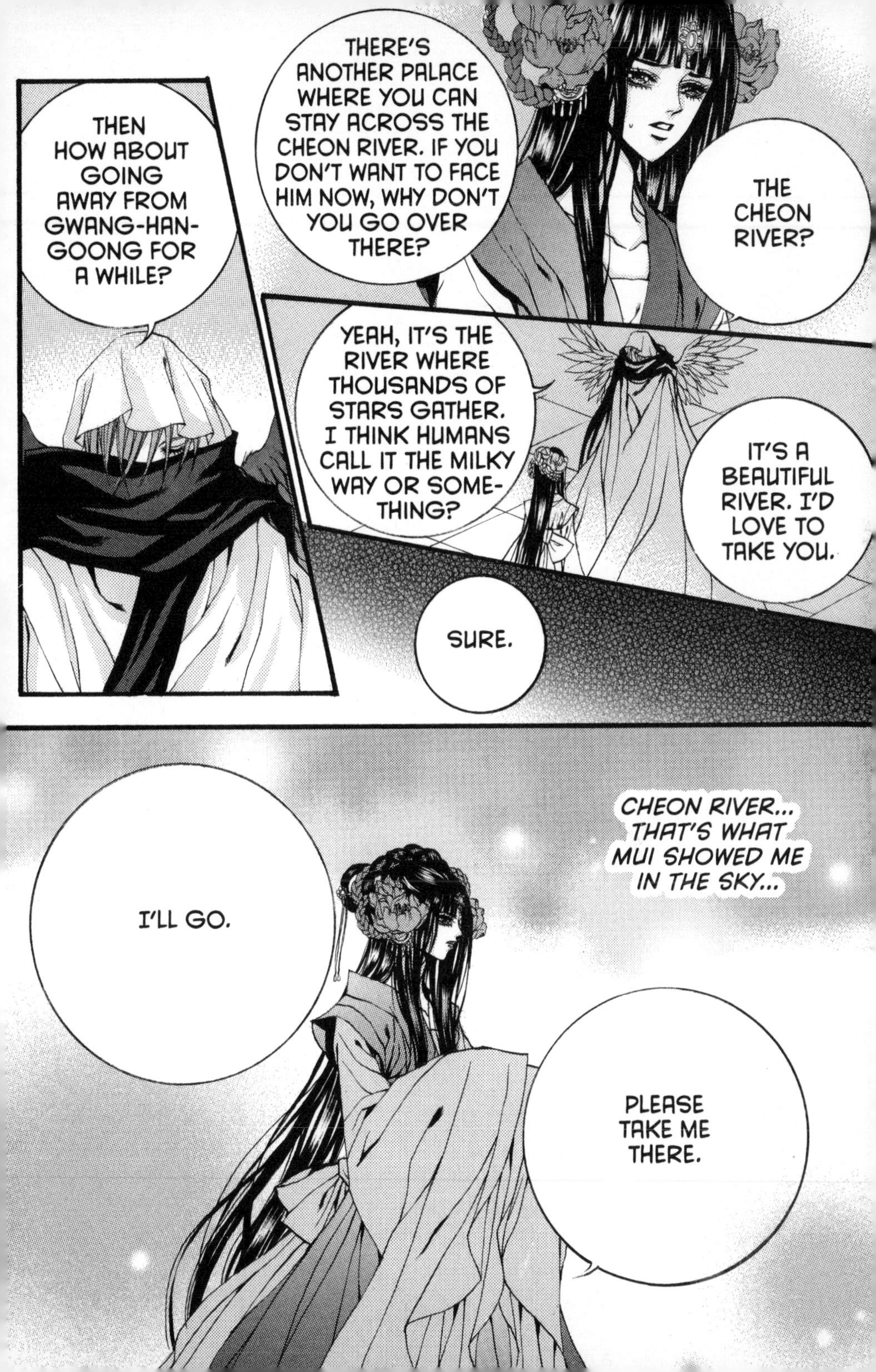

THEN HOW ABOUT GOING AWAY FROM GWANG-HAN-GOONG FOR A WHILE?
THERE'S ANOTHER PALACE WHERE YOU CAN STAY ACROSS THE CHEON RIVER. IF YOU DON'T WANT TO FACE HIM NOW, WHY DON'T YOU GO OVER THERE?
THE CHEON RIVER?
YEAH, IT'S THE RIVER WHERE THOUSANDS OF STARS GATHER. I THINK HUMANS CALL IT THE MILKY WAY OR SOME-THING?
IT'S A BEAUTIFUL RIVER. I'D LOVE TO TAKE YOU.
SURE.
I'LL GO.
CHEON RIVER... THAT'S WHAT MUI SHOWED ME IN THE SKY...
PLEASE TAKE ME THERE.

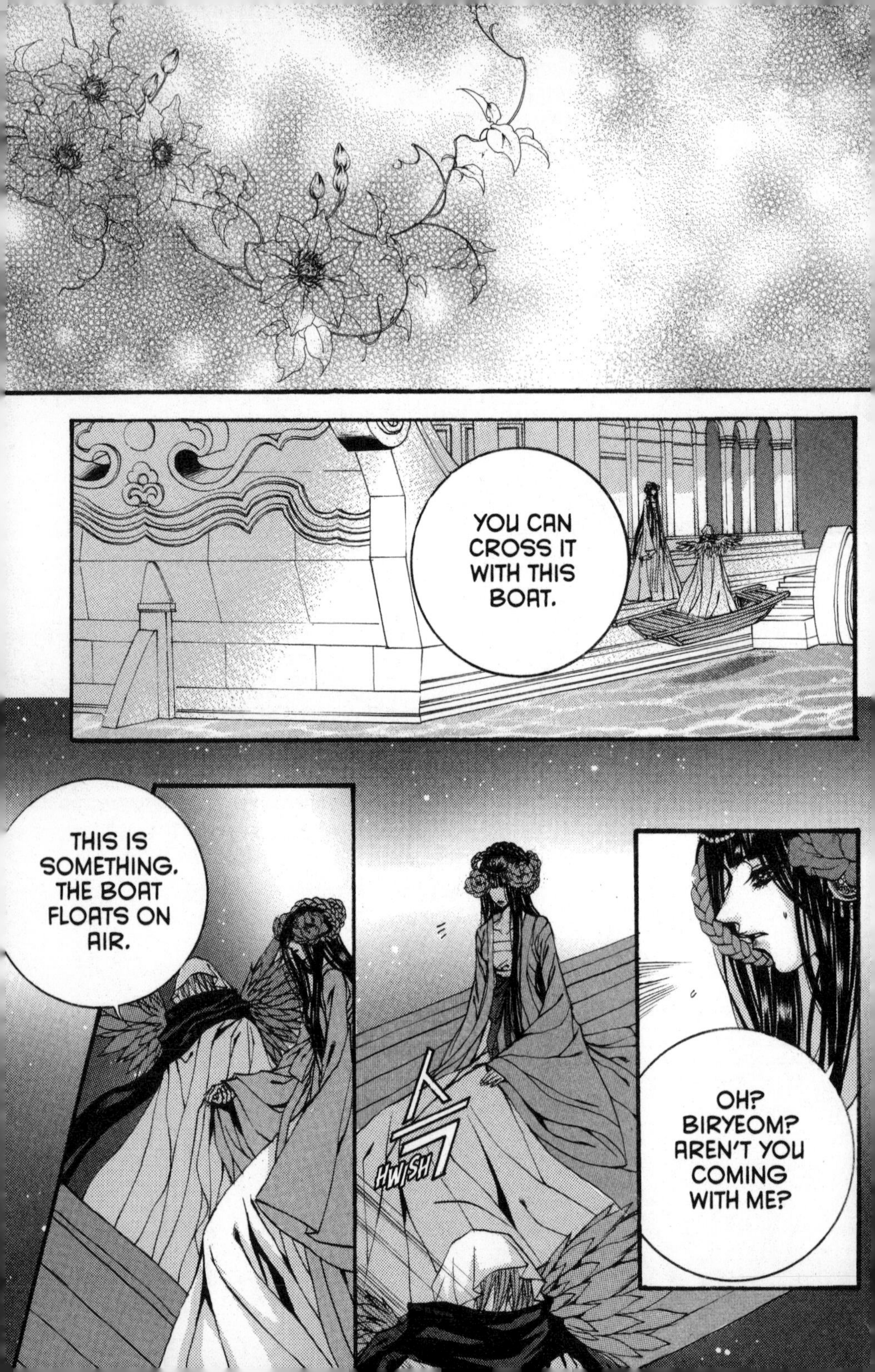

YOU CAN CROSS IT WITH THIS BOAT.
THIS IS SOMETHING. THE BOAT FLOATS ON AIR.
HWISH
OH? BIRYEOM? AREN'T YOU COMING WITH ME?

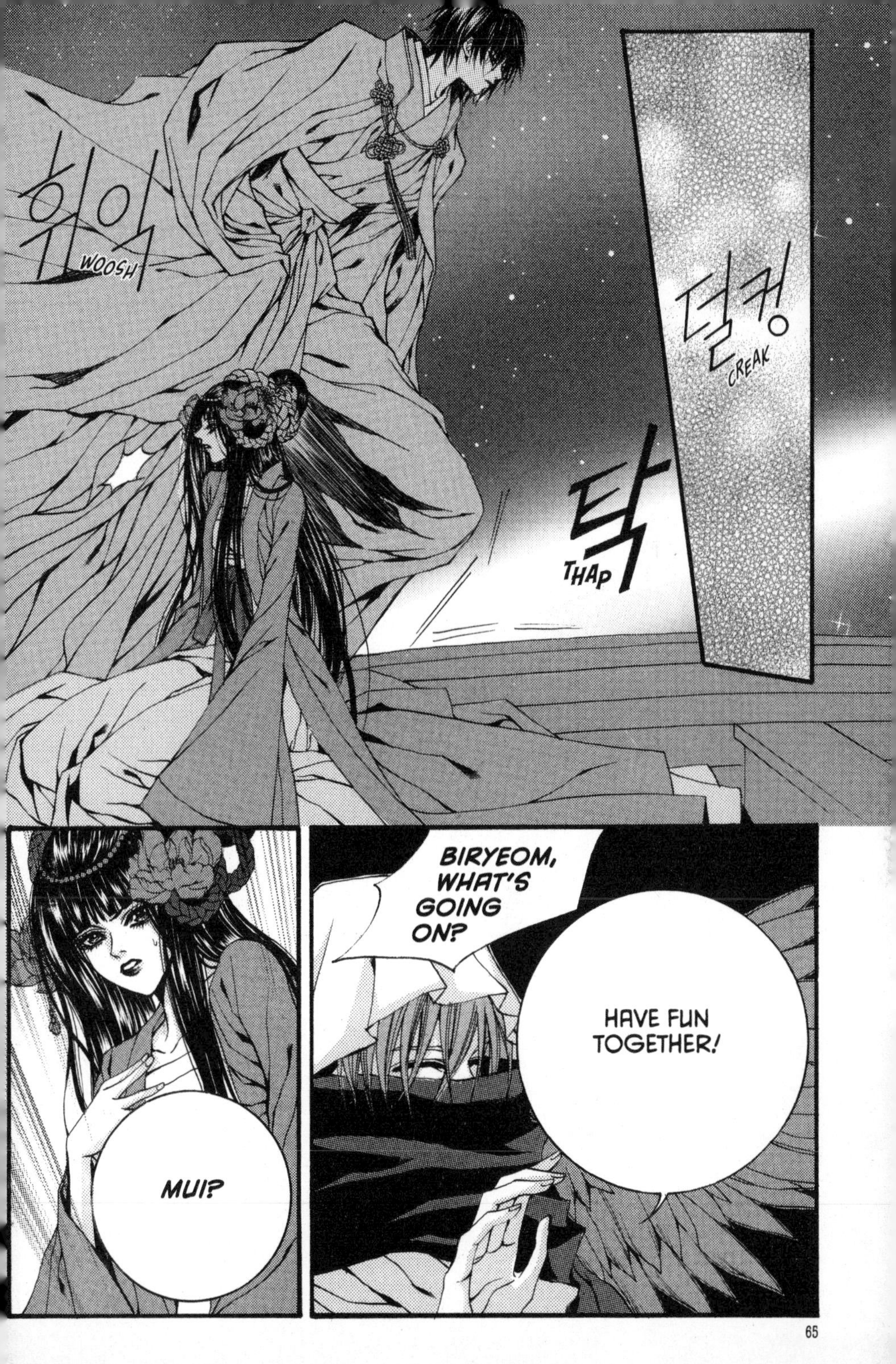
덜컹
CREAK
훠억
WOOSH
탁
THAP
BIRYEOM, WHAT'S GOING ON?
HAVE FUN TOGETHER!
MUI?

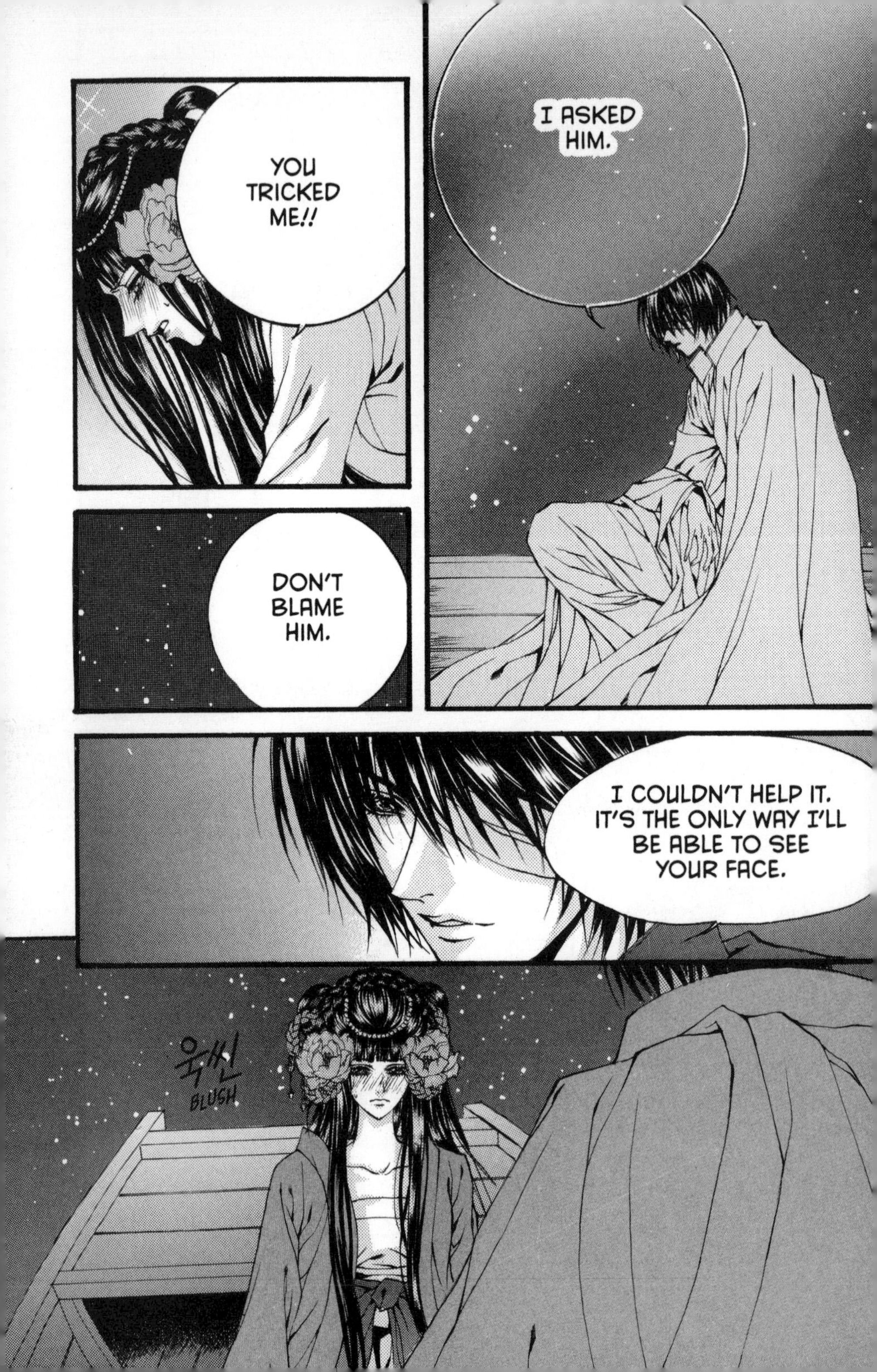
I ASKED HIM.
YOU TRICKED ME!!
DON'T BLAME HIM.
I COULDN'T HELP IT. IT'S THE ONLY WAY I'LL BE ABLE TO SEE YOUR FACE.
BLUSH

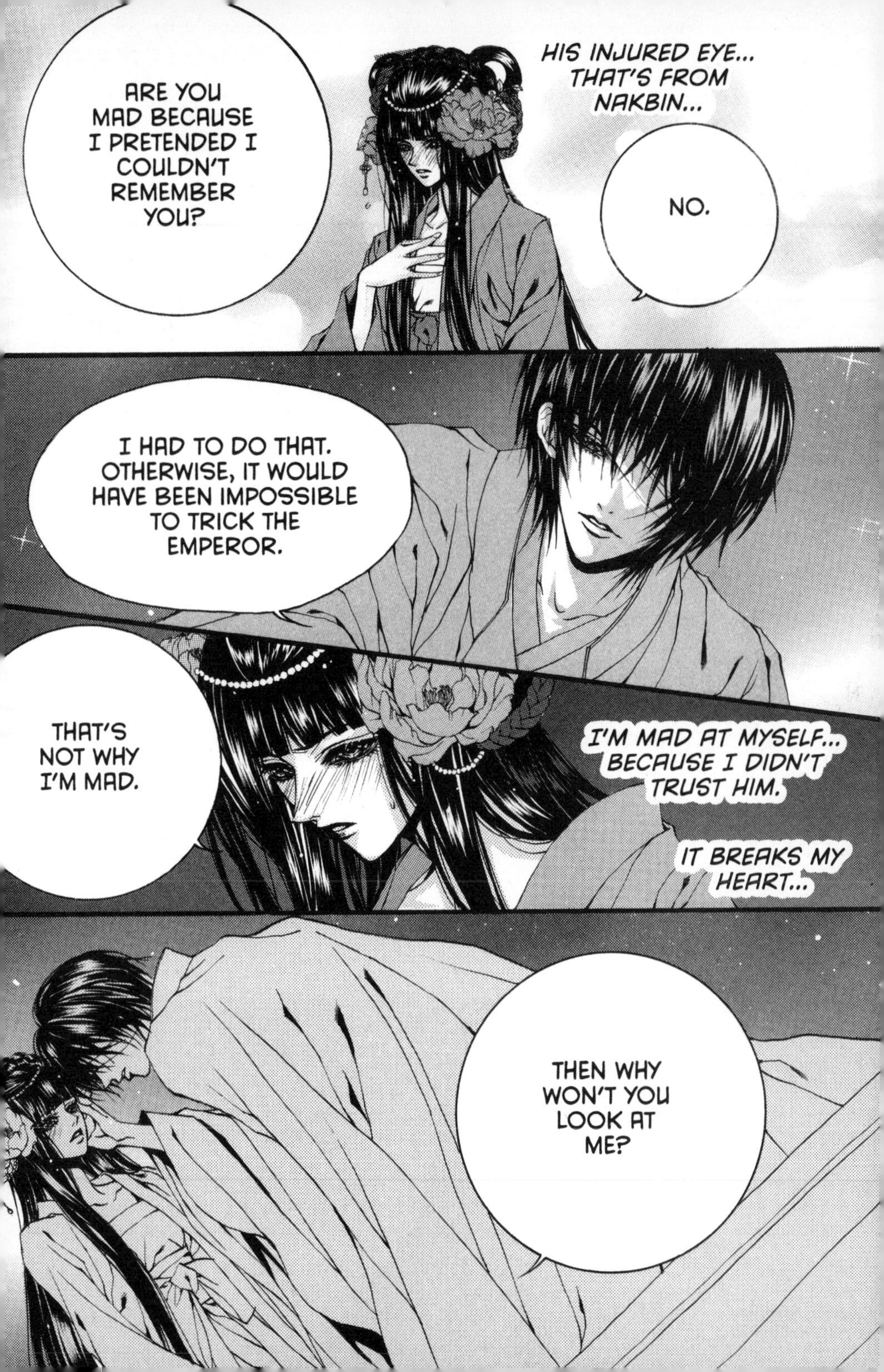
ARE YOU MAD BECAUSE I PRETENDED I COULDN'T REMEMBER YOU?
HIS INJURED EYE... THAT'S FROM NAKBIN...
NO.
I HAD TO DO THAT. OTHERWISE, IT WOULD HAVE BEEN IMPOSSIBLE TO TRICK THE EMPEROR.
THAT'S NOT WHY I'M MAD.
I'M MAD AT MYSELF... BECAUSE I DIDN'T TRUST HIM.
IT BREAKS MY HEART...
THEN WHY WON'T YOU LOOK AT ME?

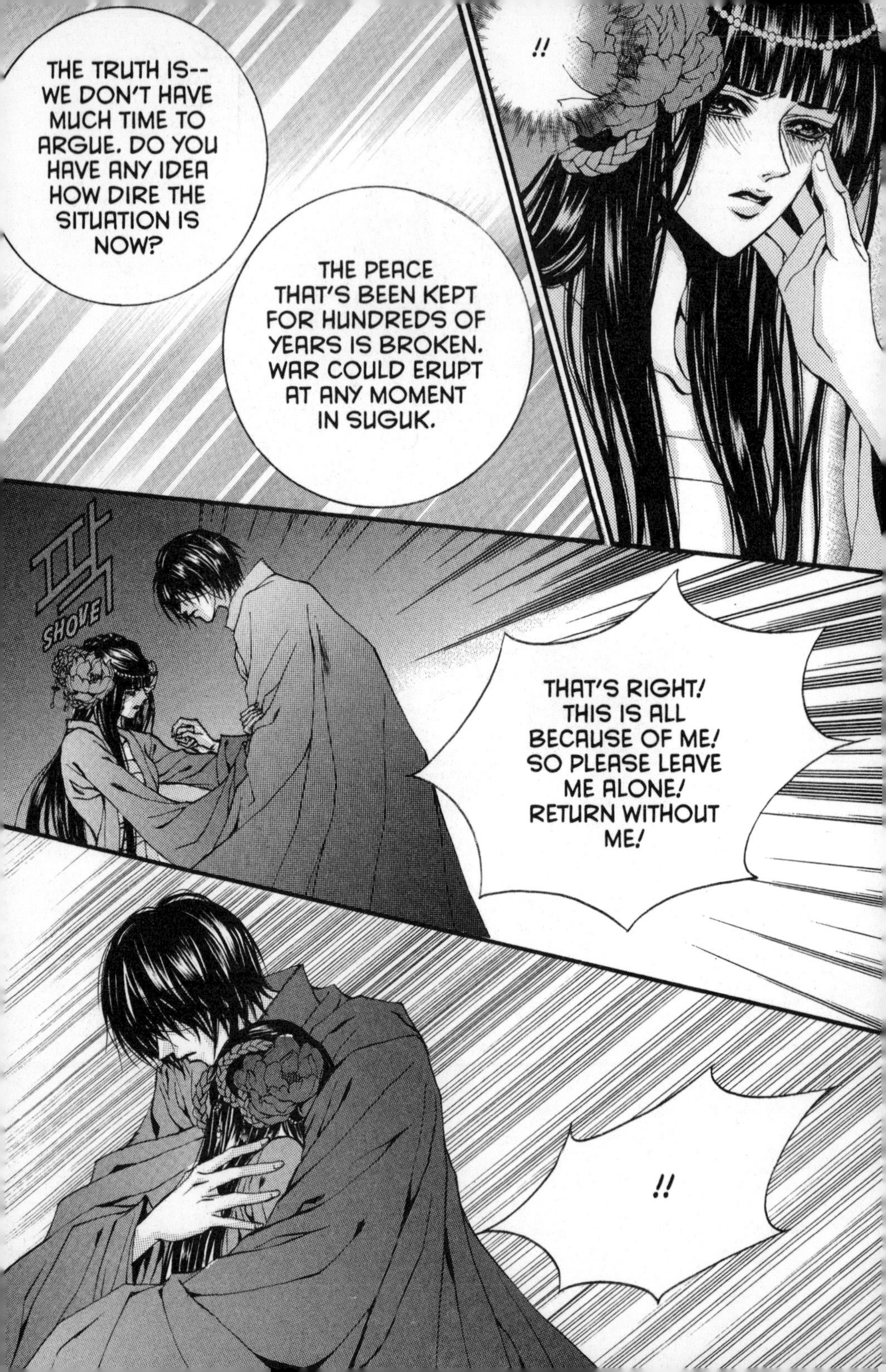
THE TRUTH IS--WE DON'T HAVE MUCH TIME TO ARGUE. DO YOU HAVE ANY IDEA HOW DIRE THE SITUATION IS NOW?
THE PEACE THAT'S BEEN KEPT FOR HUNDREDS OF YEARS IS BROKEN. WAR COULD ERUPT AT ANY MOMENT IN SUGUK.
!!
SHOVE
THAT'S RIGHT! THIS IS ALL BECAUSE OF ME! SO PLEASE LEAVE ME ALONE! RETURN WITHOUT ME!
!!

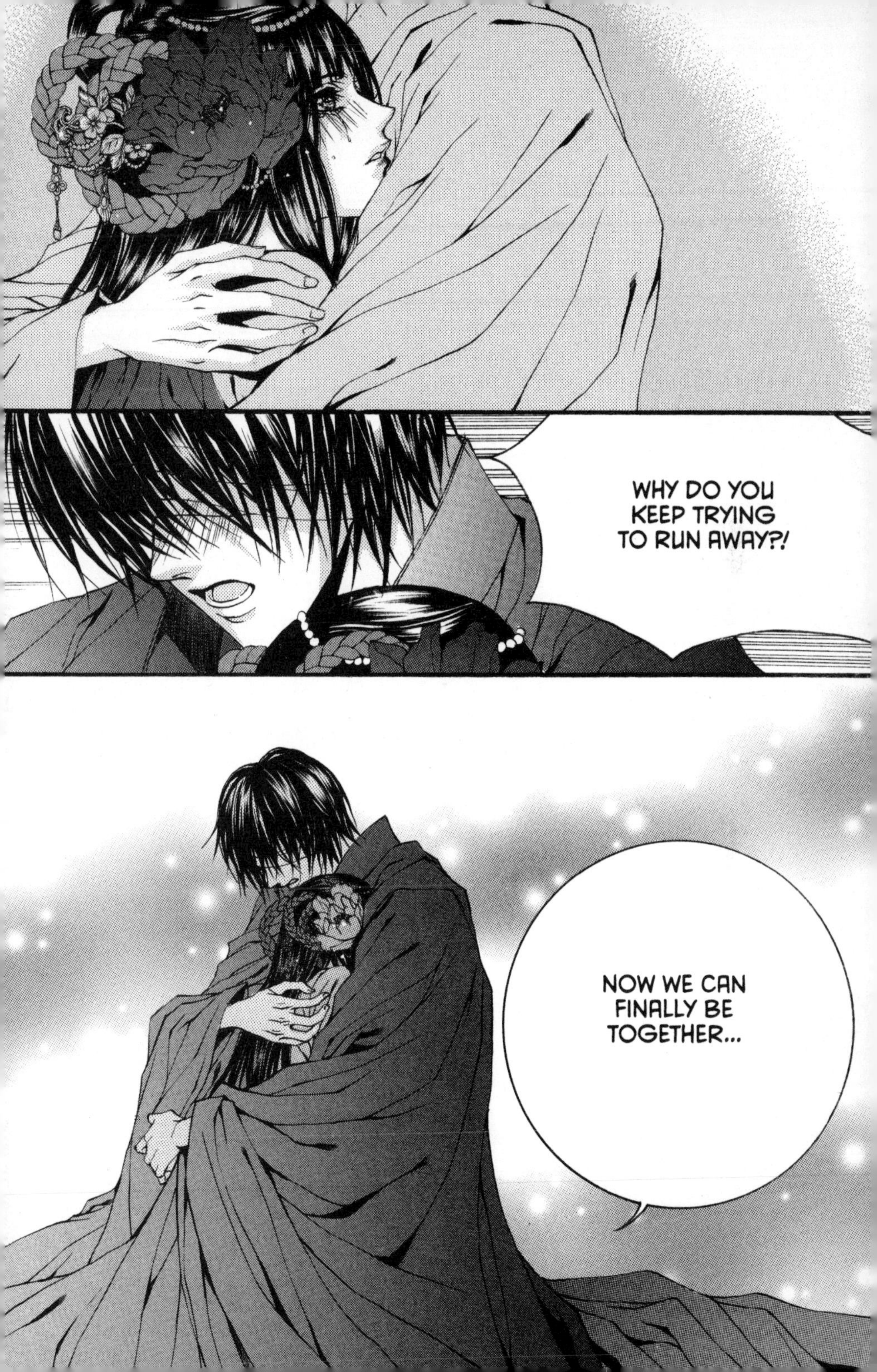
WHY DO YOU KEEP TRYING TO RUN AWAY?!
NOW WE CAN FINALLY BE TOGETHER...

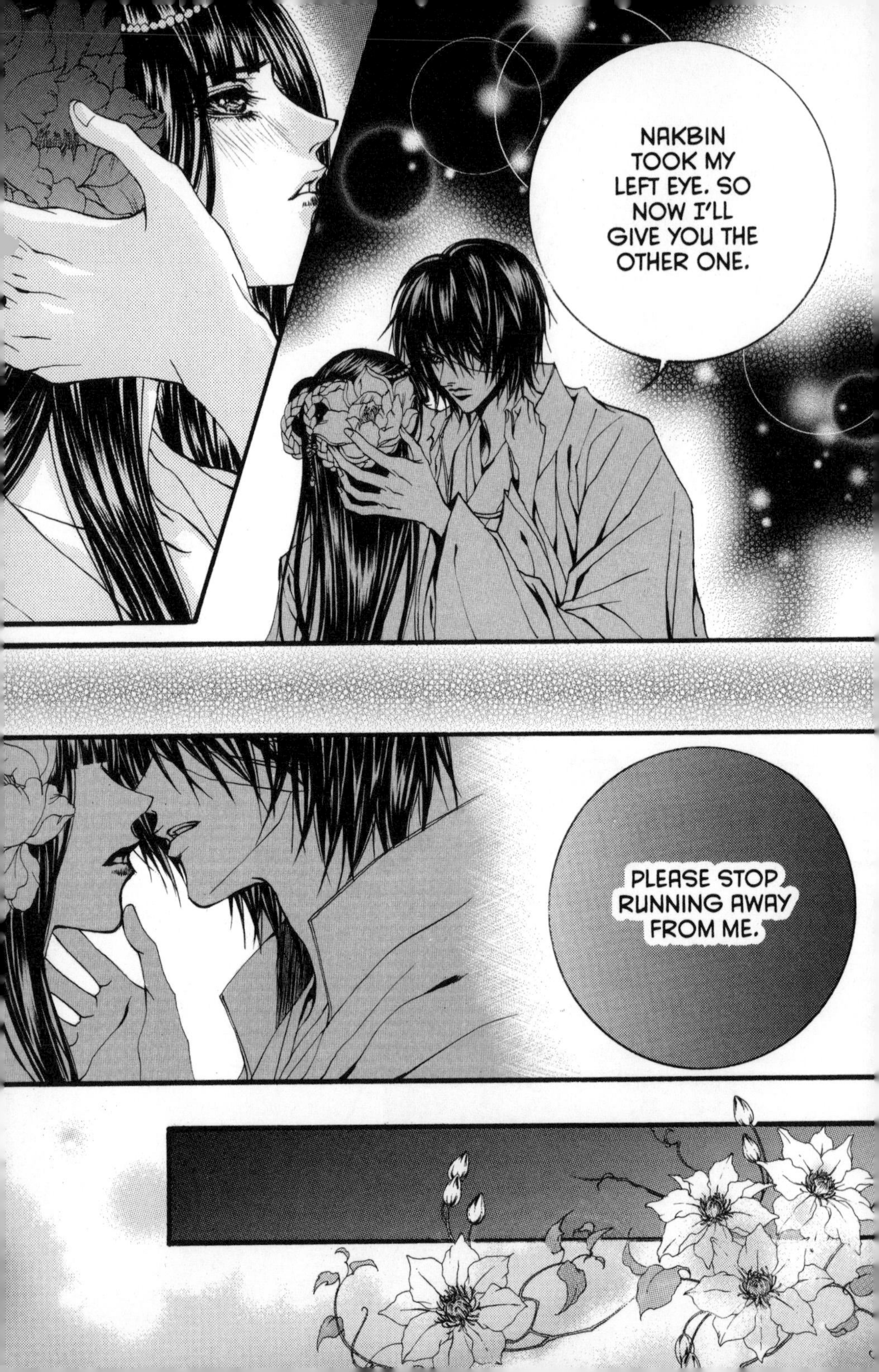
NAKBIN TOOK MY LEFT EYE. SO NOW I'LL GIVE YOU THE OTHER ONE.
PLEASE STOP RUNNING AWAY FROM ME.

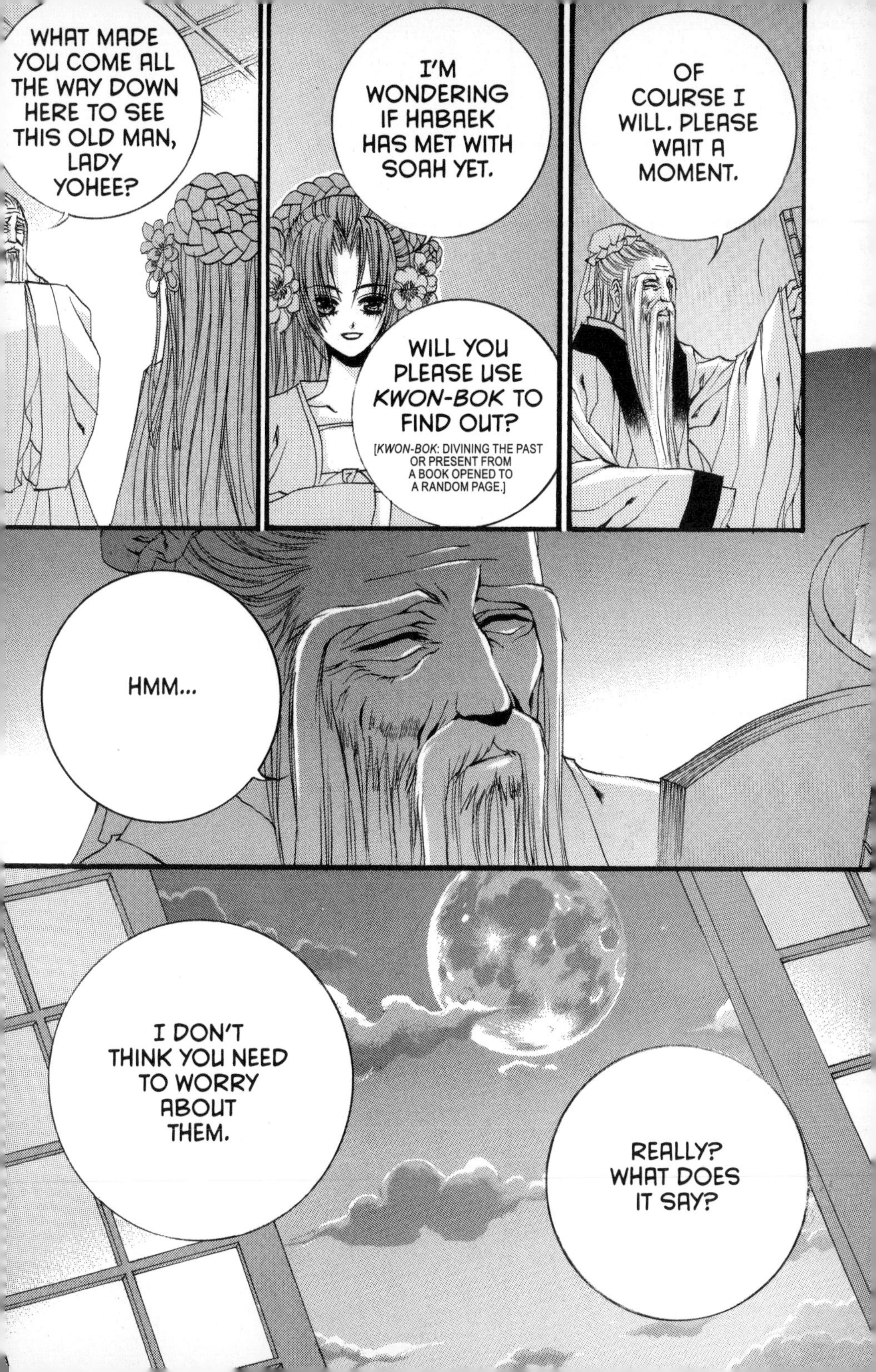
WHAT MADE YOU COME ALL THE WAY DOWN HERE TO SEE THIS OLD MAN, LADY YOHEE?
I'M WONDERING IF HABAEK HAS MET WITH SOAH YET.
WILL YOU PLEASE USE KWON-BOK TO FIND OUT?
[KWON-BOK: DIVINING THE PAST OR PRESENT FROM A BOOK OPENED TO A RANDOM PAGE.]
OF COURSE I WILL. PLEASE WAIT A MOMENT.
HMM...
I DON'T THINK YOU NEED TO WORRY ABOUT THEM.
REALLY? WHAT DOES IT SAY?

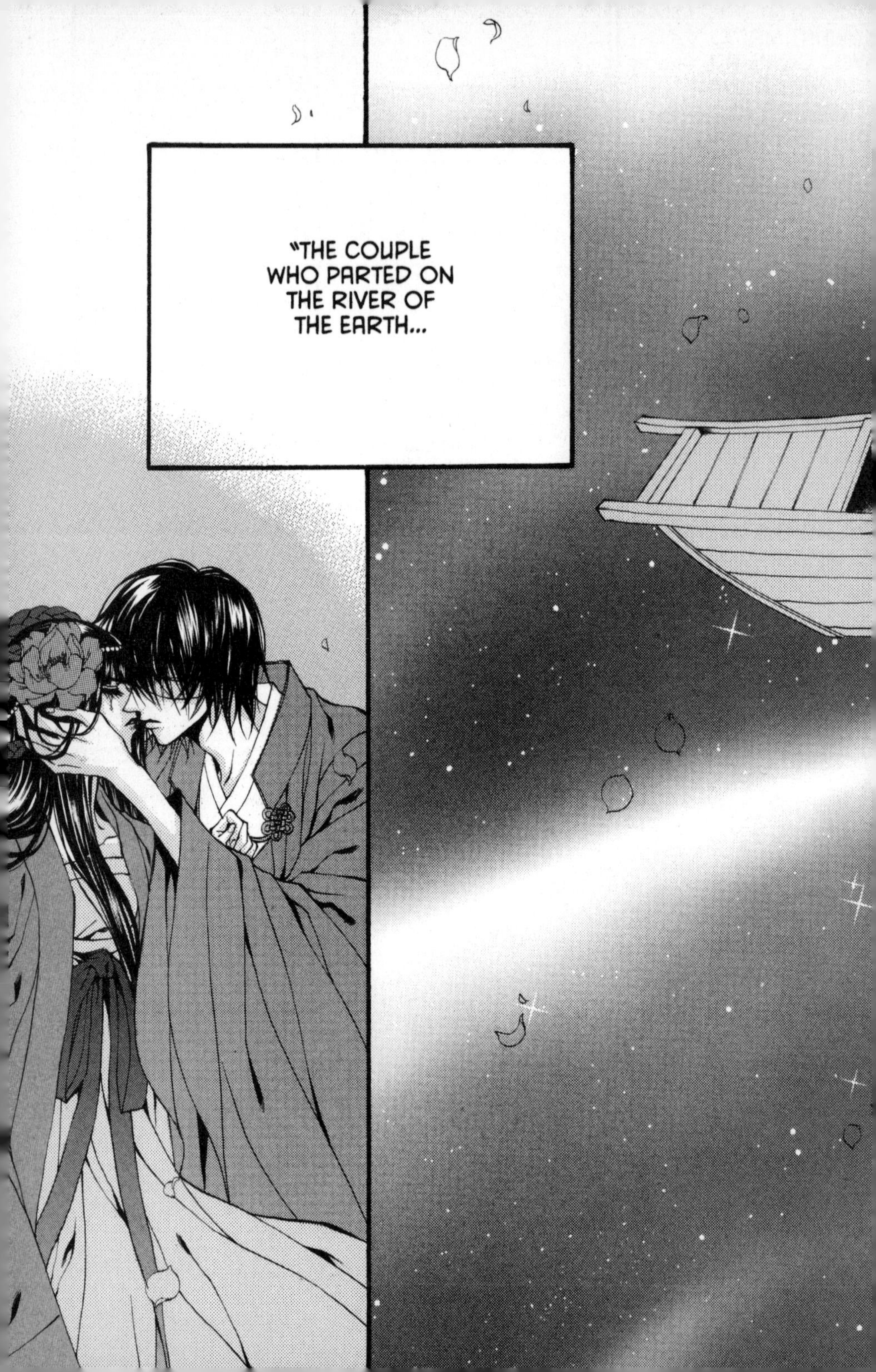
"THE COUPLE WHO PARTED ON THE RIVER OF THE EARTH...

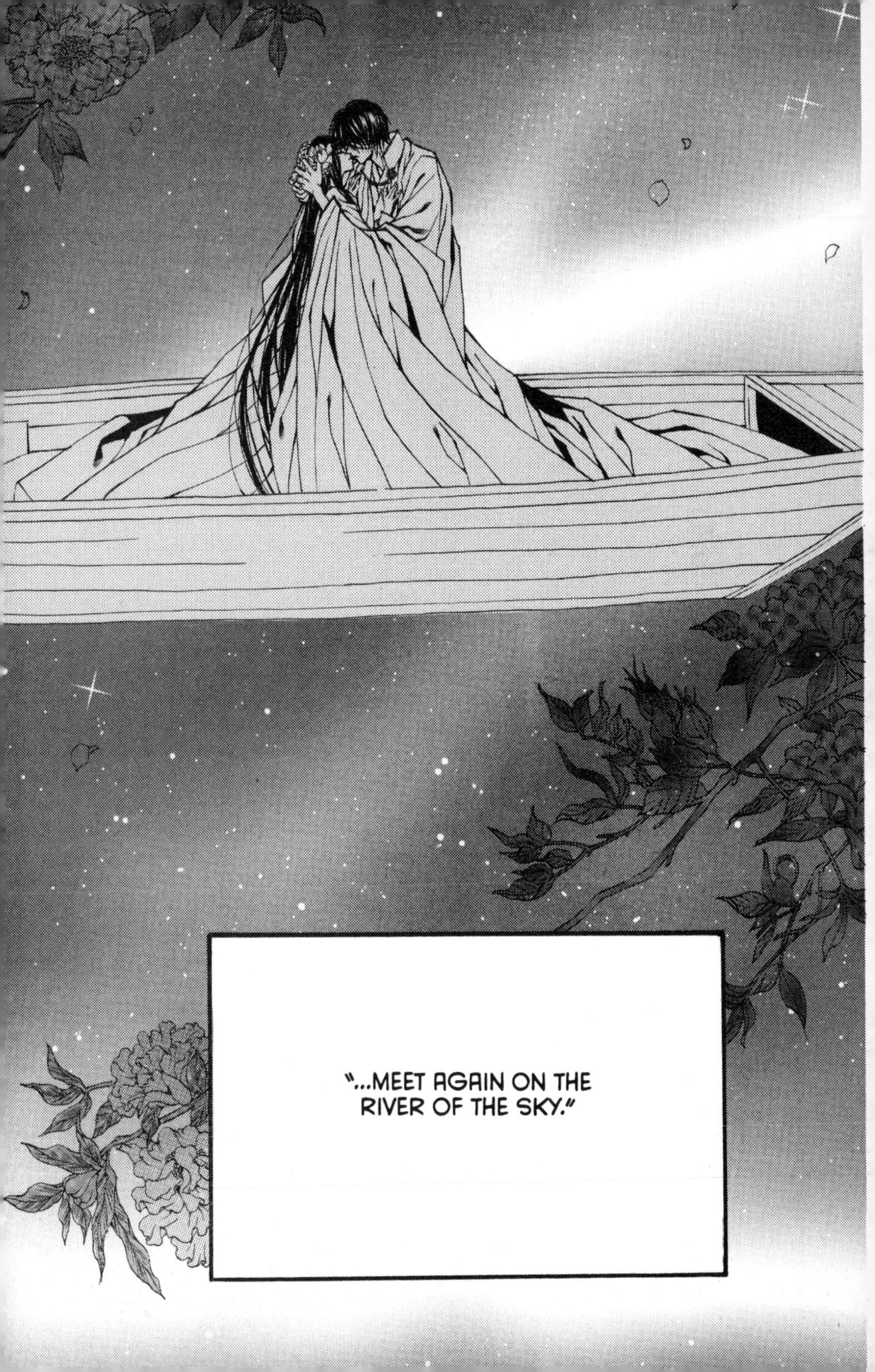
"...MEET AGAIN ON THE RIVER OF THE SKY."

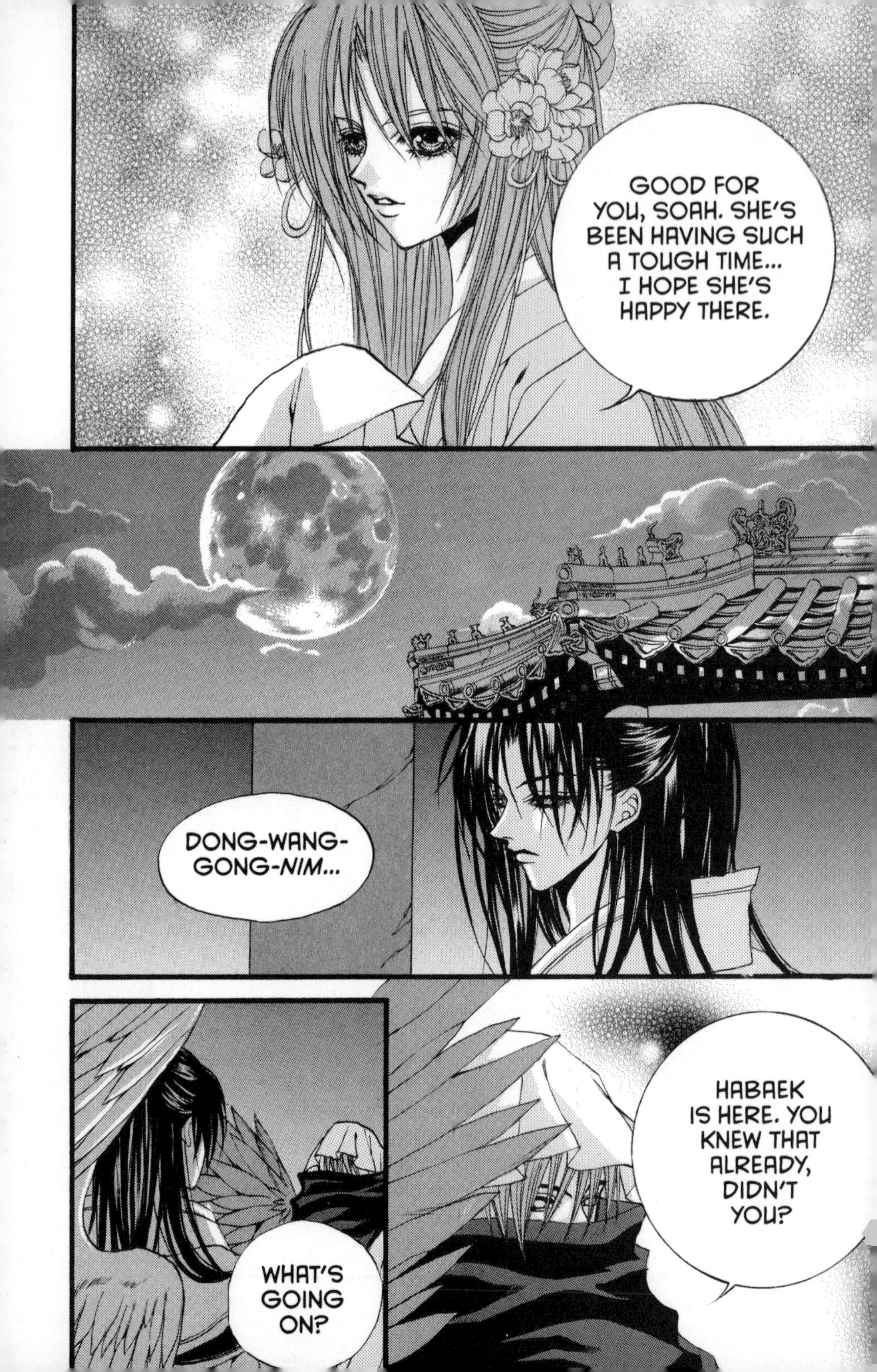
GOOD FOR YOU, SOAH. SHE'S BEEN HAVING SUCH A TOUGH TIME... I HOPE SHE'S HAPPY THERE.
DONG-WANG-GONG-*NIM*...
HABAEK IS HERE. YOU KNEW THAT ALREADY, DIDN'T YOU?
WHAT'S GOING ON?

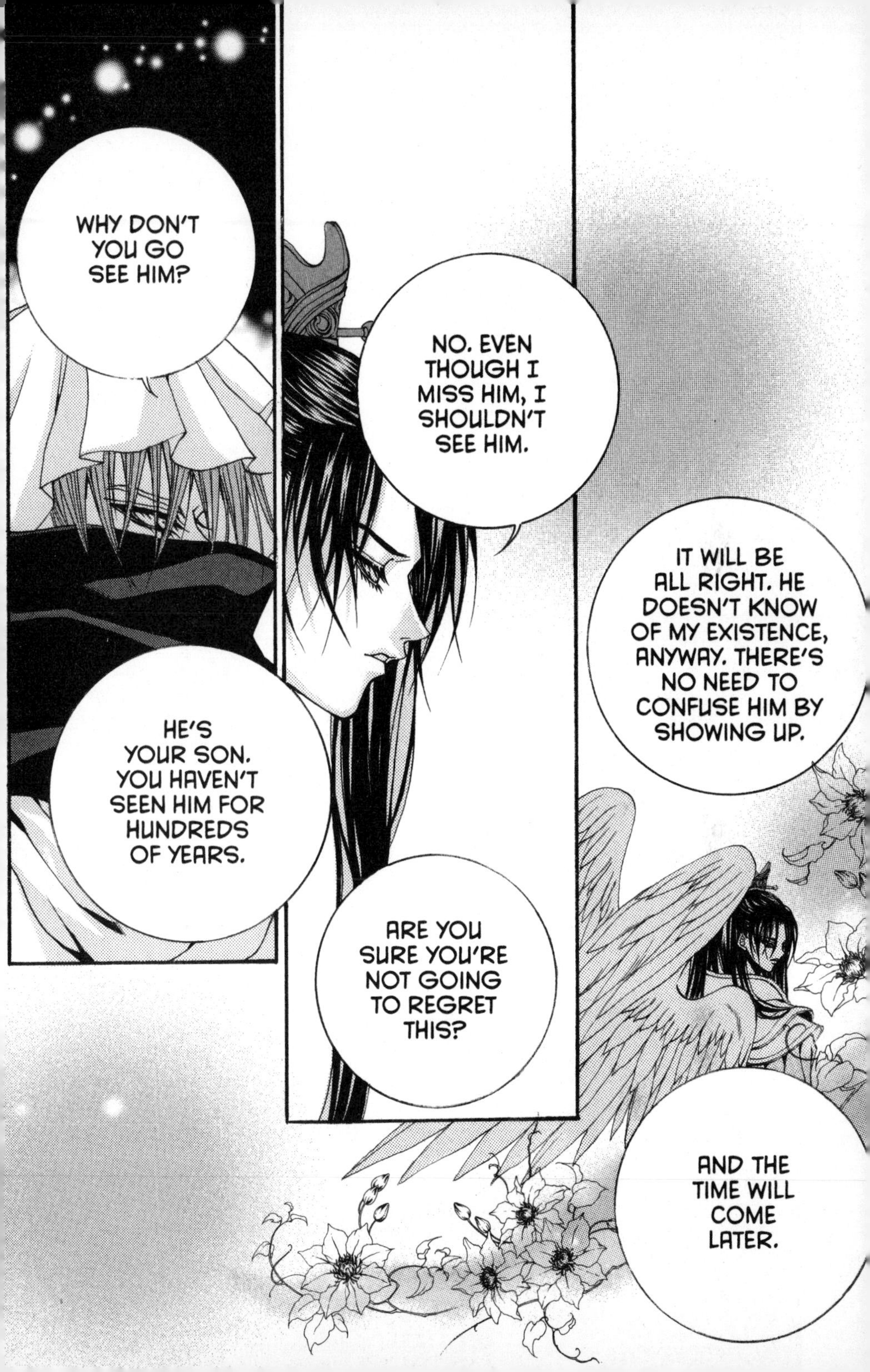
WHY DON'T YOU GO SEE HIM?
NO. EVEN THOUGH I MISS HIM, I SHOULDN'T SEE HIM.
HE'S YOUR SON. YOU HAVEN'T SEEN HIM FOR HUNDREDS OF YEARS.
IT WILL BE ALL RIGHT. HE DOESN'T KNOW OF MY EXISTENCE, ANYWAY. THERE'S NO NEED TO CONFUSE HIM BY SHOWING UP.
ARE YOU SURE YOU'RE NOT GOING TO REGRET THIS?
AND THE TIME WILL COME LATER.

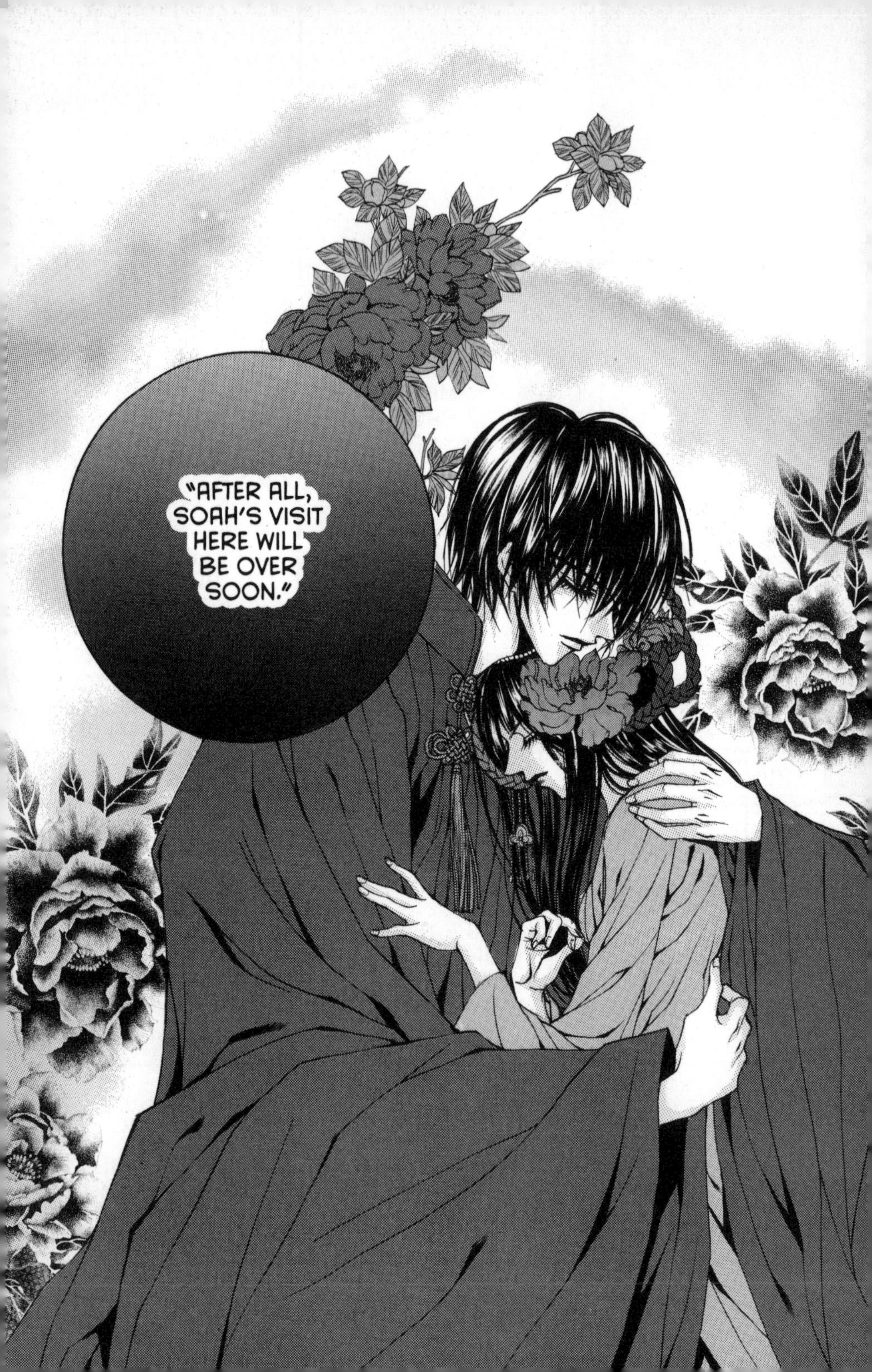
"AFTER ALL, SOAH'S VISIT HERE WILL BE OVER SOON."

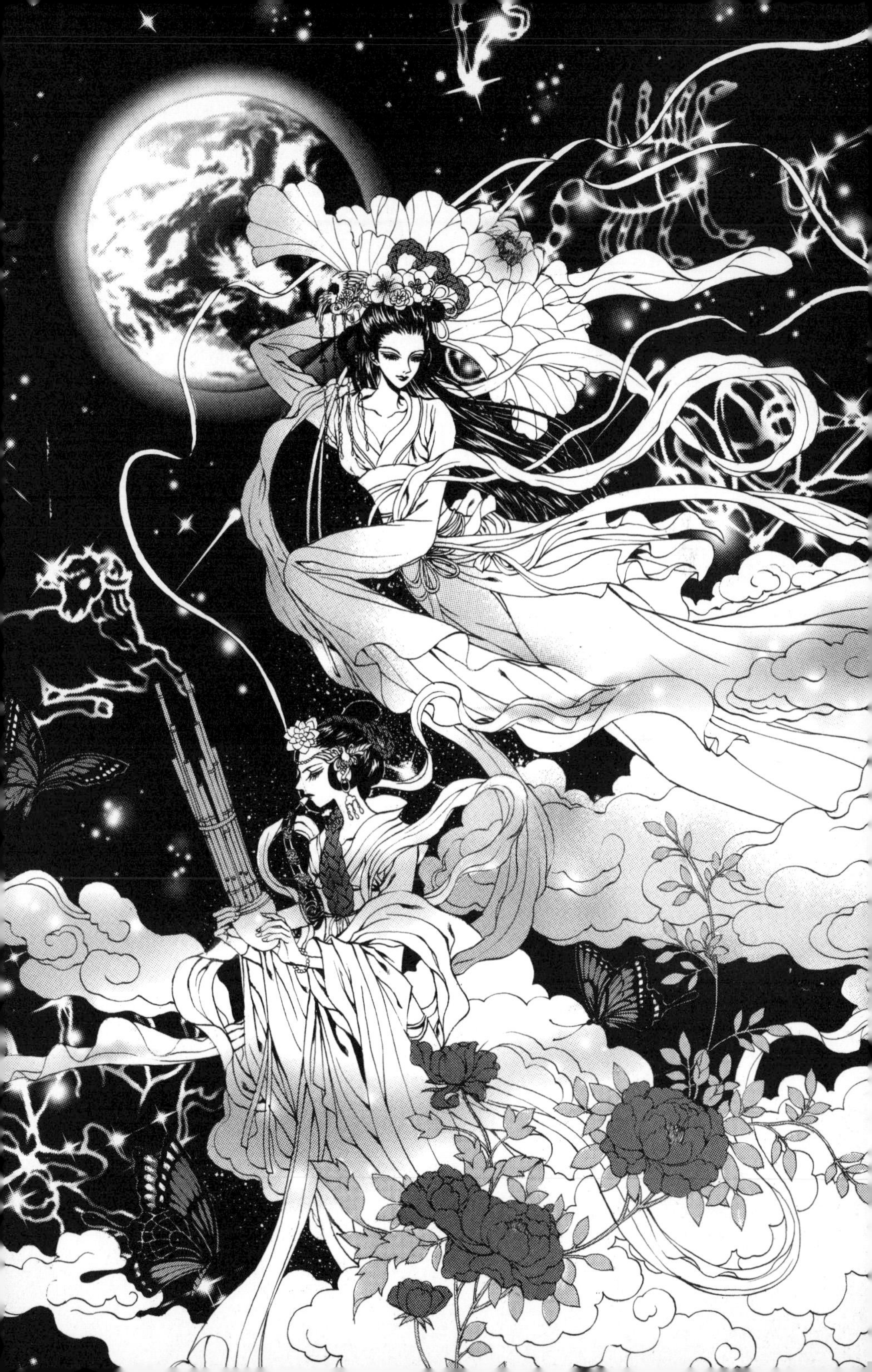

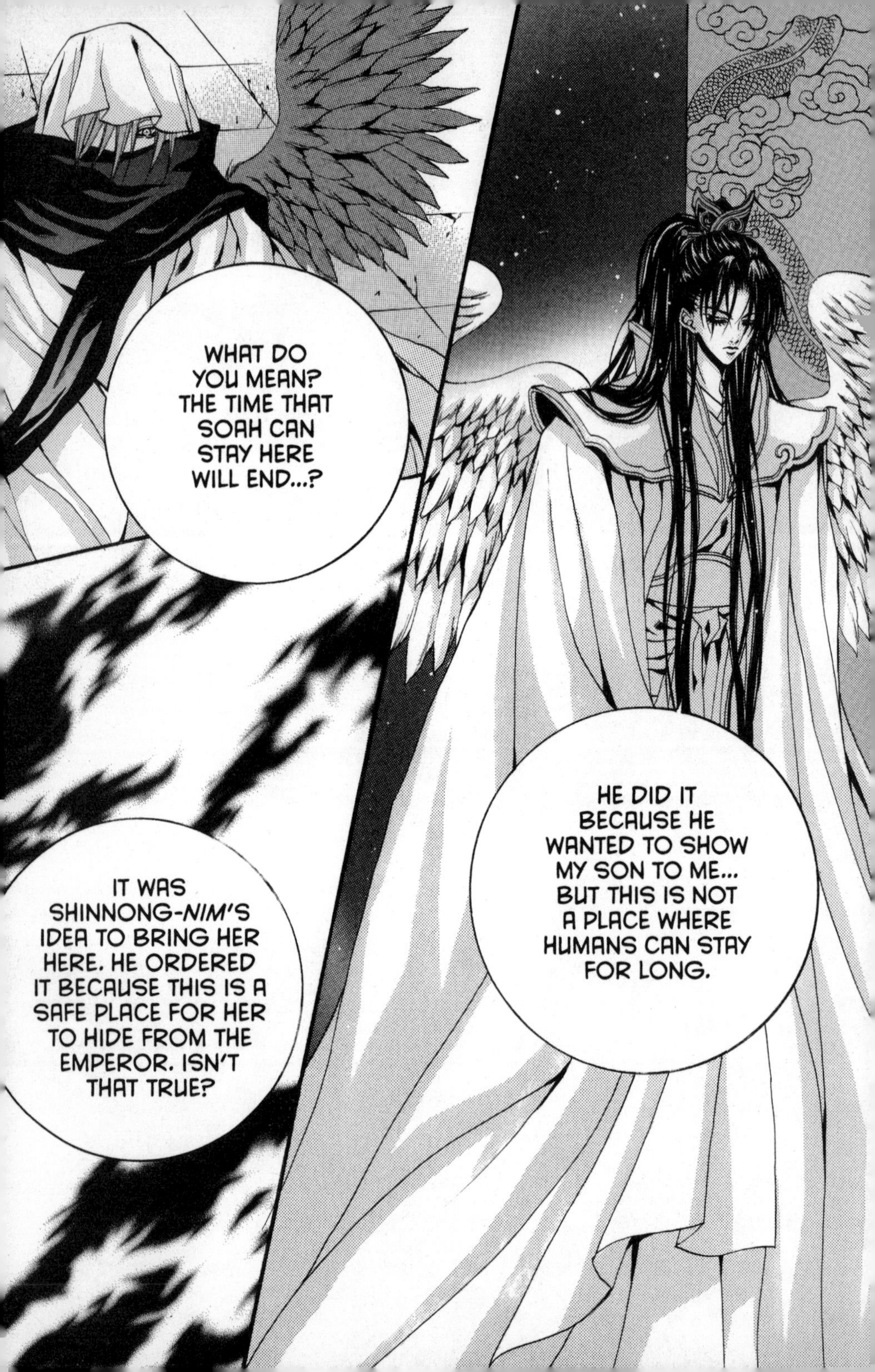
WHAT DO YOU MEAN? THE TIME THAT SOAH CAN STAY HERE WILL END...?
IT WAS SHINNONG-*NIM*'S IDEA TO BRING HER HERE. HE ORDERED IT BECAUSE THIS IS A SAFE PLACE FOR HER TO HIDE FROM THE EMPEROR. ISN'T THAT TRUE?
HE DID IT BECAUSE HE WANTED TO SHOW MY SON TO ME... BUT THIS IS NOT A PLACE WHERE HUMANS CAN STAY FOR LONG.

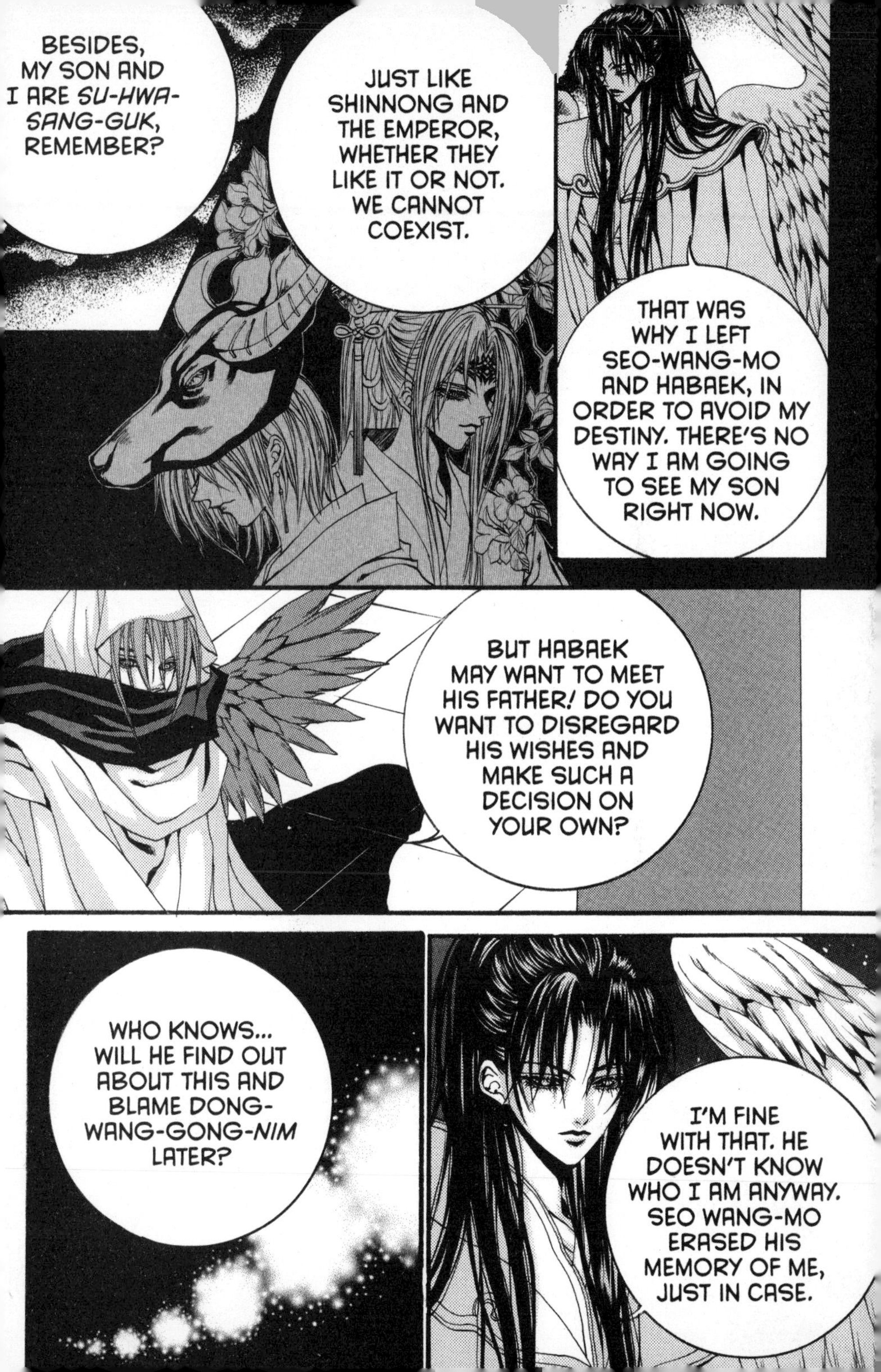
BESIDES, MY SON AND I ARE *SU-HWA-SANG-GUK*, REMEMBER?
JUST LIKE SHINNONG AND THE EMPEROR, WHETHER THEY LIKE IT OR NOT. WE CANNOT COEXIST.
THAT WAS WHY I LEFT SEO-WANG-MO AND HABAEK, IN ORDER TO AVOID MY DESTINY. THERE'S NO WAY I AM GOING TO SEE MY SON RIGHT NOW.
BUT HABAEK MAY WANT TO MEET HIS FATHER! DO YOU WANT TO DISREGARD HIS WISHES AND MAKE SUCH A DECISION ON YOUR OWN?
WHO KNOWS... WILL HE FIND OUT ABOUT THIS AND BLAME DONG-WANG-GONG-*NIM* LATER?
I'M FINE WITH THAT. HE DOESN'T KNOW WHO I AM ANYWAY. SEO WANG-MO ERASED HIS MEMORY OF ME, JUST IN CASE.

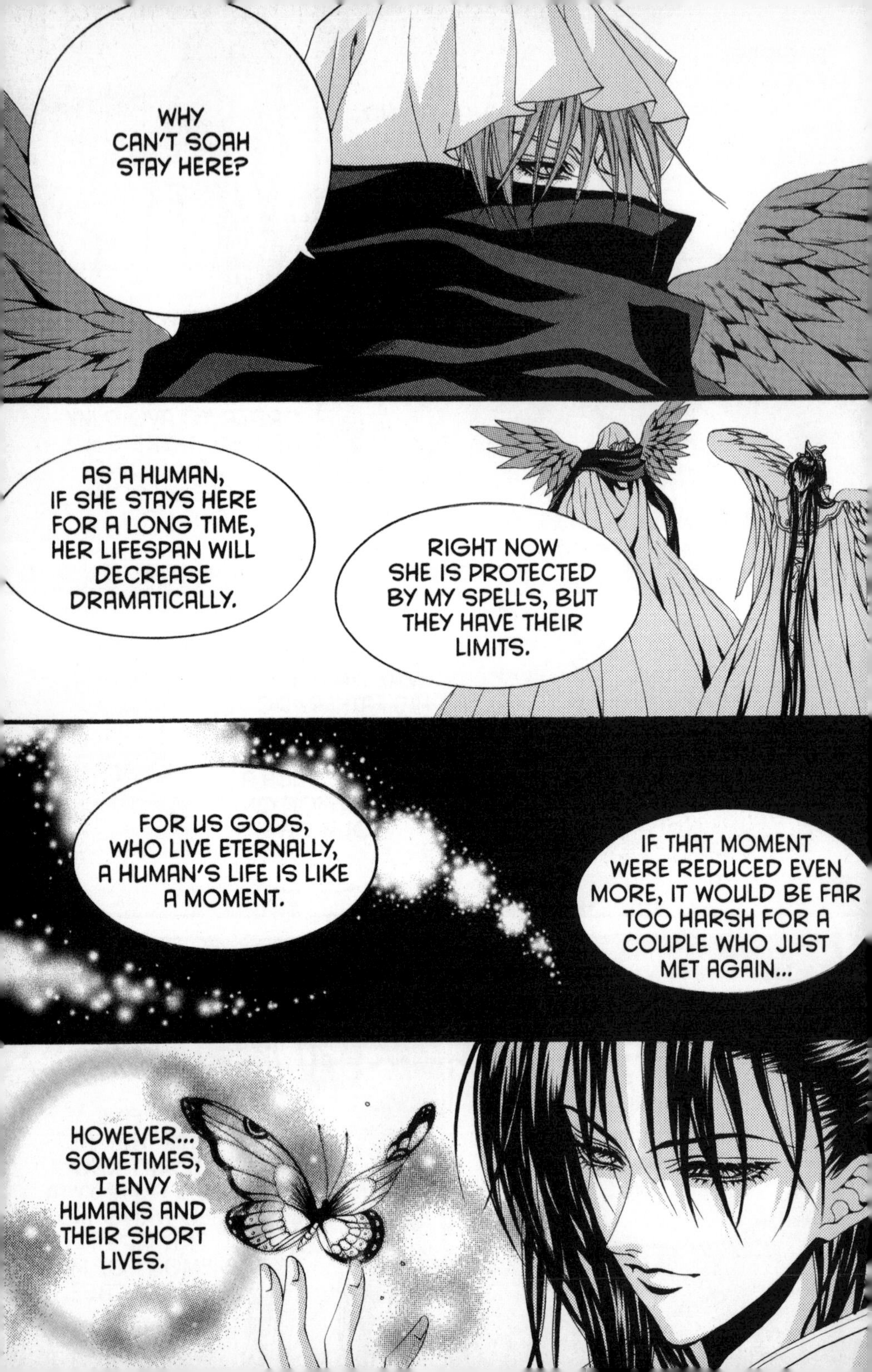
WHY CAN'T SOAH STAY HERE?
AS A HUMAN, IF SHE STAYS HERE FOR A LONG TIME, HER LIFESPAN WILL DECREASE DRAMATICALLY.
RIGHT NOW SHE IS PROTECTED BY MY SPELLS, BUT THEY HAVE THEIR LIMITS.
FOR US GODS, WHO LIVE ETERNALLY, A HUMAN'S LIFE IS LIKE A MOMENT.
IF THAT MOMENT WERE REDUCED EVEN MORE, IT WOULD BE FAR TOO HARSH FOR A COUPLE WHO JUST MET AGAIN...
HOWEVER... SOMETIMES, I ENVY HUMANS AND THEIR SHORT LIVES.

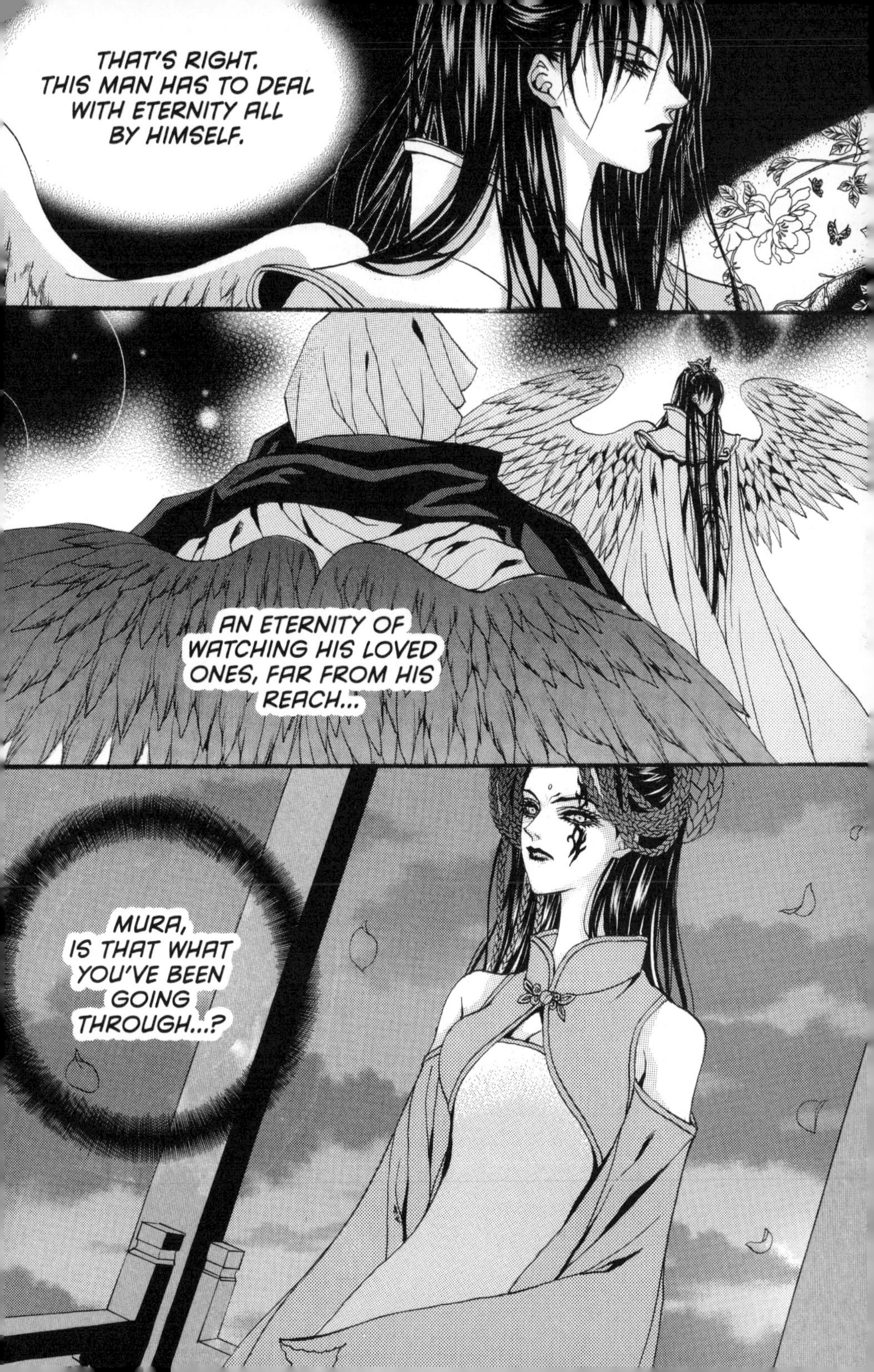
THAT'S RIGHT. THIS MAN HAS TO DEAL WITH ETERNITY ALL BY HIMSELF.
AN ETERNITY OF WATCHING HIS LOVED ONES, FAR FROM HIS REACH...
MURA, IS THAT WHAT YOU'VE BEEN GOING THROUGH...?

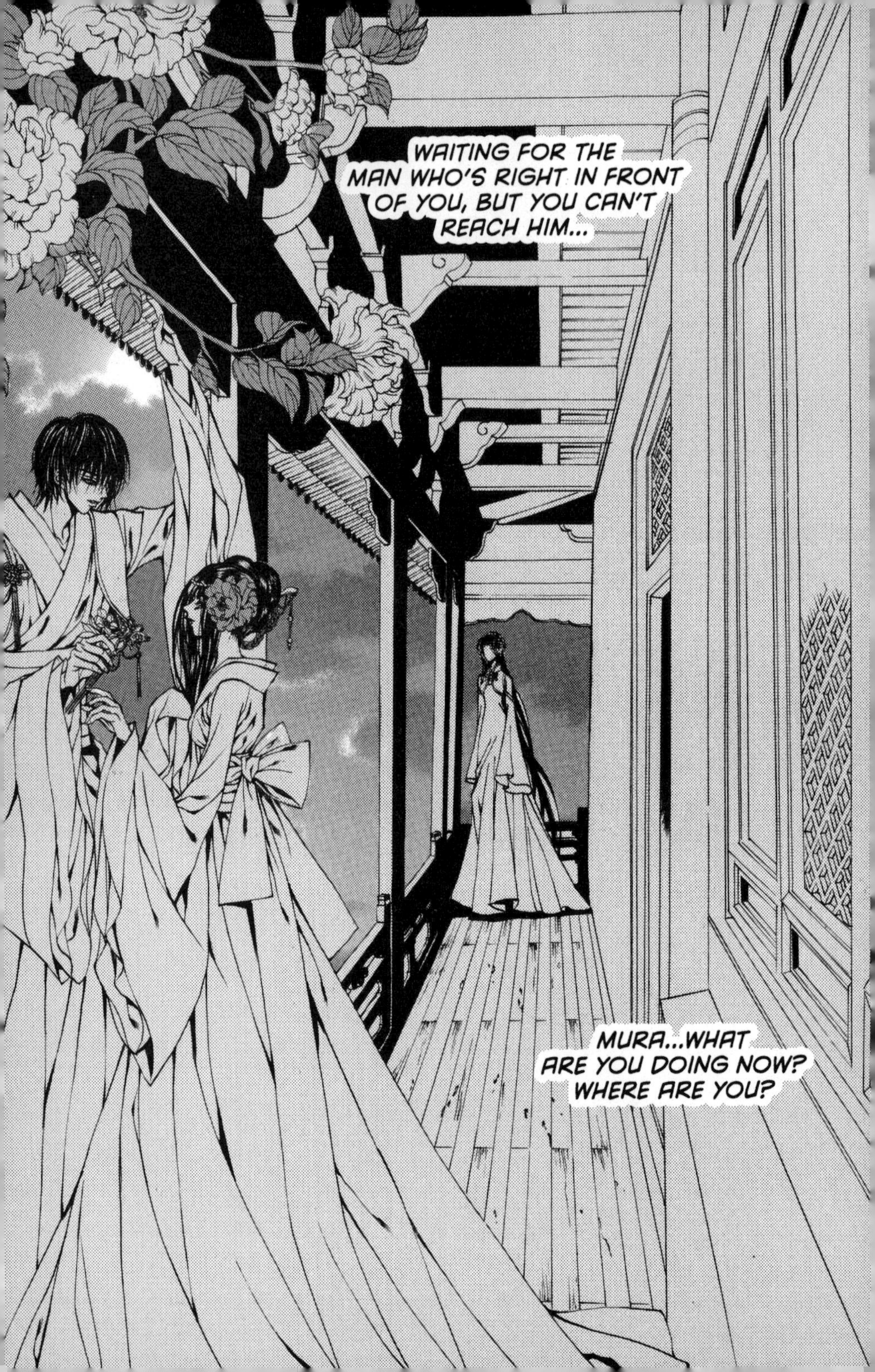
WAITING FOR THE MAN WHO'S RIGHT IN FRONT OF YOU, BUT YOU CAN'T REACH HIM...
MURA...WHAT ARE YOU DOING NOW? WHERE ARE YOU?

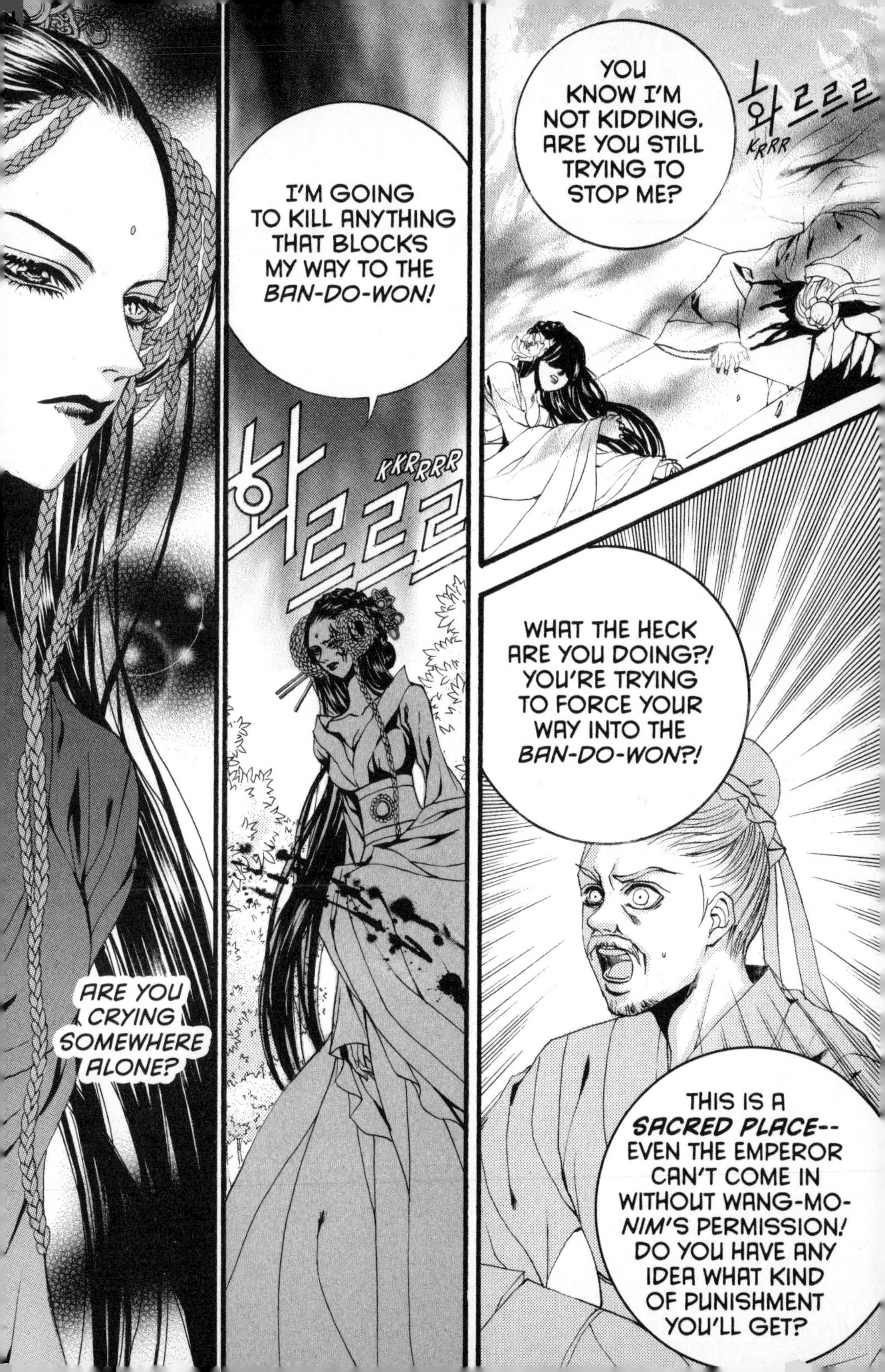
ARE YOU CRYING SOMEWHERE ALONE?
I'M GOING TO KILL ANYTHING THAT BLOCKS MY WAY TO THE *BAN-DO-WON!*
화르르르
KKRRRR
YOU KNOW I'M NOT KIDDING. ARE YOU STILL TRYING TO STOP ME?
화르르르
KRRR
WHAT THE HECK ARE YOU DOING?! YOU'RE TRYING TO FORCE YOUR WAY INTO THE *BAN-DO-WON?!*
THIS IS A ***SACRED PLACE***-- EVEN THE EMPEROR CAN'T COME IN WITHOUT WANG-MO-*NIM'*S PERMISSION! DO YOU HAVE ANY IDEA WHAT KIND OF PUNISHMENT YOU'LL GET?

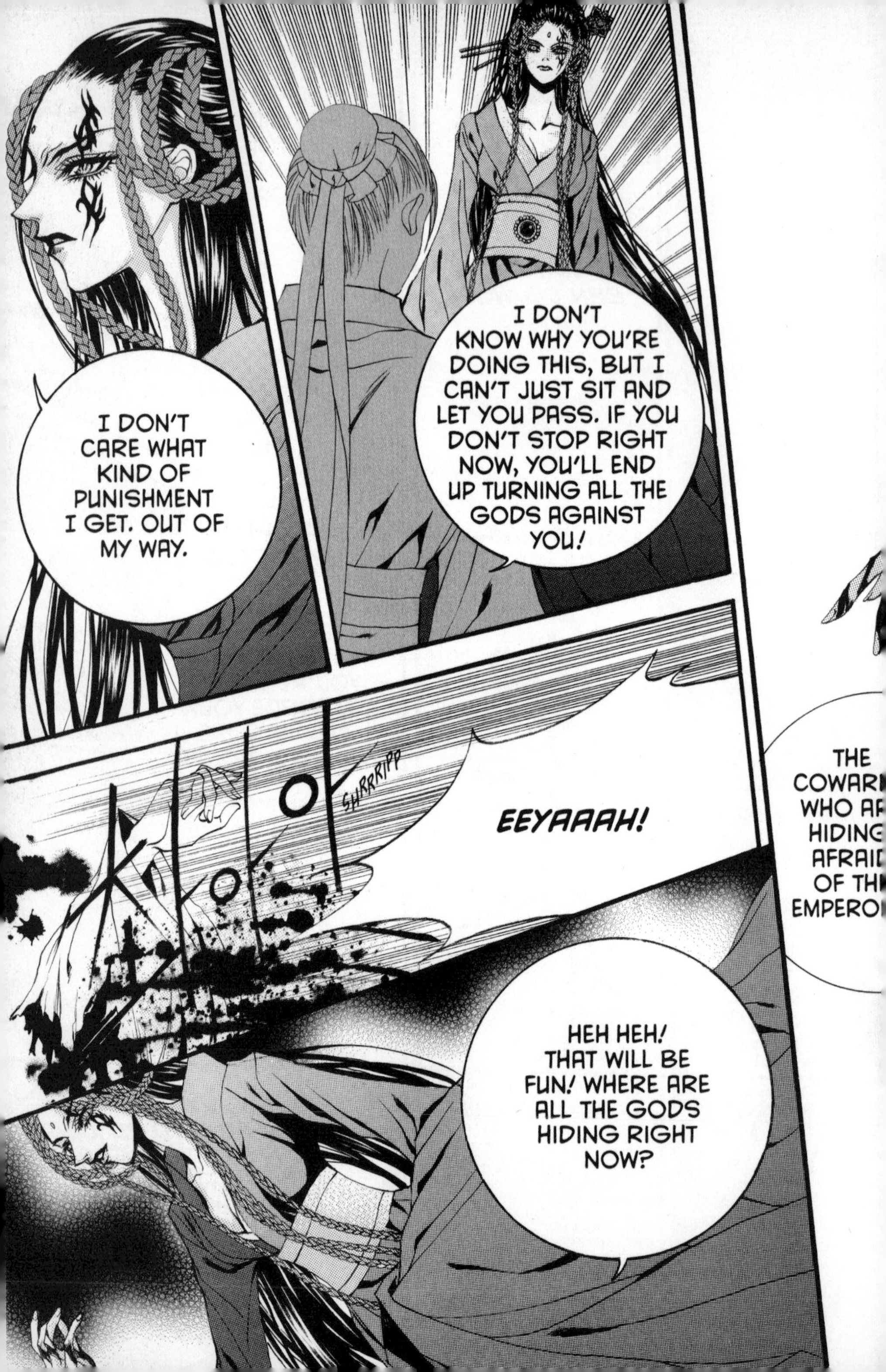
I DON'T KNOW WHY YOU'RE DOING THIS, BUT I CAN'T JUST SIT AND LET YOU PASS. IF YOU DON'T STOP RIGHT NOW, YOU'LL END UP TURNING ALL THE GODS AGAINST YOU!
I DON'T CARE WHAT KIND OF PUNISHMENT I GET. OUT OF MY WAY.
SHRRRIPP
EEYAAAH!
HEH HEH! THAT WILL BE FUN! WHERE ARE ALL THE GODS HIDING RIGHT NOW?
THE COWAR WHO AR HIDING AFRAID OF TH EMPERO

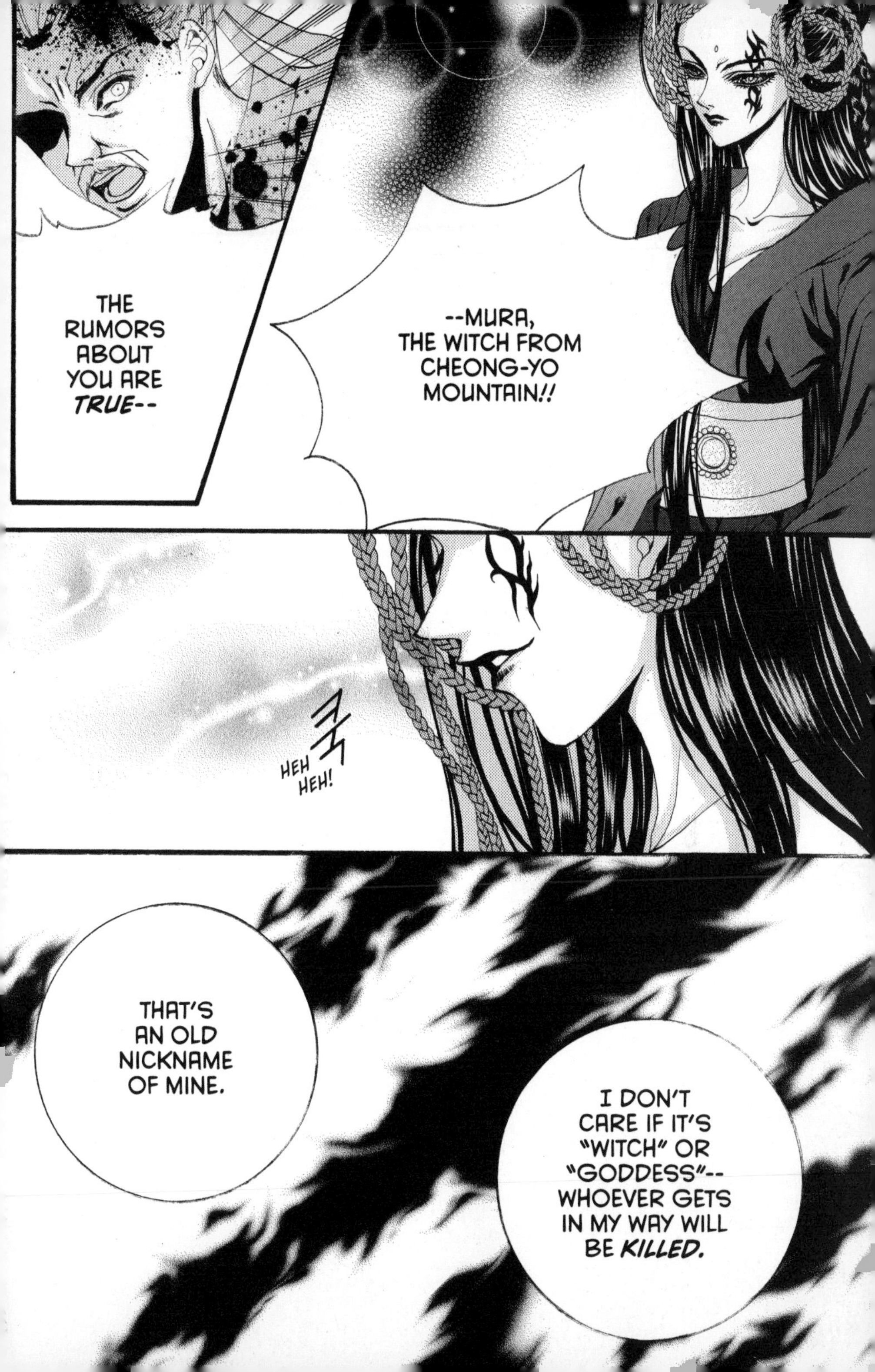
THE RUMORS ABOUT YOU ARE TRUE--
--MURA, THE WITCH FROM CHEONG-YO MOUNTAIN!!
크
HEH HEH!
THAT'S AN OLD NICKNAME OF MINE.
I DON'T CARE IF IT'S "WITCH" OR "GODDESS"-- WHOEVER GETS IN MY WAY WILL BE KILLED.

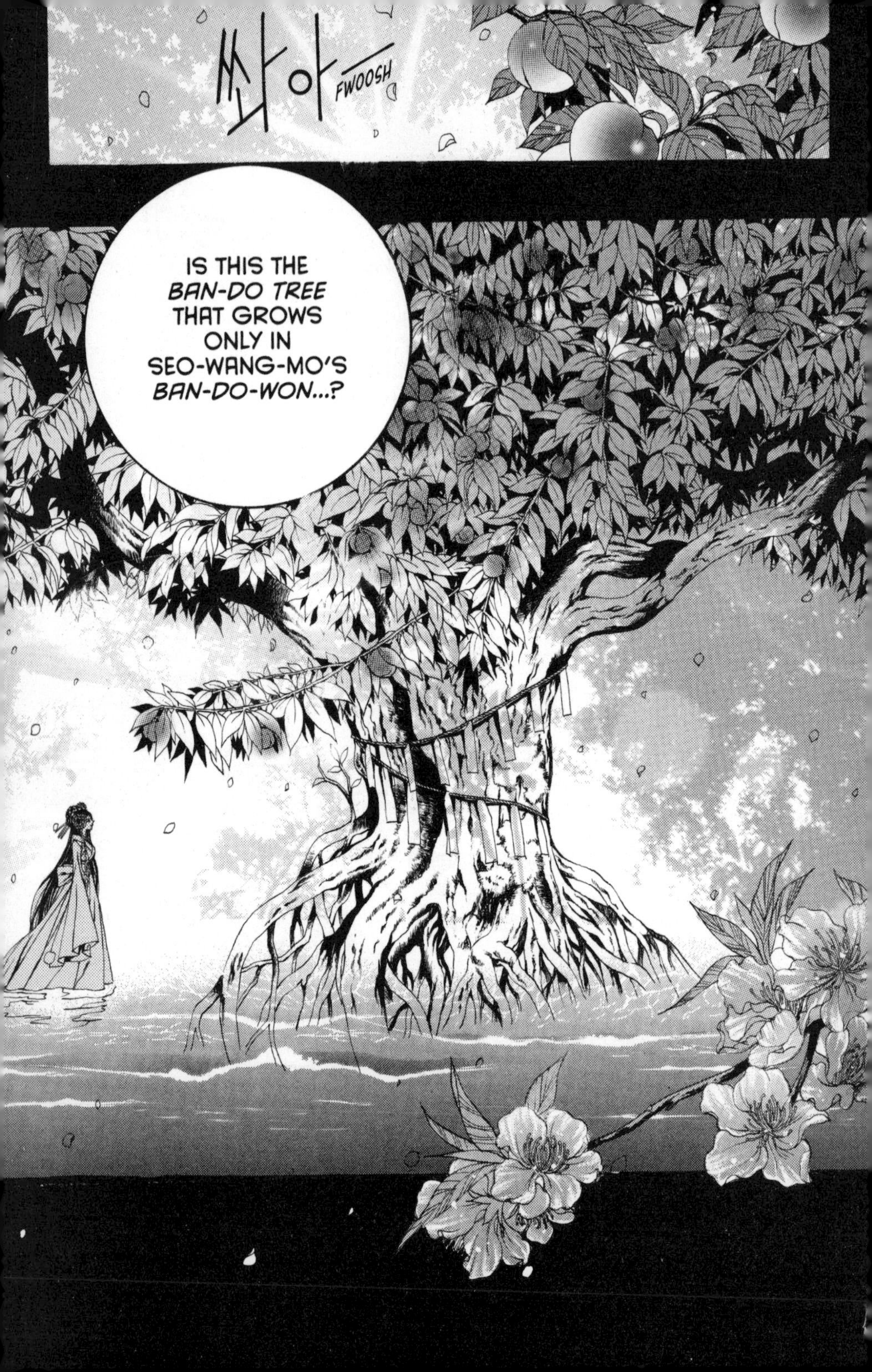
쏴아
FWOOSH
IS THIS THE *BAN-DO TREE* THAT GROWS ONLY IN SEO-WANG-MO'S *BAN-DO-WON*...?

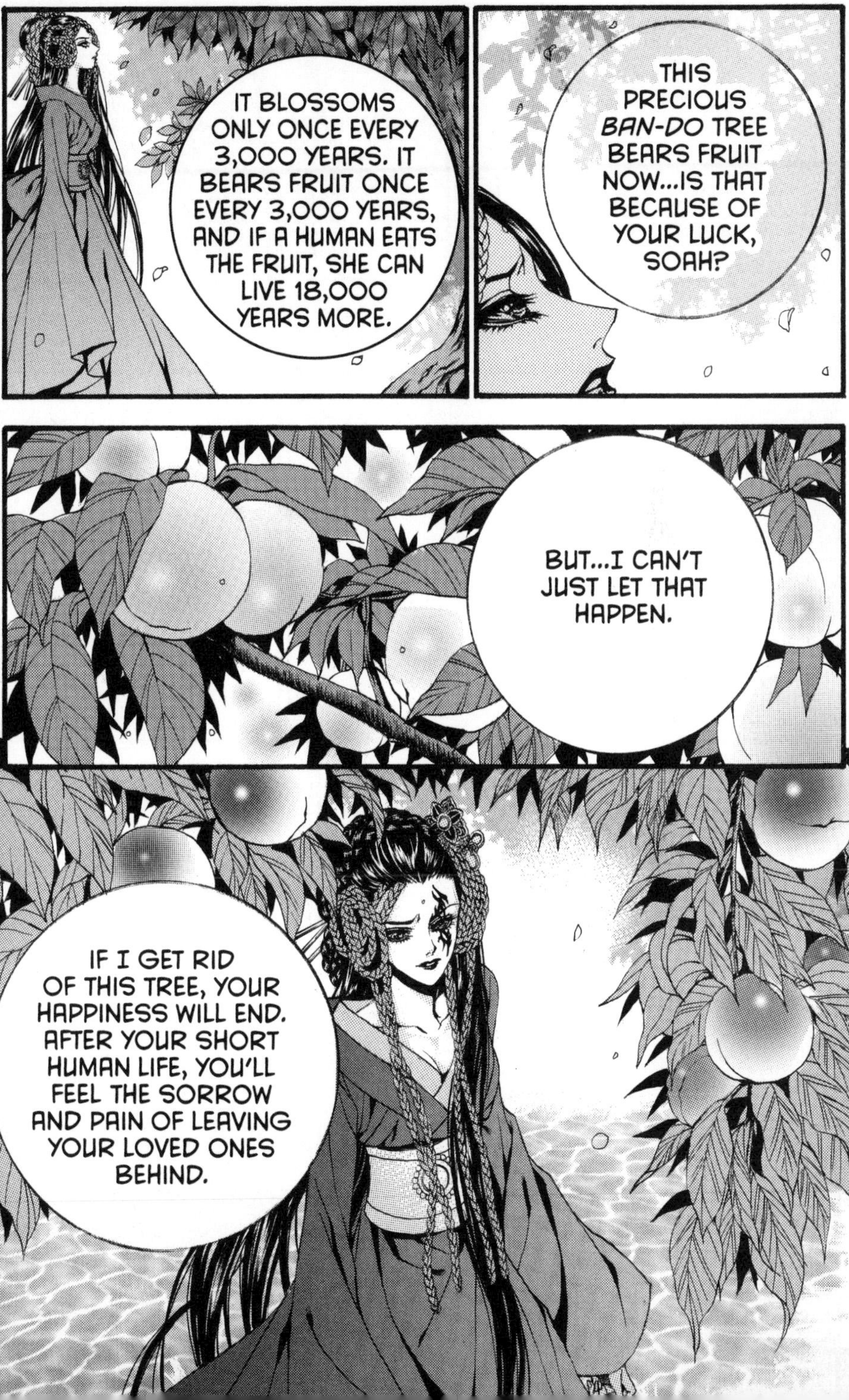
IT BLOSSOMS ONLY ONCE EVERY 3,000 YEARS. IT BEARS FRUIT ONCE EVERY 3,000 YEARS, AND IF A HUMAN EATS THE FRUIT, SHE CAN LIVE 18,000 YEARS MORE.
THIS PRECIOUS *BAN-DO* TREE BEARS FRUIT NOW...IS THAT BECAUSE OF YOUR LUCK, SOAH?
BUT...I CAN'T JUST LET THAT HAPPEN.
IF I GET RID OF THIS TREE, YOUR HAPPINESS WILL END. AFTER YOUR SHORT HUMAN LIFE, YOU'LL FEEL THE SORROW AND PAIN OF LEAVING YOUR LOVED ONES BEHIND.

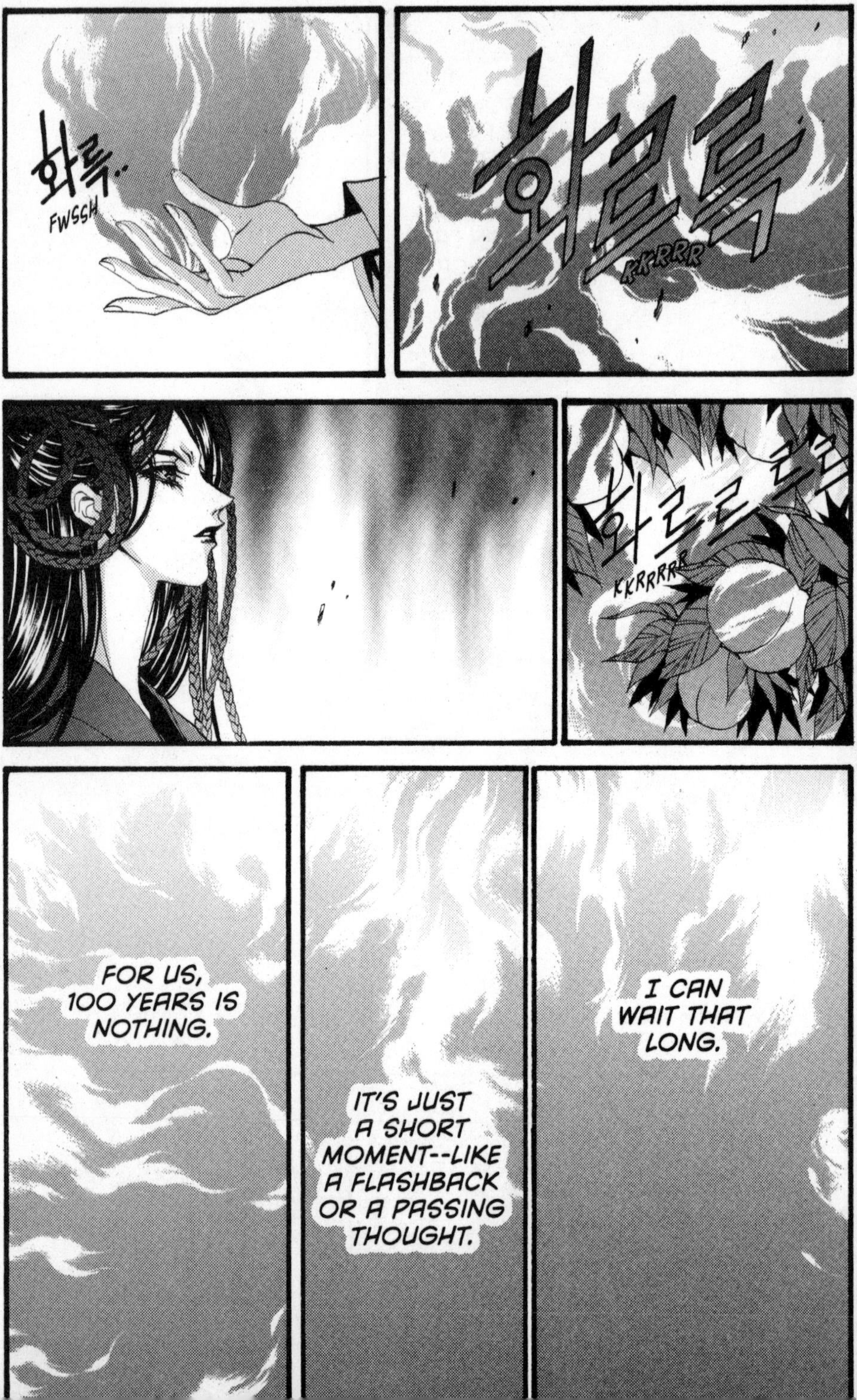
화륵..
FWSSH
화르륵
KKRRR
KKRRRRR
FOR US, 100 YEARS IS NOTHING.
IT'S JUST A SHORT MOMENT--LIKE A FLASHBACK OR A PASSING THOUGHT.
I CAN WAIT THAT LONG.

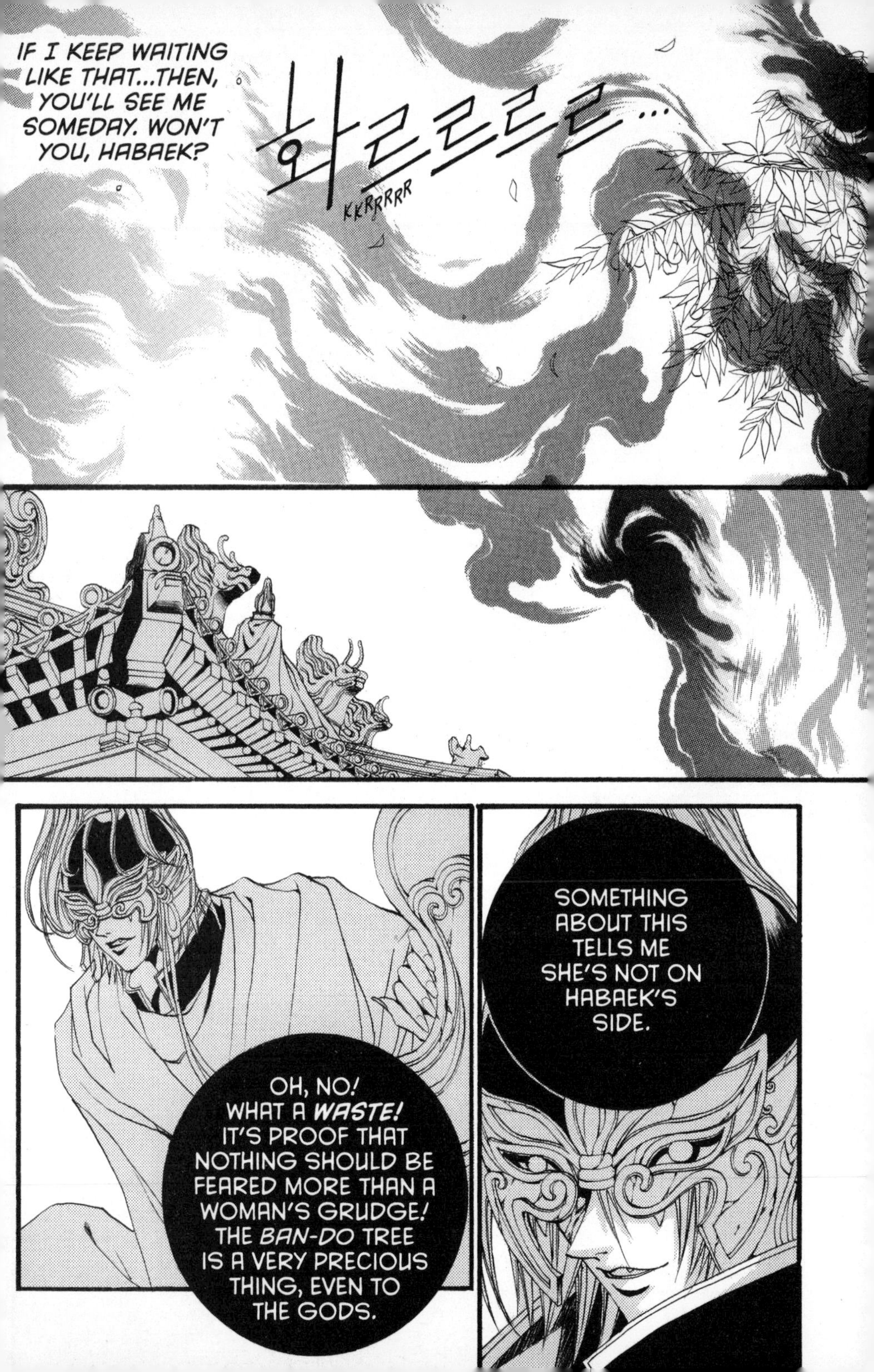
IF I KEEP WAITING LIKE THAT...THEN, YOU'LL SEE ME SOMEDAY. WON'T YOU, HABAEK?
화르르르르...
KKRRRRR
OH, NO! WHAT A *WASTE!* IT'S PROOF THAT NOTHING SHOULD BE FEARED MORE THAN A WOMAN'S GRUDGE! THE *BAN-DO* TREE IS A VERY PRECIOUS THING, EVEN TO THE GODS.
SOMETHING ABOUT THIS TELLS ME SHE'S NOT ON HABAEK'S SIDE.

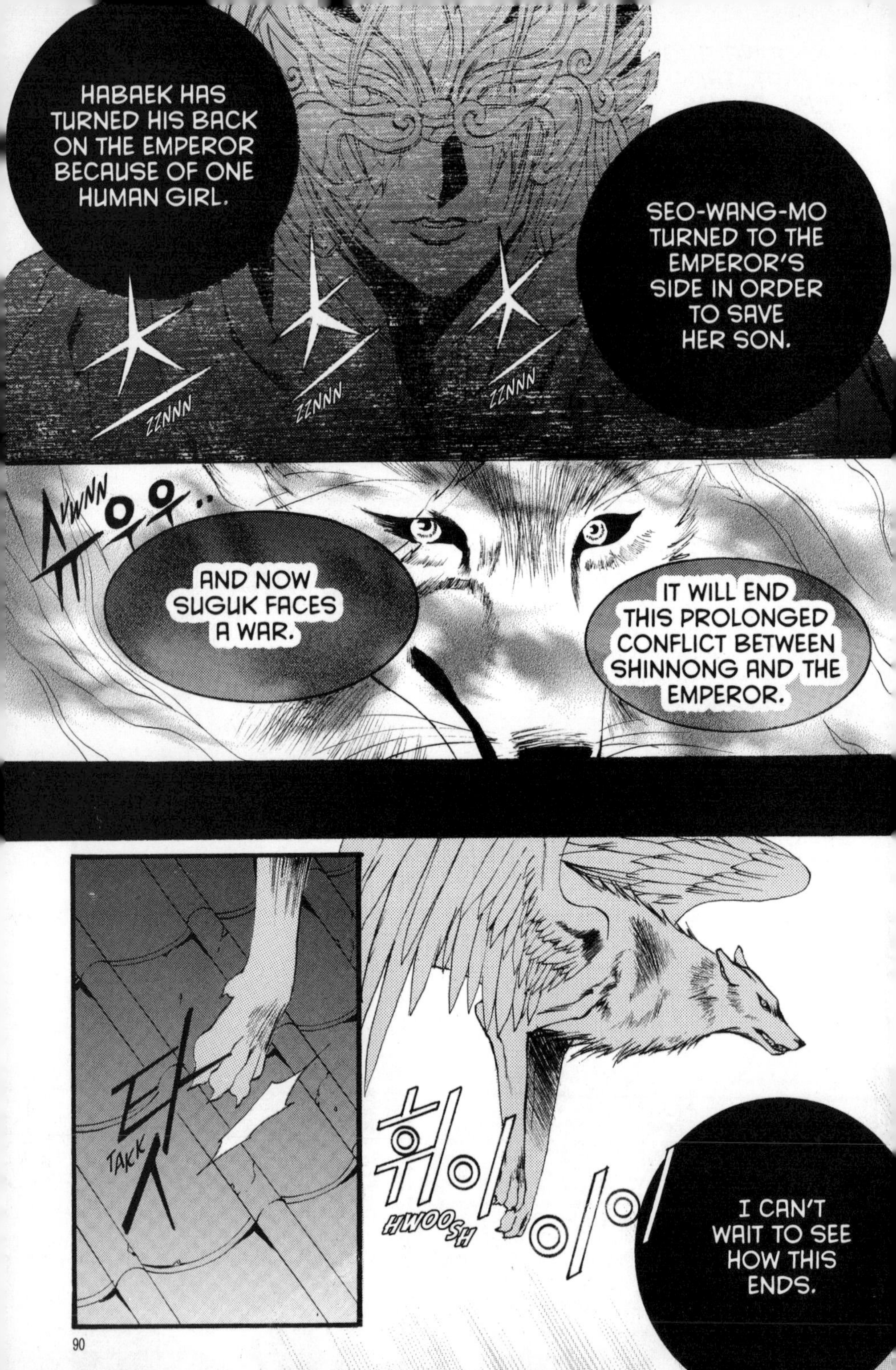
HABAEK HAS TURNED HIS BACK ON THE EMPEROR BECAUSE OF ONE HUMAN GIRL.
SEO-WANG-MO TURNED TO THE EMPEROR'S SIDE IN ORDER TO SAVE HER SON.
ZZNNN
ZZNNN
ZZNNN
AVWNN
우우..
AND NOW SUGUK FACES A WAR.
IT WILL END THIS PROLONGED CONFLICT BETWEEN SHINNONG AND THE EMPEROR.
탁
TAKK
휘이이이
HWOOSH
I CAN'T WAIT TO SEE HOW THIS ENDS.

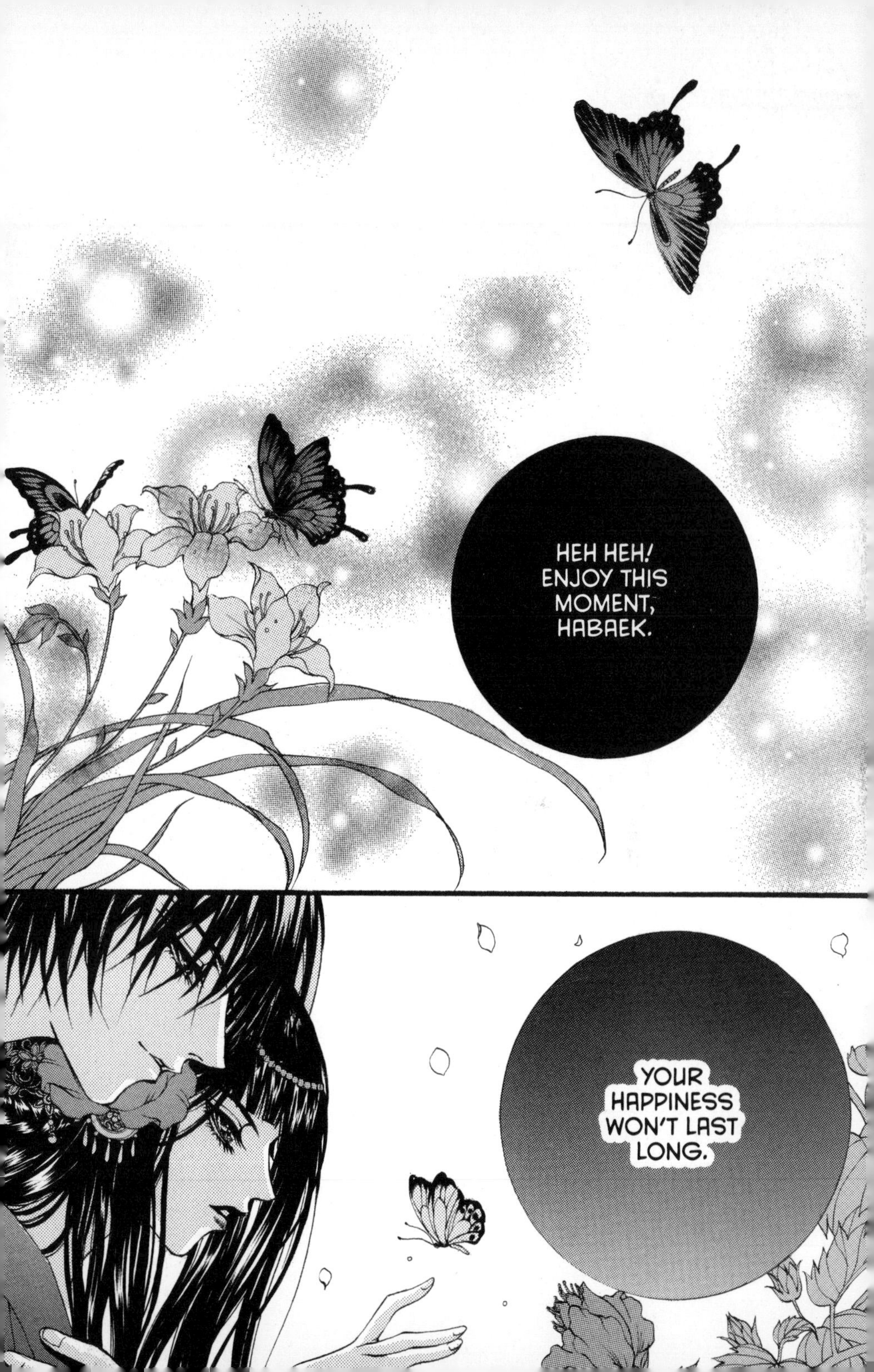
HEH HEH! ENJOY THIS MOMENT, HABAEK.
YOUR HAPPINESS WON'T LAST LONG.

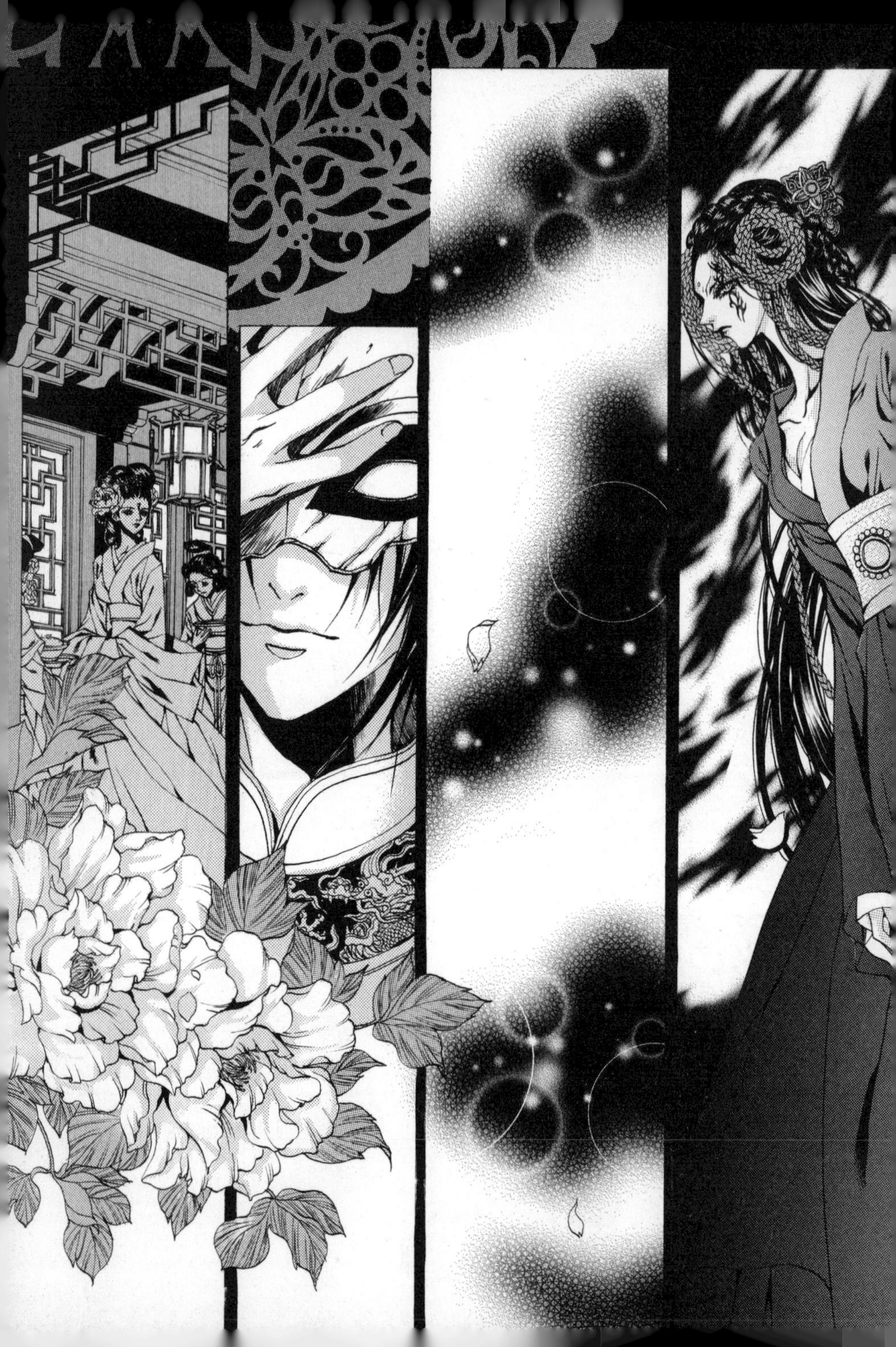

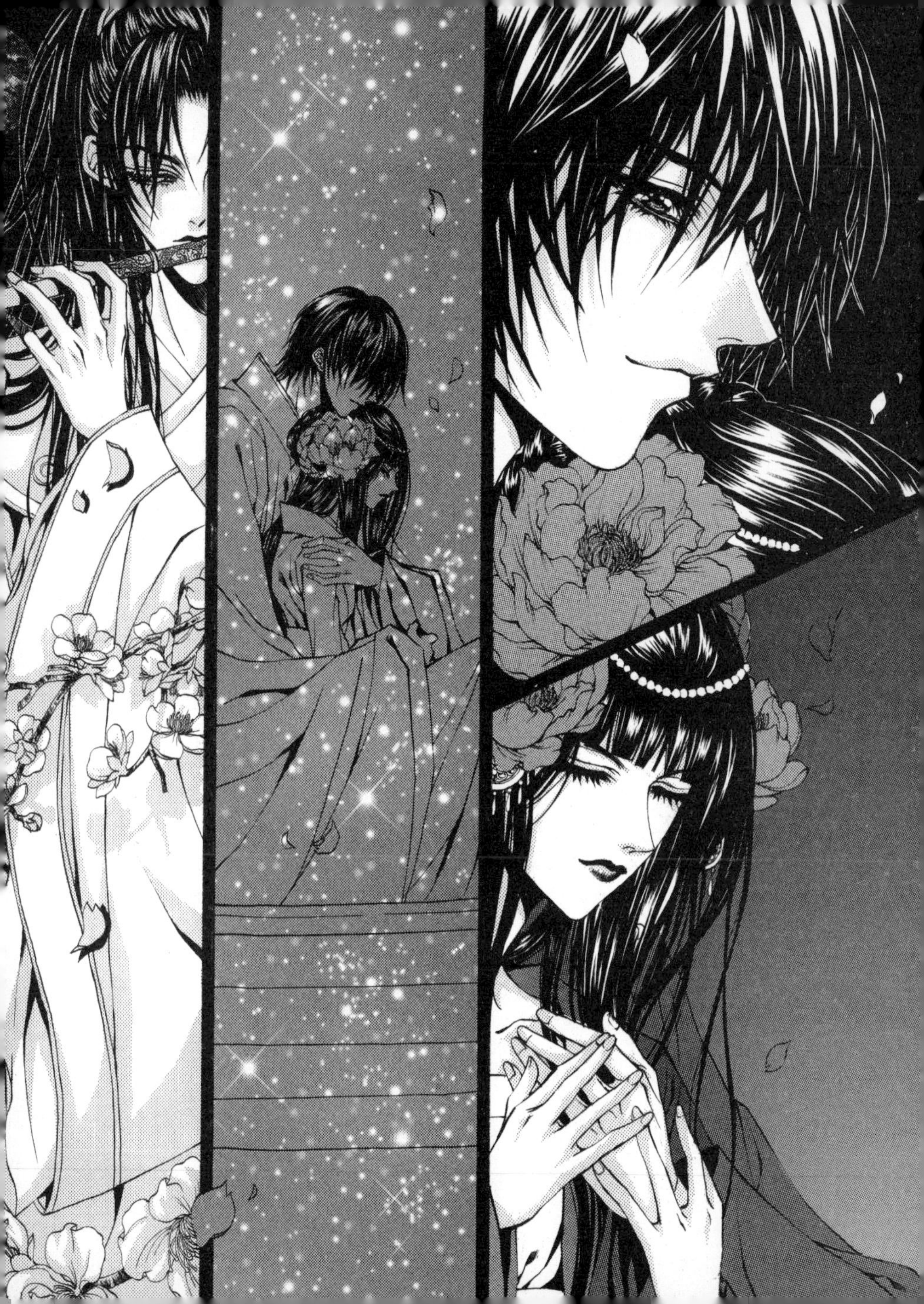

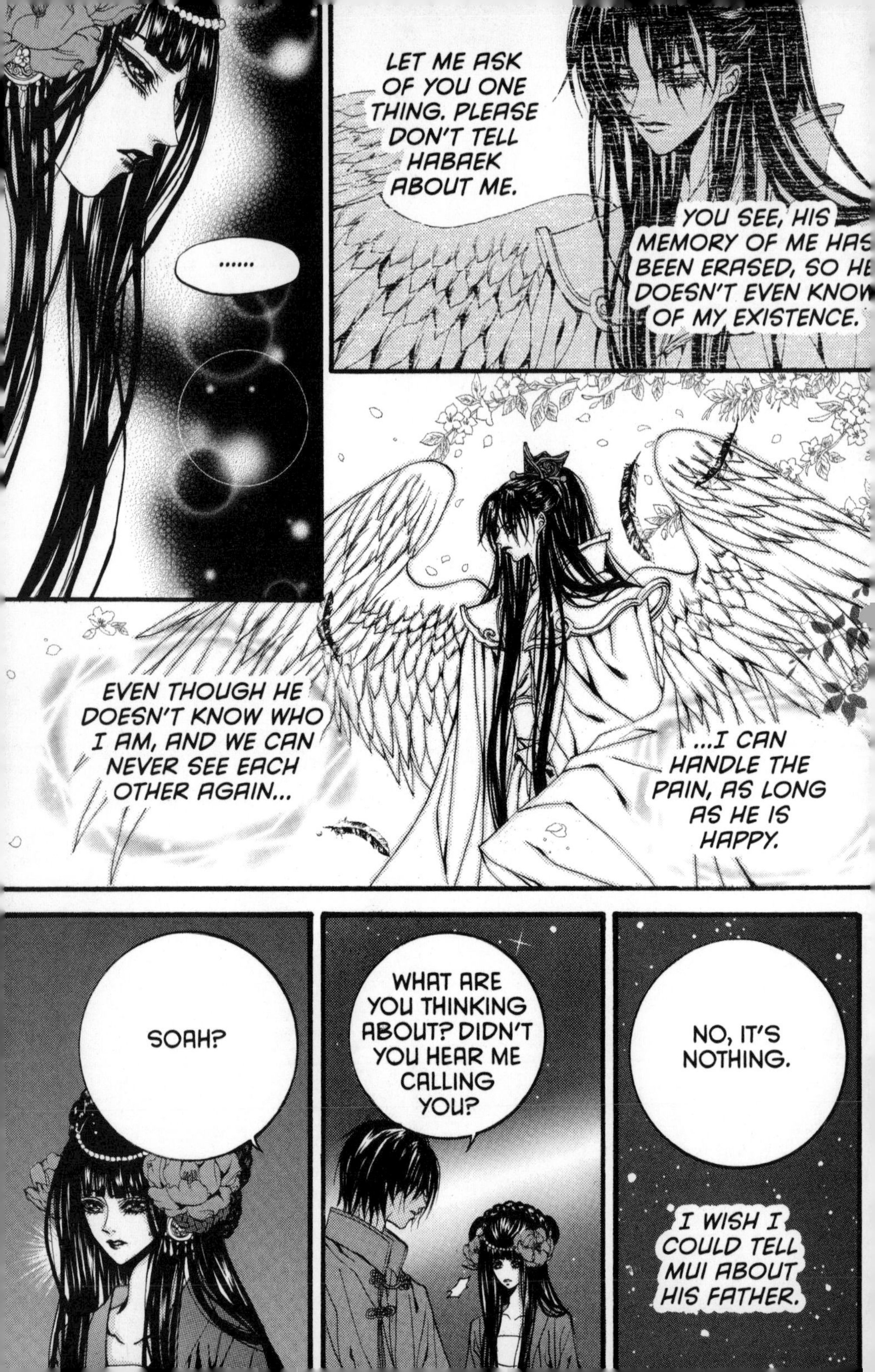

LET ME ASK OF YOU ONE THING. PLEASE DON'T TELL HABAEK ABOUT ME.
......
YOU SEE, HIS MEMORY OF ME HAS BEEN ERASED, SO HE DOESN'T EVEN KNOW OF MY EXISTENCE.
EVEN THOUGH HE DOESN'T KNOW WHO I AM, AND WE CAN NEVER SEE EACH OTHER AGAIN...
...I CAN HANDLE THE PAIN, AS LONG AS HE IS HAPPY.
SOAH?
WHAT ARE YOU THINKING ABOUT? DIDN'T YOU HEAR ME CALLING YOU?
NO, IT'S NOTHING.
I WISH I COULD TELL MUI ABOUT HIS FATHER.

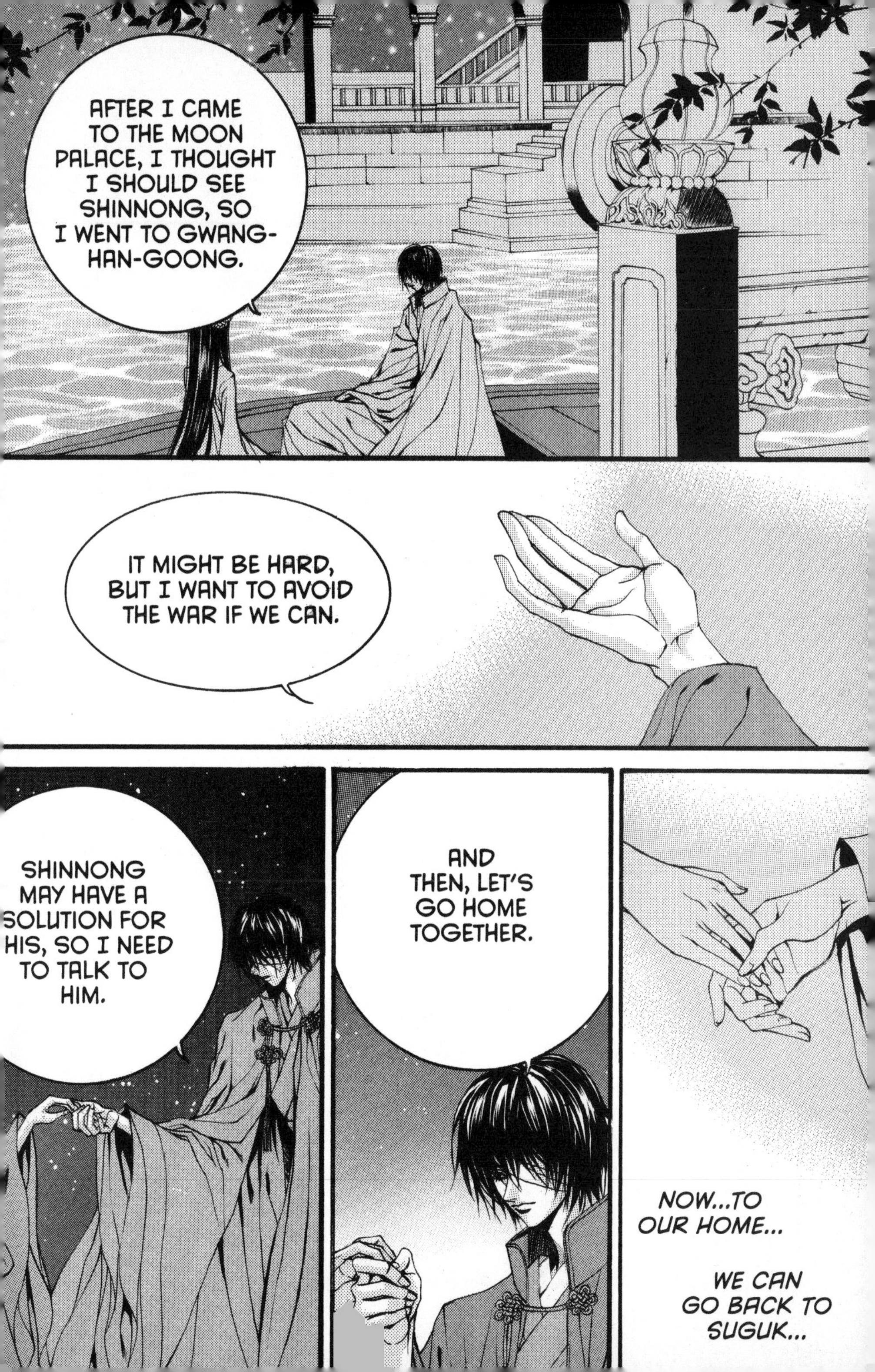
AFTER I CAME TO THE MOON PALACE, I THOUGHT I SHOULD SEE SHINNONG, SO I WENT TO GWANG-HAN-GOONG.
IT MIGHT BE HARD, BUT I WANT TO AVOID THE WAR IF WE CAN.
SHINNONG MAY HAVE A SOLUTION FOR HIS, SO I NEED TO TALK TO HIM.
AND THEN, LET'S GO HOME TOGETHER.
NOW...TO OUR HOME...
WE CAN GO BACK TO SUGUK...

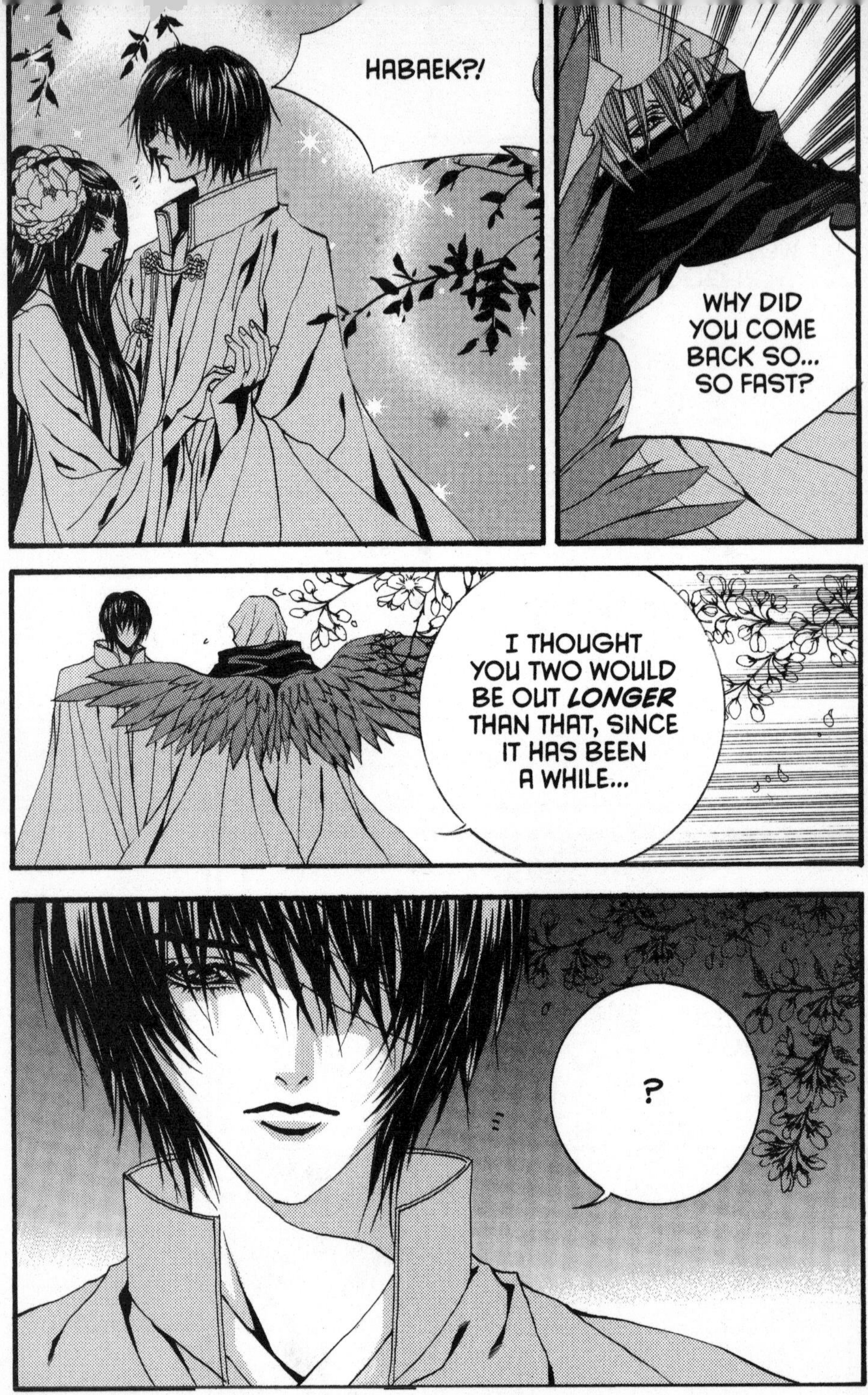
HABAEK?!
WHY DID YOU COME BACK SO... SO FAST?
I THOUGHT YOU TWO WOULD BE OUT *LONGER* THAN THAT, SINCE IT HAS BEEN A WHILE...
?

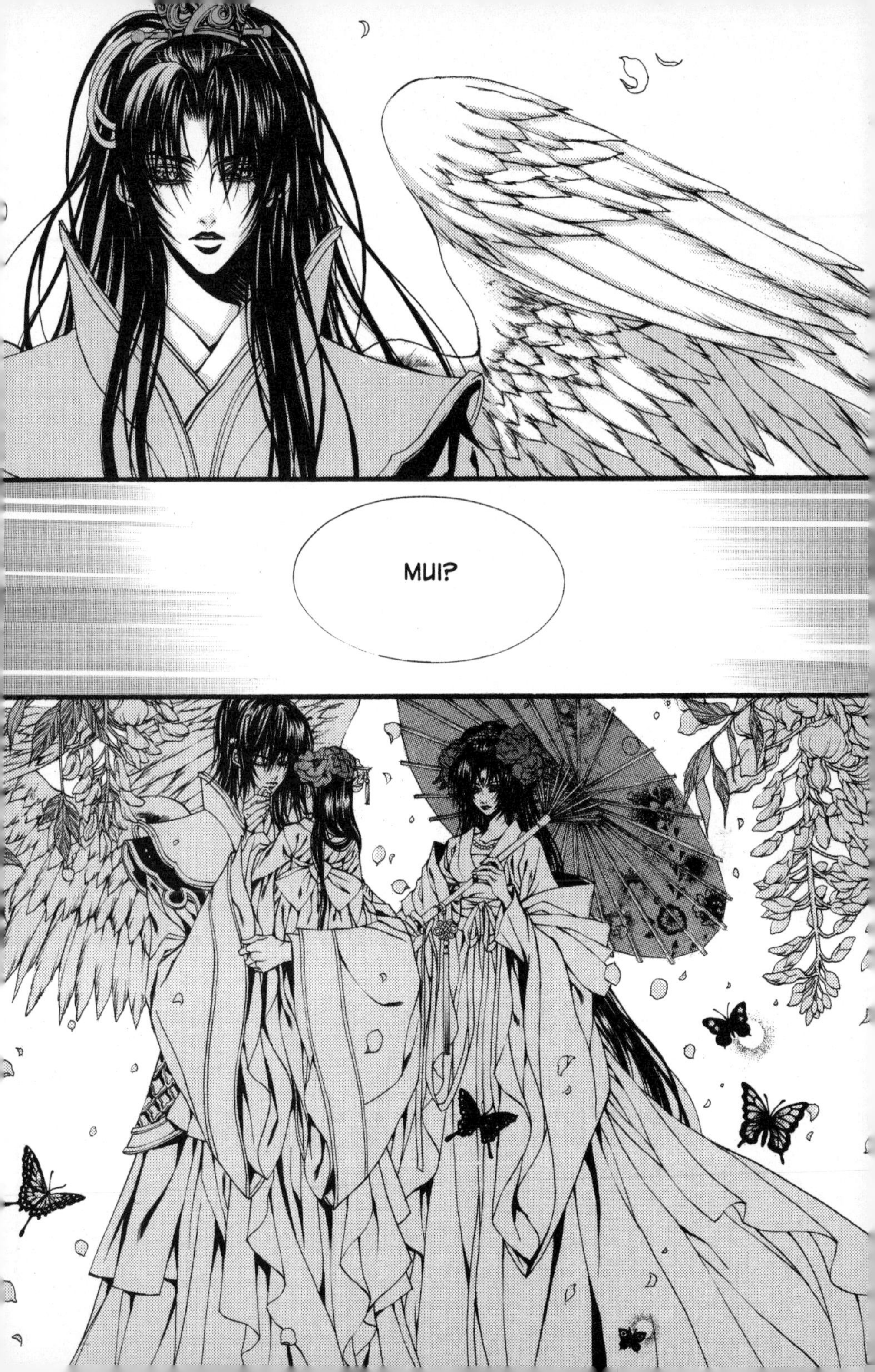
MUI?

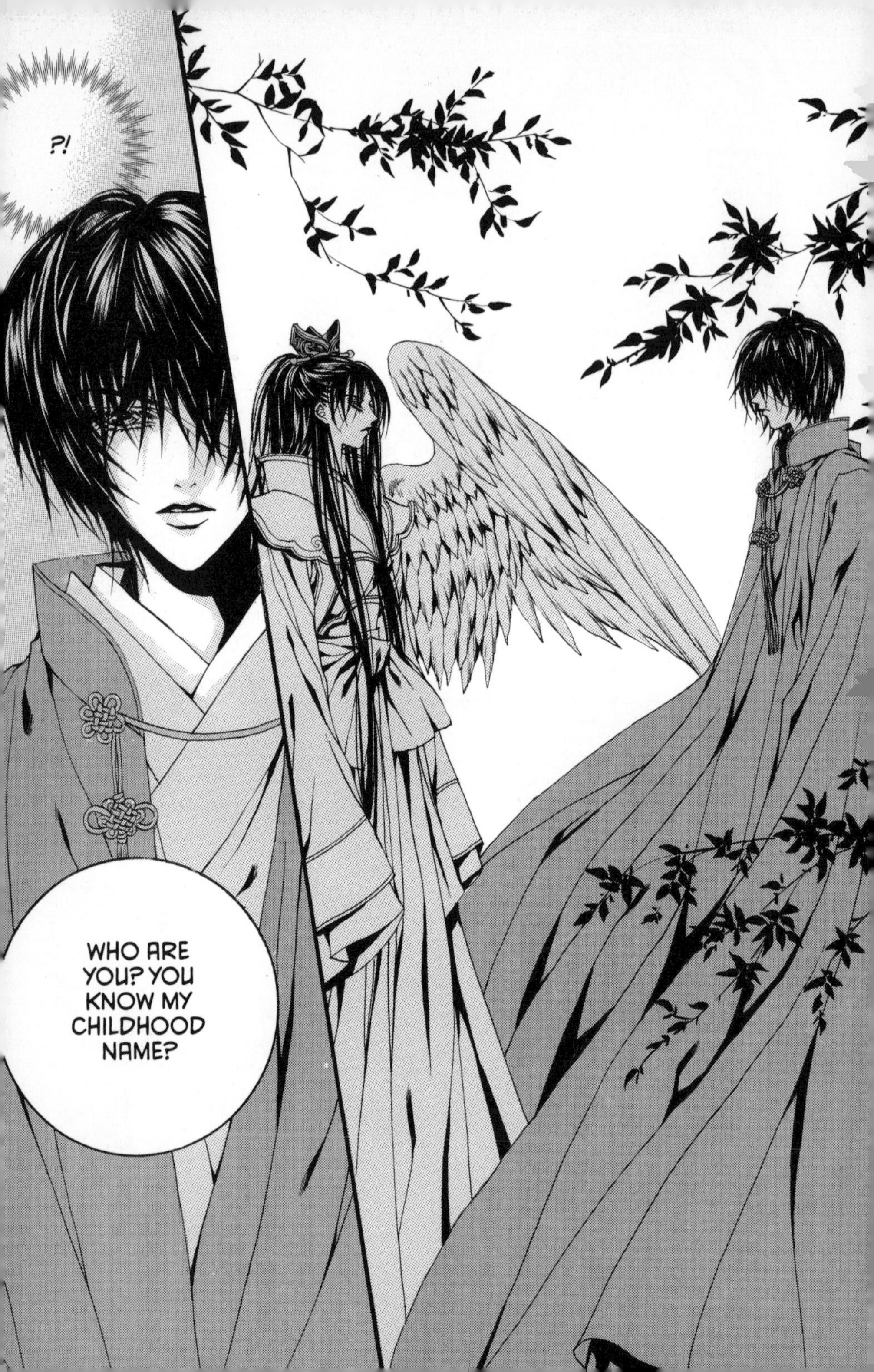
?!
WHO ARE YOU? YOU KNOW MY CHILDHOOD NAME?

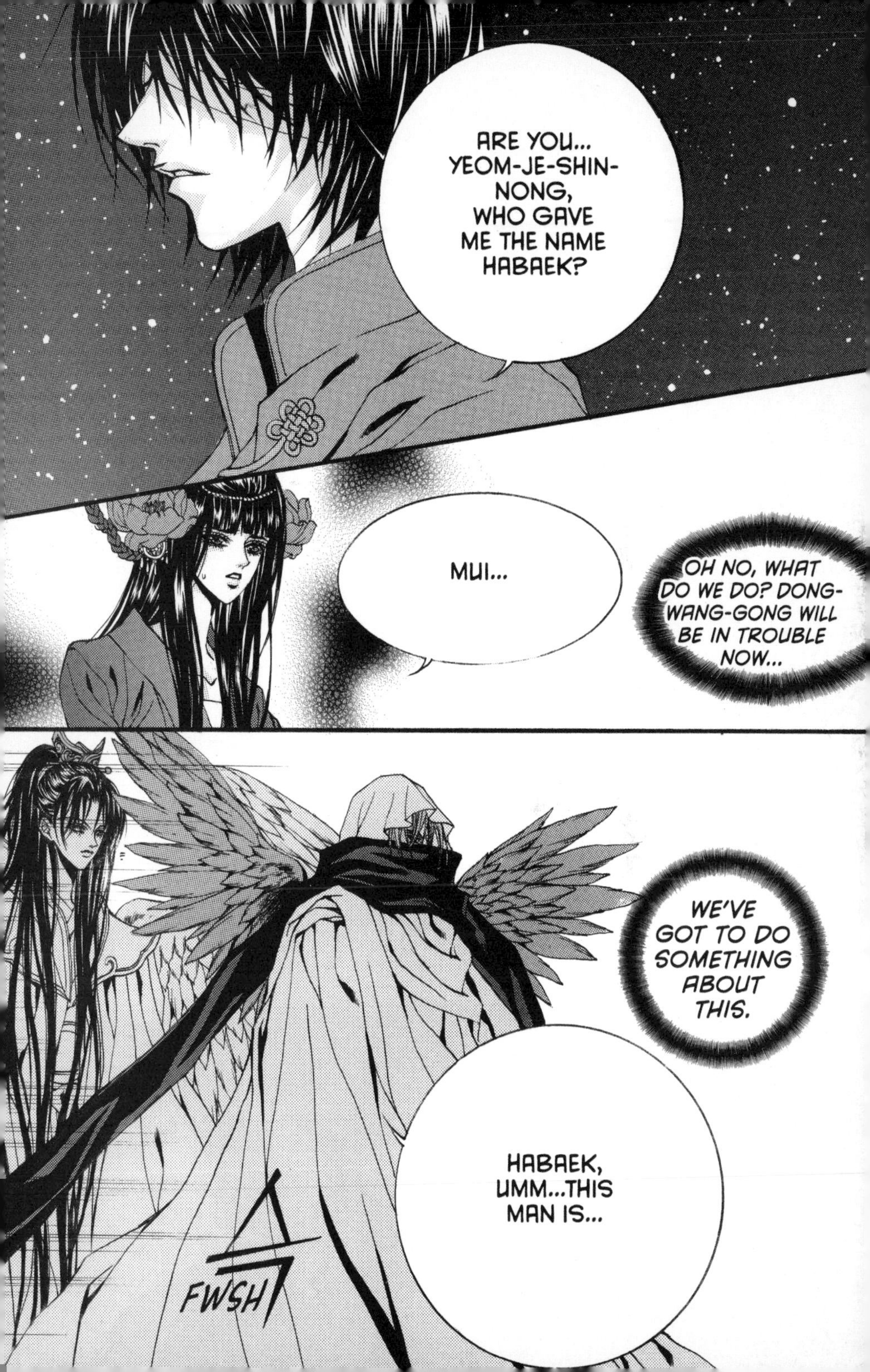
ARE YOU... YEOM-JE-SHIN-NONG, WHO GAVE ME THE NAME HABAEK?
MUI...
OH NO, WHAT DO WE DO? DONG-WANG-GONG WILL BE IN TROUBLE NOW...
WE'VE GOT TO DO SOMETHING ABOUT THIS.
HABAEK, UMM...THIS MAN IS...
FWSH

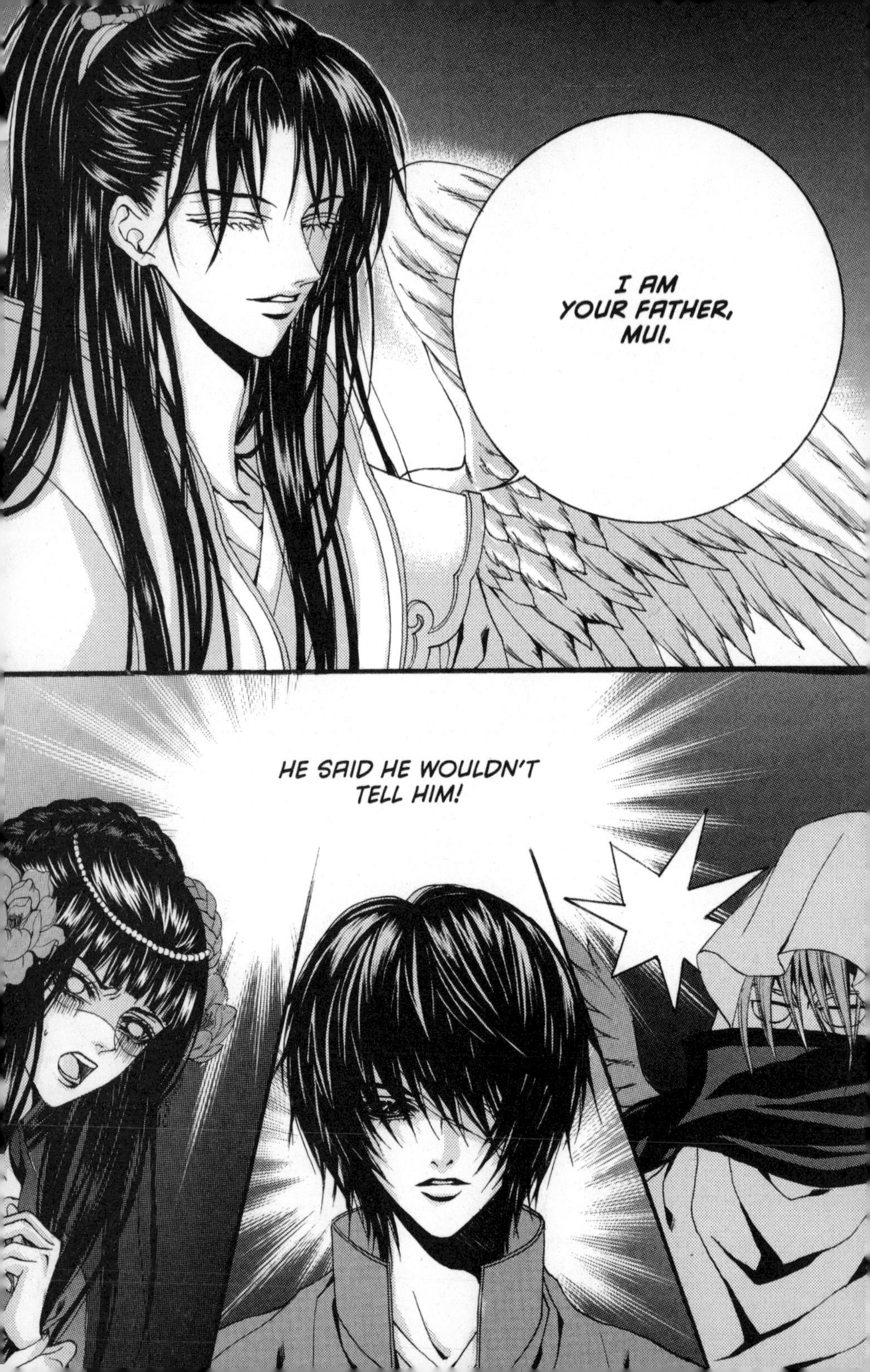
I AM YOUR FATHER, MUI.
HE SAID HE WOULDN'T TELL HIM!

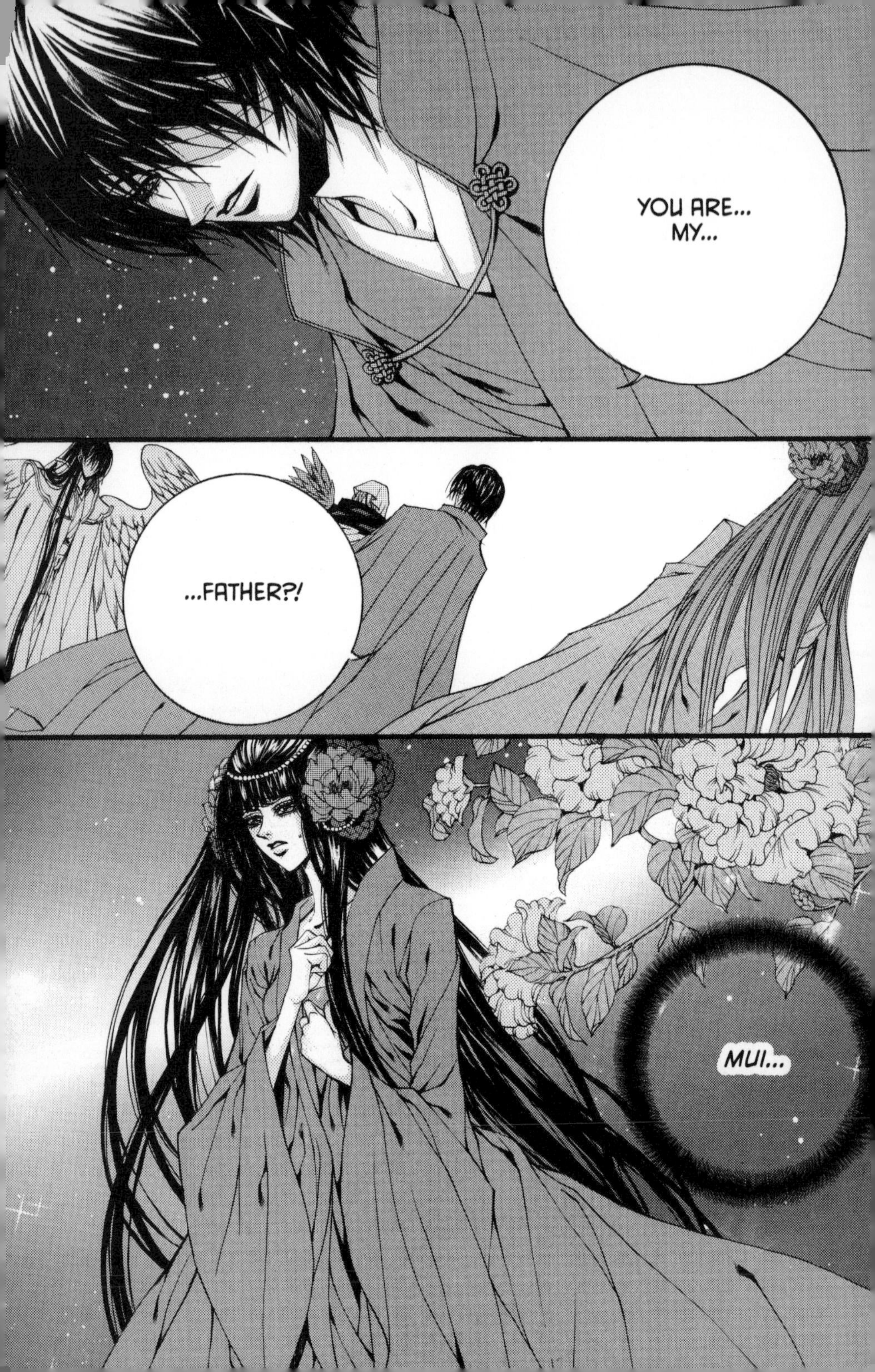
YOU ARE... MY...
...FATHER?!
MUI...

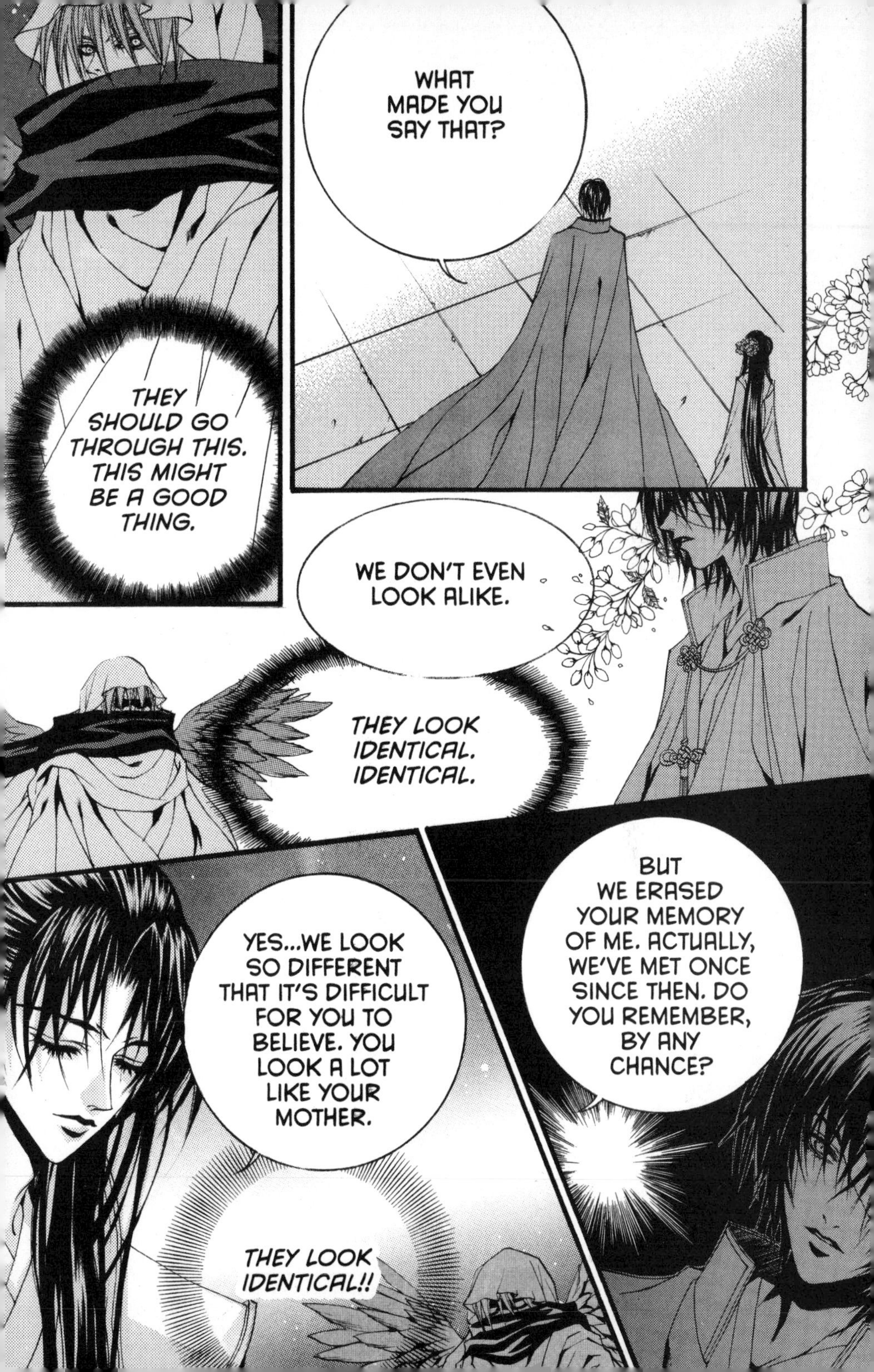
WHAT MADE YOU SAY THAT?
THEY SHOULD GO THROUGH THIS. THIS MIGHT BE A GOOD THING.
WE DON'T EVEN LOOK ALIKE.
THEY LOOK IDENTICAL. IDENTICAL.
BUT WE ERASED YOUR MEMORY OF ME. ACTUALLY, WE'VE MET ONCE SINCE THEN. DO YOU REMEMBER, BY ANY CHANCE?
YES...WE LOOK SO DIFFERENT THAT IT'S DIFFICULT FOR YOU TO BELIEVE. YOU LOOK A LOT LIKE YOUR MOTHER.
THEY LOOK IDENTICAL!!

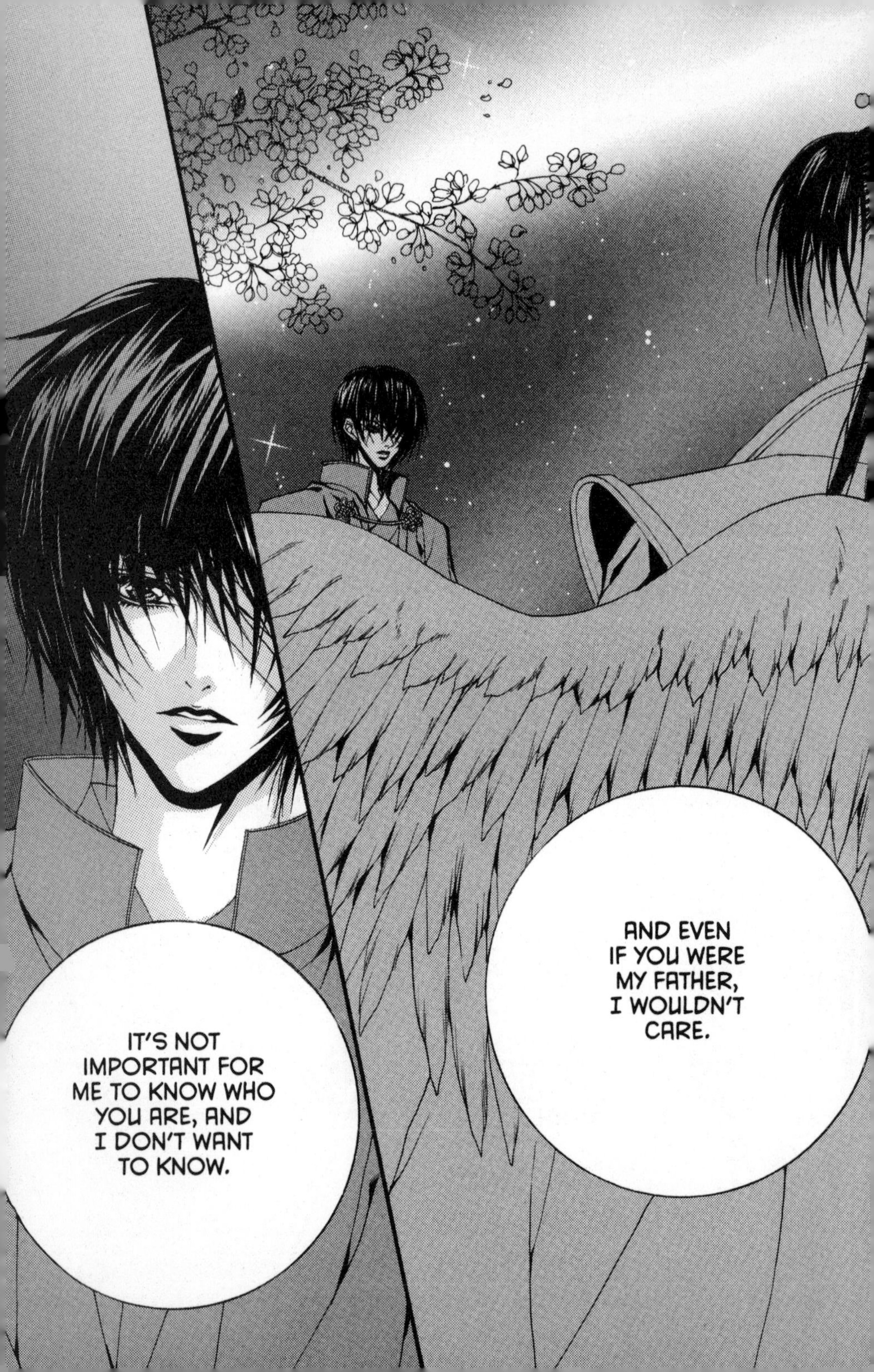
AND EVEN IF YOU WERE MY FATHER, I WOULDN'T CARE.
IT'S NOT IMPORTANT FOR ME TO KNOW WHO YOU ARE, AND I DON'T WANT TO KNOW.

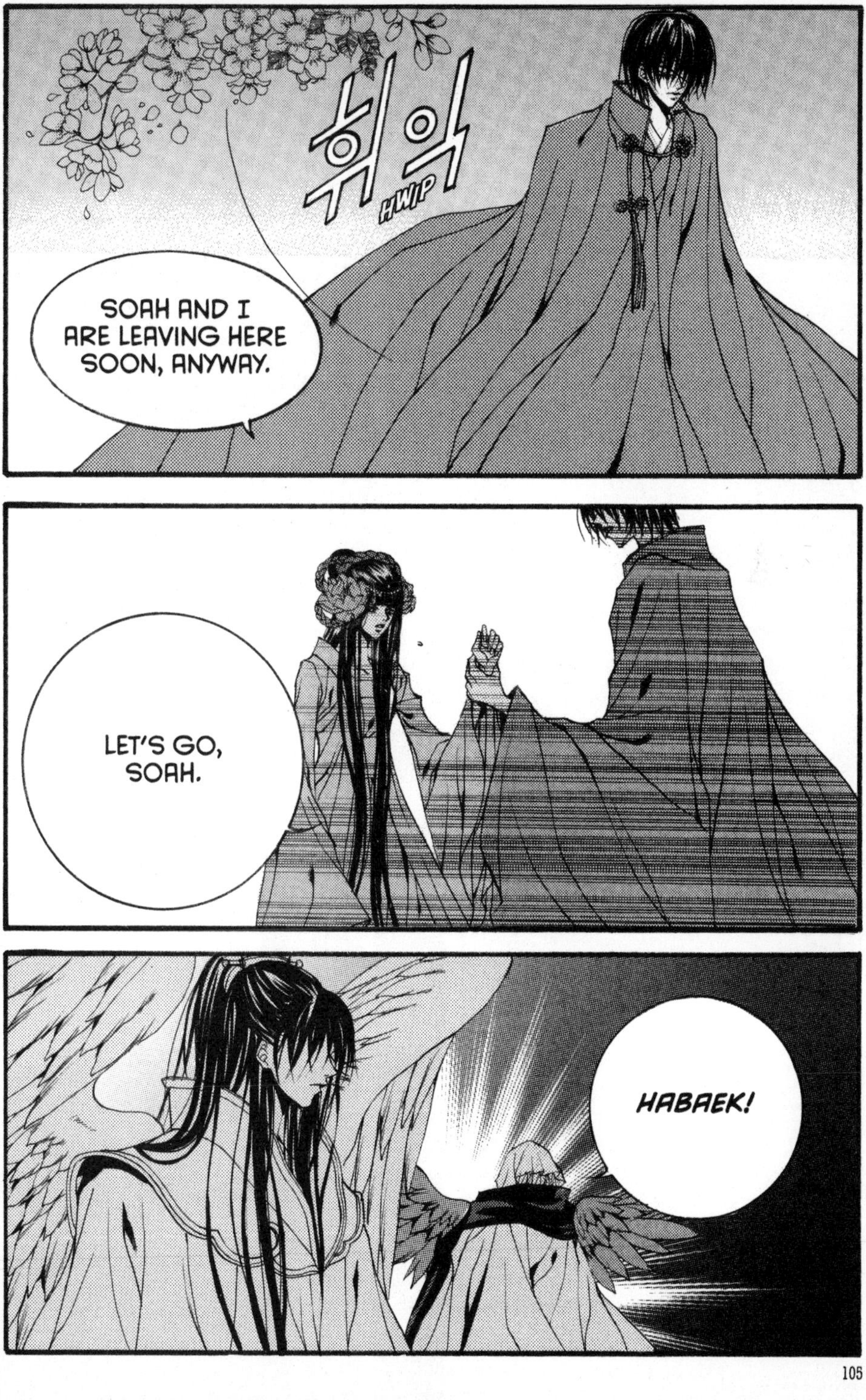
휘익
HWIP
SOAH AND I ARE LEAVING HERE SOON, ANYWAY.
LET'S GO, SOAH.
HABAEK!

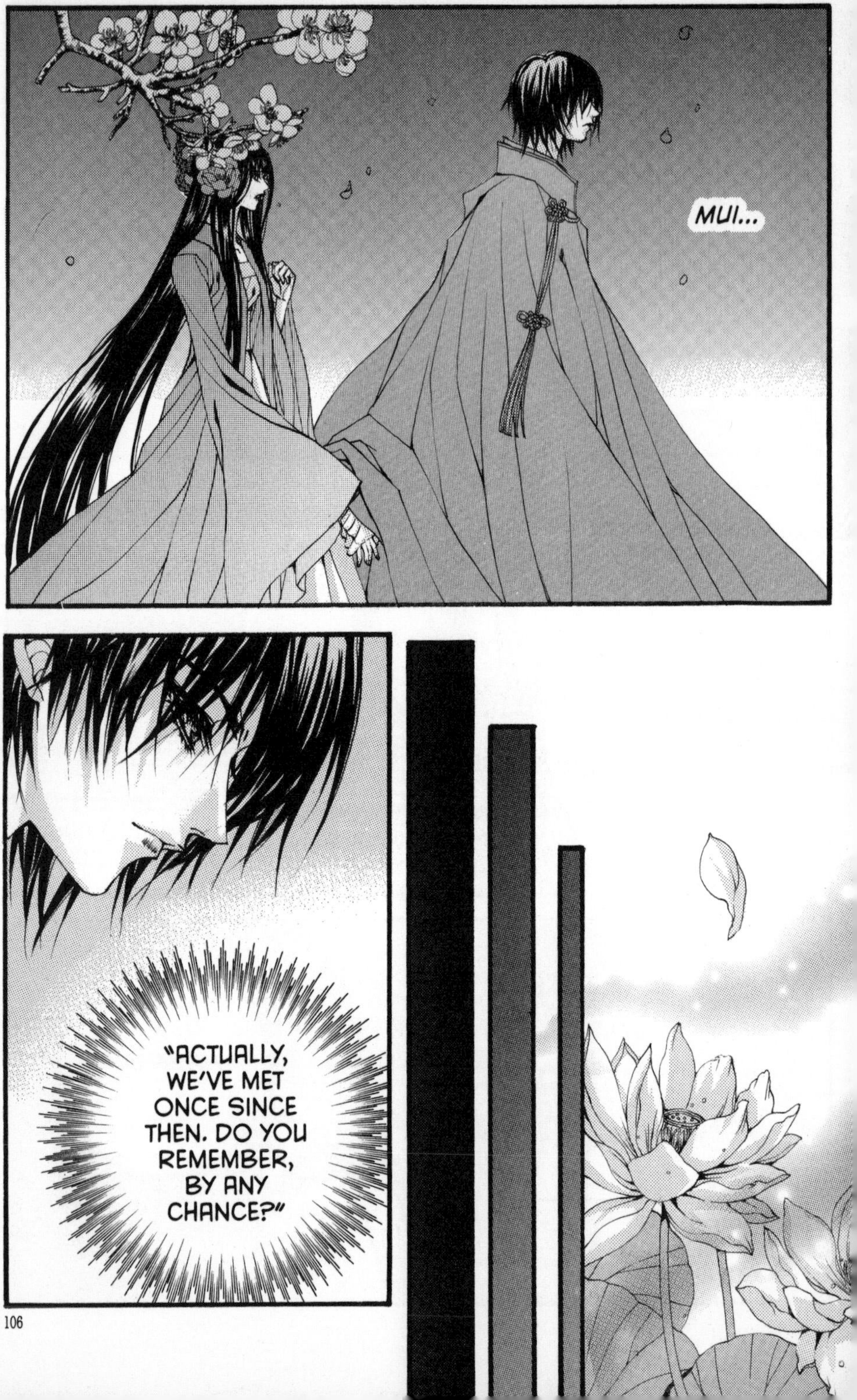
MUI...
"ACTUALLY, WE'VE MET ONCE SINCE THEN. DO YOU REMEMBER, BY ANY CHANCE?"

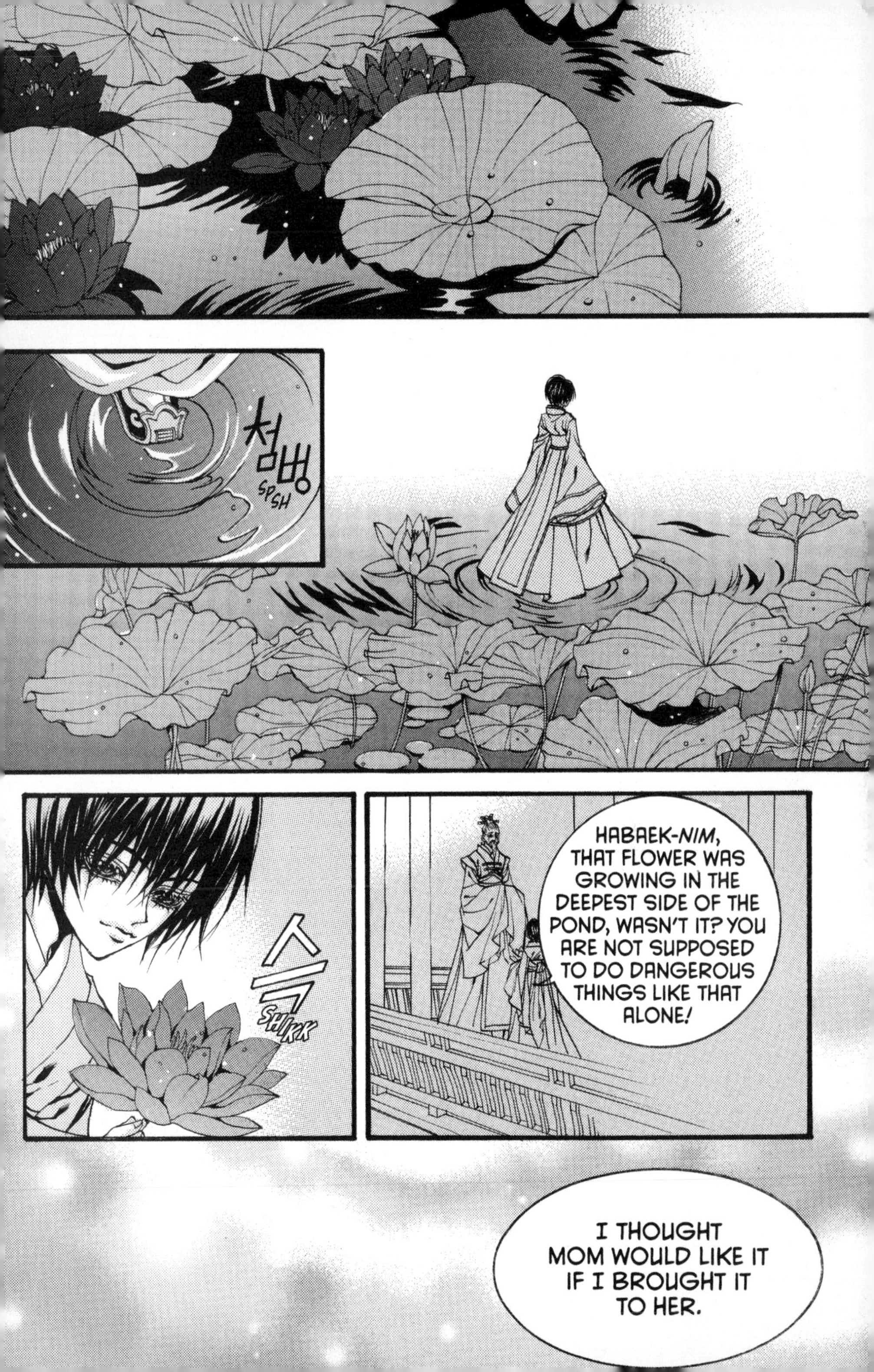
첨벙
SPSH
슥
SHIKK
HABAEK-*NIM*, THAT FLOWER WAS GROWING IN THE DEEPEST SIDE OF THE POND, WASN'T IT? YOU ARE NOT SUPPOSED TO DO DANGEROUS THINGS LIKE THAT ALONE!
I THOUGHT MOM WOULD LIKE IT IF I BROUGHT IT TO HER.

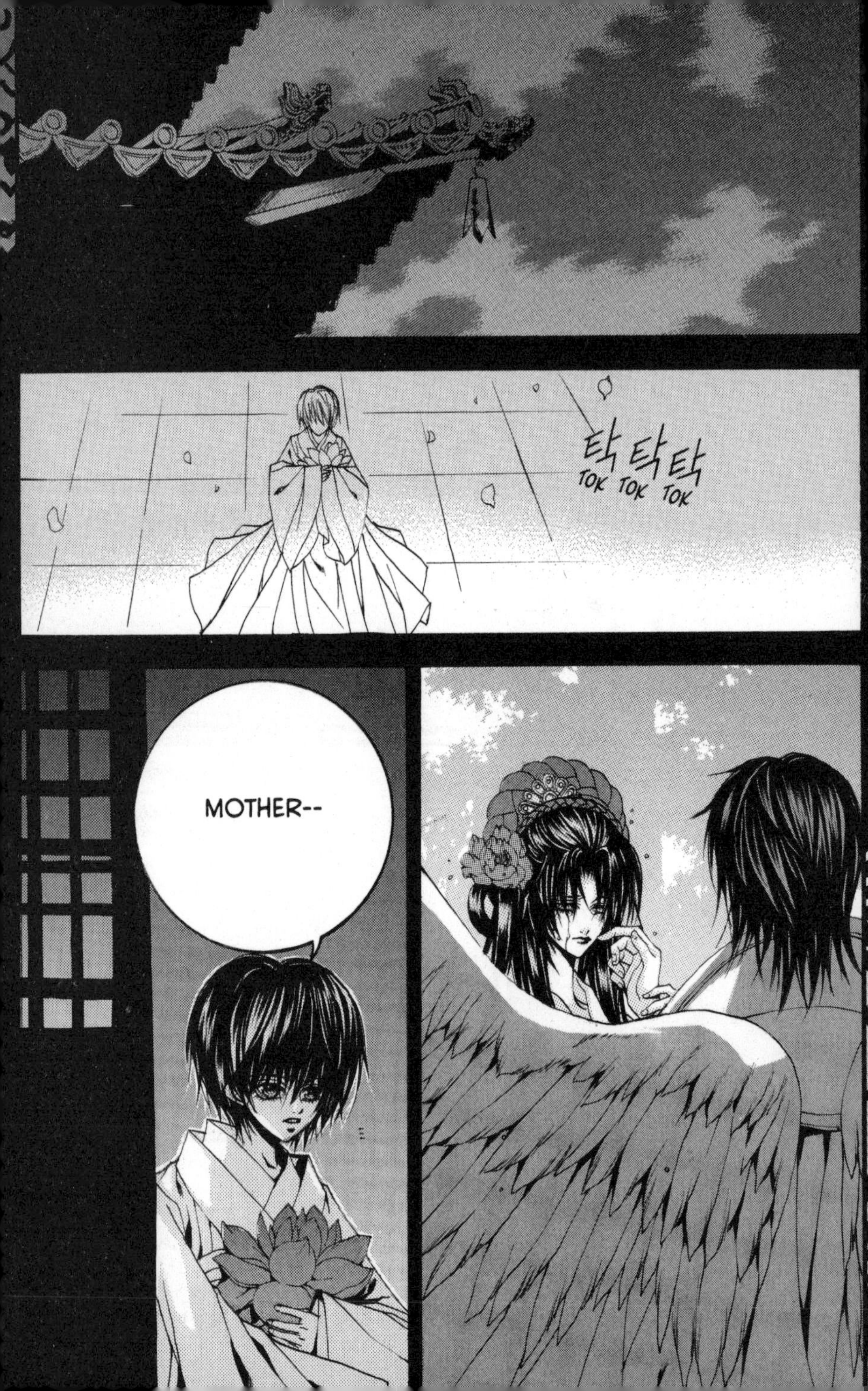

탁 탁 탁
TOK TOK TOK
MOTHER--

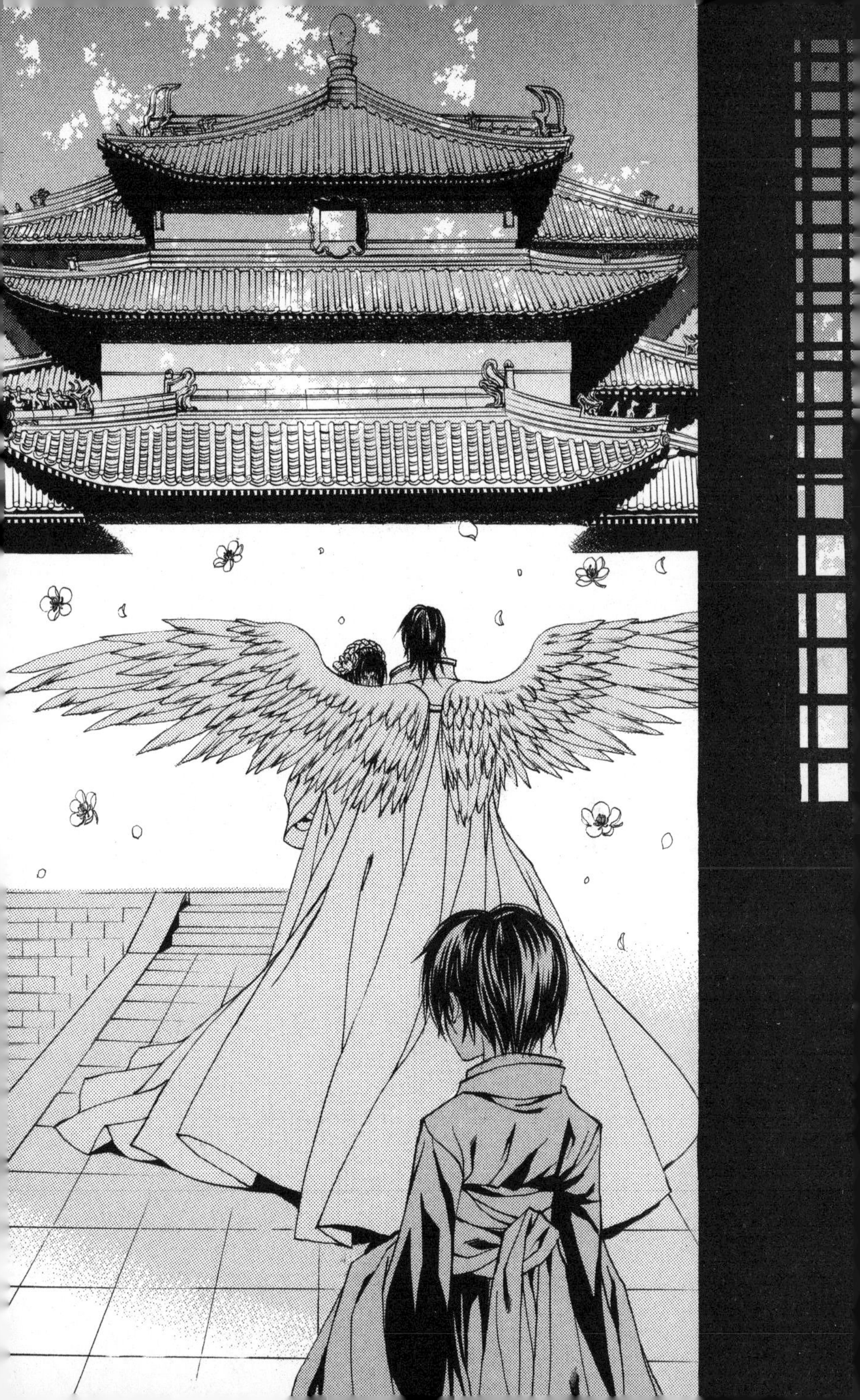

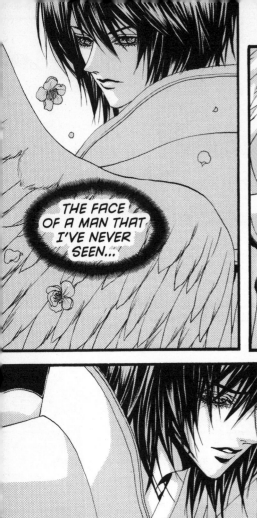

THE FACE OF A MAN THAT I'VE NEVER SEEN...

FWSH

FLINCH 움찔

FROM NOW ON, YOU SHOULD PROTEC YOUR MOTHER.

BIG HAND, WARM ARMS.

I COULD TELL--VAGUELY-- WHO HE WAS.

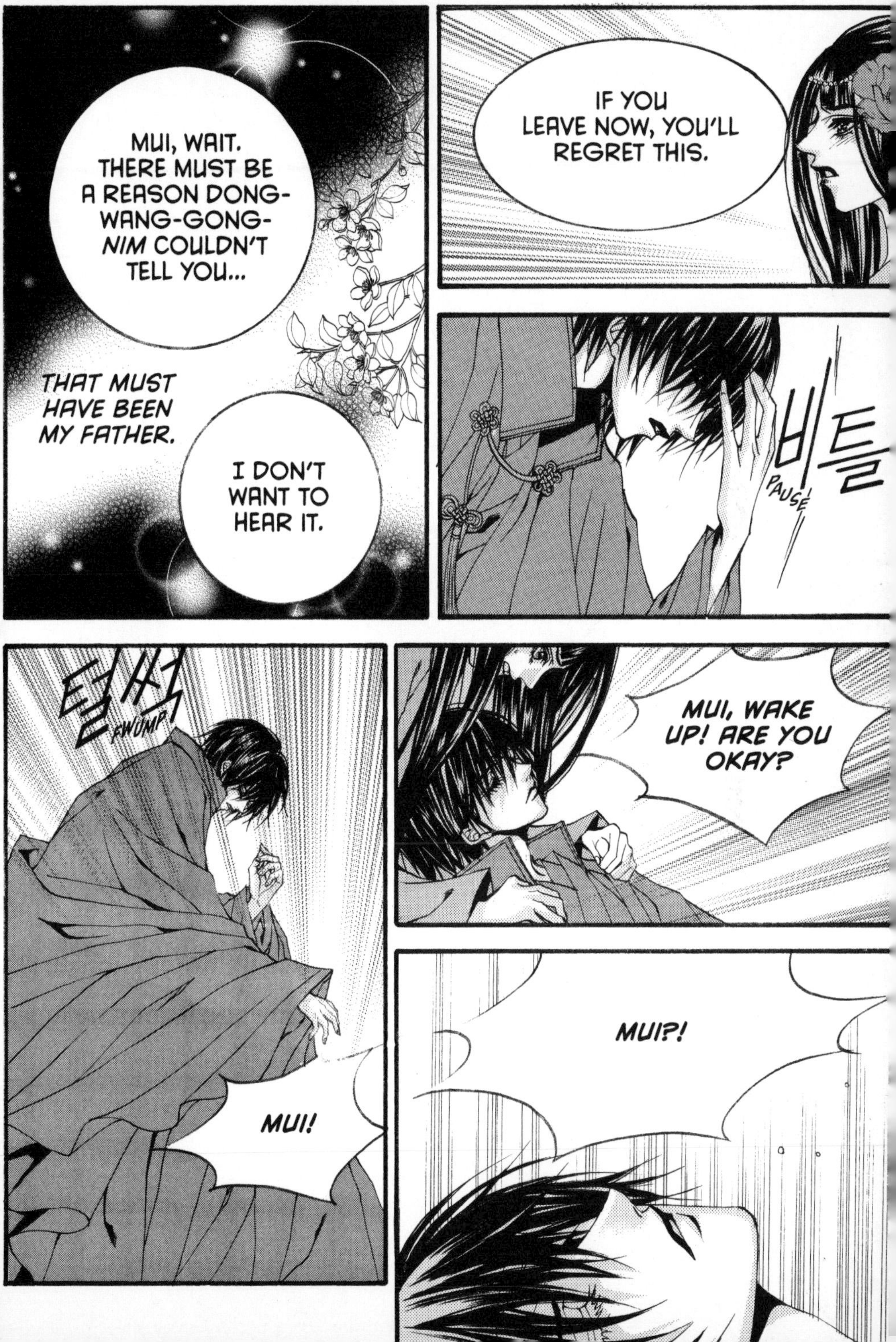
MUI, WAIT. THERE MUST BE A REASON DONG-WANG-GONG-*NIM* COULDN'T TELL YOU...
THAT MUST HAVE BEEN MY FATHER.
I DON'T WANT TO HEAR IT.
IF YOU LEAVE NOW, YOU'LL REGRET THIS.
비틀
PAUSE
털썩
FWUMP
MUI!
MUI, WAKE UP! ARE YOU OKAY?
MUI?!

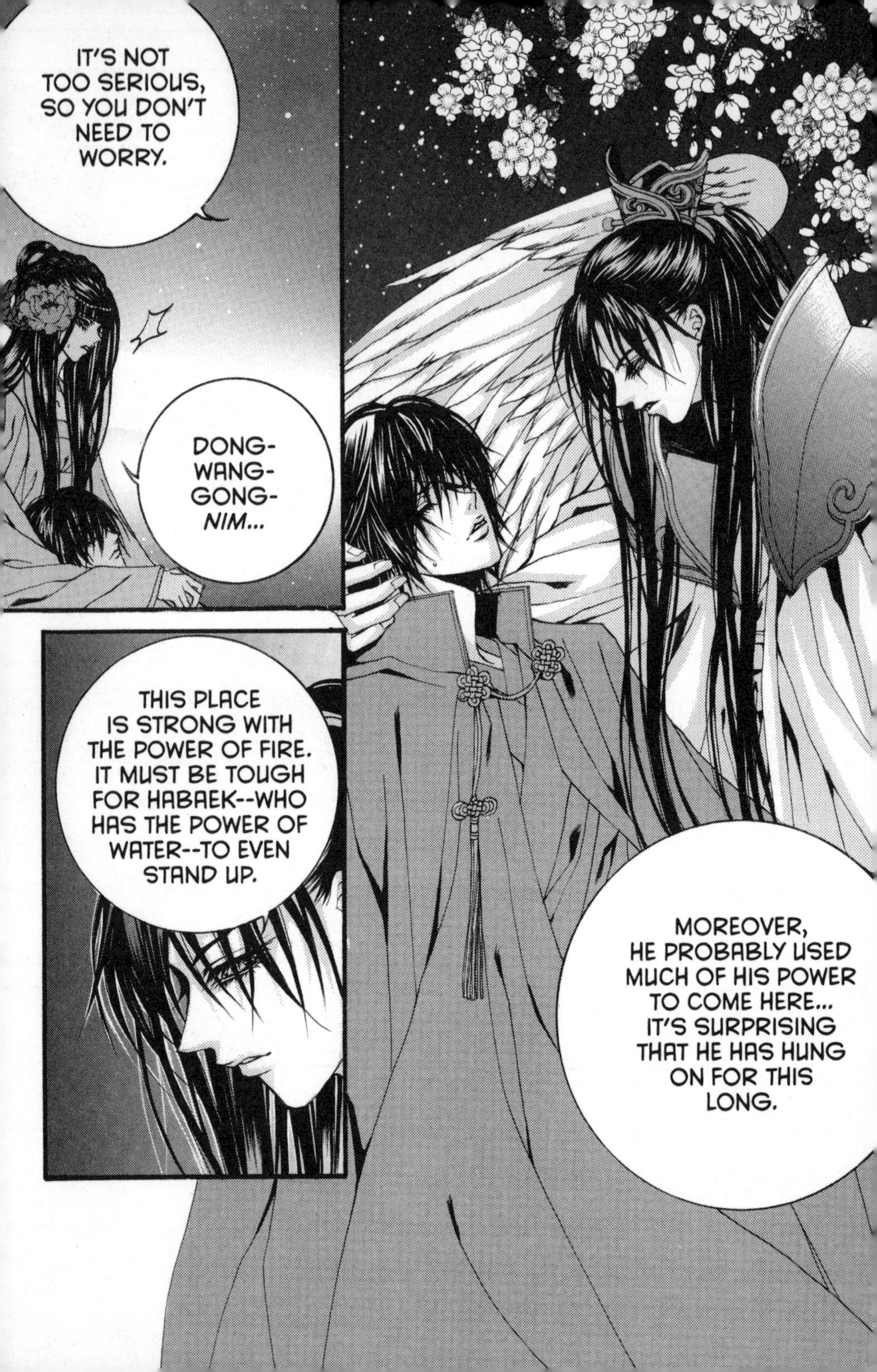
IT'S NOT TOO SERIOUS, SO YOU DON'T NEED TO WORRY.
DONG-WANG-GONG-*NIM*...
THIS PLACE IS STRONG WITH THE POWER OF FIRE. IT MUST BE TOUGH FOR HABAEK--WHO HAS THE POWER OF WATER--TO EVEN STAND UP.
MOREOVER, HE PROBABLY USED MUCH OF HIS POWER TO COME HERE... IT'S SURPRISING THAT HE HAS HUNG ON FOR THIS LONG.

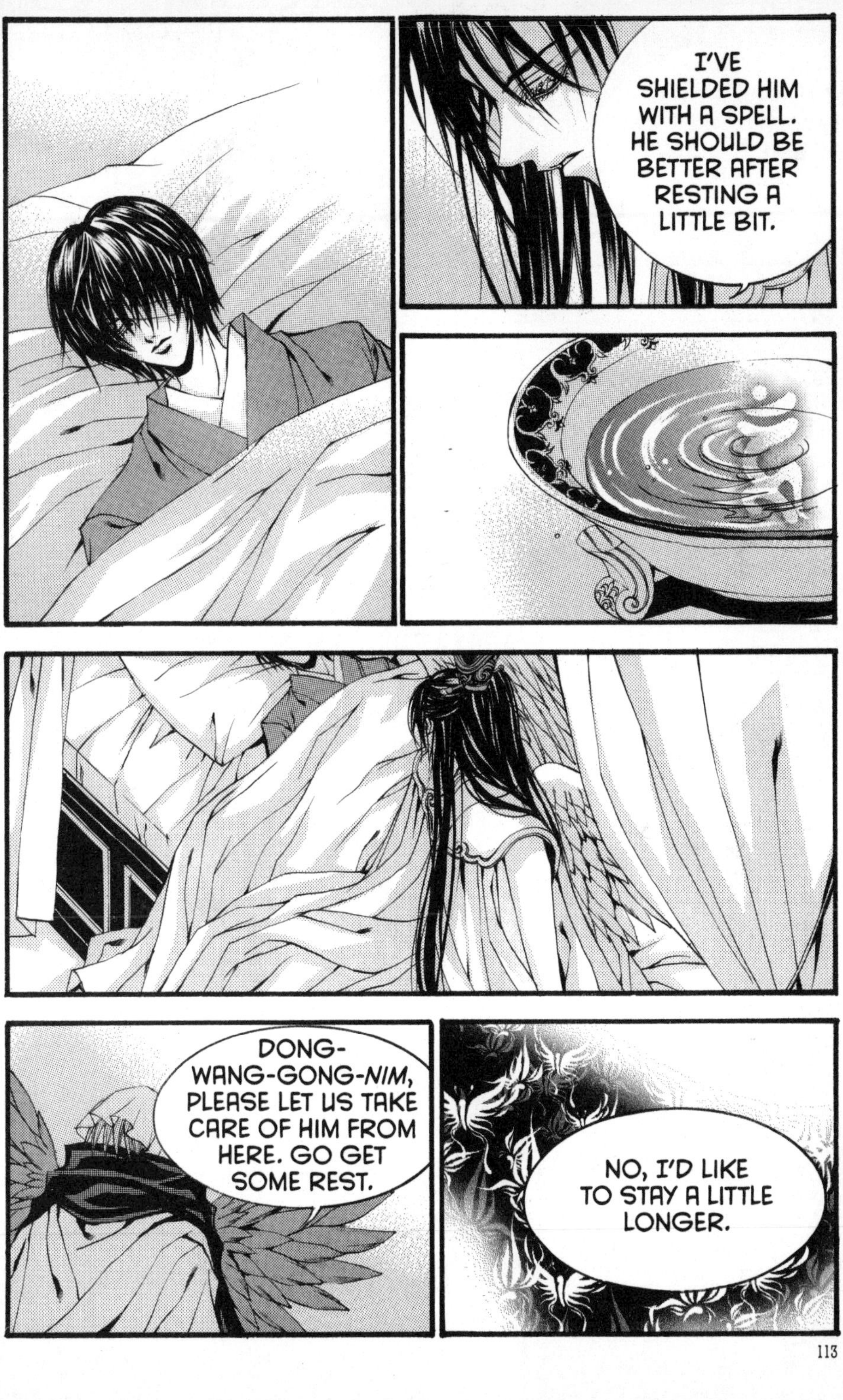
I'VE SHIELDED HIM WITH A SPELL. HE SHOULD BE BETTER AFTER RESTING A LITTLE BIT.
DONG-WANG-GONG-*NIM*, PLEASE LET US TAKE CARE OF HIM FROM HERE. GO GET SOME REST.
NO, I'D LIKE TO STAY A LITTLE LONGER.

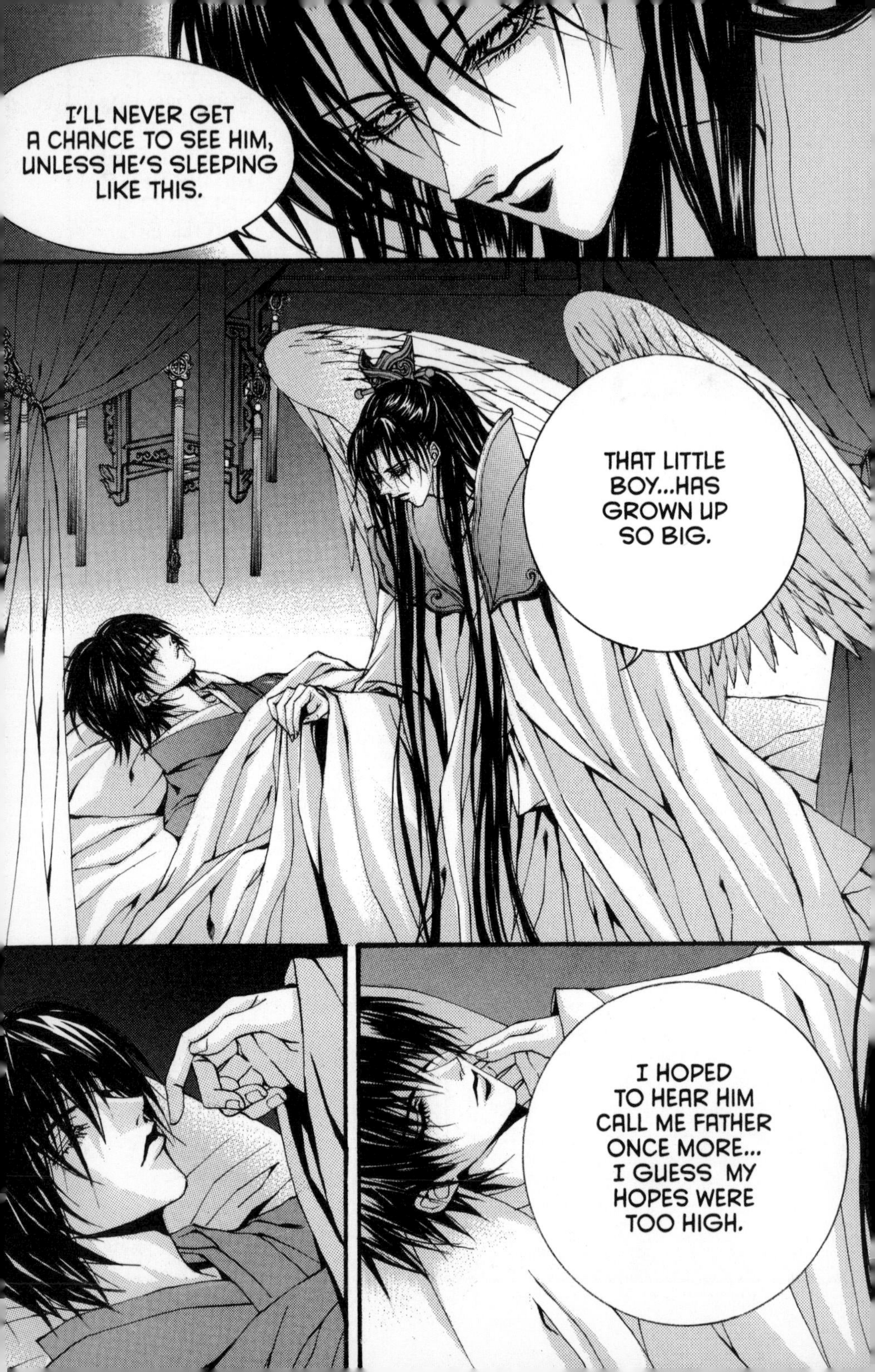
I'LL NEVER GET A CHANCE TO SEE HIM, UNLESS HE'S SLEEPING LIKE THIS.
THAT LITTLE BOY...HAS GROWN UP SO BIG.
I HOPED TO HEAR HIM CALL ME FATHER ONCE MORE... I GUESS MY HOPES WERE TOO HIGH.

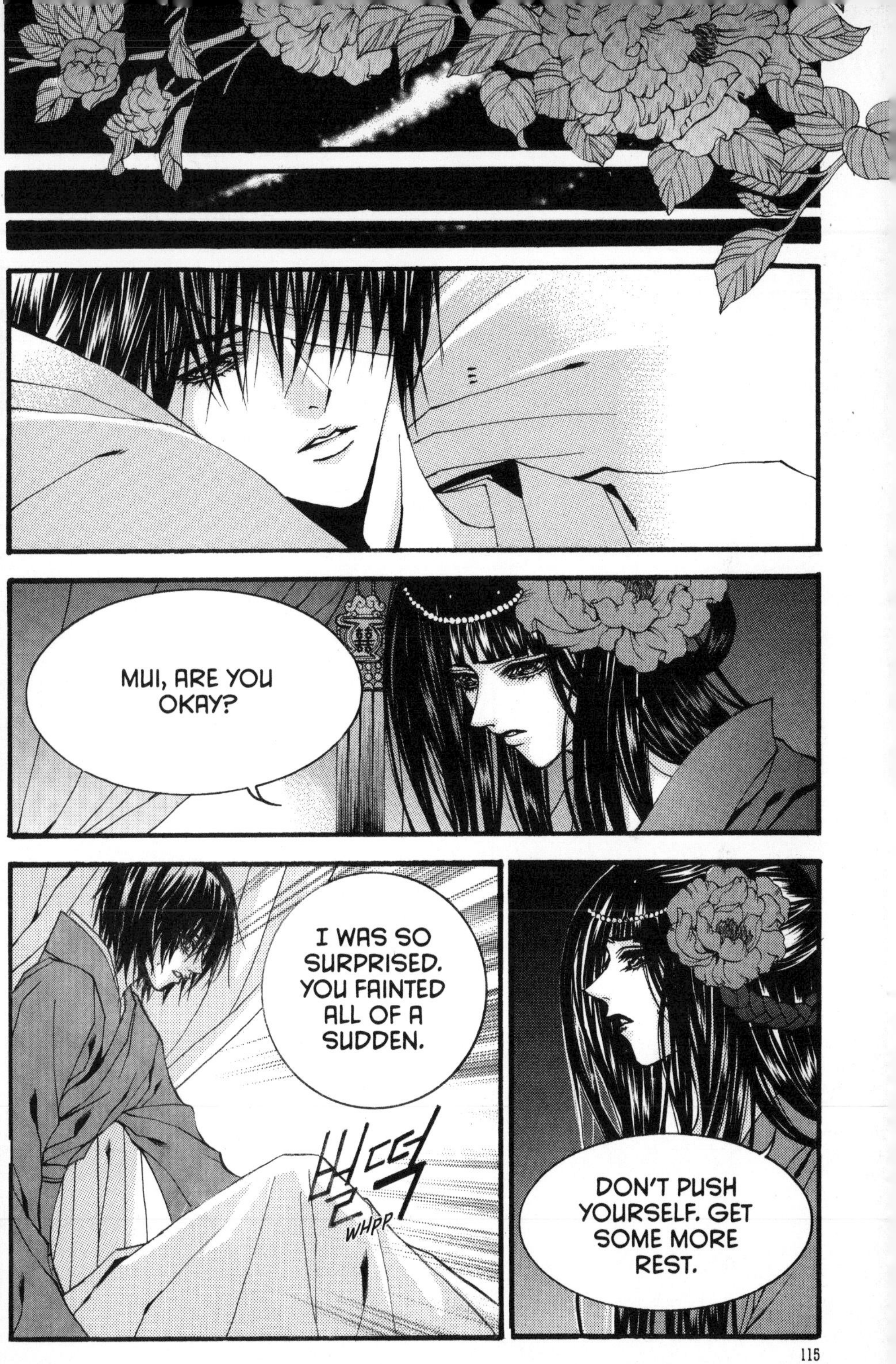
MUI, ARE YOU OKAY?
I WAS SO SURPRISED. YOU FAINTED ALL OF A SUDDEN.
WHPP
DON'T PUSH YOURSELF. GET SOME MORE REST.

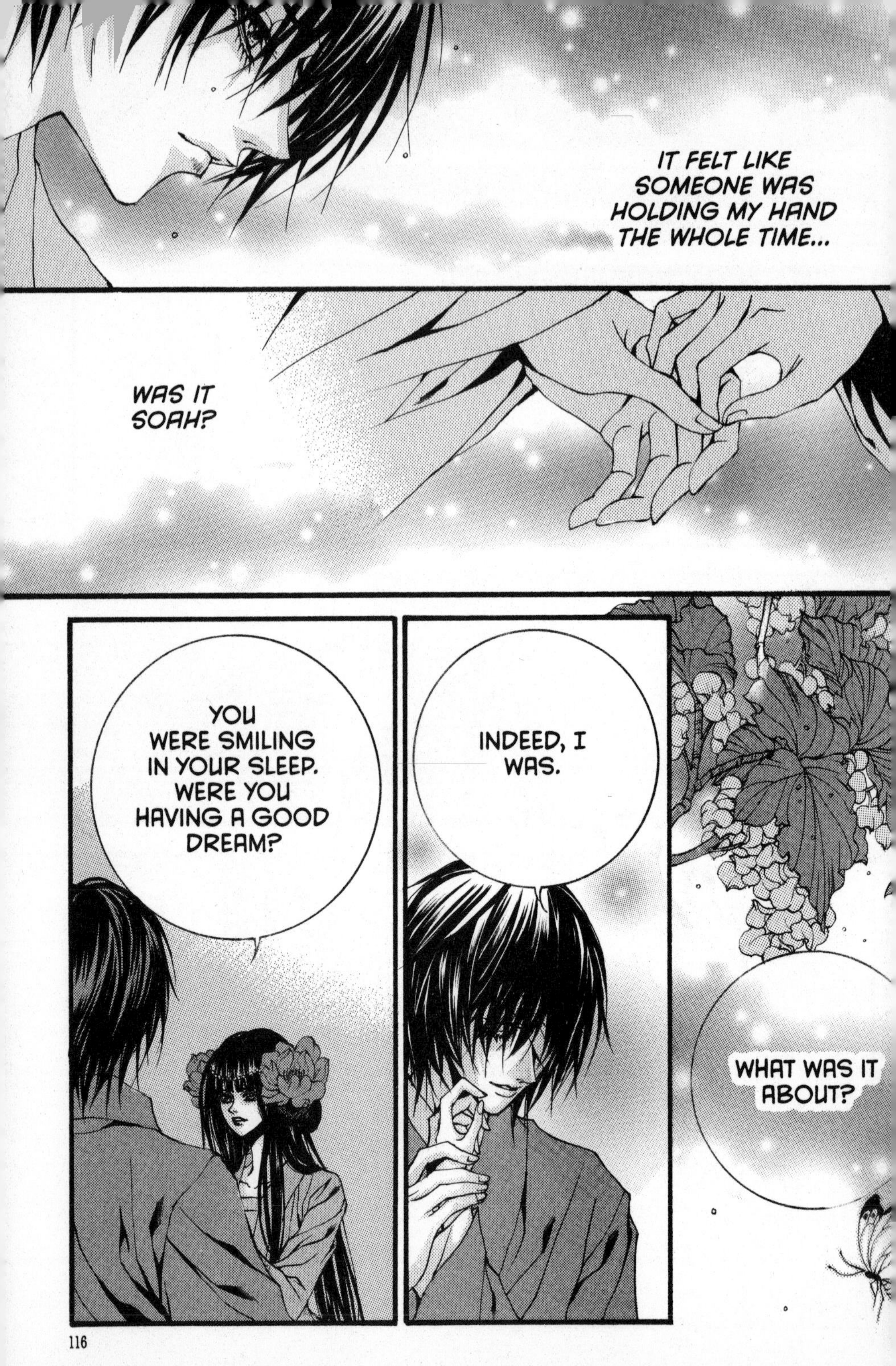
IT FELT LIKE SOMEONE WAS HOLDING MY HAND THE WHOLE TIME...
WAS IT SOAH?
YOU WERE SMILING IN YOUR SLEEP. WERE YOU HAVING A GOOD DREAM?
INDEED, I WAS.
WHAT WAS IT ABOUT?

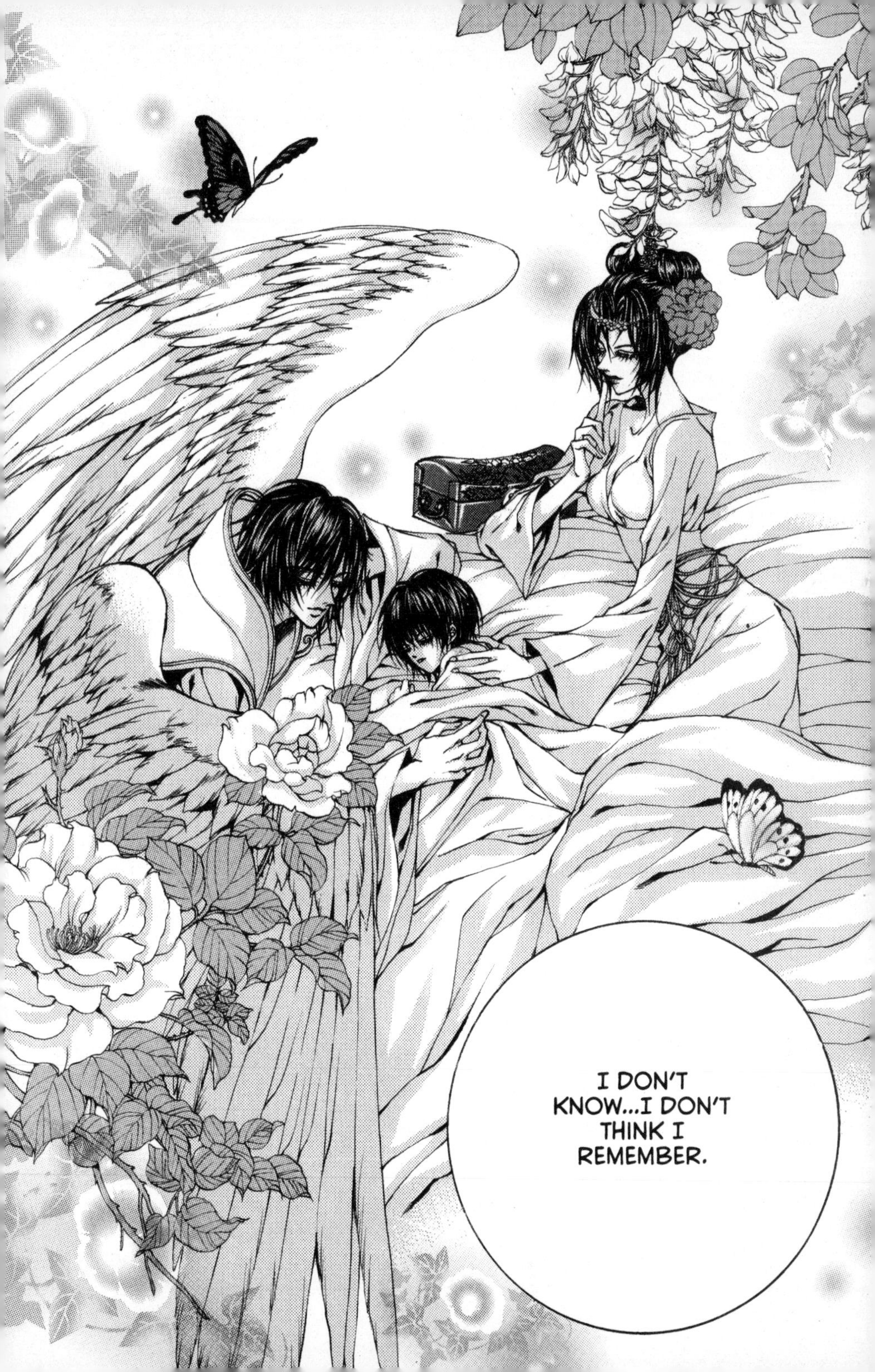
I DON'T KNOW...I DON'T THINK I REMEMBER.

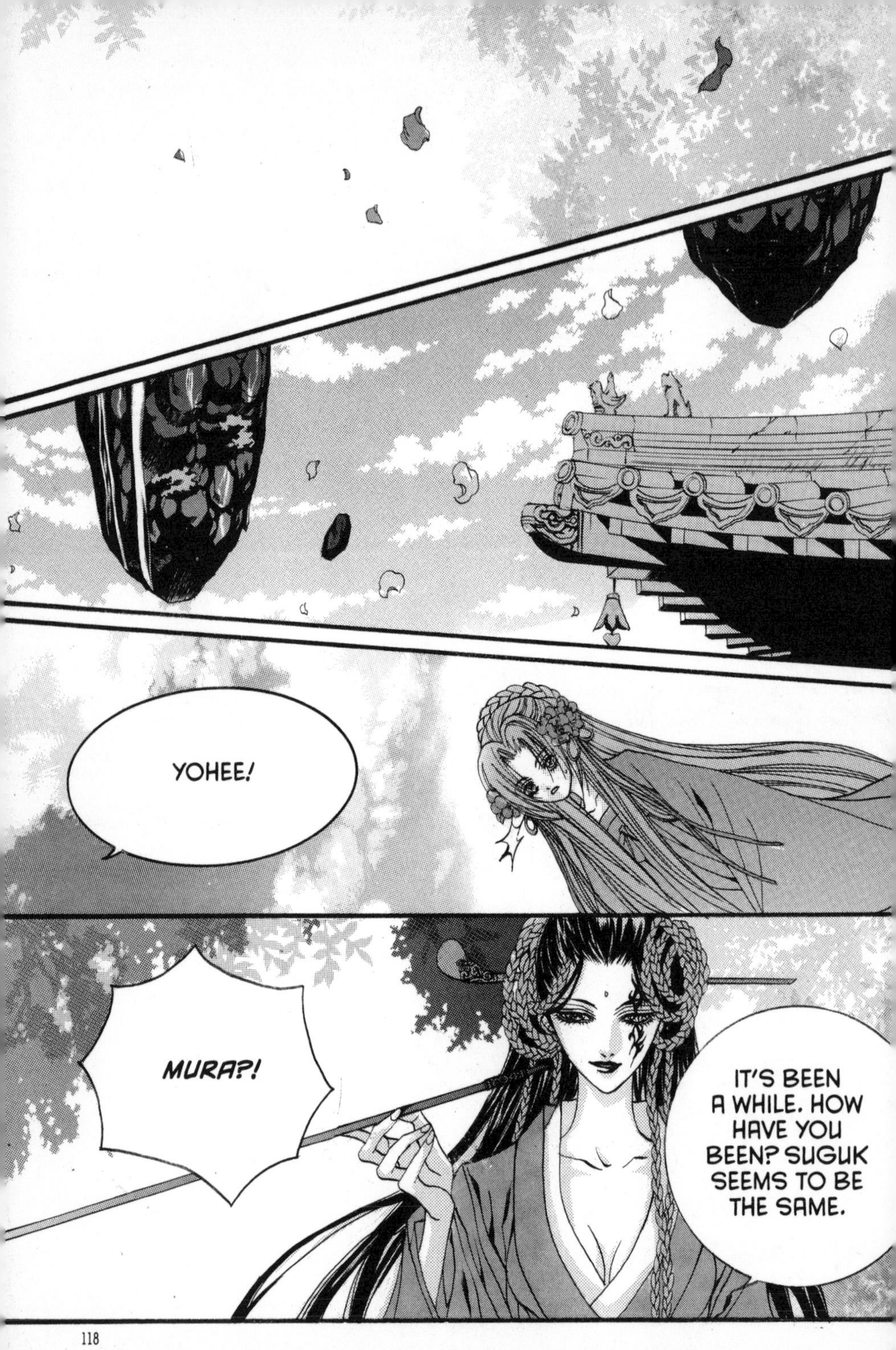
YOHEE!
MURA?!
IT'S BEEN A WHILE. HOW HAVE YOU BEEN? SUGUK SEEMS TO BE THE SAME.

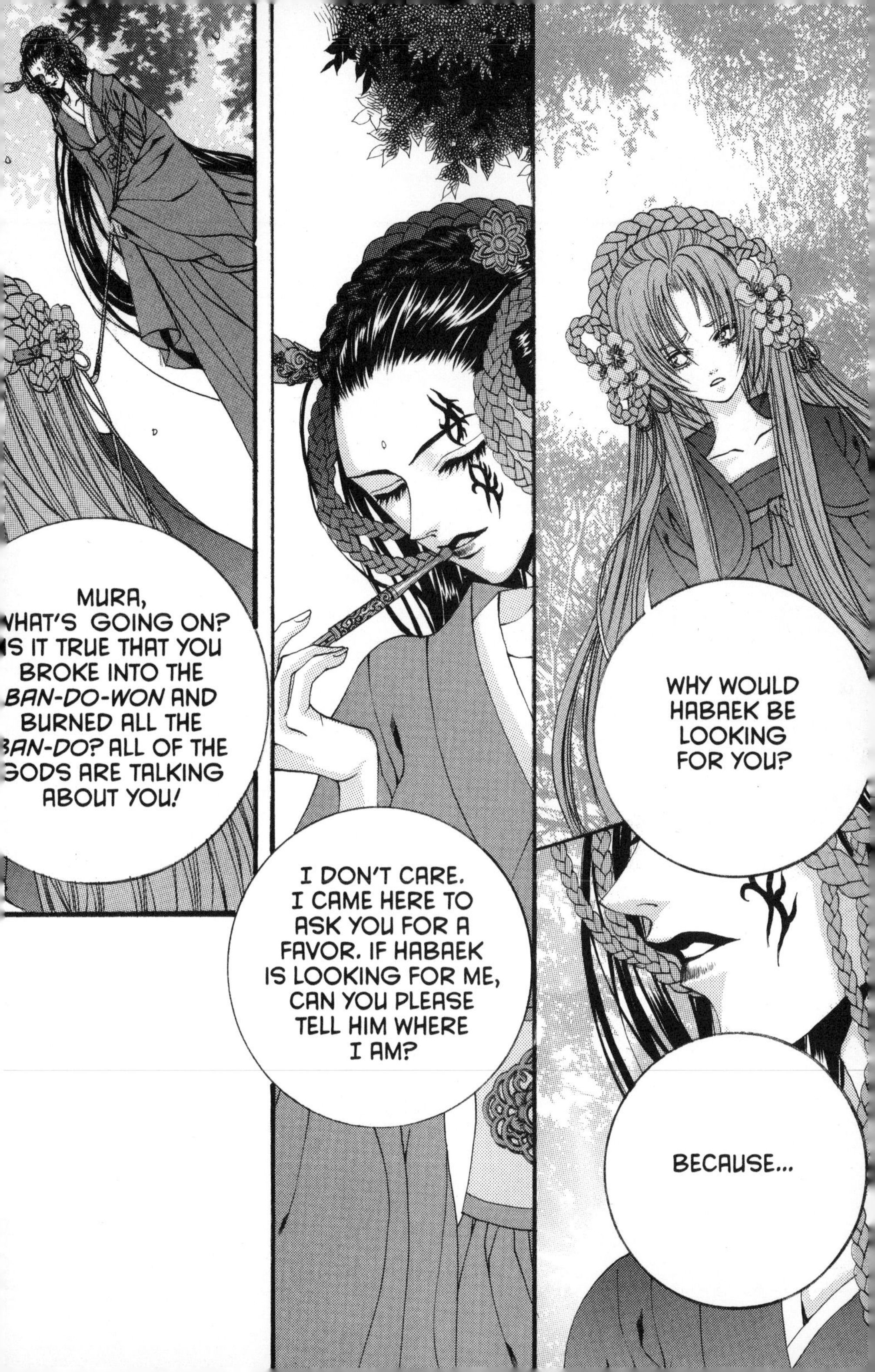
MURA, WHAT'S GOING ON? IS IT TRUE THAT YOU BROKE INTO THE *BAN-DO-WON* AND BURNED ALL THE *BAN-DO*? ALL OF THE GODS ARE TALKING ABOUT YOU!
I DON'T CARE. I CAME HERE TO ASK YOU FOR A FAVOR. IF HABAEK IS LOOKING FOR ME, CAN YOU PLEASE TELL HIM WHERE I AM?
WHY WOULD HABAEK BE LOOKING FOR YOU?
BECAUSE...

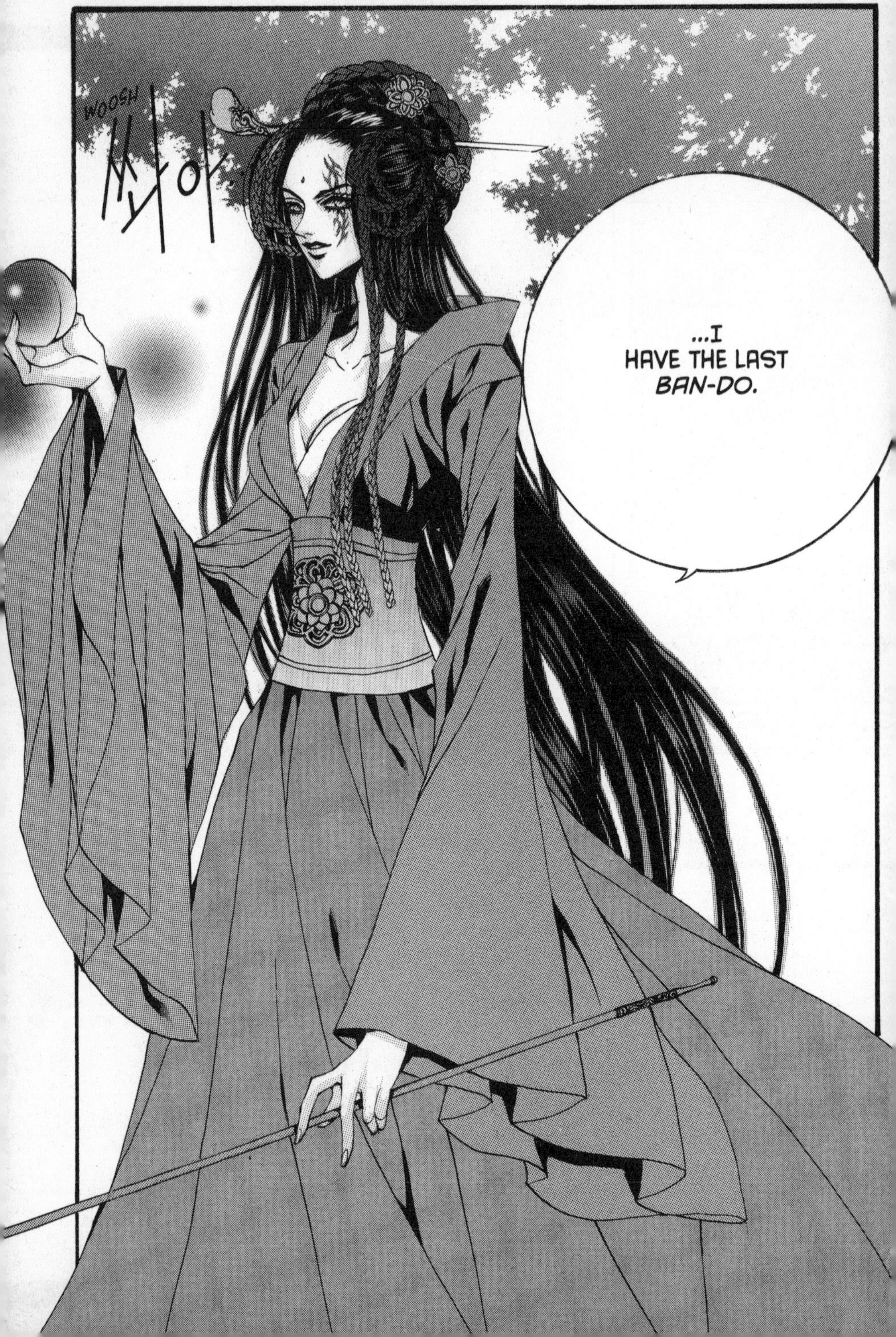
쏴아
WOOSH
...I HAVE THE LAST BAN-DO.

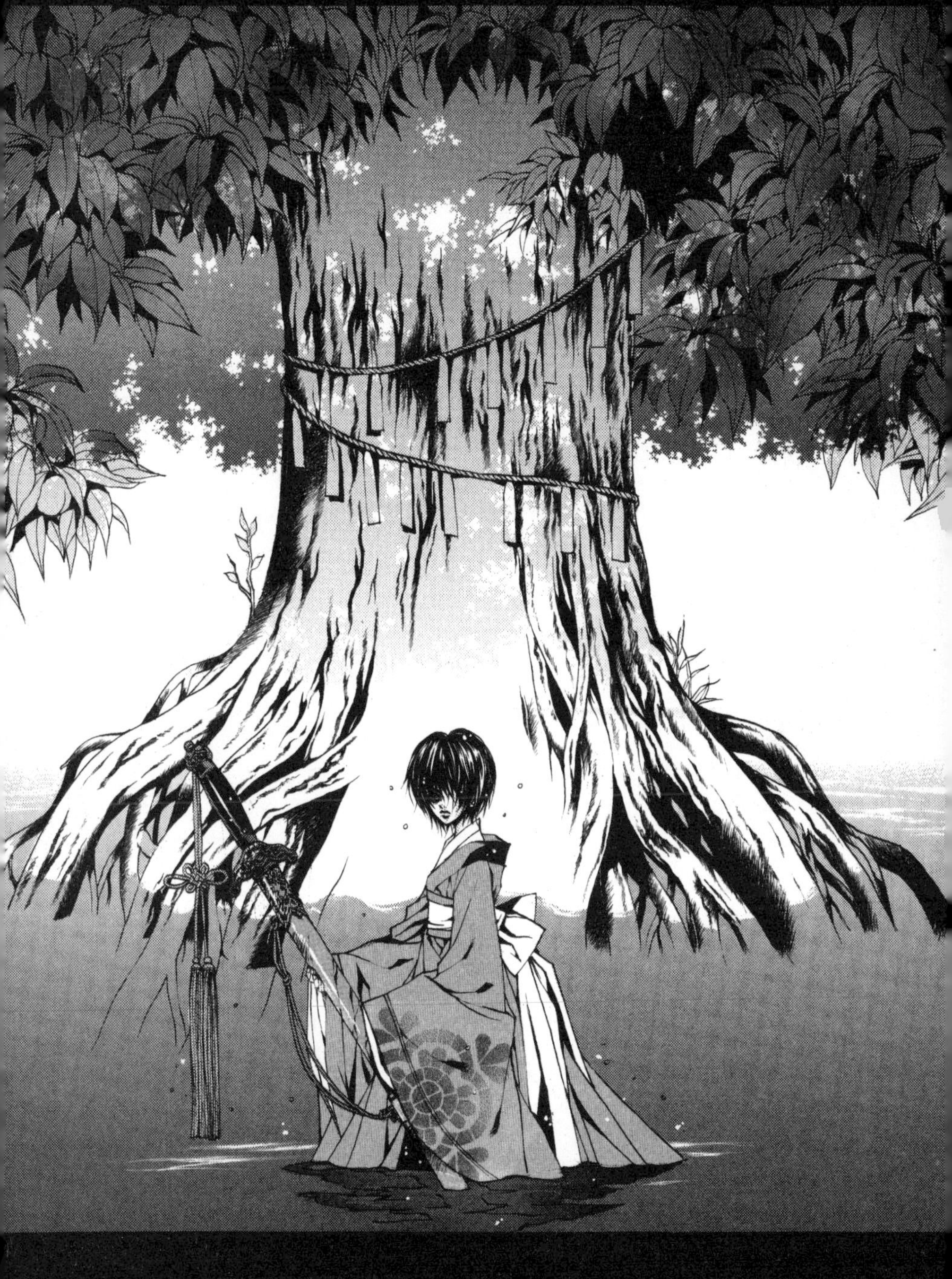

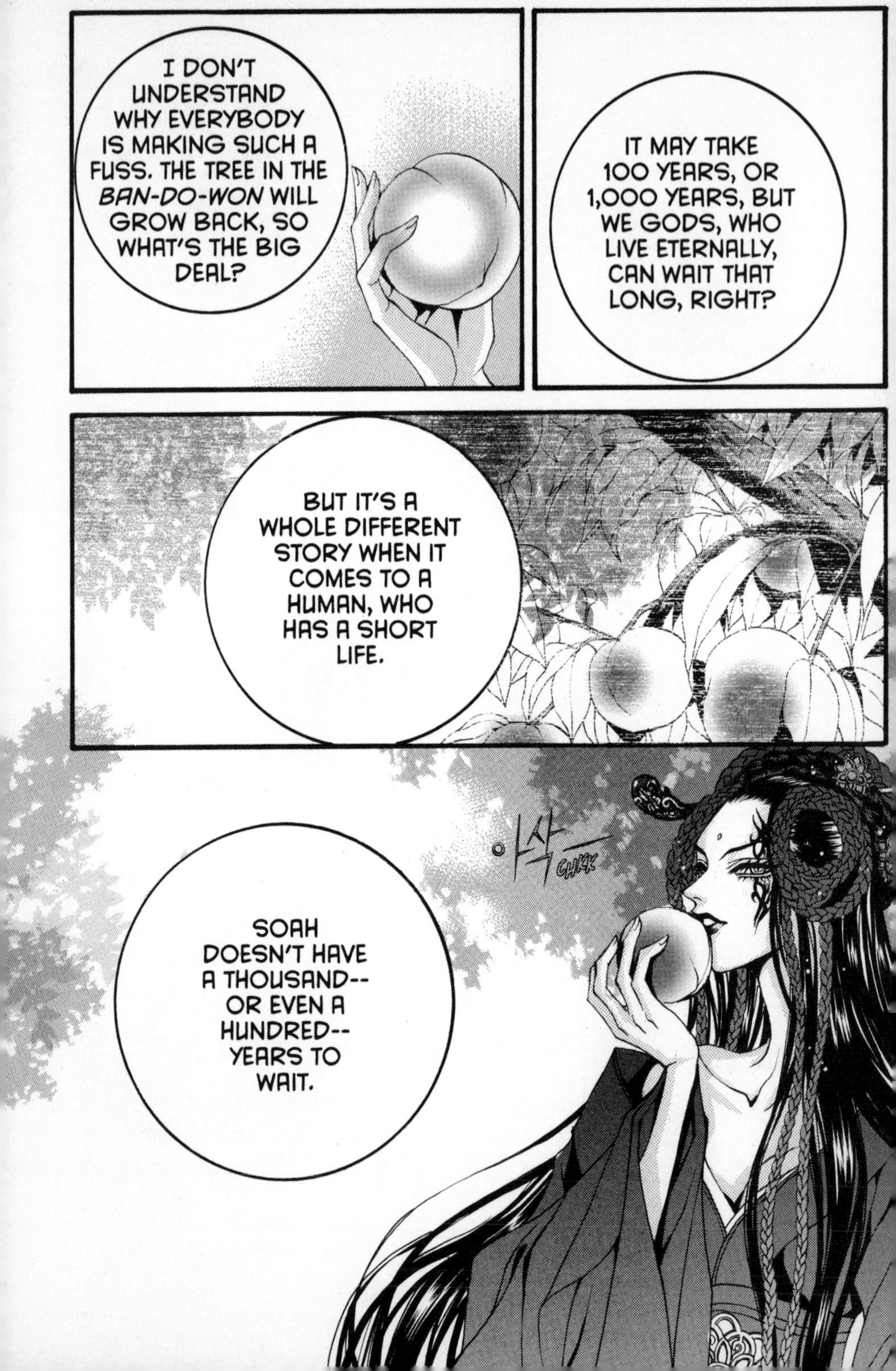

I DON'T UNDERSTAND WHY EVERYBODY IS MAKING SUCH A FUSS. THE TREE IN THE *BAN-DO-WON* WILL GROW BACK, SO WHAT'S THE BIG DEAL?
IT MAY TAKE 100 YEARS, OR 1,000 YEARS, BUT WE GODS, WHO LIVE ETERNALLY, CAN WAIT THAT LONG, RIGHT?
BUT IT'S A WHOLE DIFFERENT STORY WHEN IT COMES TO A HUMAN, WHO HAS A SHORT LIFE.
아삭
CHIKK
SOAH DOESN'T HAVE A THOUSAND-- OR EVEN A HUNDRED-- YEARS TO WAIT.

WHY SO SERIOUS, YOHEE? THIS IS JUST A REGULAR PEACH. THE REAL *BAN-DO* IS STORED SAFELY AWAY SOMEWHERE, SO NO WORRIES...

THIS IS *TOO MUCH,* MURA.

ARE YOU DOING THIS BECAUSE YOU REALLY LOVE HABAEK? THIS *OBSESSION* IS WRONG.

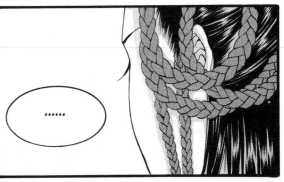

......

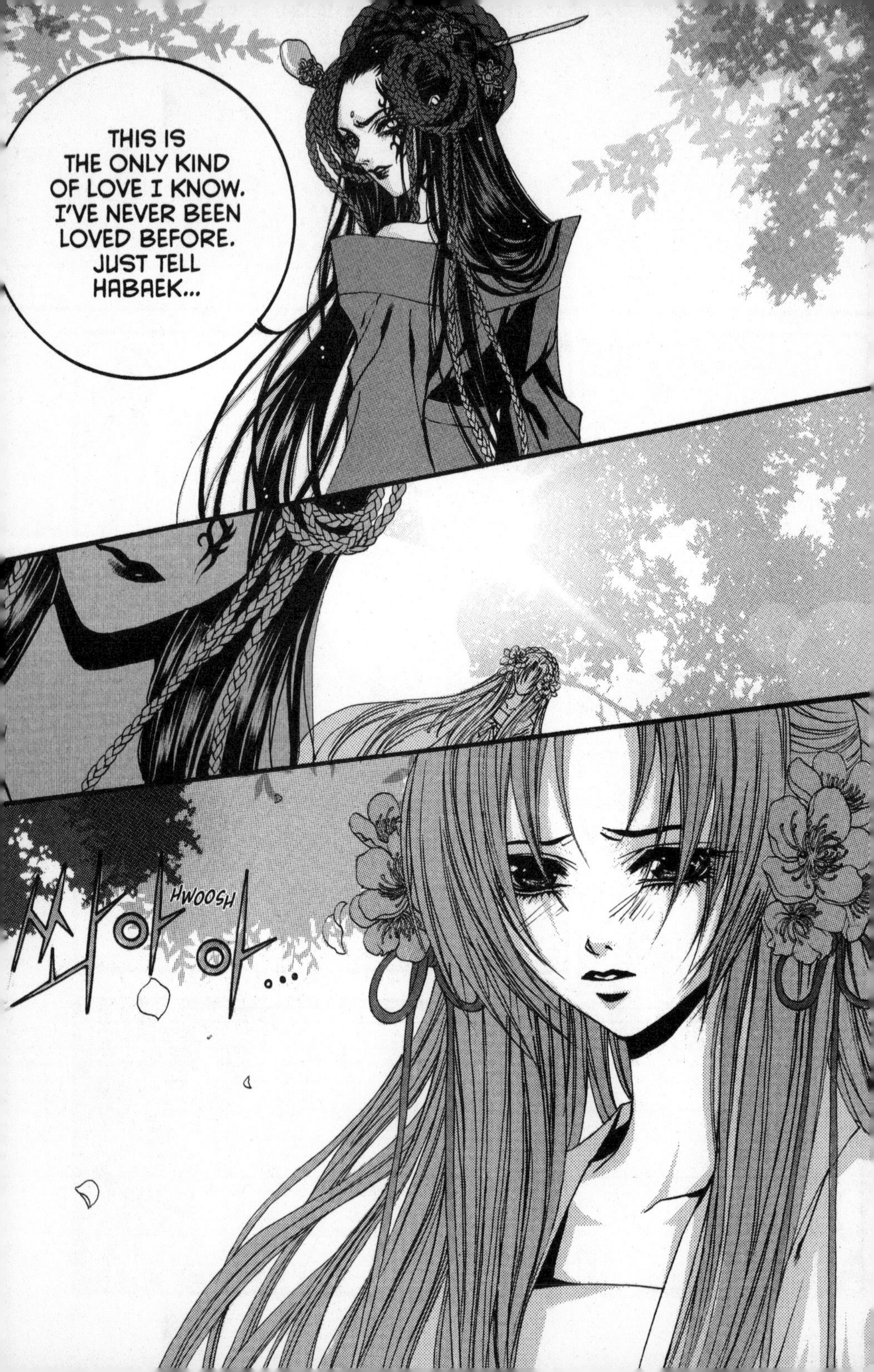
THIS IS THE ONLY KIND OF LOVE I KNOW. I'VE NEVER BEEN LOVED BEFORE. JUST TELL HABAEK...
HWOOSH

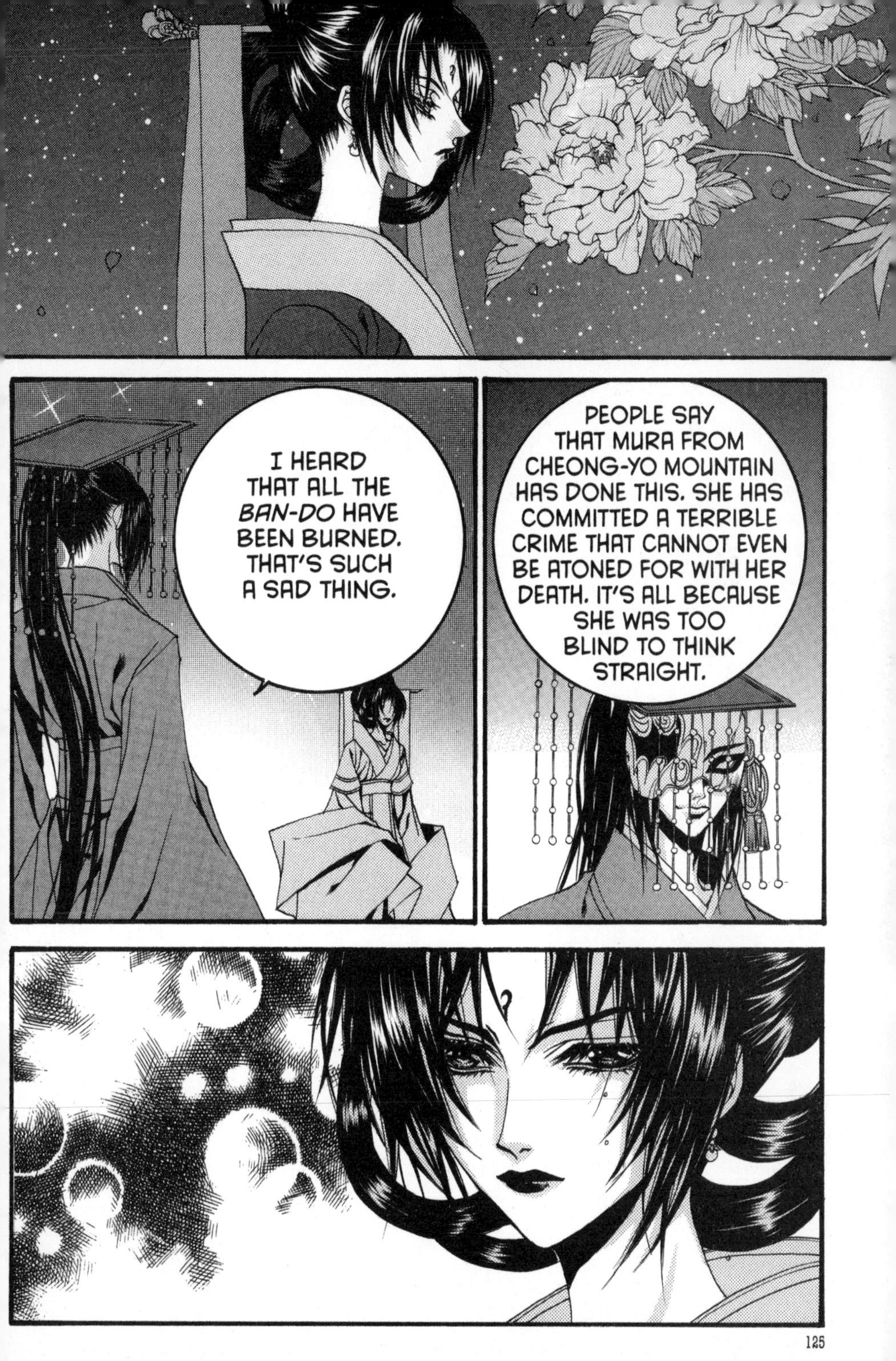
I HEARD THAT ALL THE *BAN-DO* HAVE BEEN BURNED. THAT'S SUCH A SAD THING.
PEOPLE SAY THAT MURA FROM CHEONG-YO MOUNTAIN HAS DONE THIS. SHE HAS COMMITTED A TERRIBLE CRIME THAT CANNOT EVEN BE ATONED FOR WITH HER DEATH. IT'S ALL BECAUSE SHE WAS TOO BLIND TO THINK STRAIGHT.

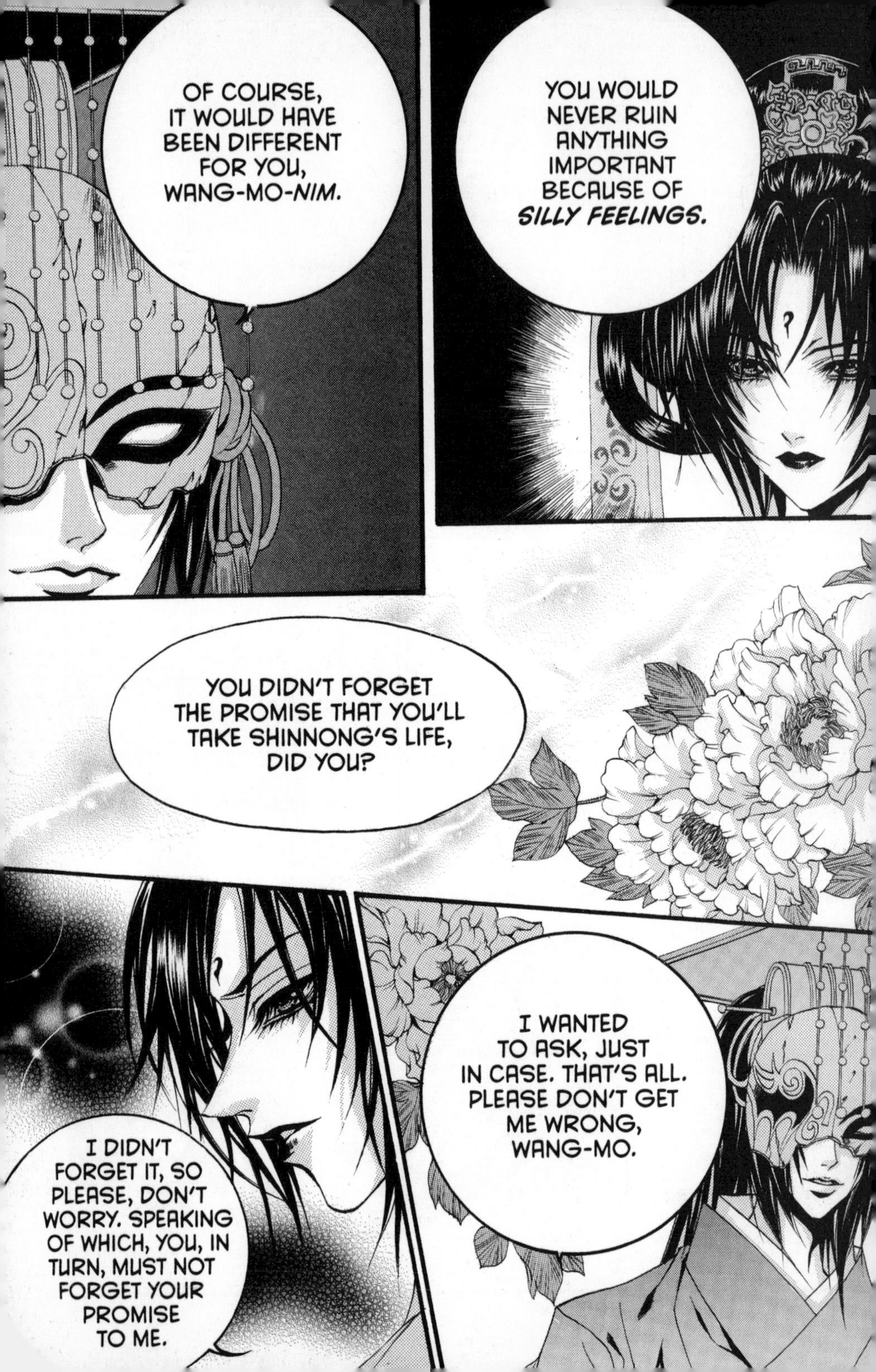
OF COURSE, IT WOULD HAVE BEEN DIFFERENT FOR YOU, WANG-MO-*NIM*.
YOU WOULD NEVER RUIN ANYTHING IMPORTANT BECAUSE OF *SILLY FEELINGS*.
YOU DIDN'T FORGET THE PROMISE THAT YOU'LL TAKE SHINNONG'S LIFE, DID YOU?
I WANTED TO ASK, JUST IN CASE. THAT'S ALL. PLEASE DON'T GET ME WRONG, WANG-MO.
I DIDN'T FORGET IT, SO PLEASE, DON'T WORRY. SPEAKING OF WHICH, YOU, IN TURN, MUST NOT FORGET YOUR PROMISE TO ME.

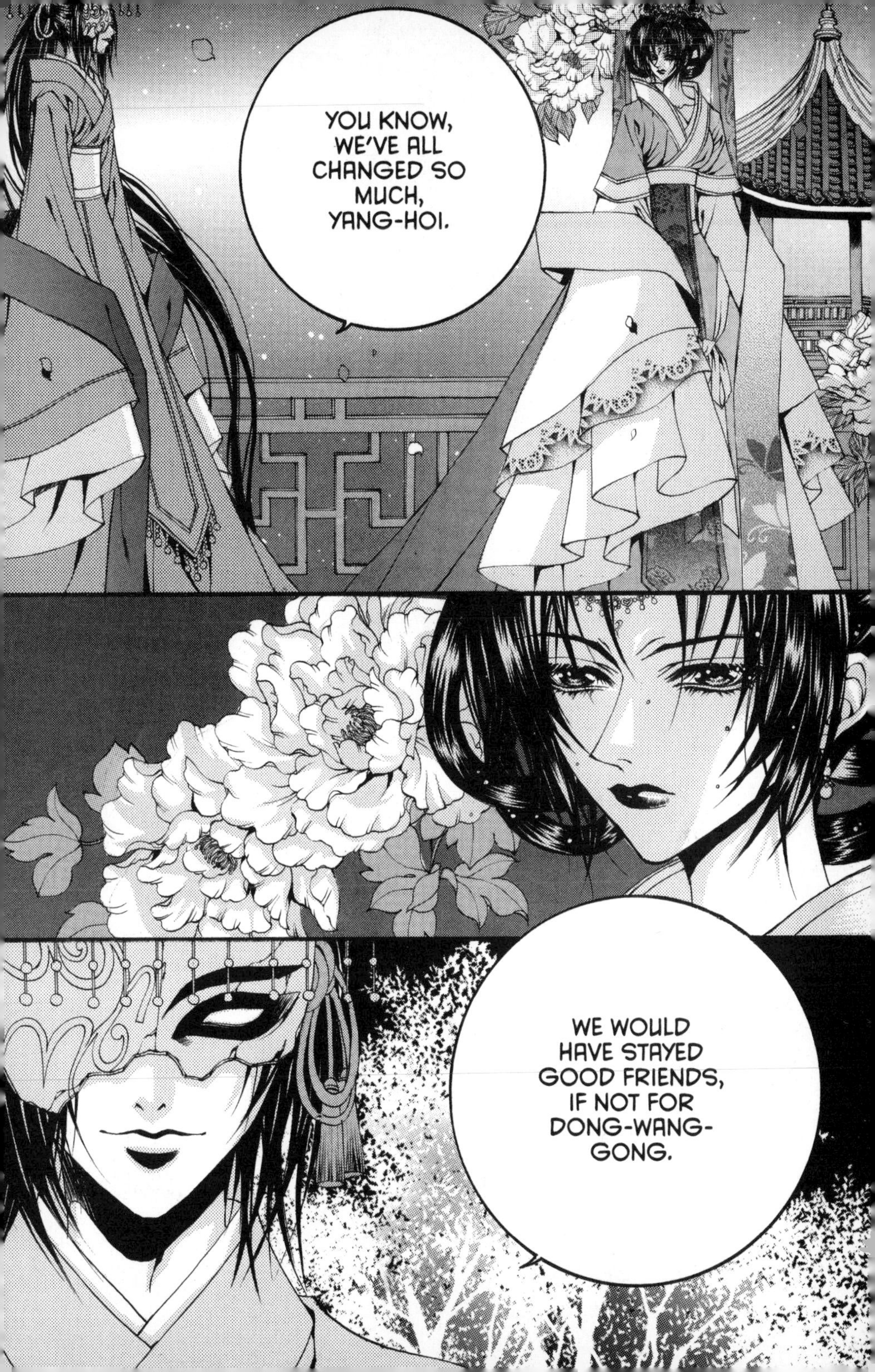
YOU KNOW, WE'VE ALL CHANGED SO MUCH, YANG-HOI.
WE WOULD HAVE STAYED GOOD FRIENDS, IF NOT FOR DONG-WANG-GONG.

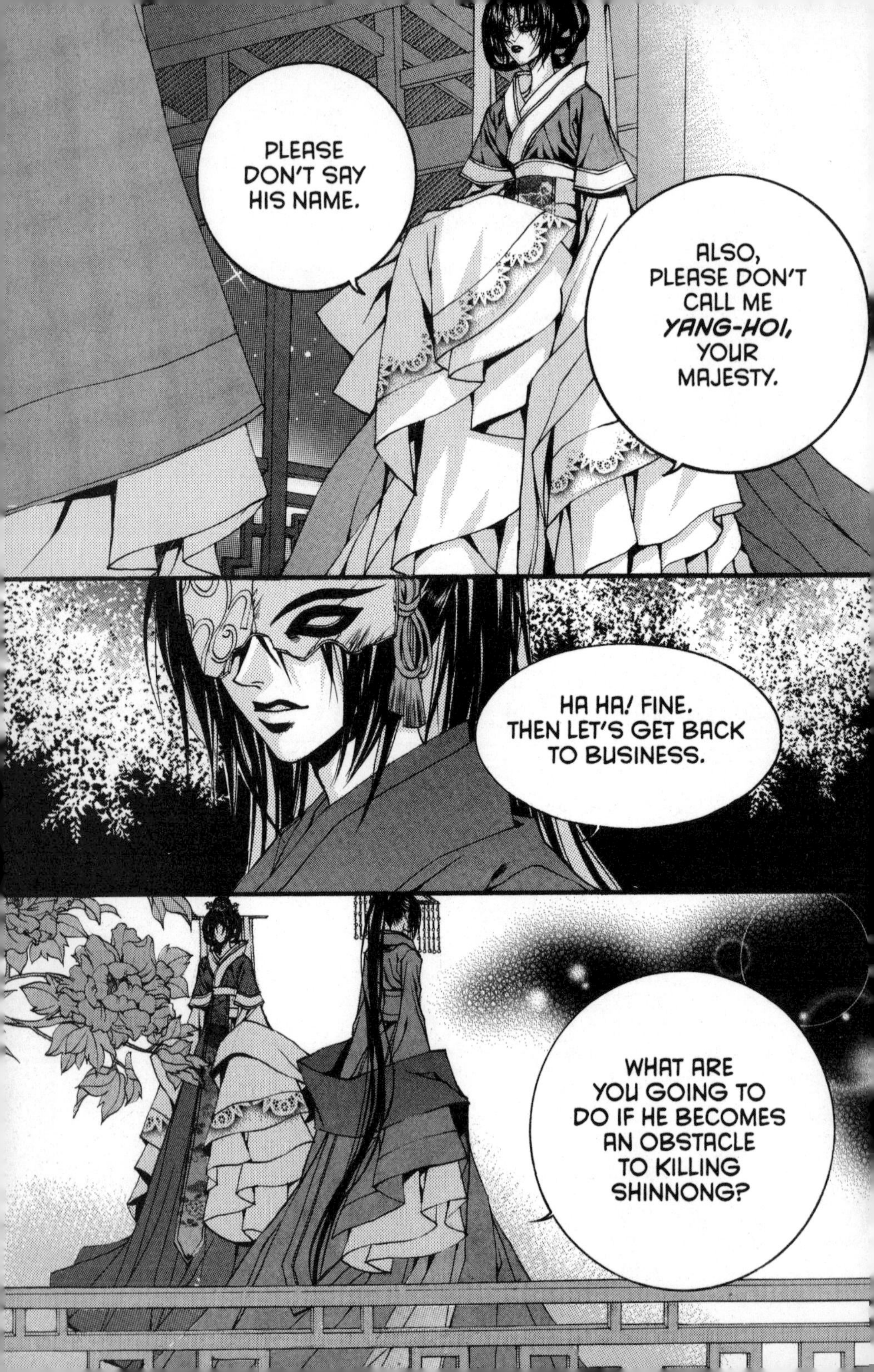
PLEASE DON'T SAY HIS NAME.
ALSO, PLEASE DON'T CALL ME *YANG-HOI,* YOUR MAJESTY.
HA HA! FINE. THEN LET'S GET BACK TO BUSINESS.
WHAT ARE YOU GOING TO DO IF HE BECOMES AN OBSTACLE TO KILLING SHINNONG?

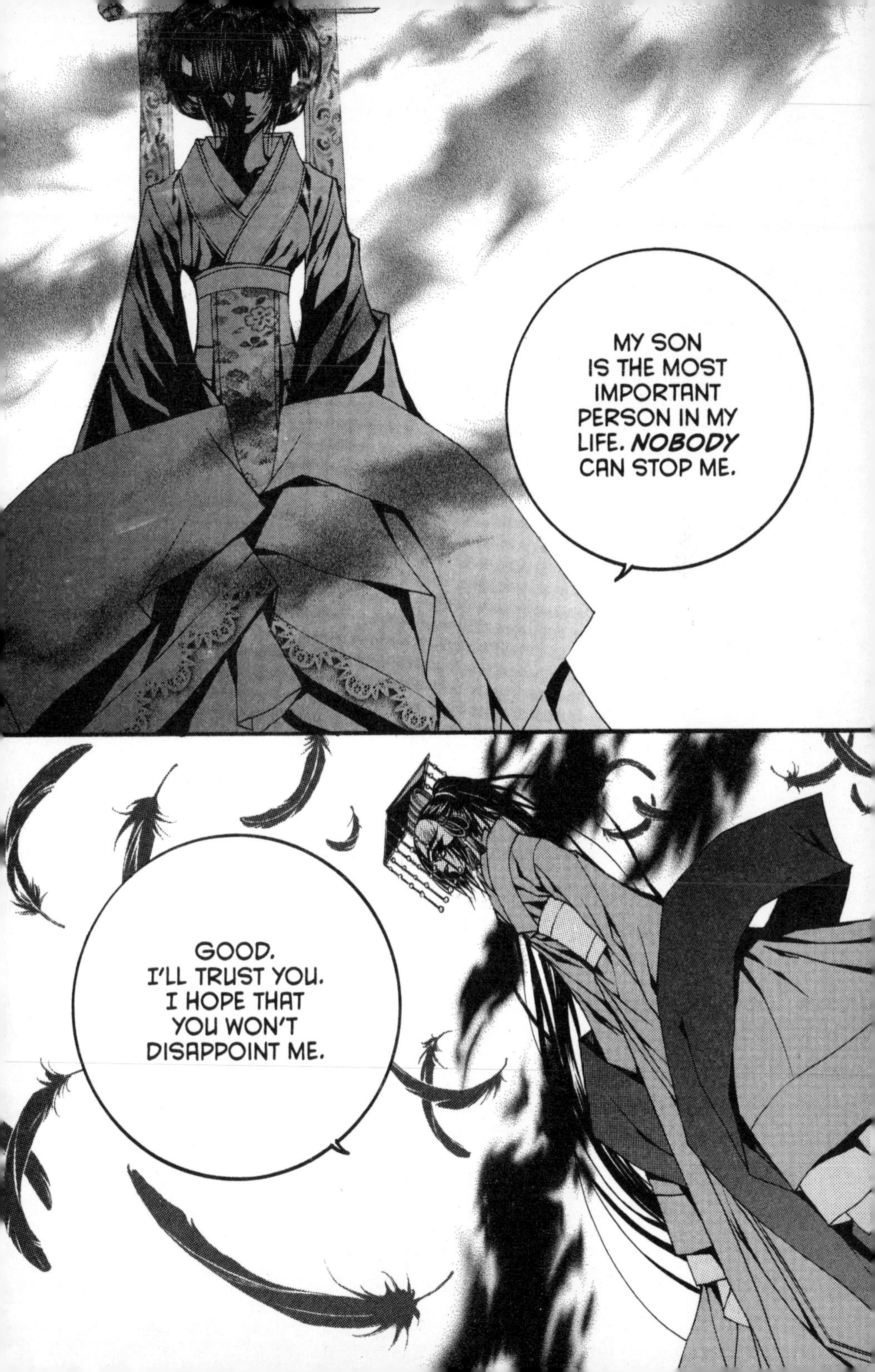
MY SON IS THE MOST IMPORTANT PERSON IN MY LIFE. *NOBODY* CAN STOP ME.
GOOD. I'LL TRUST YOU. I HOPE THAT YOU WON'T DISAPPOINT ME.

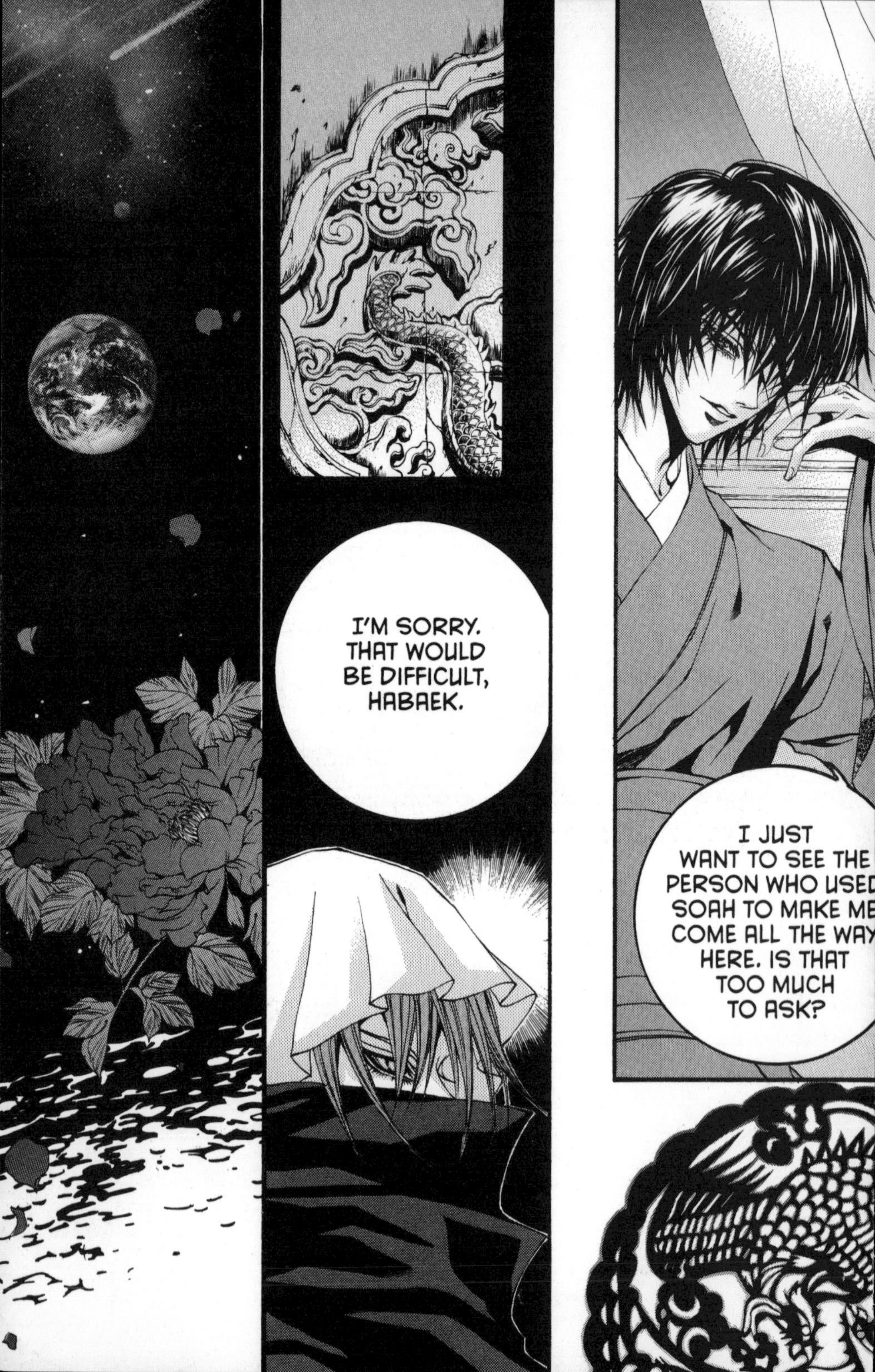
I JUST WANT TO SEE THE PERSON WHO USED SOAH TO MAKE ME COME ALL THE WAY HERE. IS THAT TOO MUCH TO ASK?
I'M SORRY. THAT WOULD BE DIFFICULT, HABAEK.

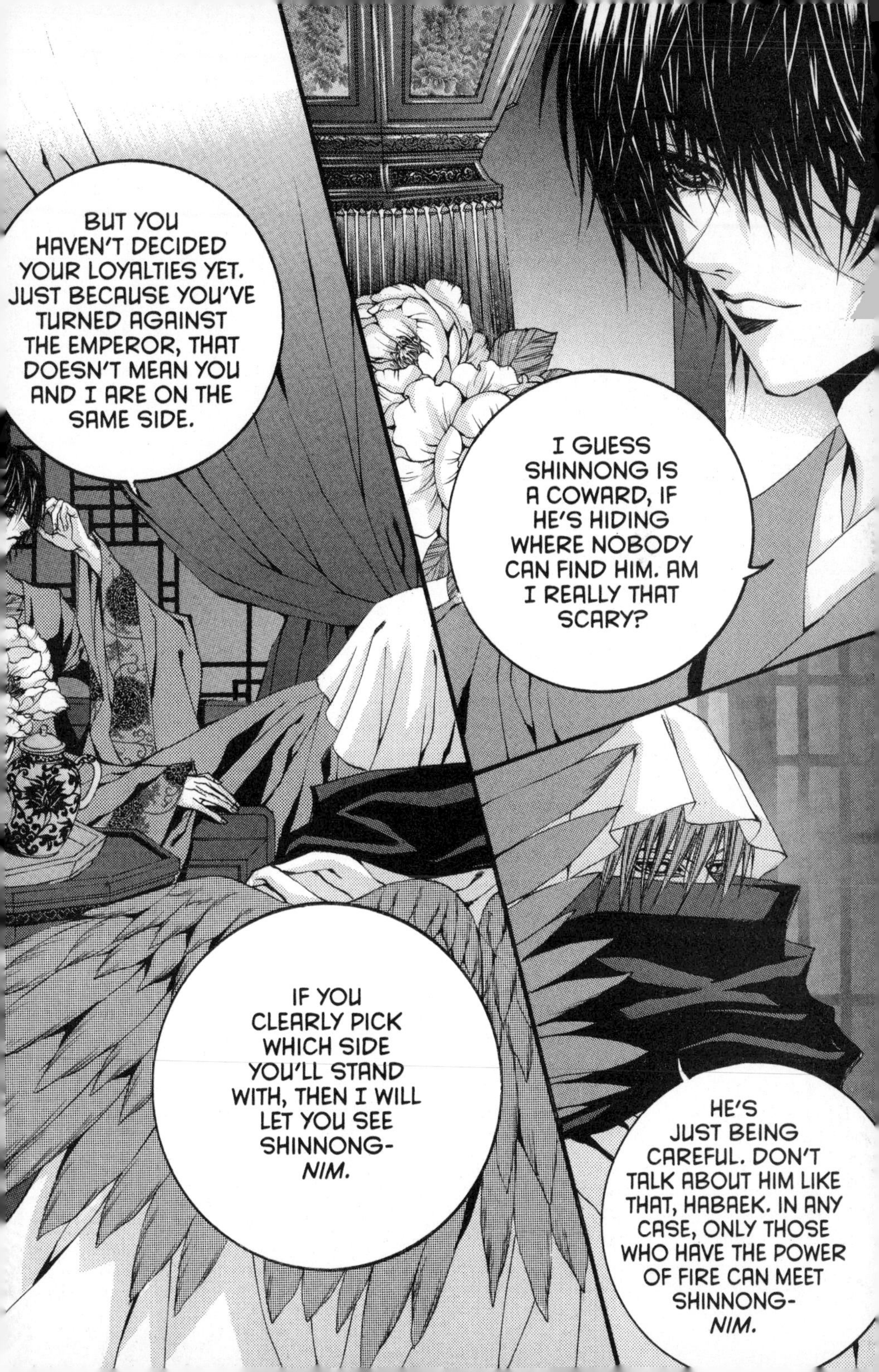
BUT YOU HAVEN'T DECIDED YOUR LOYALTIES YET. JUST BECAUSE YOU'VE TURNED AGAINST THE EMPEROR, THAT DOESN'T MEAN YOU AND I ARE ON THE SAME SIDE.
I GUESS SHINNONG IS A COWARD, IF HE'S HIDING WHERE NOBODY CAN FIND HIM. AM I REALLY THAT SCARY?
IF YOU CLEARLY PICK WHICH SIDE YOU'LL STAND WITH, THEN I WILL LET YOU SEE SHINNONG-*NIM.*
HE'S JUST BEING CAREFUL. DON'T TALK ABOUT HIM LIKE THAT, HABAEK. IN ANY CASE, ONLY THOSE WHO HAVE THE POWER OF FIRE CAN MEET SHINNONG-*NIM.*

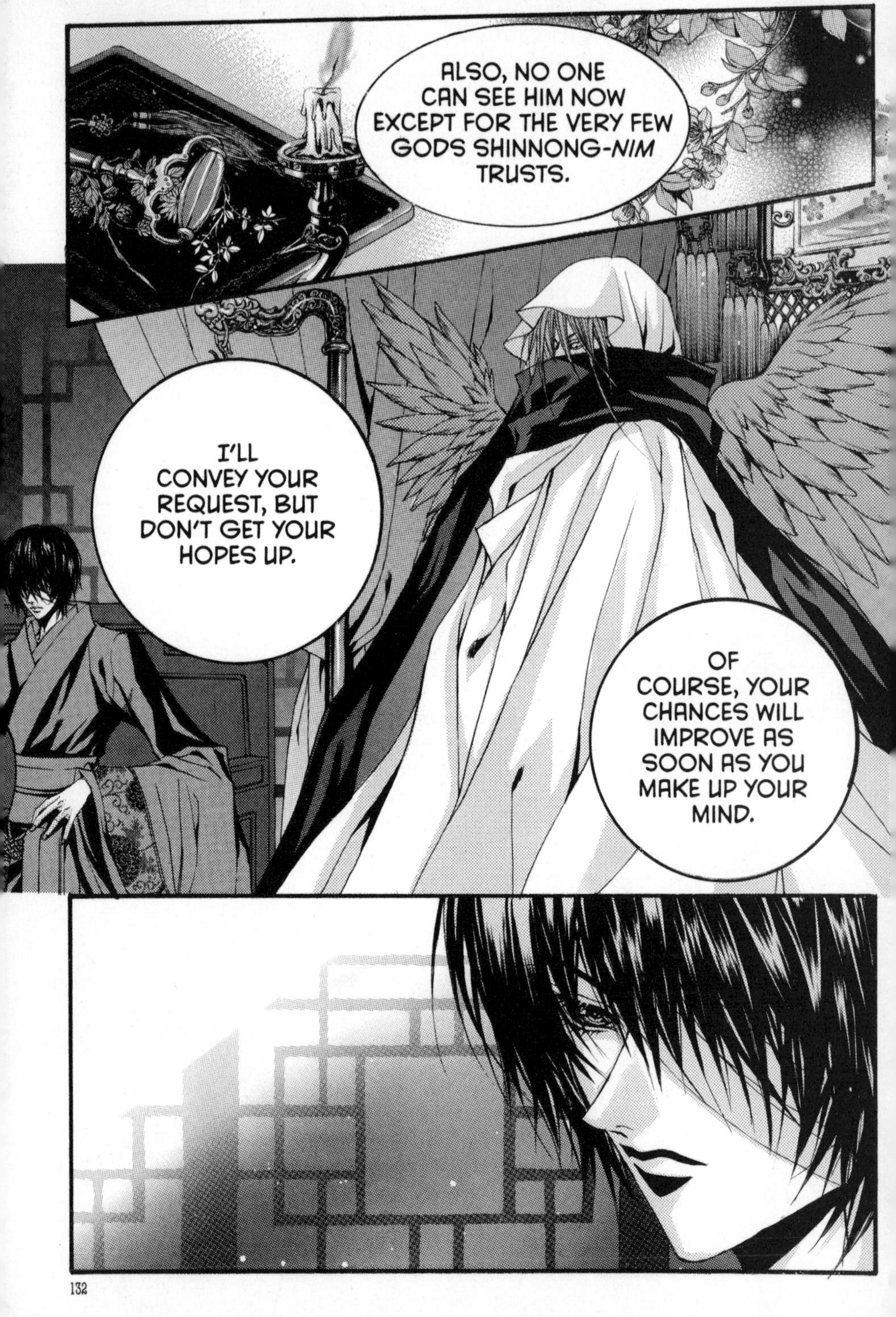
ALSO, NO ONE CAN SEE HIM NOW EXCEPT FOR THE VERY FEW GODS SHINNONG-*NIM* TRUSTS.
I'LL CONVEY YOUR REQUEST, BUT DON'T GET YOUR HOPES UP.
OF COURSE, YOUR CHANCES WILL IMPROVE AS SOON AS YOU MAKE UP YOUR MIND.

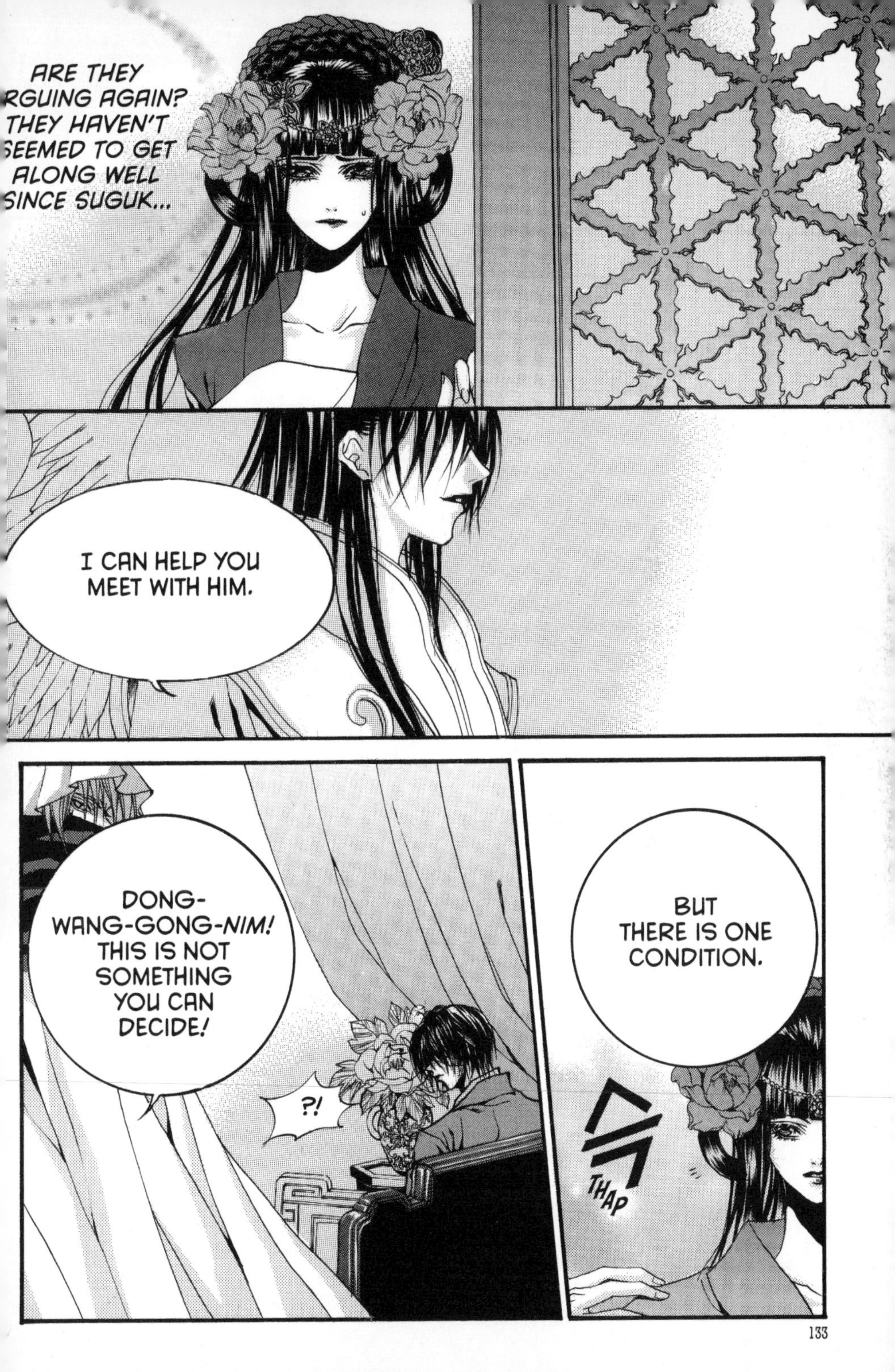
ARE THEY RGUING AGAIN? THEY HAVEN'T SEEMED TO GET ALONG WELL SINCE SUGUK...
I CAN HELP YOU MEET WITH HIM.
DONG-WANG-GONG-NIM! THIS IS NOT SOMETHING YOU CAN DECIDE!
?!
BUT THERE IS ONE CONDITION.
THAP

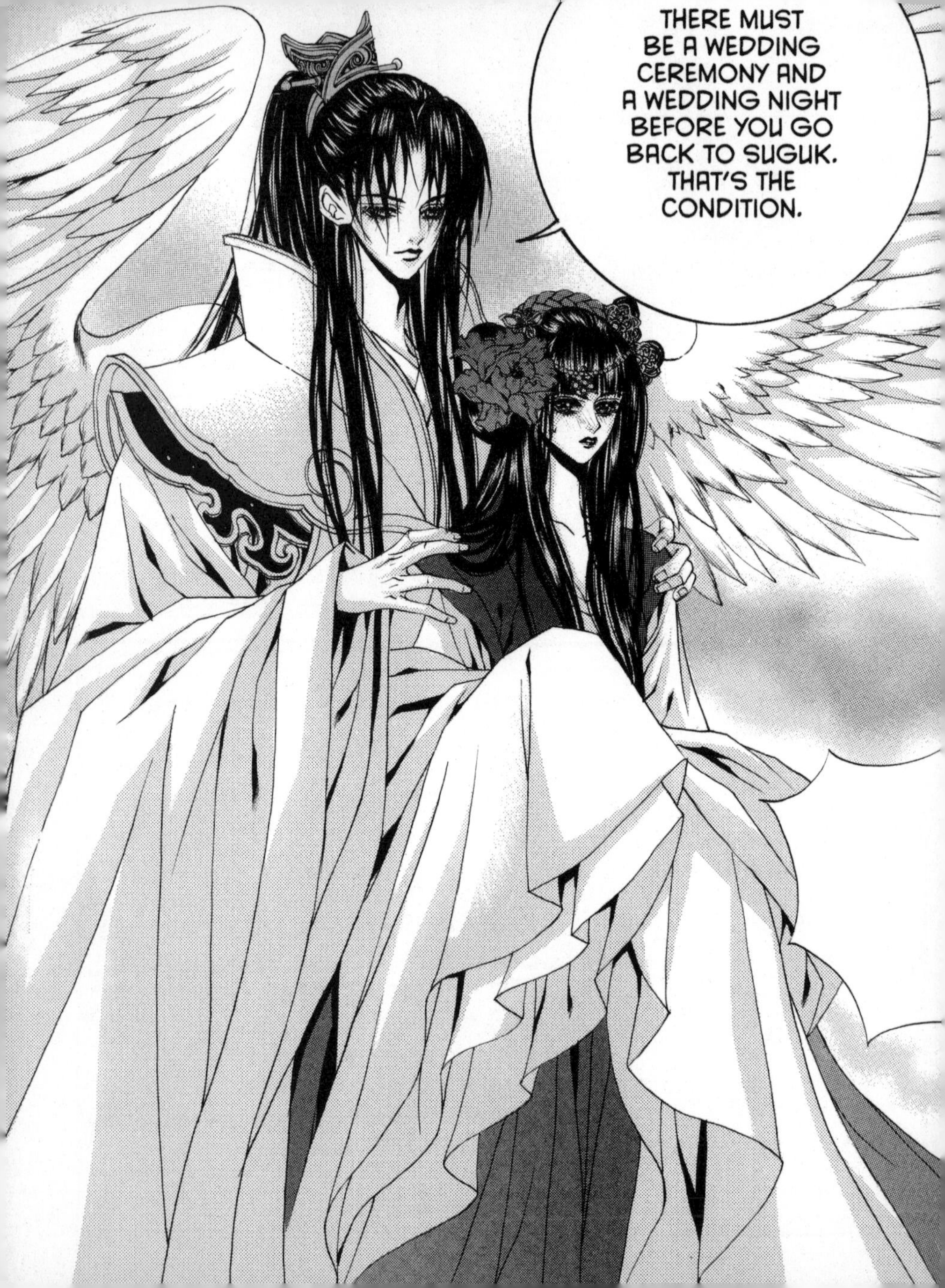
THERE MUST BE A WEDDING CEREMONY AND A WEDDING NIGHT BEFORE YOU GO BACK TO SUGUK. THAT'S THE CONDITION.

BRIDE of the WATER GOD

BRIDE of the WATER GOD

 GAIDEN (BONUS STORY): **DONG-SHIM-CHO**

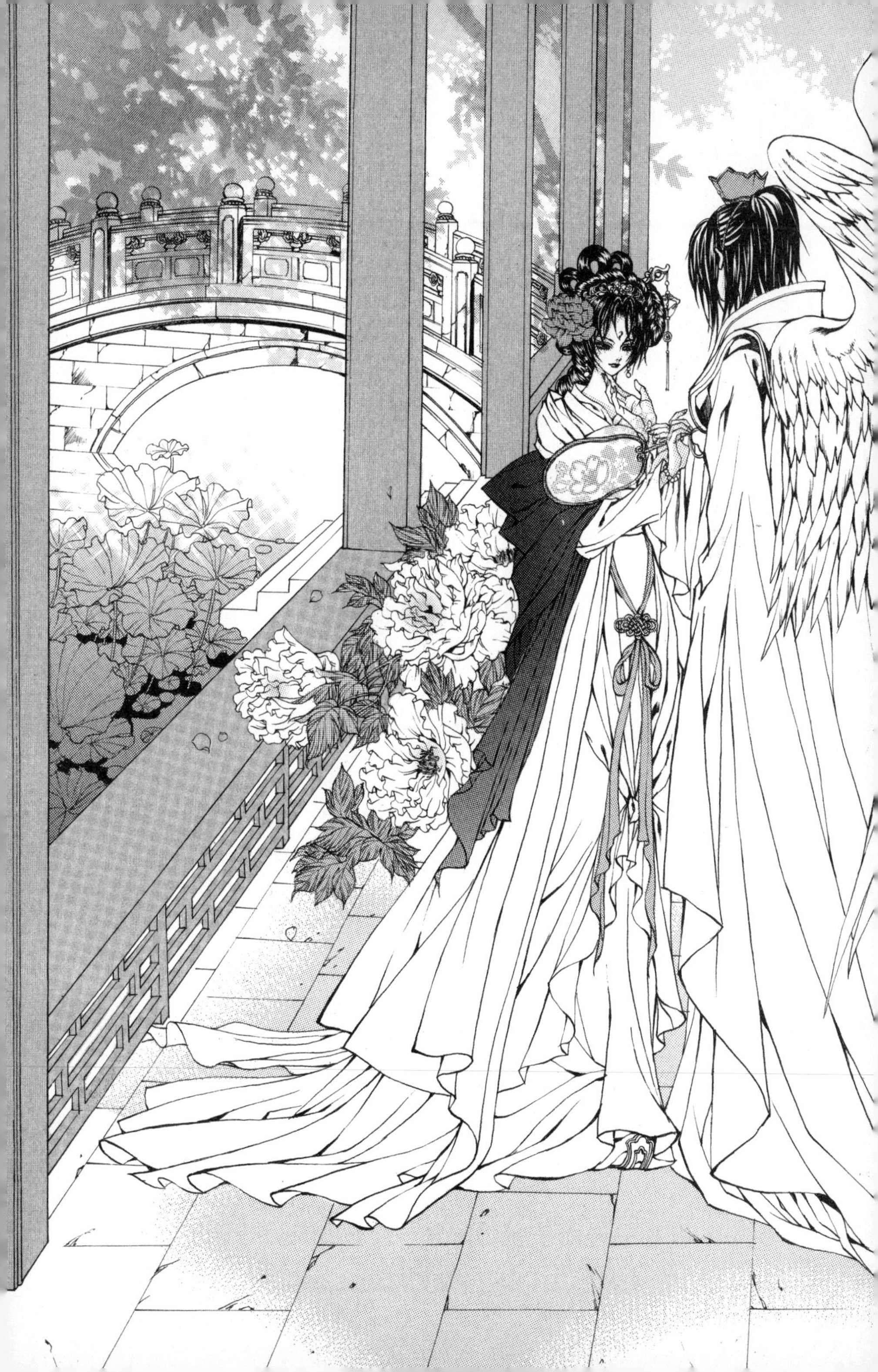

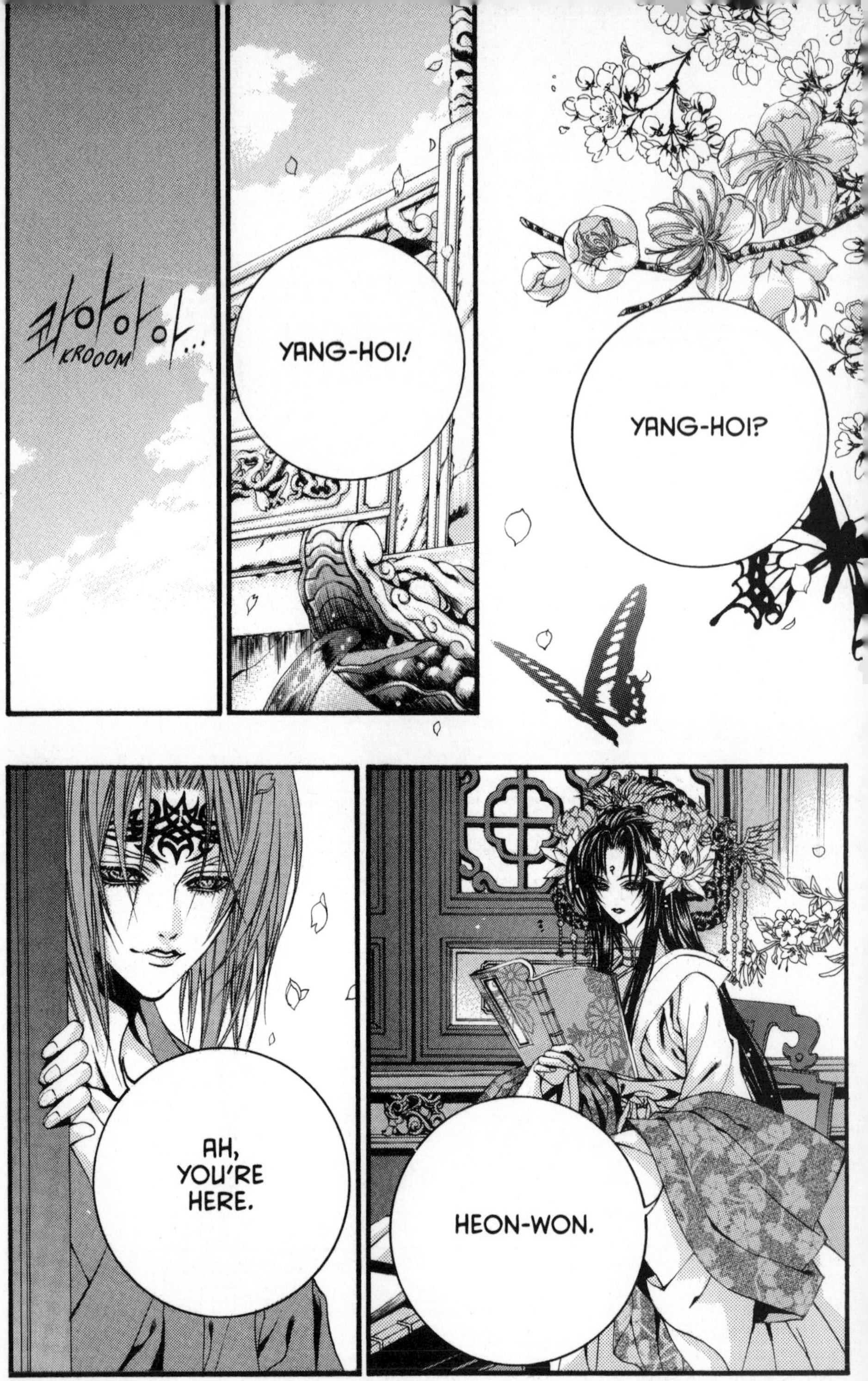

콰아아아...
KROOOM
YANG-HOI!
YANG-HOI?
AH, YOU'RE HERE.
HEON-WON.

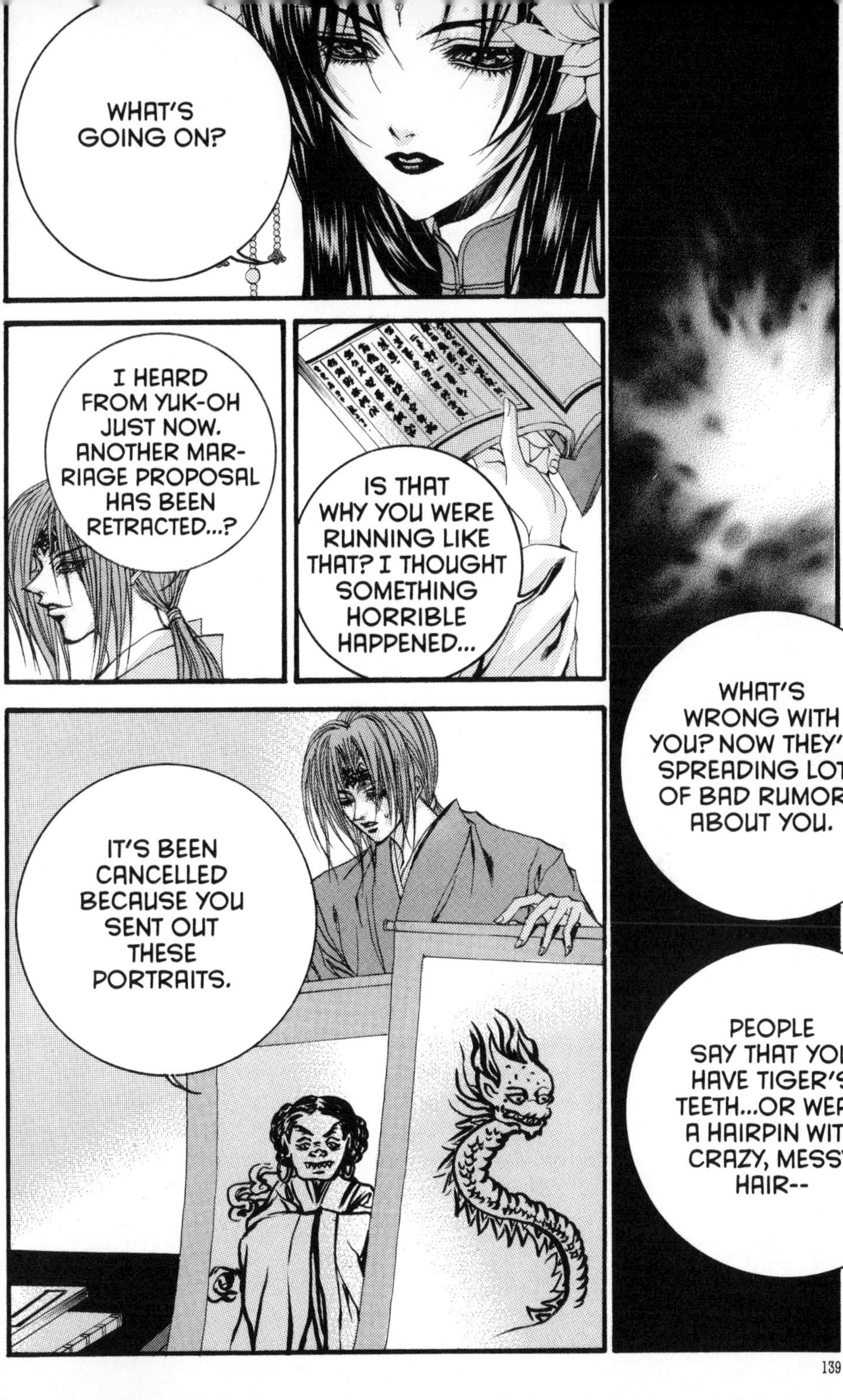
WHAT'S GOING ON?
I HEARD FROM YUK-OH JUST NOW. ANOTHER MAR-RIAGE PROPOSAL HAS BEEN RETRACTED...?
IS THAT WHY YOU WERE RUNNING LIKE THAT? I THOUGHT SOMETHING HORRIBLE HAPPENED...
IT'S BEEN CANCELLED BECAUSE YOU SENT OUT THESE PORTRAITS.
WHAT'S WRONG WITH YOU? NOW THEY'RE SPREADING LOTS OF BAD RUMORS ABOUT YOU.
PEOPLE SAY THAT YOU HAVE TIGER'S TEETH...OR WEAR A HAIRPIN WITH CRAZY, MESSY HAIR--

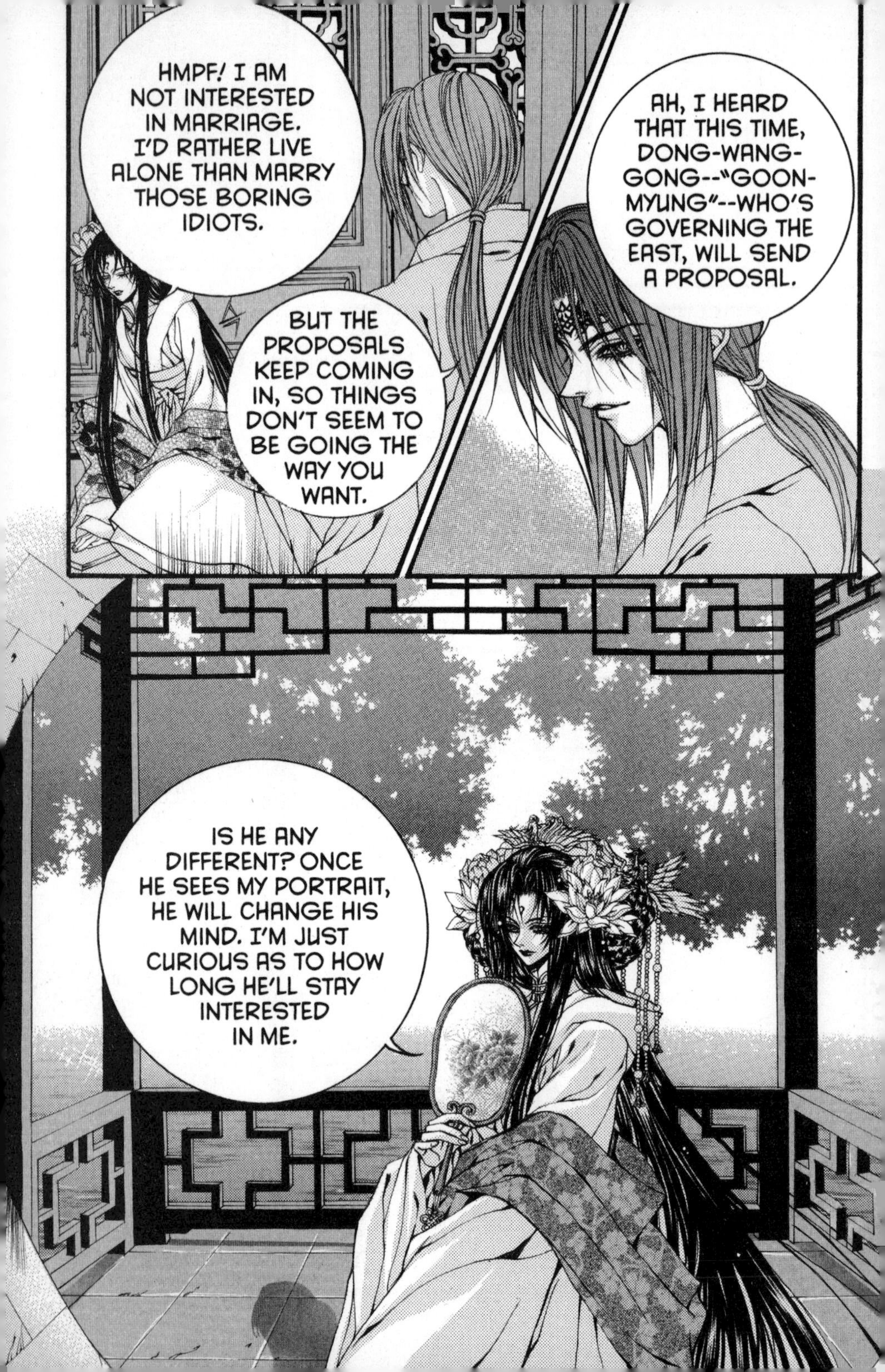
AH, I HEARD THAT THIS TIME, DONG-WANG-GONG--"GOON-MYUNG"--WHO'S GOVERNING THE EAST, WILL SEND A PROPOSAL.
HMPF! I AM NOT INTERESTED IN MARRIAGE. I'D RATHER LIVE ALONE THAN MARRY THOSE BORING IDIOTS.
BUT THE PROPOSALS KEEP COMING IN, SO THINGS DON'T SEEM TO BE GOING THE WAY YOU WANT.
IS HE ANY DIFFERENT? ONCE HE SEES MY PORTRAIT, HE WILL CHANGE HIS MIND. I'M JUST CURIOUS AS TO HOW LONG HE'LL STAY INTERESTED IN ME.

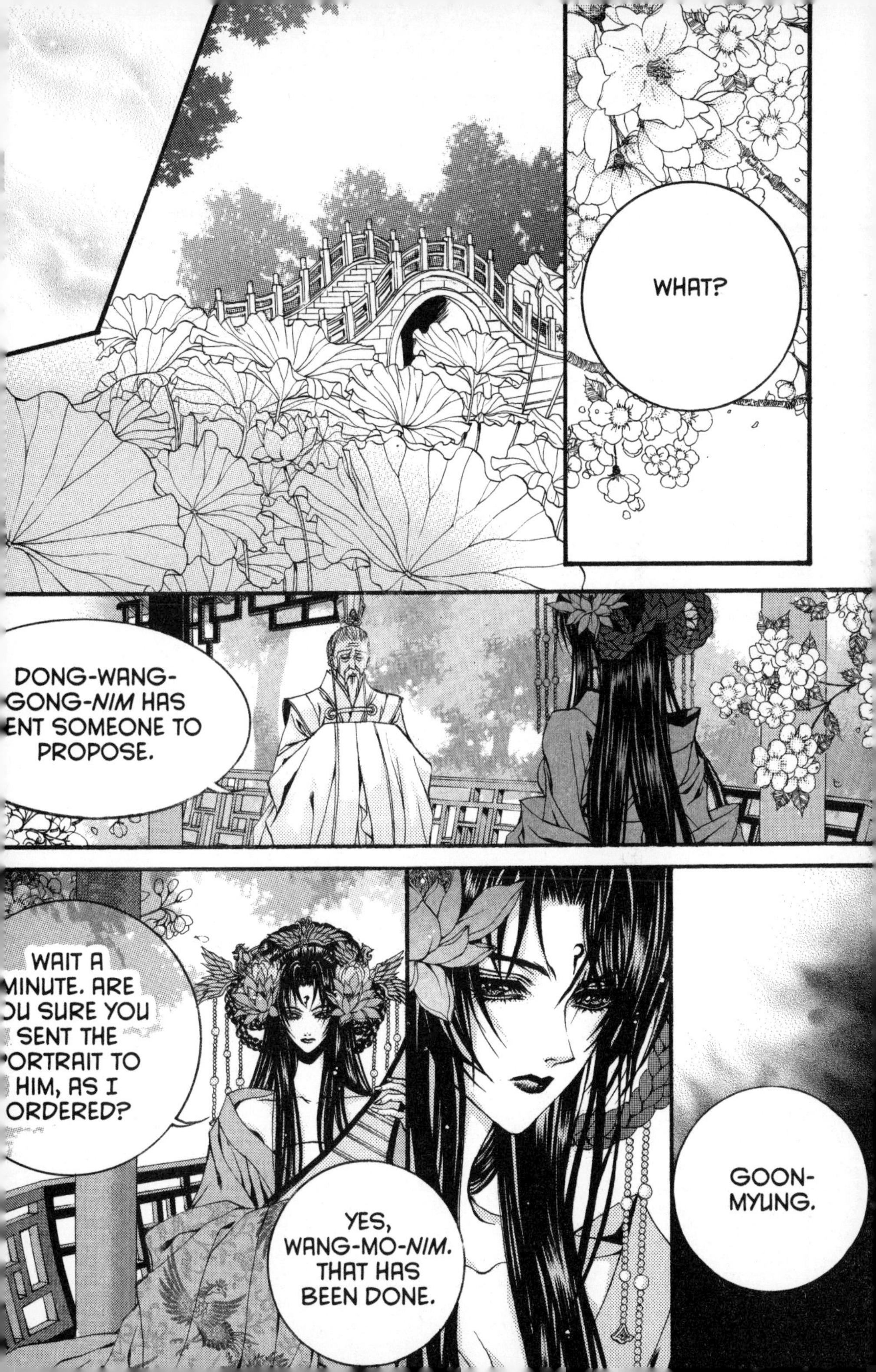
WHAT?
DONG-WANG-GONG-*NIM* HAS ENT SOMEONE TO PROPOSE.
WAIT A MINUTE. ARE OU SURE YOU SENT THE ORTRAIT TO HIM, AS I ORDERED?
YES, WANG-MO-*NIM*. THAT HAS BEEN DONE.
GOON-MYUNG.

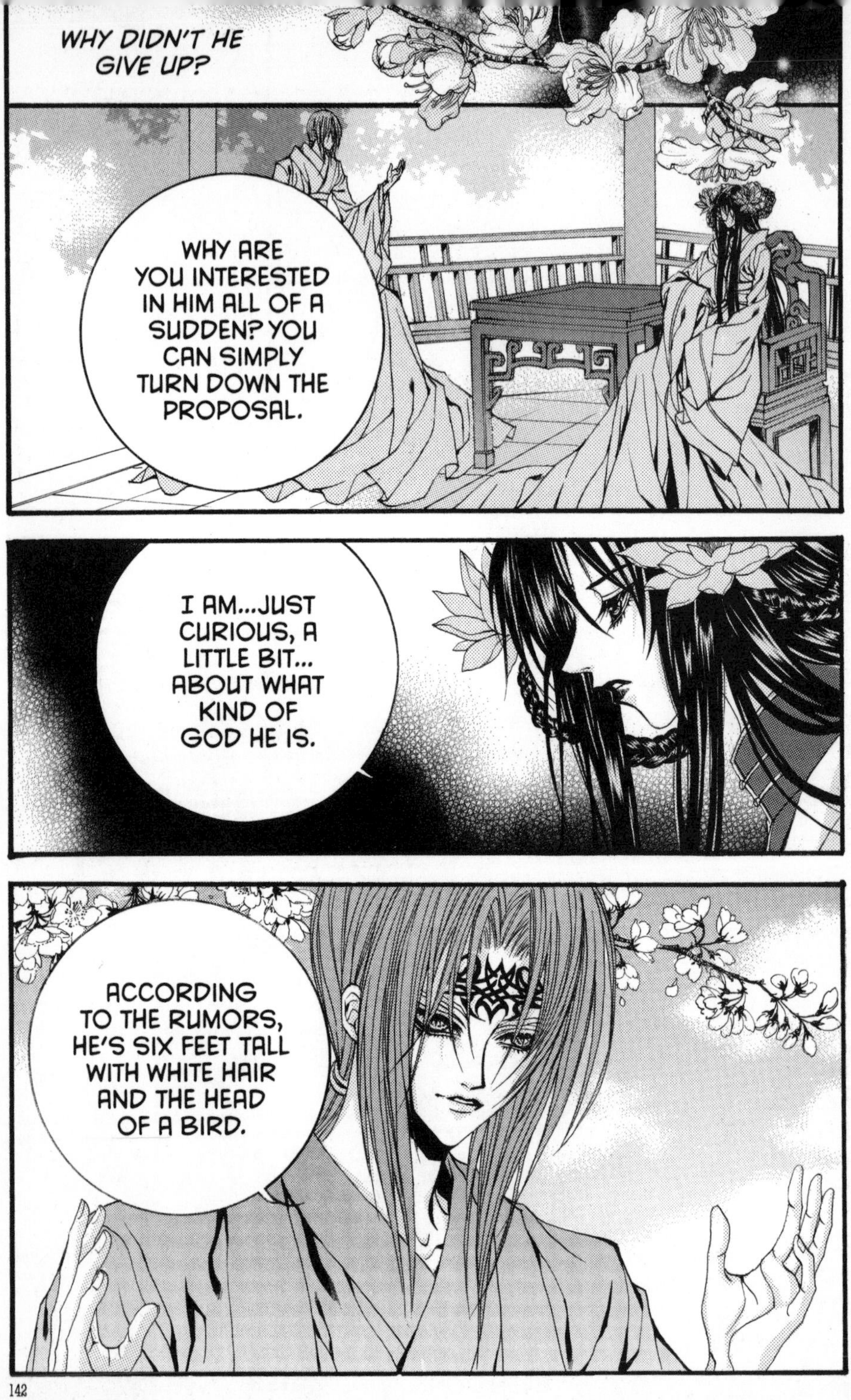
WHY DIDN'T HE GIVE UP?
WHY ARE YOU INTERESTED IN HIM ALL OF A SUDDEN? YOU CAN SIMPLY TURN DOWN THE PROPOSAL.
I AM...JUST CURIOUS, A LITTLE BIT... ABOUT WHAT KIND OF GOD HE IS.
ACCORDING TO THE RUMORS, HE'S SIX FEET TALL WITH WHITE HAIR AND THE HEAD OF A BIRD.

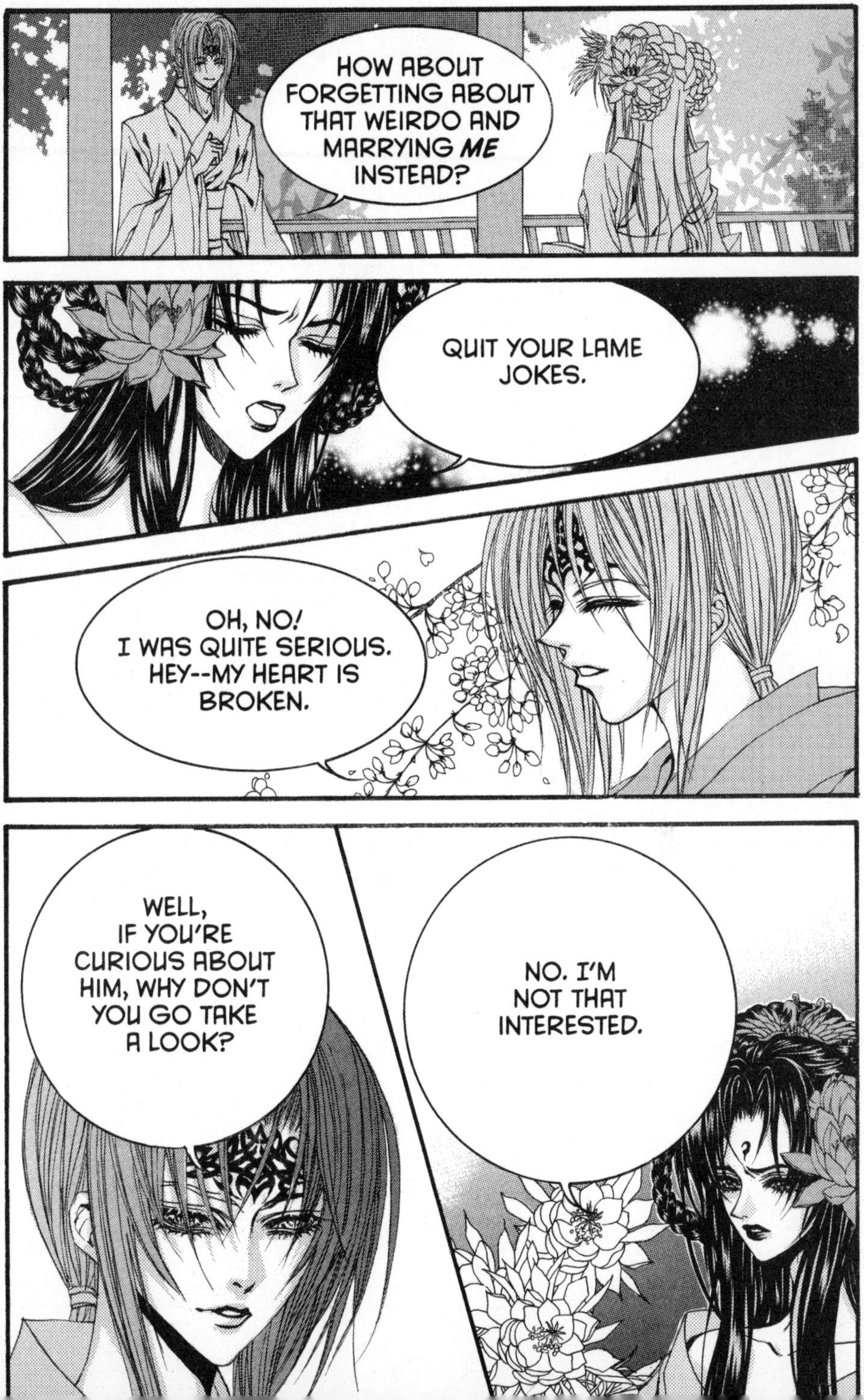
HOW ABOUT FORGETTING ABOUT THAT WEIRDO AND MARRYING *ME* INSTEAD?
QUIT YOUR LAME JOKES.
OH, NO! I WAS QUITE SERIOUS. HEY--MY HEART IS BROKEN.
WELL, IF YOU'RE CURIOUS ABOUT HIM, WHY DON'T YOU GO TAKE A LOOK?
NO. I'M NOT THAT INTERESTED.

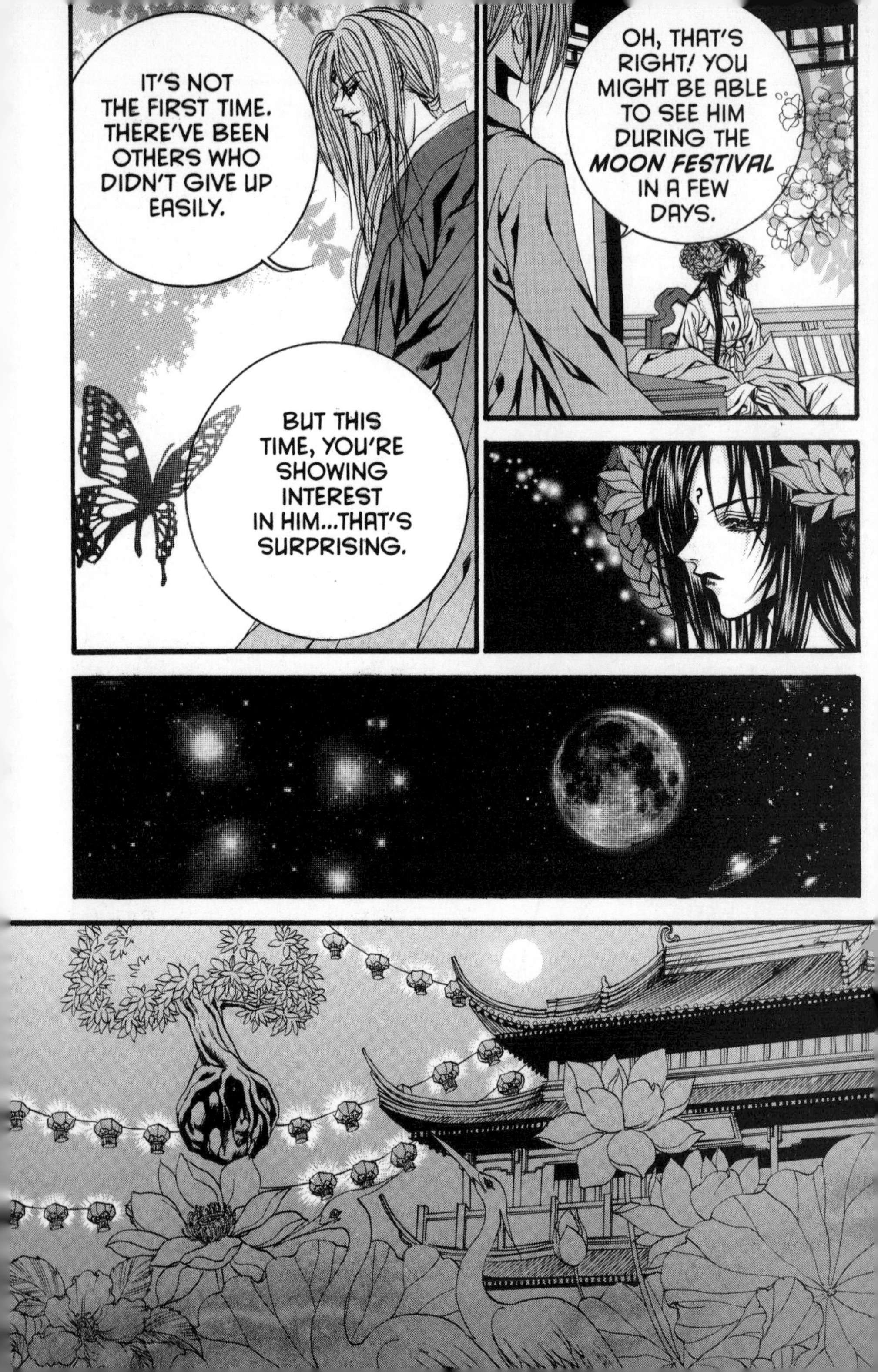
IT'S NOT THE FIRST TIME. THERE'VE BEEN OTHERS WHO DIDN'T GIVE UP EASILY.
BUT THIS TIME, YOU'RE SHOWING INTEREST IN HIM...THAT'S SURPRISING.
OH, THAT'S RIGHT! YOU MIGHT BE ABLE TO SEE HIM DURING THE *MOON FESTIVAL* IN A FEW DAYS.

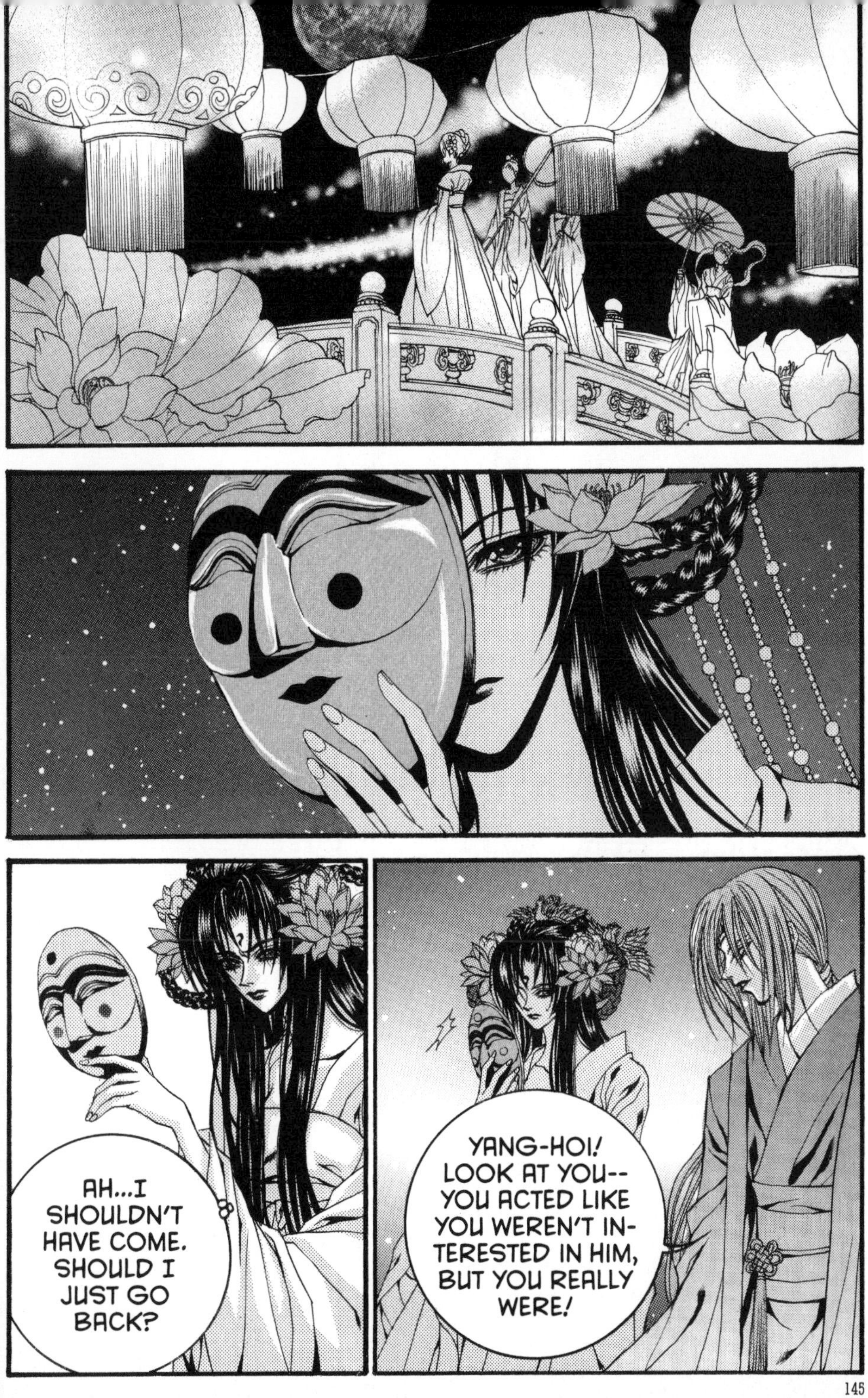
AH...I SHOULDN'T HAVE COME. SHOULD I JUST GO BACK?
YANG-HOI! LOOK AT YOU-- YOU ACTED LIKE YOU WEREN'T IN-TERESTED IN HIM, BUT YOU REALLY WERE!

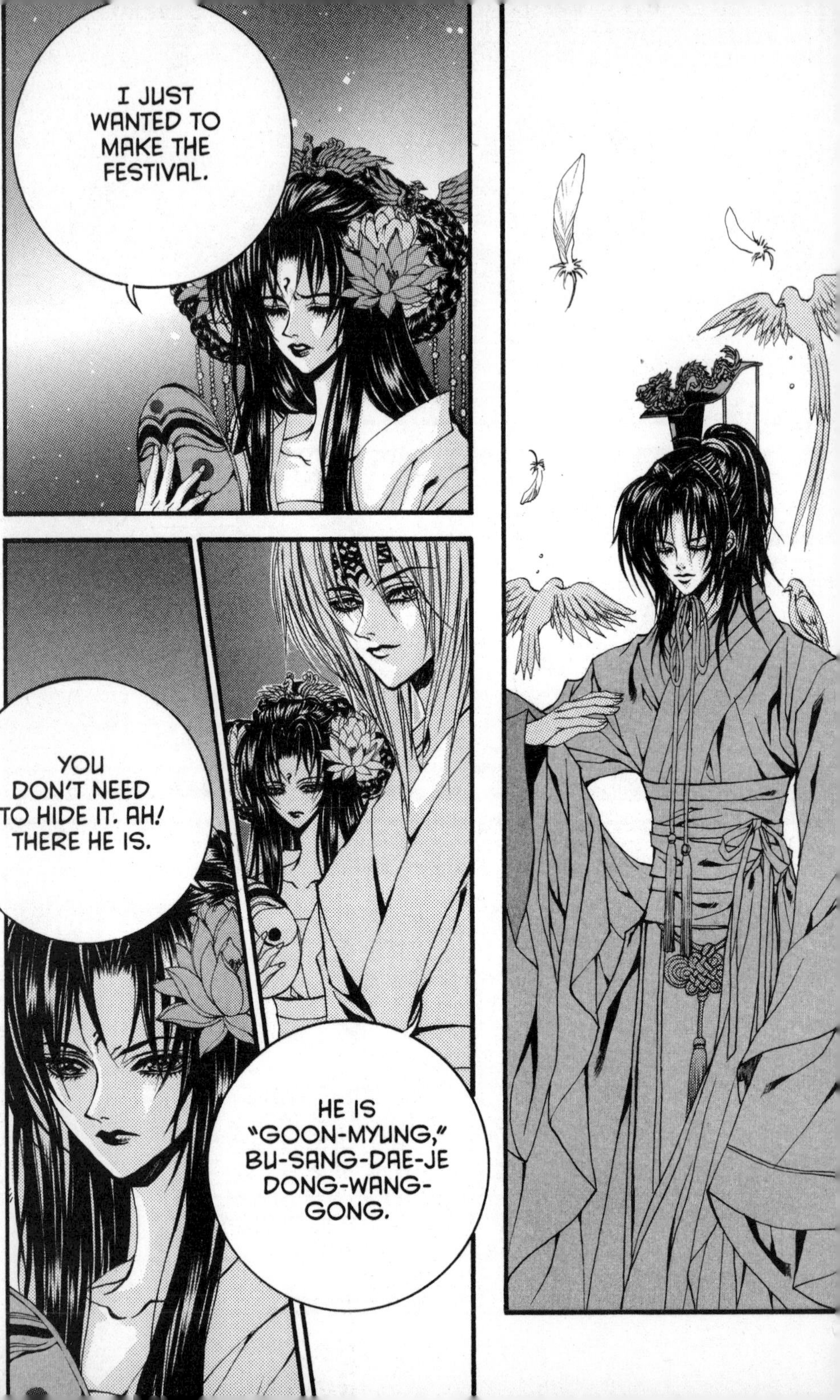
I JUST WANTED TO MAKE THE FESTIVAL.
YOU DON'T NEED TO HIDE IT. AH! THERE HE IS.
HE IS "GOON-MYUNG," BU-SANG-DAE-JE DONG-WANG-GONG.

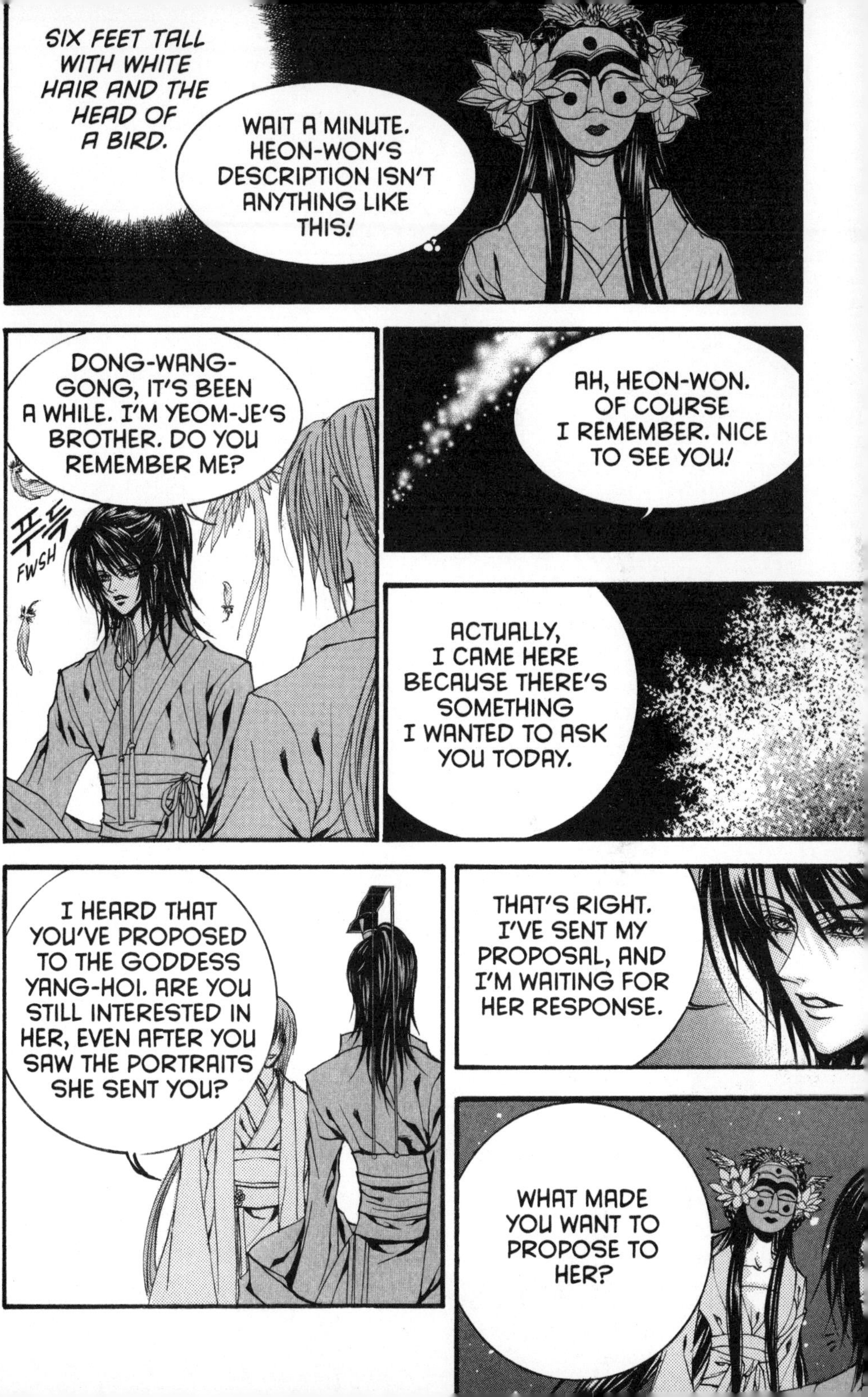
SIX FEET TALL WITH WHITE HAIR AND THE HEAD OF A BIRD.
WAIT A MINUTE. HEON-WON'S DESCRIPTION ISN'T ANYTHING LIKE THIS!
DONG-WANG-GONG, IT'S BEEN A WHILE. I'M YEOM-JE'S BROTHER. DO YOU REMEMBER ME?
푸득
FWSH
AH, HEON-WON. OF COURSE I REMEMBER. NICE TO SEE YOU!
ACTUALLY, I CAME HERE BECAUSE THERE'S SOMETHING I WANTED TO ASK YOU TODAY.
I HEARD THAT YOU'VE PROPOSED TO THE GODDESS YANG-HOI. ARE YOU STILL INTERESTED IN HER, EVEN AFTER YOU SAW THE PORTRAITS SHE SENT YOU?
THAT'S RIGHT. I'VE SENT MY PROPOSAL, AND I'M WAITING FOR HER RESPONSE.
WHAT MADE YOU WANT TO PROPOSE TO HER?

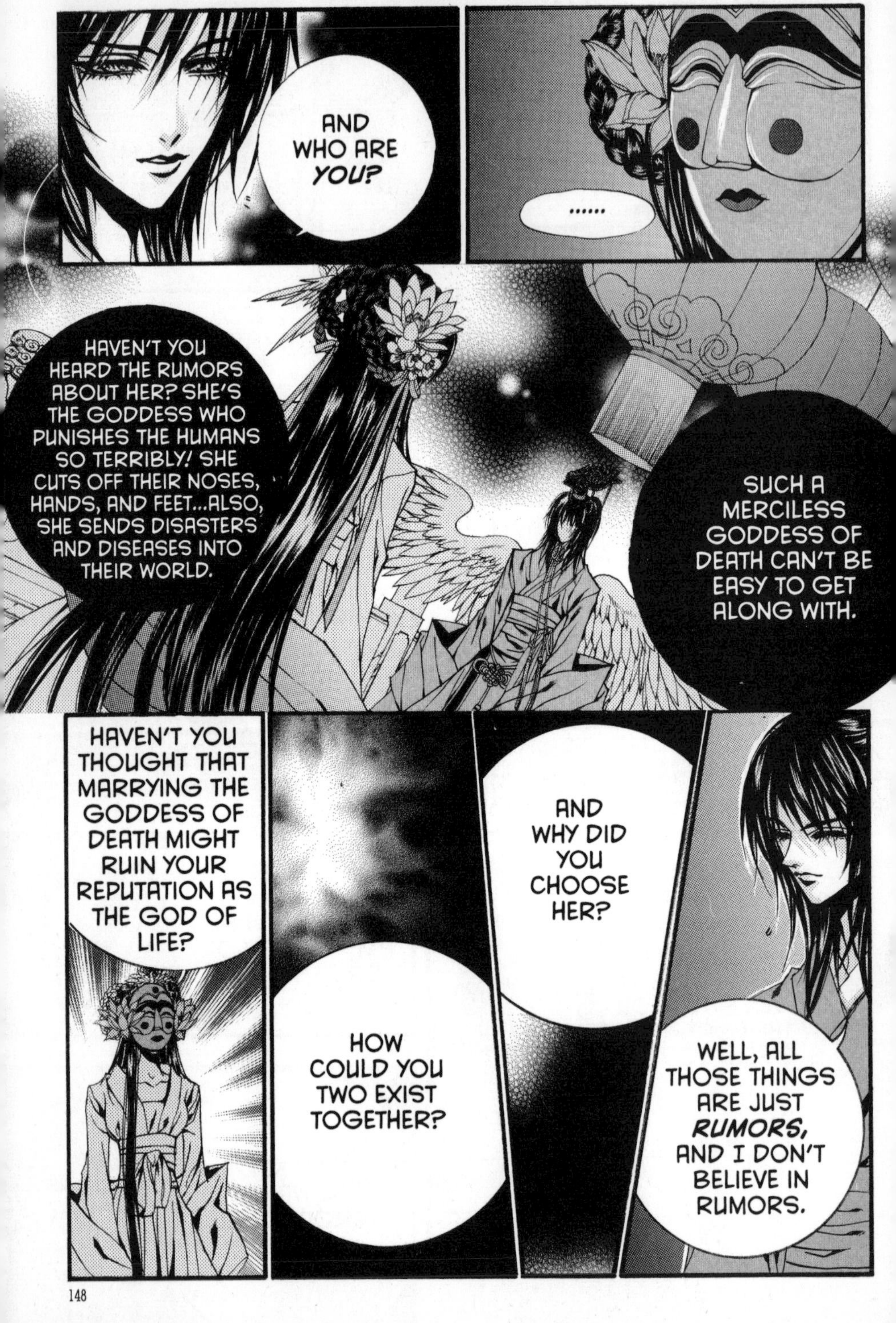
AND WHO ARE *YOU?*
......
HAVEN'T YOU HEARD THE RUMORS ABOUT HER? SHE'S THE GODDESS WHO PUNISHES THE HUMANS SO TERRIBLY! SHE CUTS OFF THEIR NOSES, HANDS, AND FEET...ALSO, SHE SENDS DISASTERS AND DISEASES INTO THEIR WORLD.
SUCH A MERCILESS GODDESS OF DEATH CAN'T BE EASY TO GET ALONG WITH.
HAVEN'T YOU THOUGHT THAT MARRYING THE GODDESS OF DEATH MIGHT RUIN YOUR REPUTATION AS THE GOD OF LIFE?
AND WHY DID YOU CHOOSE HER?
HOW COULD YOU TWO EXIST TOGETHER?
WELL, ALL THOSE THINGS ARE JUST *RUMORS,* AND I DON'T BELIEVE IN RUMORS.

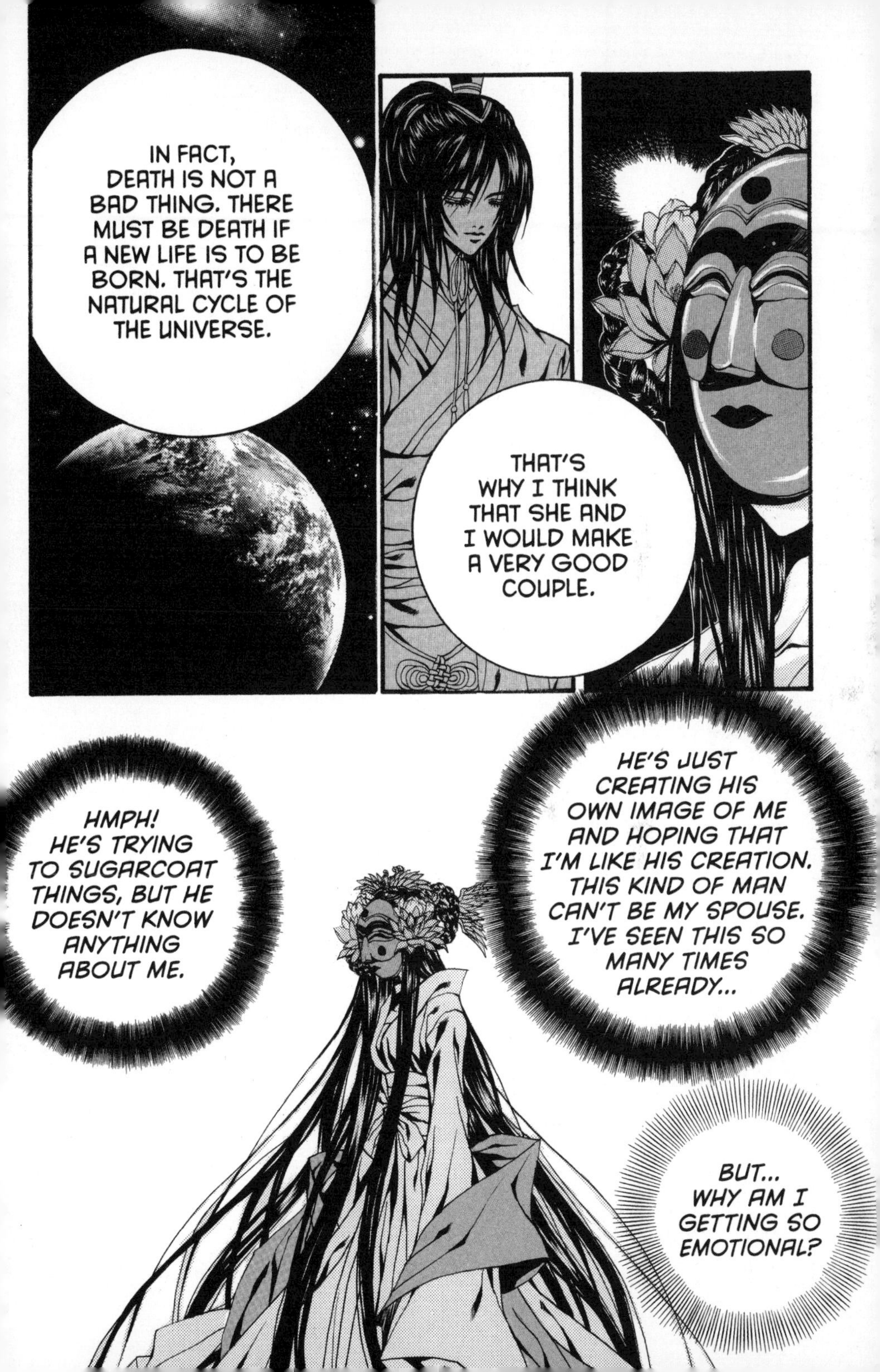
IN FACT, DEATH IS NOT A BAD THING. THERE MUST BE DEATH IF A NEW LIFE IS TO BE BORN. THAT'S THE NATURAL CYCLE OF THE UNIVERSE.
THAT'S WHY I THINK THAT SHE AND I WOULD MAKE A VERY GOOD COUPLE.
HE'S JUST CREATING HIS OWN IMAGE OF ME AND HOPING THAT I'M LIKE HIS CREATION. THIS KIND OF MAN CAN'T BE MY SPOUSE. I'VE SEEN THIS SO MANY TIMES ALREADY...
HMPH! HE'S TRYING TO SUGARCOAT THINGS, BUT HE DOESN'T KNOW ANYTHING ABOUT ME.
BUT... WHY AM I GETTING SO EMOTIONAL?

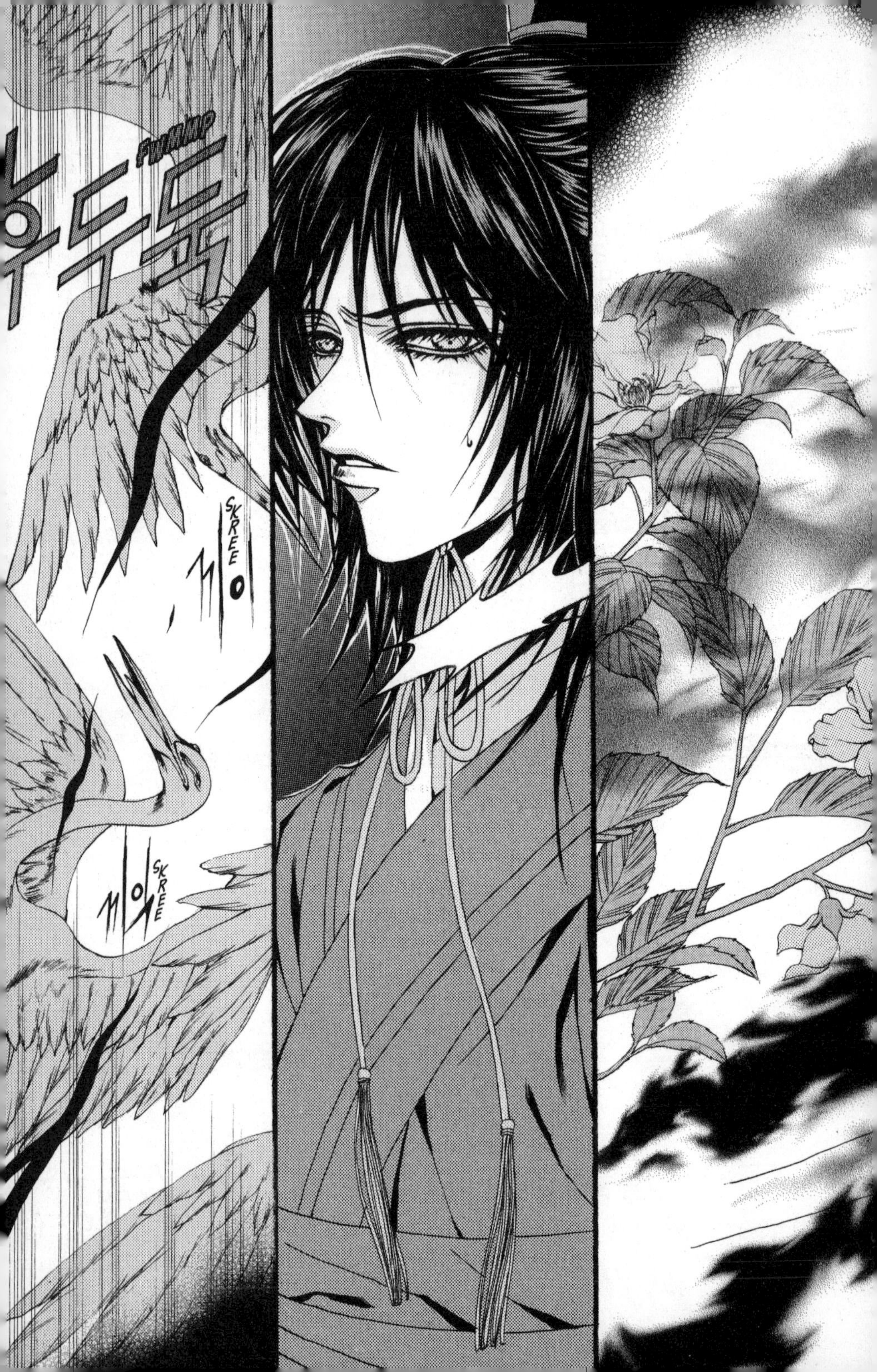
후드득
FWMMP
SKREE
끼이
SKREE

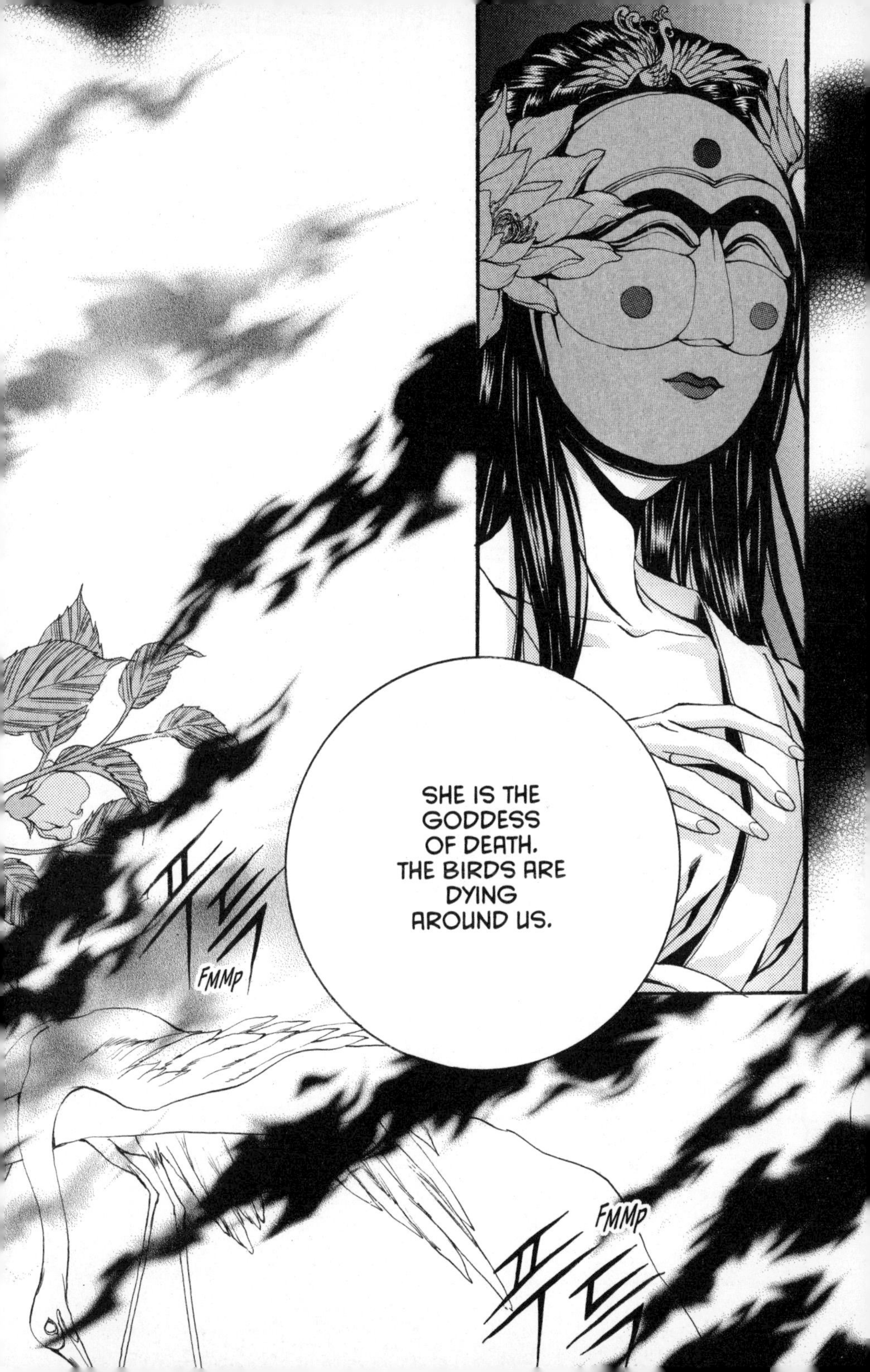

SHE IS THE GODDESS OF DEATH. THE BIRDS ARE DYING AROUND US.
FMMP
FMMP

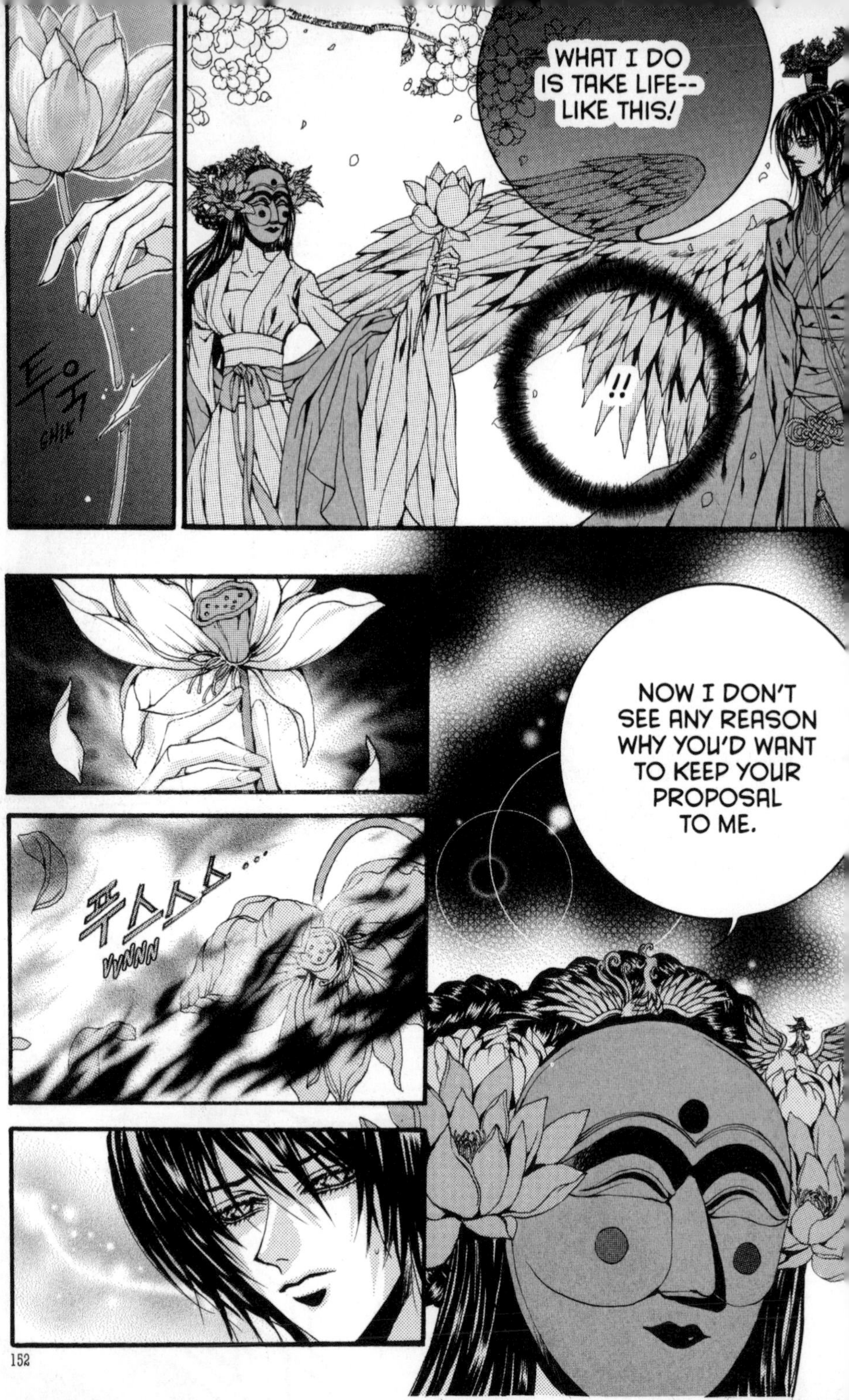
WHAT I DO IS TAKE LIFE-- LIKE THIS!
투욱
CHIK
!!
NOW I DON'T SEE ANY REASON WHY YOU'D WANT TO KEEP YOUR PROPOSAL TO ME.
푸스스스...
WHNN

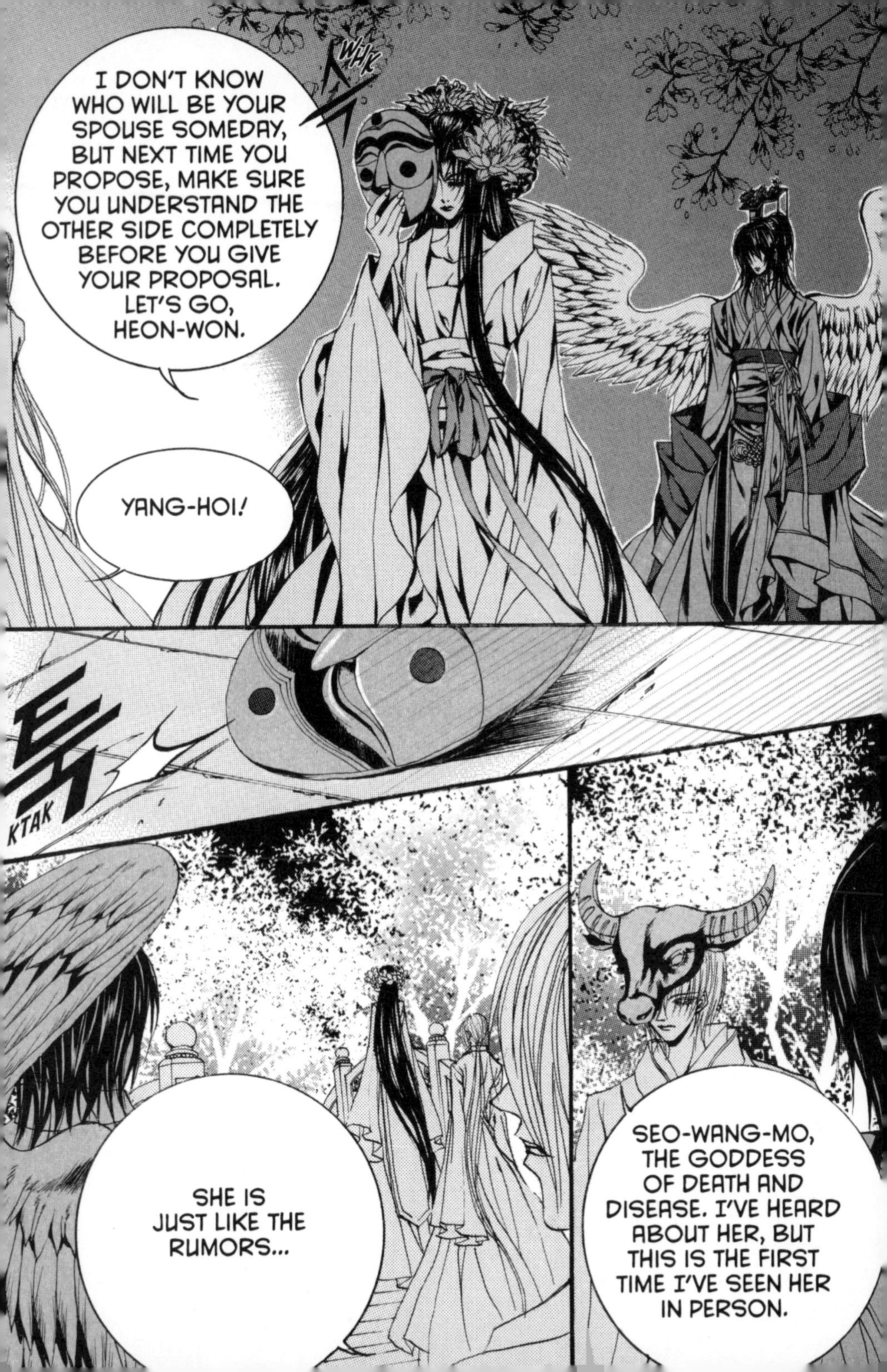
WHK
I DON'T KNOW WHO WILL BE YOUR SPOUSE SOMEDAY, BUT NEXT TIME YOU PROPOSE, MAKE SURE YOU UNDERSTAND THE OTHER SIDE COMPLETELY BEFORE YOU GIVE YOUR PROPOSAL. LET'S GO, HEON-WON.
YANG-HOI!
KTAK
SEO-WANG-MO, THE GODDESS OF DEATH AND DISEASE. I'VE HEARD ABOUT HER, BUT THIS IS THE FIRST TIME I'VE SEEN HER IN PERSON.
SHE IS JUST LIKE THE RUMORS...

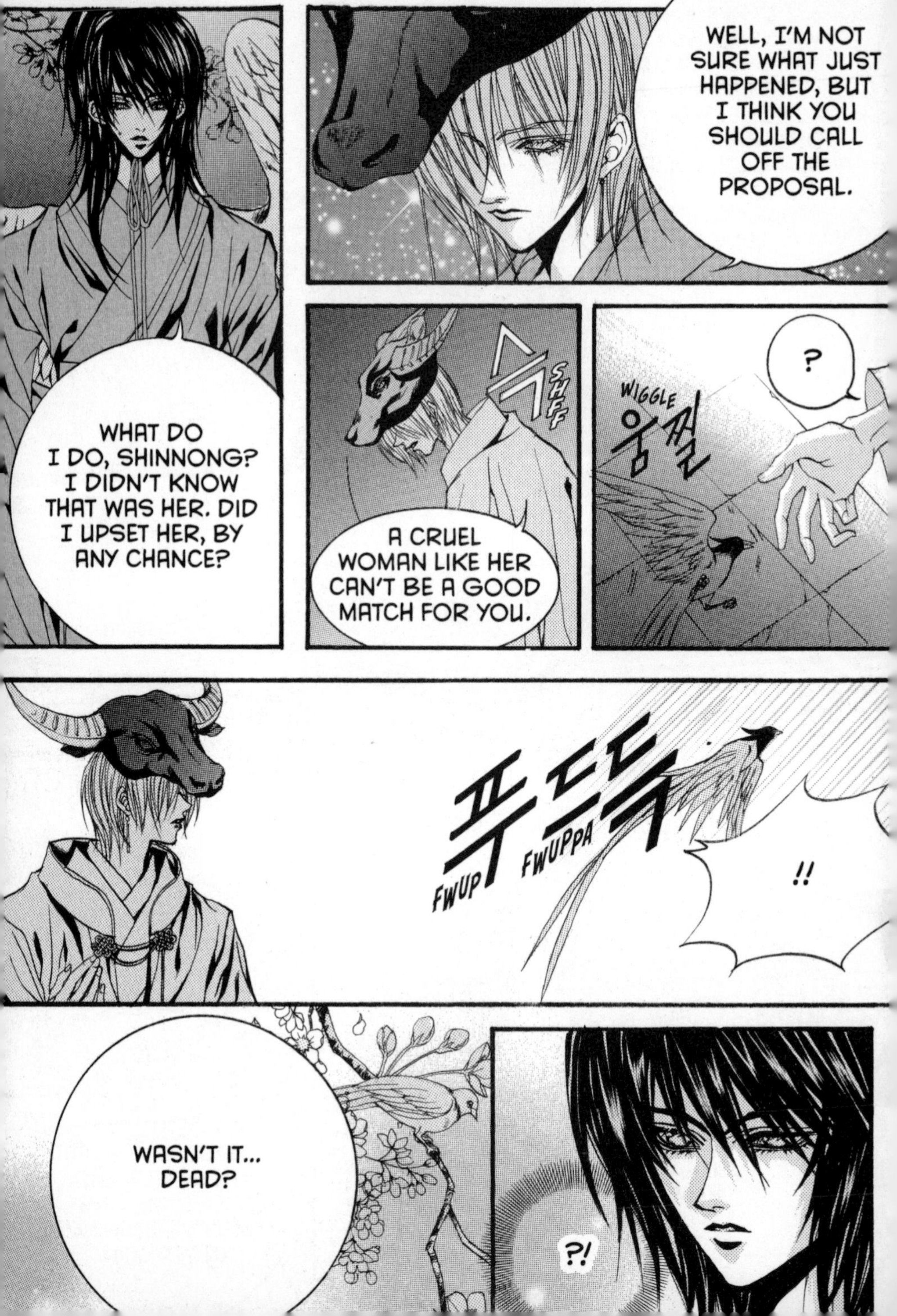
WELL, I'M NOT SURE WHAT JUST HAPPENED, BUT I THINK YOU SHOULD CALL OFF THE PROPOSAL.
WHAT DO I DO, SHINNONG? I DIDN'T KNOW THAT WAS HER. DID I UPSET HER, BY ANY CHANCE?
SHFF
A CRUEL WOMAN LIKE HER CAN'T BE A GOOD MATCH FOR YOU.
?
WIGGLE
움찔
푸드득
FWUP FWUPPA
!!
WASN'T IT... DEAD?
?!

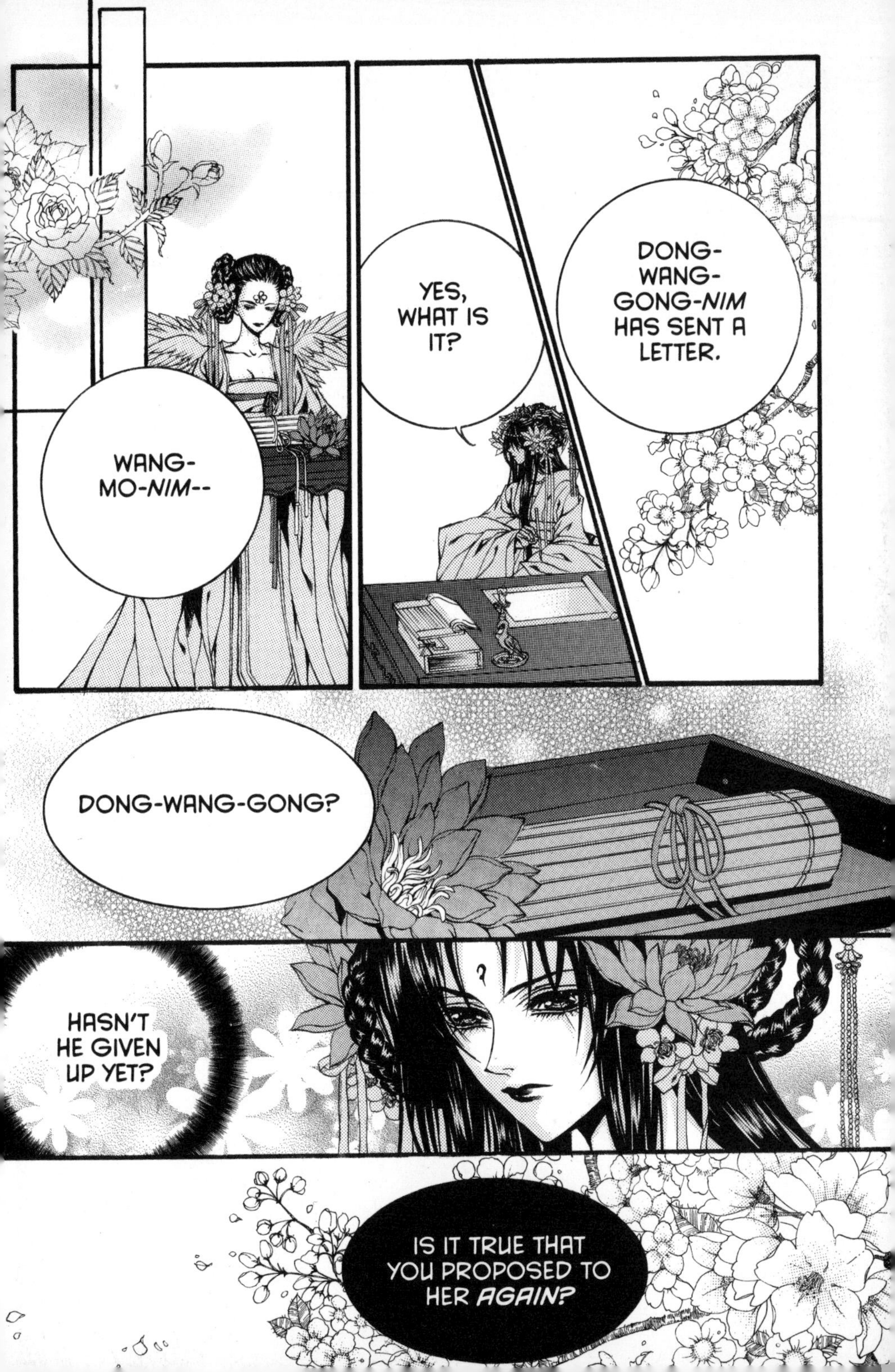
WANG-MO-*NIM*--
YES, WHAT IS IT?
DONG-WANG-GONG-*NIM* HAS SENT A LETTER.
DONG-WANG-GONG?
?
HASN'T HE GIVEN UP YET?
IS IT TRUE THAT YOU PROPOSED TO HER *AGAIN*?

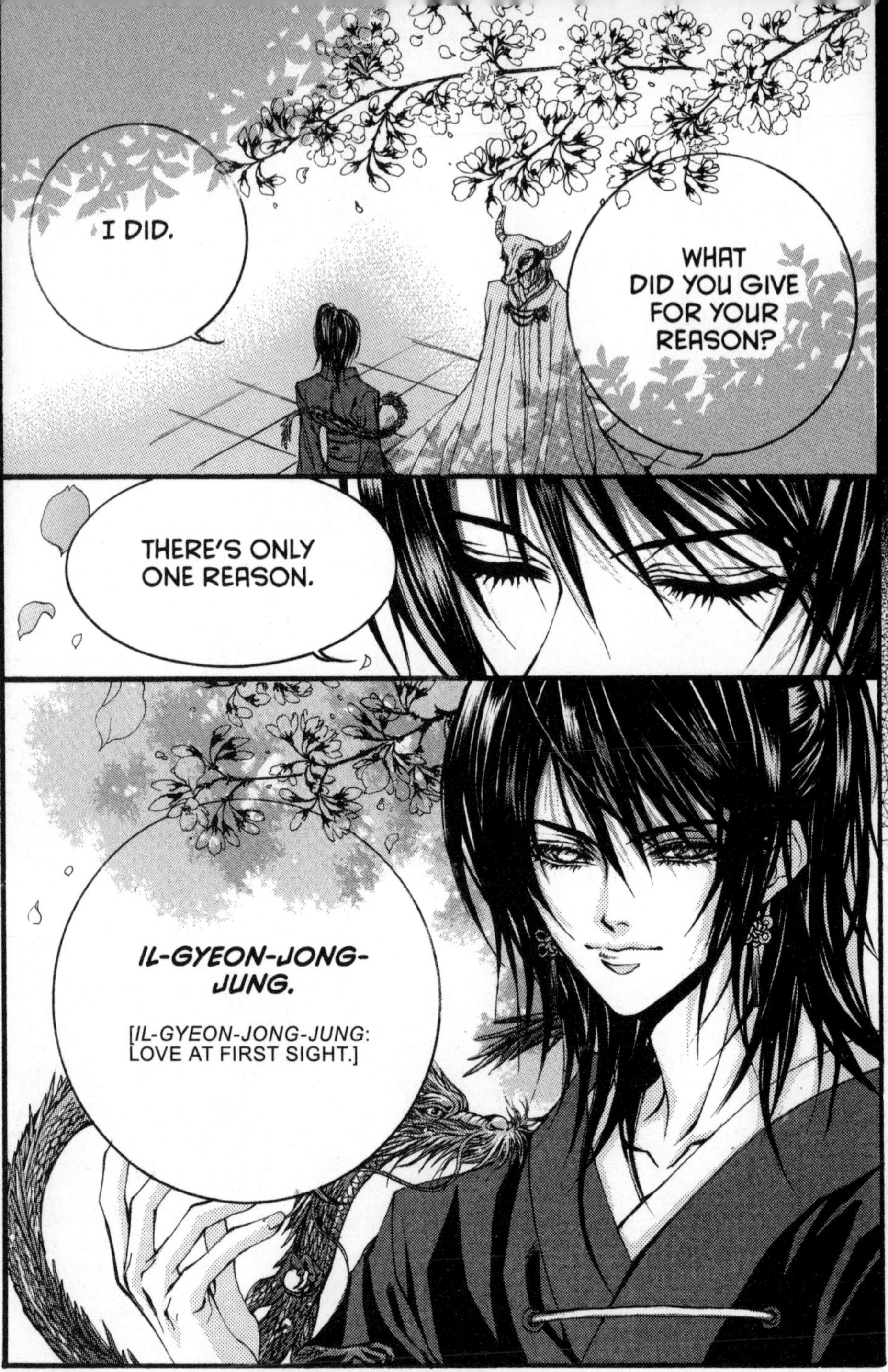
WHAT DID YOU GIVE FOR YOUR REASON?
I DID.
THERE'S ONLY ONE REASON.
IL-GYEON-JONG-JUNG.
[*IL-GYEON-JONG-JUNG*: LOVE AT FIRST SIGHT.]

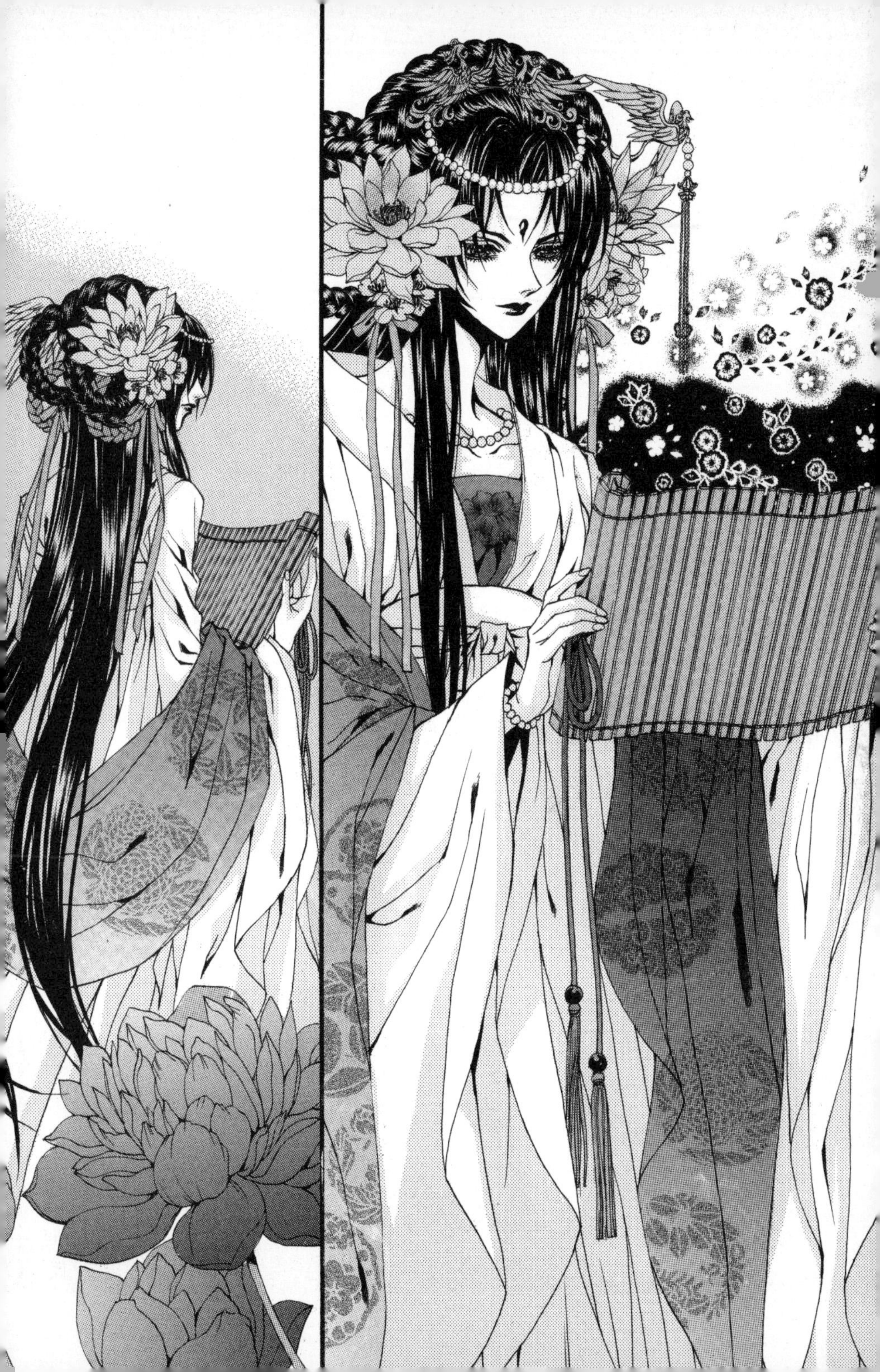

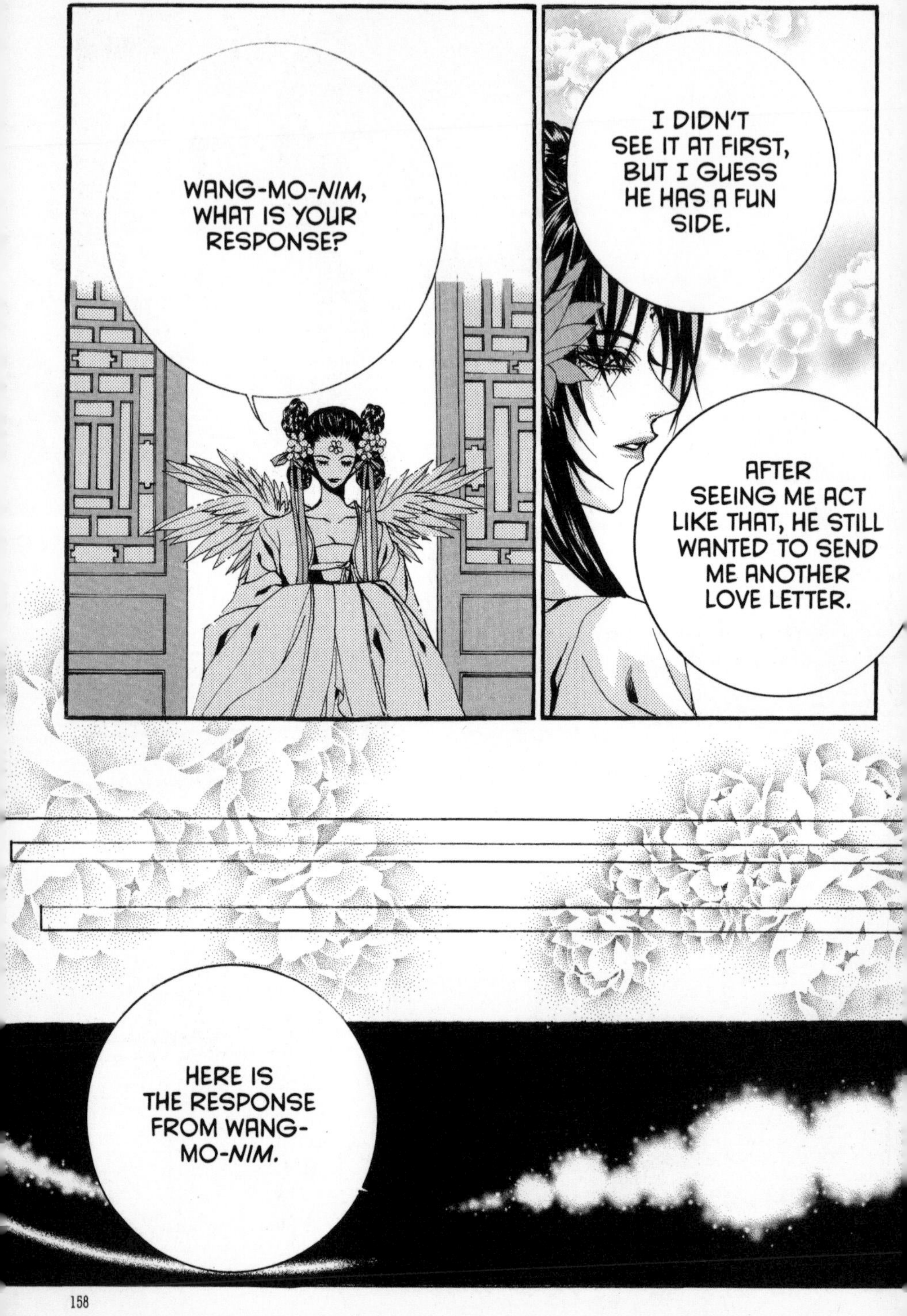
I DIDN'T SEE IT AT FIRST, BUT I GUESS HE HAS A FUN SIDE.
AFTER SEEING ME ACT LIKE THAT, HE STILL WANTED TO SEND ME ANOTHER LOVE LETTER.
WANG-MO-*NIM*, WHAT IS YOUR RESPONSE?
HERE IS THE RESPONSE FROM WANG-MO-*NIM*.

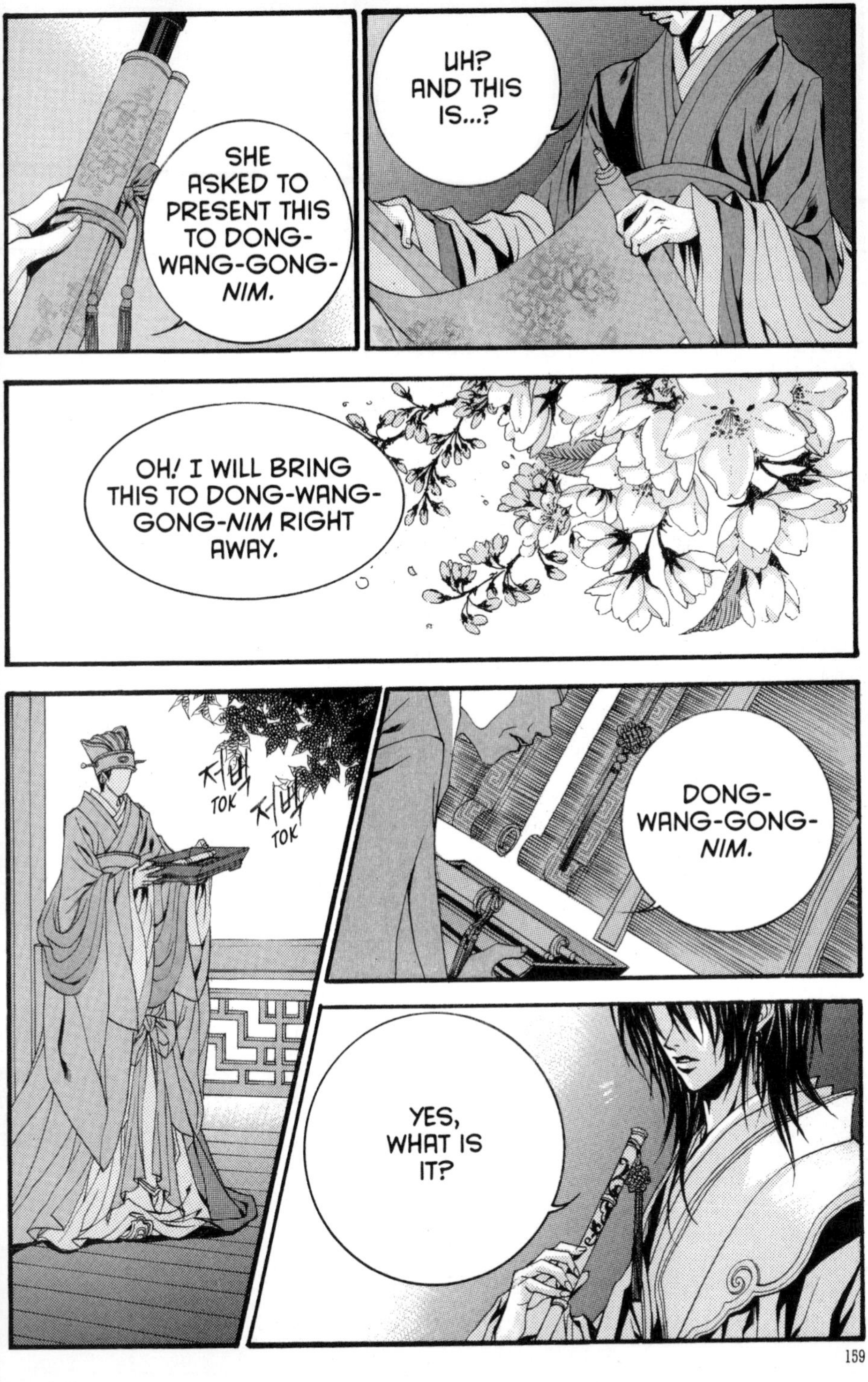
SHE ASKED TO PRESENT THIS TO DONG-WANG-GONG-*NIM.*
UH? AND THIS IS...?
OH! I WILL BRING THIS TO DONG-WANG-GONG-*NIM* RIGHT AWAY.
TOK
TOK
DONG-WANG-GONG-*NIM.*
YES, WHAT IS IT?

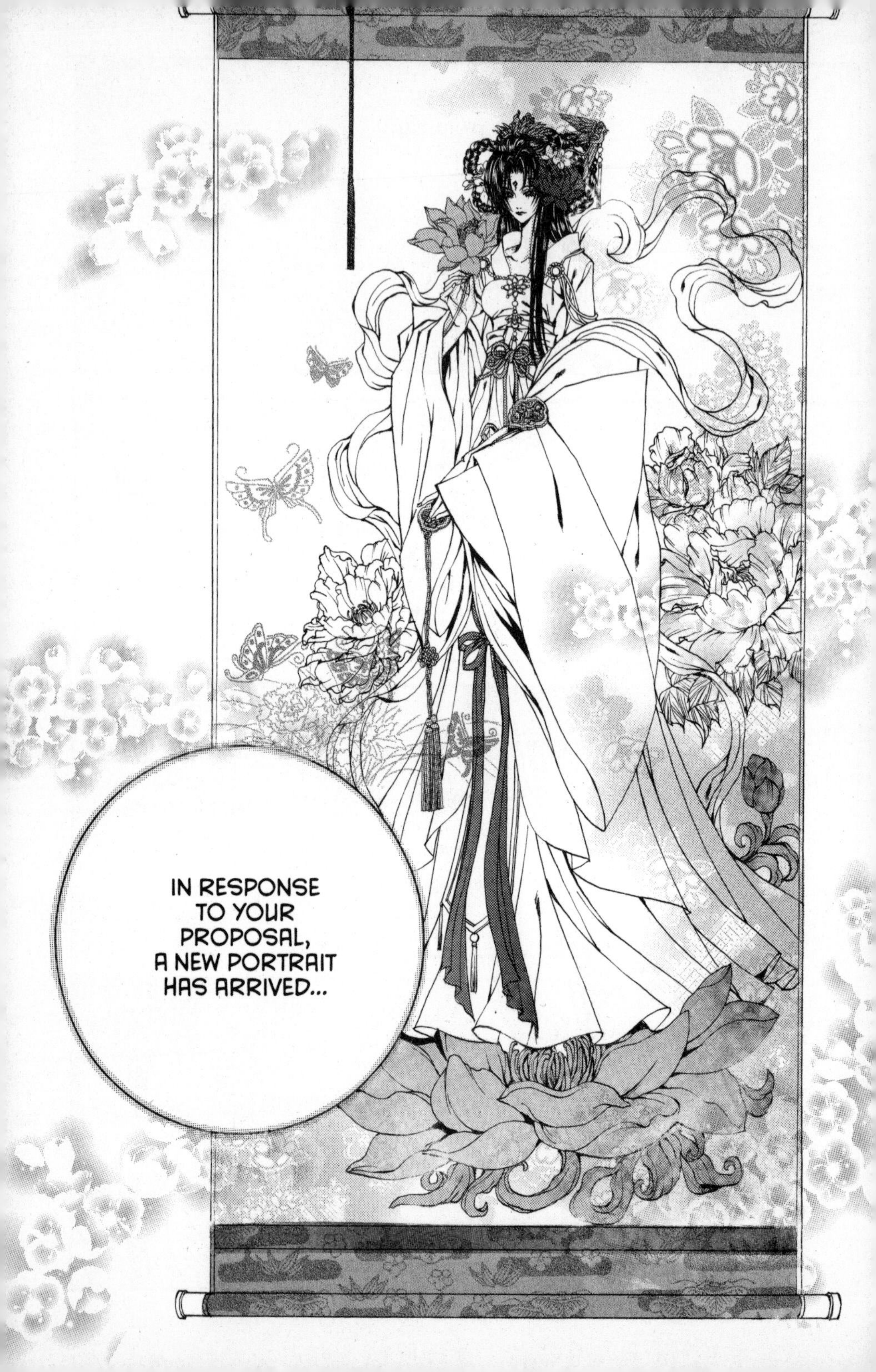
IN RESPONSE TO YOUR PROPOSAL, A NEW PORTRAIT HAS ARRIVED...

BRIDE of the WATER GOD

☆ MI-GAENG'S CLOSING DIARY ☆

("MI-GAENG" IS MI-KYUNG YUN'S NICKNAME)

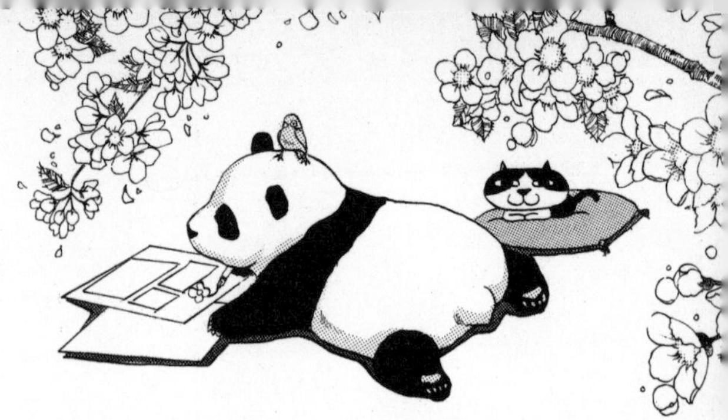

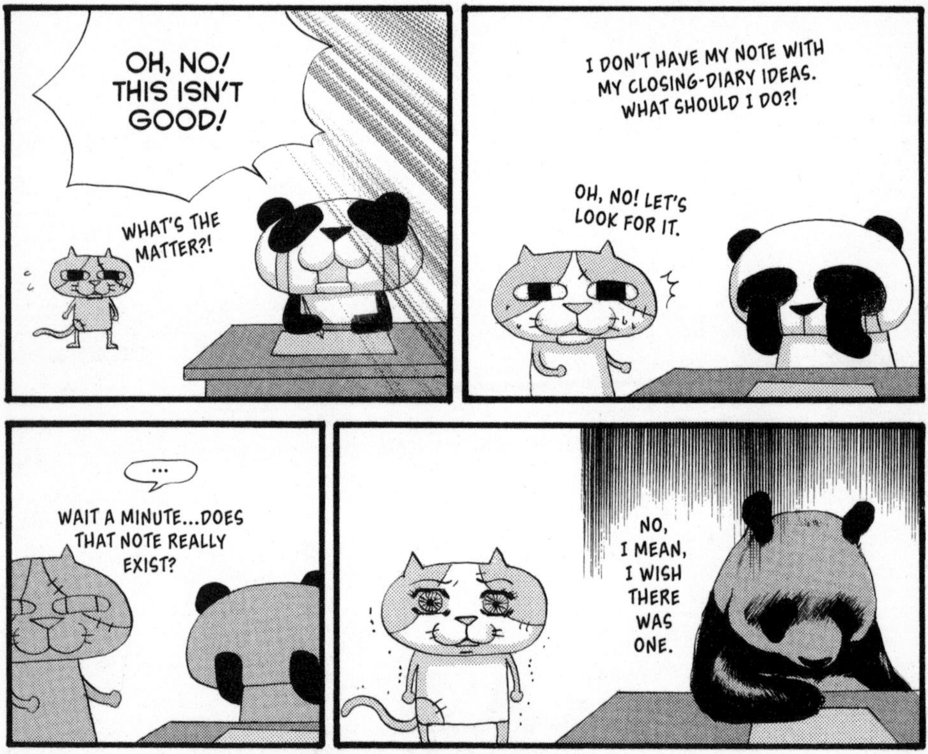
OH, NO! THIS ISN'T GOOD!
WHAT'S THE MATTER?!
I DON'T HAVE MY NOTE WITH MY CLOSING-DIARY IDEAS. WHAT SHOULD I DO?!
OH, NO! LET'S LOOK FOR IT.
...
WAIT A MINUTE...DOES THAT NOTE REALLY EXIST?
NO, I MEAN, I WISH THERE WAS ONE.
IT'S BEEN SO HARD WORKING ALONE, BECAUSE I ONLY HAVE CONVERSATIONS WITH BIRDS AND CATS.
I WANT TO TALK TO PEOPLE! SOB! SOB!

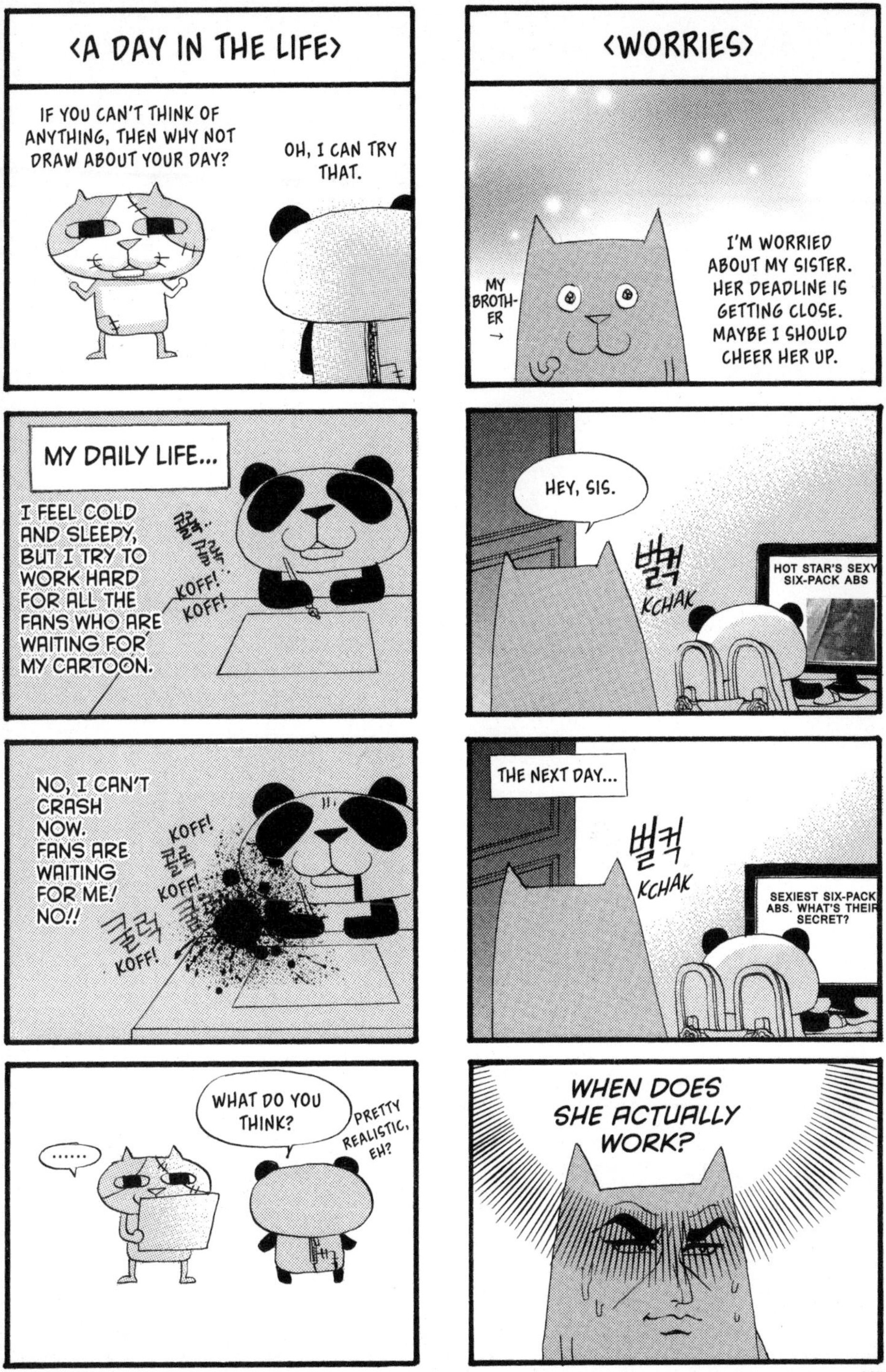
<A DAY IN THE LIFE>
IF YOU CAN'T THINK OF ANYTHING, THEN WHY NOT DRAW ABOUT YOUR DAY?
OH, I CAN TRY THAT.
MY DAILY LIFE...
I FEEL COLD AND SLEEPY, BUT I TRY TO WORK HARD FOR ALL THE FANS WHO ARE WAITING FOR MY CARTOON.
콜록.. 콜록..
KOFF! KOFF!
NO, I CAN'T CRASH NOW. FANS ARE WAITING FOR ME! NO!!
KOFF!
콜록
KOFF!
쿨럭
KOFF!
WHAT DO YOU THINK?
PRETTY REALISTIC, EH?
......
<WORRIES>
MY BROTH-ER →
I'M WORRIED ABOUT MY SISTER. HER DEADLINE IS GETTING CLOSE. MAYBE I SHOULD CHEER HER UP.
HEY, SIS.
벌컥
KCHAK
HOT STAR'S SEXY SIX-PACK ABS
THE NEXT DAY...
벌컥
KCHAK
SEXIEST SIX-PACK ABS. WHAT'S THEIR SECRET?
WHEN DOES SHE ACTUALLY WORK?

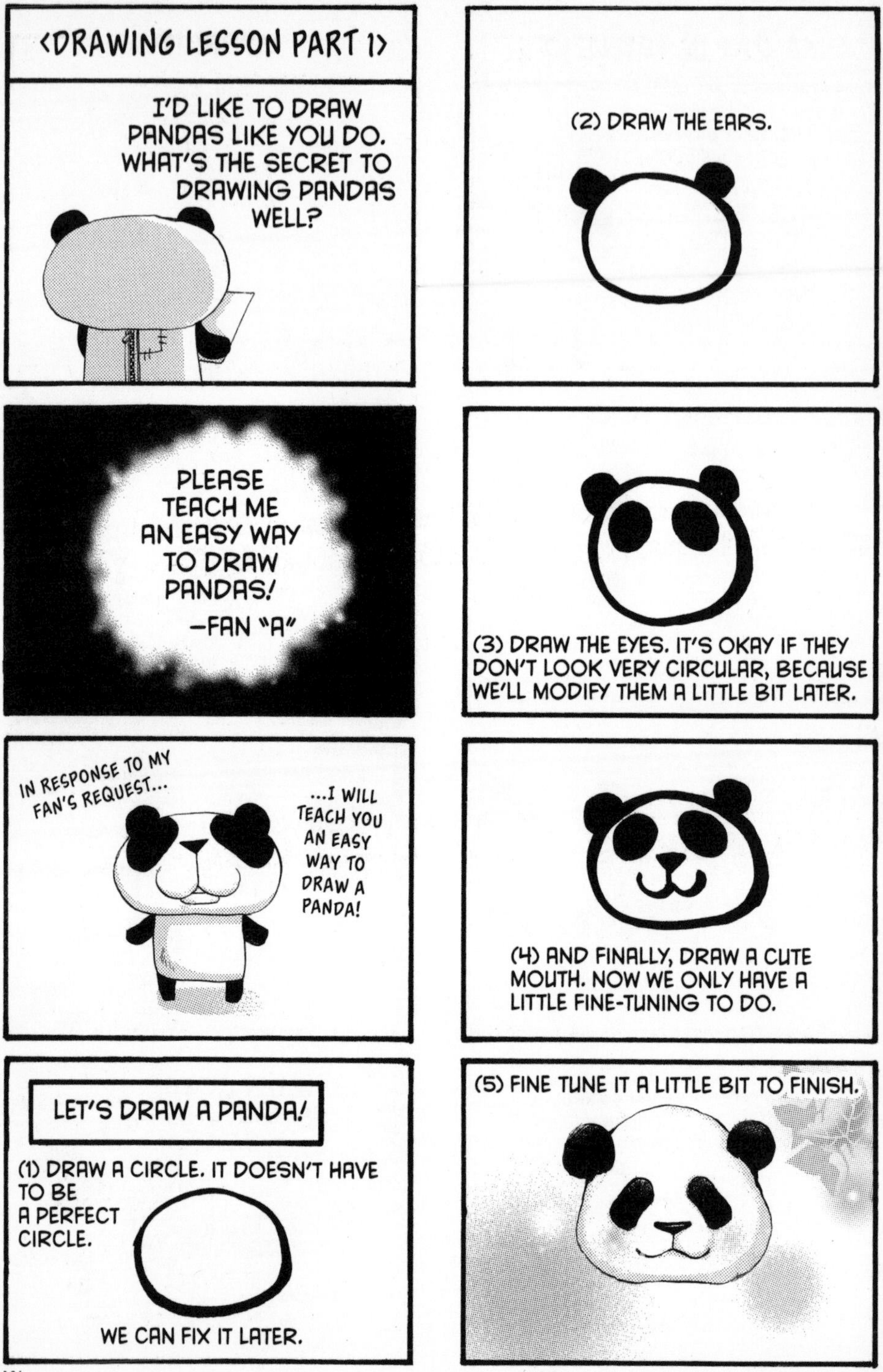
<DRAWING LESSON PART 1>
I'D LIKE TO DRAW PANDAS LIKE YOU DO. WHAT'S THE SECRET TO DRAWING PANDAS WELL?
PLEASE TEACH ME AN EASY WAY TO DRAW PANDAS! —FAN "A"
IN RESPONSE TO MY FAN'S REQUEST...
...I WILL TEACH YOU AN EASY WAY TO DRAW A PANDA!
LET'S DRAW A PANDA!
(1) DRAW A CIRCLE. IT DOESN'T HAVE TO BE A PERFECT CIRCLE.
WE CAN FIX IT LATER.
(2) DRAW THE EARS.
(3) DRAW THE EYES. IT'S OKAY IF THEY DON'T LOOK VERY CIRCULAR, BECAUSE WE'LL MODIFY THEM A LITTLE BIT LATER.
(4) AND FINALLY, DRAW A CUTE MOUTH. NOW WE ONLY HAVE A LITTLE FINE-TUNING TO DO.
(5) FINE TUNE IT A LITTLE BIT TO FINISH.

ISN'T IT EASY? PLEASE, EVERYBODY TRY IT!

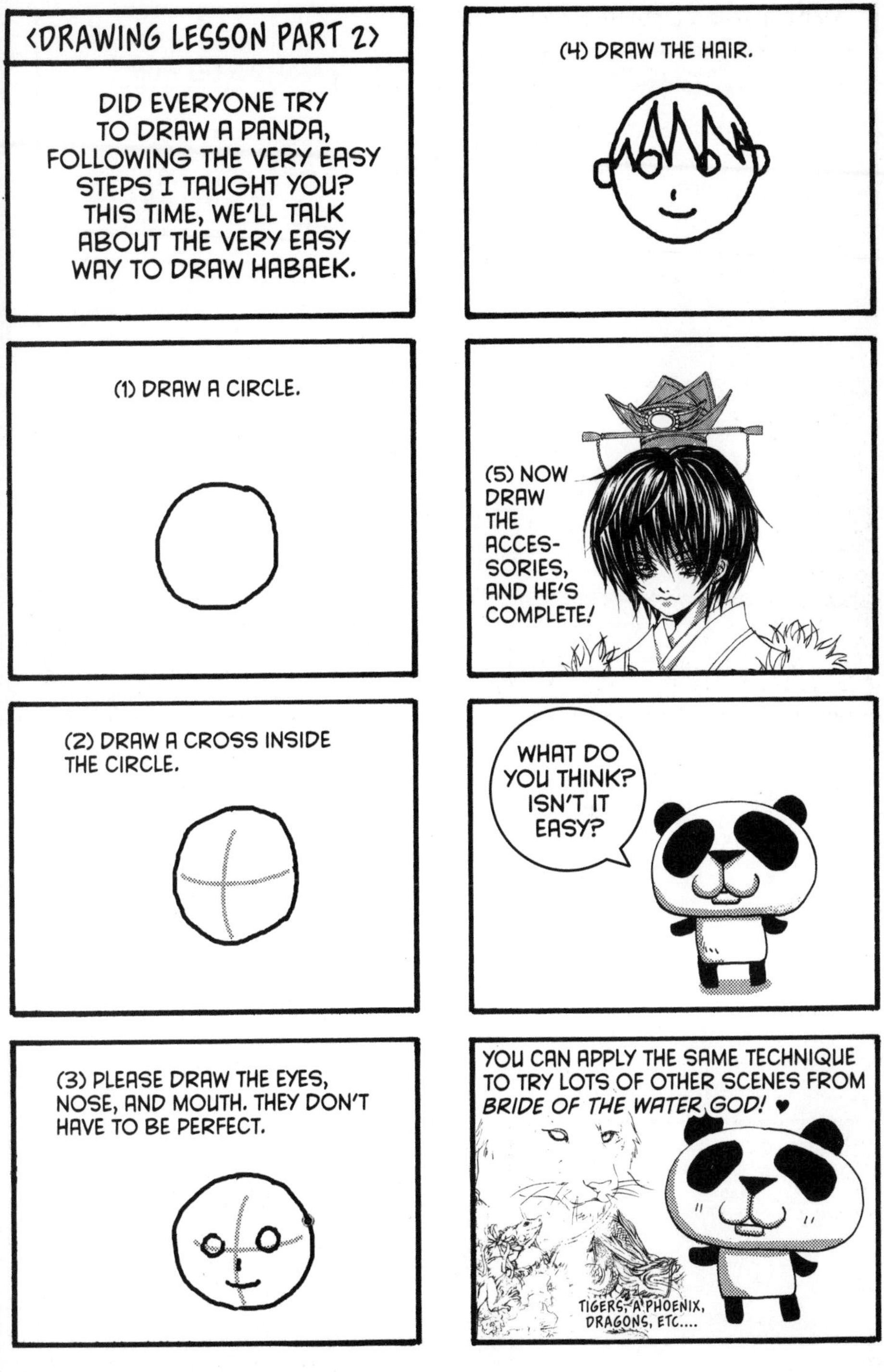
<DRAWING LESSON PART 2>
DID EVERYONE TRY TO DRAW A PANDA, FOLLOWING THE VERY EASY STEPS I TAUGHT YOU? THIS TIME, WE'LL TALK ABOUT THE VERY EASY WAY TO DRAW HABAEK.
(1) DRAW A CIRCLE.
(2) DRAW A CROSS INSIDE THE CIRCLE.
(3) PLEASE DRAW THE EYES, NOSE, AND MOUTH. THEY DON'T HAVE TO BE PERFECT.
(4) DRAW THE HAIR.
(5) NOW DRAW THE ACCES-SORIES, AND HE'S COMPLETE!
WHAT DO YOU THINK? ISN'T IT EASY?
YOU CAN APPLY THE SAME TECHNIQUE TO TRY LOTS OF OTHER SCENES FROM *BRIDE OF THE WATER GOD!* ♥
TIGERS, A PHOENIX, DRAGONS, ETC....

SPECIAL NOTES SEO-WANG-MO'S BAN-DO AND BAN-DO-WON

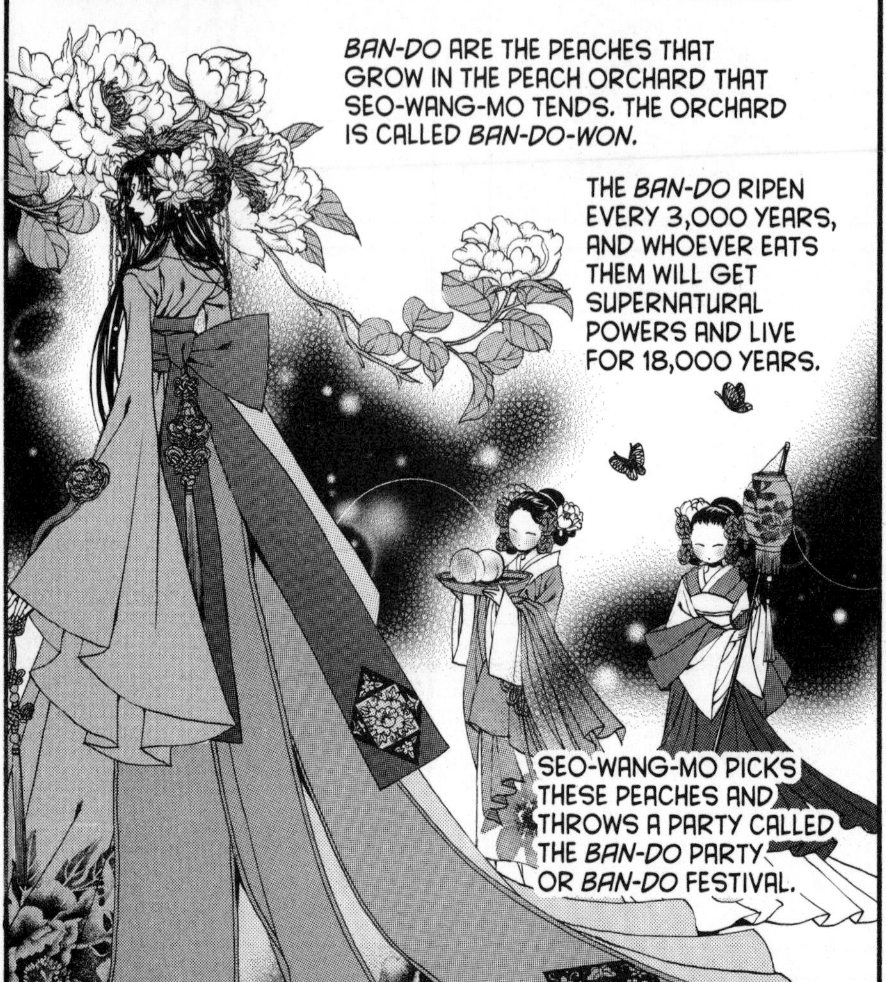

BAN-DO ARE THE PEACHES THAT GROW IN THE PEACH ORCHARD THAT SEO-WANG-MO TENDS. THE ORCHARD IS CALLED *BAN-DO-WON*.

THE *BAN-DO* RIPEN EVERY 3,000 YEARS, AND WHOEVER EATS THEM WILL GET SUPERNATURAL POWERS AND LIVE FOR 18,000 YEARS.

SEO-WANG-MO PICKS THESE PEACHES AND THROWS A PARTY CALLED THE *BAN-DO* PARTY OR *BAN-DO* FESTIVAL.

SON-O-GONG FROM *JOURNEY TO THE WEST* WAS GIVEN THE RESPONSIBILITY OF TAKING CARE OF THE *BAN-DO-WON*--BUT BECAUSE HE ATE THE FRUIT AND DRANK THE GOD'S DRINK, HE WAS LOCKED UP IN O-HAENG MOUNTAIN.

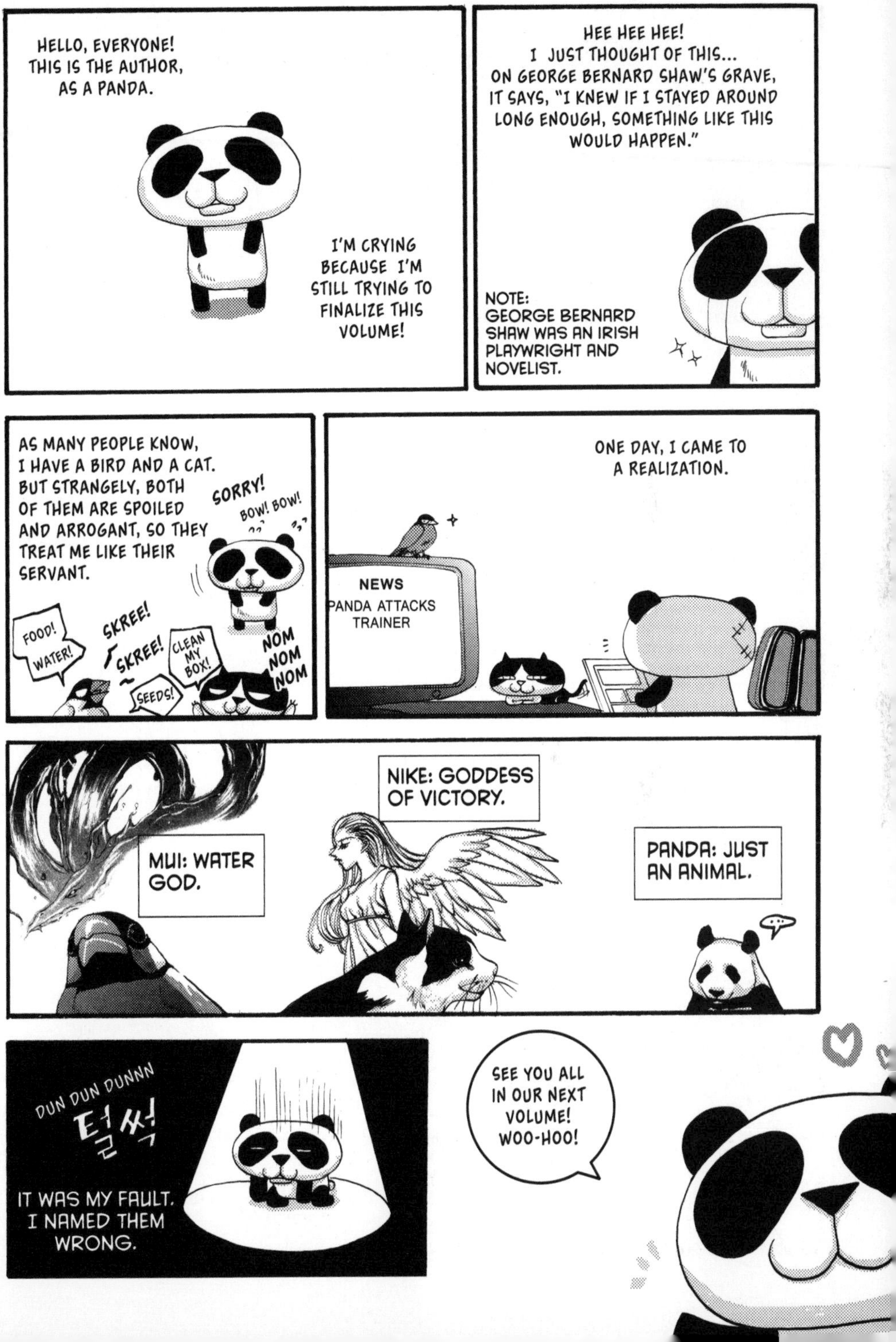
HELLO, EVERYONE! THIS IS THE AUTHOR, AS A PANDA.
I'M CRYING BECAUSE I'M STILL TRYING TO FINALIZE THIS VOLUME!
HEE HEE HEE! I JUST THOUGHT OF THIS... ON GEORGE BERNARD SHAW'S GRAVE, IT SAYS, "I KNEW IF I STAYED AROUND LONG ENOUGH, SOMETHING LIKE THIS WOULD HAPPEN."
NOTE: GEORGE BERNARD SHAW WAS AN IRISH PLAYWRIGHT AND NOVELIST.
AS MANY PEOPLE KNOW, I HAVE A BIRD AND A CAT. BUT STRANGELY, BOTH OF THEM ARE SPOILED AND ARROGANT, SO THEY TREAT ME LIKE THEIR SERVANT.
SORRY!
BOW! BOW!
FOOD! WATER!
SKREE! SKREE!
SEEDS!
CLEAN MY BOX!
NOM NOM NOM
ONE DAY, I CAME TO A REALIZATION.
NEWS
PANDA ATTACKS TRAINER
NIKE: GODDESS OF VICTORY.
MUI: WATER GOD.
PANDA: JUST AN ANIMAL.
DUN DUN DUNNN
털썩
IT WAS MY FAULT. I NAMED THEM WRONG.
SEE YOU ALL IN OUR NEXT VOLUME! WOO-HOO!

We tend to neglect that which is around us all the time, often taking things for granted. Why do we only realize how precious a relationship is after we've lost one? Today, I feel grateful and have renewed appreciation for all the people around me. Thank you for standing by my side and sticking with me, everyone!

—Mi-Kyung Yun

CREATOR PROFILE

Born on October 14, 1980. Majored in Animation at Mokwon University.

Received the silver medal for Seoul Media Group's "Shin-in-gong-mo-jeon" ("New Artist Debut Competition") for *Na-eu Ji-gu Bang-moon-gi* (*The Journey of My Earth Visit*) in 2003.

Received a "Shin-in-sang" ("Best New Artist") award from the Dokja-manhwa-daesang organization for *Railroad* in 2004.

Won the Korean "Manhwa of Today" award for *Bride of the Water God* in 2007.

Currently publishing *Bride of the Water God* serially in the Korean comics magazine *Wink*.

BRIDE of the WATER GOD

When Soah's impoverished, desperate village decides to sacrifice her to the Water God Habaek to end a long drought, they believe that drowning one beautiful girl will save their entire community and bring much-needed rain. Not only is Soah surprised to be *rescued* by the Water God instead of killed; she never imagined she'd be a welcomed guest in Habaek's magical kingdom, where an exciting new life awaits her! Most surprising, however, is the Water God himself, and how very different he is from the monster Soah imagined . . .

Created by Mi-Kyung Yun, who received the "Best New Artist" award in 2004 from the esteemed *Dokja-manhwa-daesang* organization, *Bride of the Water God* was the top-selling *shoujo* manhwa in Korea in 2006!

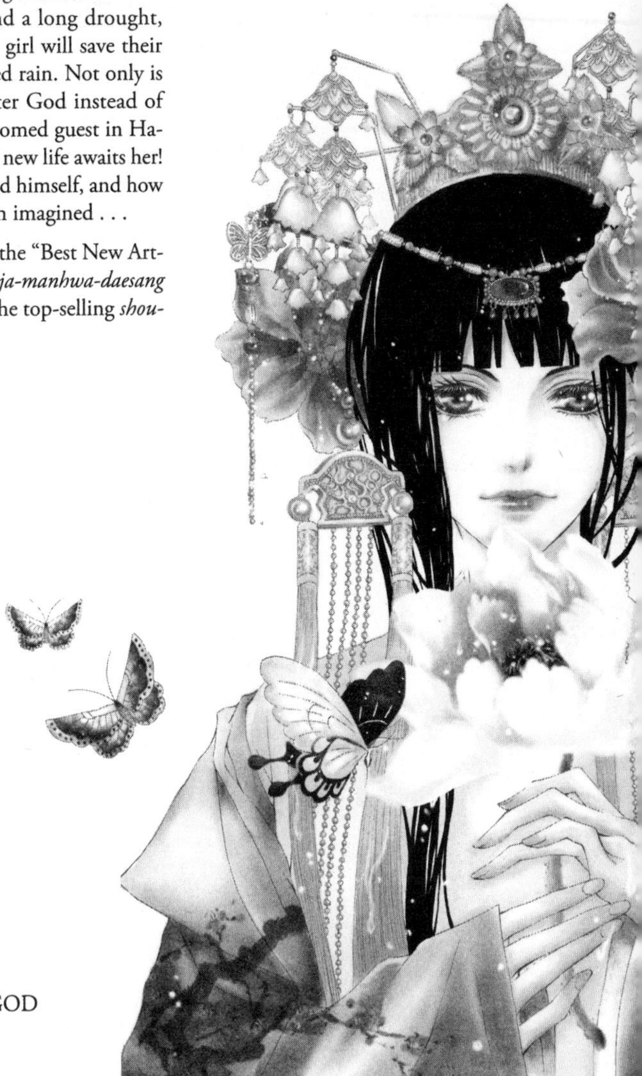

Volume 1
ISBN 978-1-59307-849-2

Volume 2
ISBN 978-1-59307-883-6

Volume 3
ISBN 978-1-59582-305-2

Volume 4
ISBN 978-1-59582-378-6

Volume 5
ISBN 978-1-59582-445-5

Volume 6
ISBN 978-1-59582-605-3

Volume 7
ISBN 978-1-59582-668-8

Volume 8
ISBN 978-1-59582-687-9

Volume 9
ISBN 978-1-59582-688-6

Volume 10
ISBN 978-1-59582-873-6

Volume 11
ISBN 978-1-59582-874-3

$9.99 each

Previews for BRIDE OF THE WATER GOD and other DARK HORSE MANHWA titles can be found at darkhorse.com!

DARK HORSE MANHWA

AVAILABLE AT YOUR LOCAL COMICS SHOP OR BOOKSTORE! TO FIND A COMICS SHOP IN YOUR AREA, CALL 1-888-266-4226.

For more information or to order direct visit darkhorse.com or call 1-800-862-0052 Mon.–Fri. 9 AM to 5 PM Pacific Time. *Prices and availability subject to change without notice.

PARK JOONG-KI'S

S•H•A•M•A•N WARRIOR

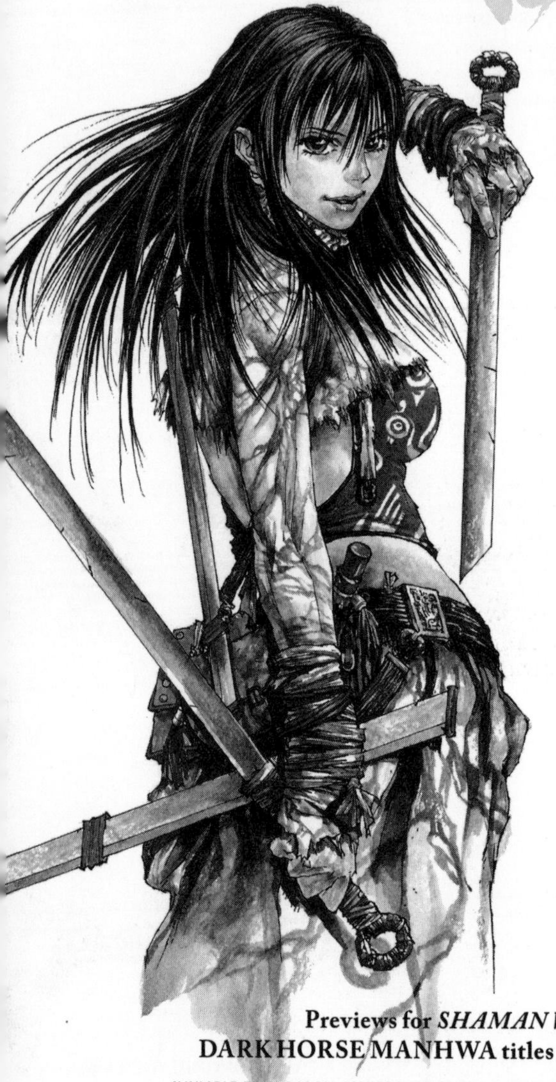

A lavishly illustrated fantasy series with violent, breakneck action sequences and imaginative, memorable characters! Outlawed by the kingdom they once served, the Shaman Warriors of Kugai are a dying breed of disturbingly powerful, mystical fighting machines. As a young Shaman Warrior, Yaki's inherited powers have yet to awaken, but the heartless leaders of Kugai are determined to kill her and put an end to her legendary bloodline. When Batu—her hotheaded guardian—sneaks through dangerous territories to hunt the Death Lord who assassinated Yaki's father, the girl embarks on her own treacherous path of self-discovery.

Volume 1 ISBN 978-1-59307-638-2

Volume 2 ISBN 978-1-59307-749-5

Volume 3 ISBN 978-1-59307-769-3

Volume 4 ISBN 978-1-59307-819-5

Volume 5 ISBN 978-1-59307-859-1

Volume 6 ISBN 978-1-59307-895-9

Volume 7 ISBN 978-1-59582-332-8

Volume 8 ISBN 978-1-59582-381-6

Volume 9 ISBN 978-1-59582-453-0

$12.99 each

Previews for *SHAMAN WARRIOR* and other DARK HORSE MANHWA titles can be found at darkhorse.com!

AVAILABLE AT YOUR LOCAL COMICS SHOP OR BOOKSTORE. To find a comics shop in your area, call 1-888-266-4226.
For more information or to order direct: On the web: darkhorse.com. E-mail: mailorder@darkhorse.com.
Phone: 1-800-862-0052 Mon.–Fri. 9 AM to 5 PM Pacific Time.

DARK HORSE MANHWA

BY KIM YOUNG-OH

Banya

the explosive delivery man

With a worldwide war raging between humans and monsters, the young delivery men and women of the Gaya Desert Post Office do not pledge allegiance to any country or king. They are banded together by a pledge to *deliver* . . . "Fast. Precise. Secure." Banya, the craziest and craftiest of the bunch, will stop at nothing to get a job done. All five volumes are now available, so check out the complete series!

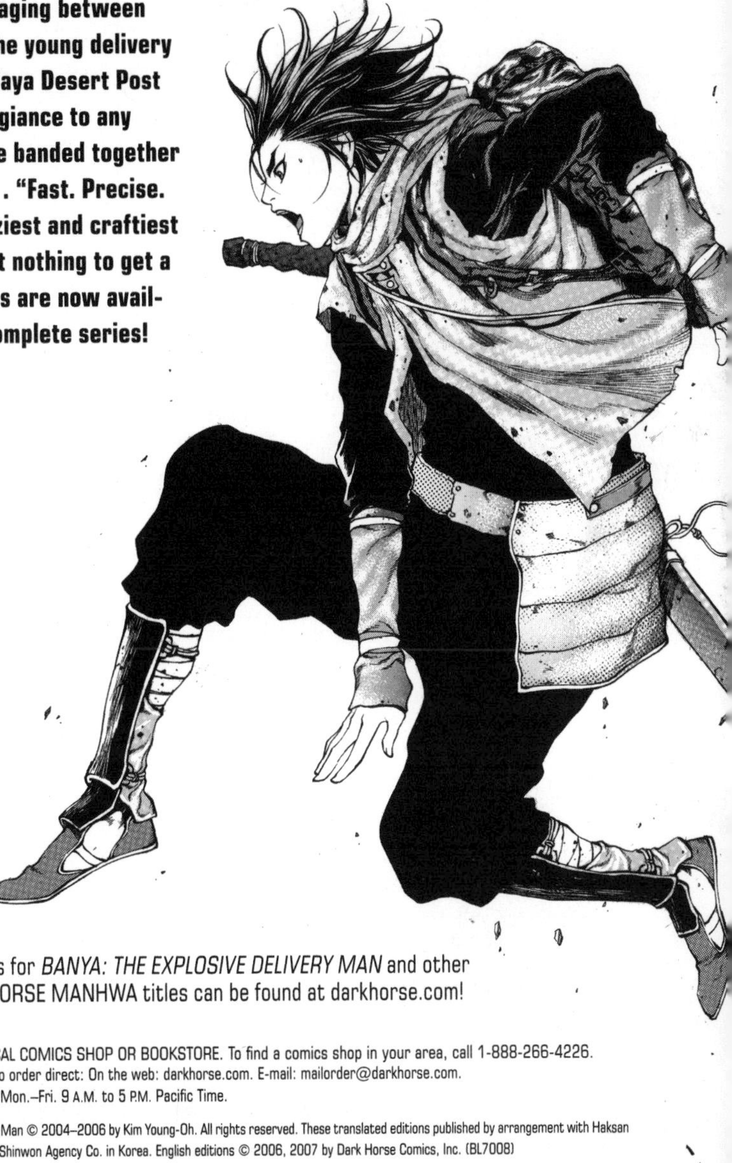

Volume 1
ISBN 978-1-59307-614-6

Volume 2
ISBN 978-1-59307-688-7

Volume 3
ISBN 978-1-59307-705-1

Volume 4
ISBN 978-1-59307-774-7

Volume 5
ISBN 978-1-59307-841-6

$12.95 EACH!

Previews for *BANYA: THE EXPLOSIVE DELIVERY MAN* and other DARK HORSE MANHWA titles can be found at darkhorse.com!

DARK HORSE MANHWA

AVAILABLE AT YOUR LOCAL COMICS SHOP OR BOOKSTORE. To find a comics shop in your area, call 1-888-266-4226.
For more information or to order direct: On the web: darkhorse.com. E-mail: mailorder@darkhorse.com.
Phone: 1-800-862-0052 Mon.–Fri. 9 A.M. to 5 P.M. Pacific Time.

publisher
Mike Richardson

editor
Philip R. Simon

assistant editor
Everett Patterson

digital production
Christianne Goudreau

collection designers
David Nestelle & Tina Alessi

Special thanks to Davey Estrada, Michael Gombos, Heejeong Haas, and Cara Niece.

English-language version produced by DARK HORSE COMICS.

BRIDE OF THE WATER GOD Volume 11

Dark Horse Manhwa, a division of Dark Horse Comics, Inc.
10956 SE Main Street, Milwaukie, OR 97222
DarkHorse.com

To find a comics shop in your area, call the
Comic Shop Locator Service toll-free at 1-888-266-4226

First edition: May 2012
ISBN 978-1-59582-874-3

1 3 5 7 9 10 8 6 4 2
Printed at Lake Book Manufacturing, Inc., Melrose Park, IL, USA